"… someone always had a camera …"
Private Photography in East Germany, 1980–2000

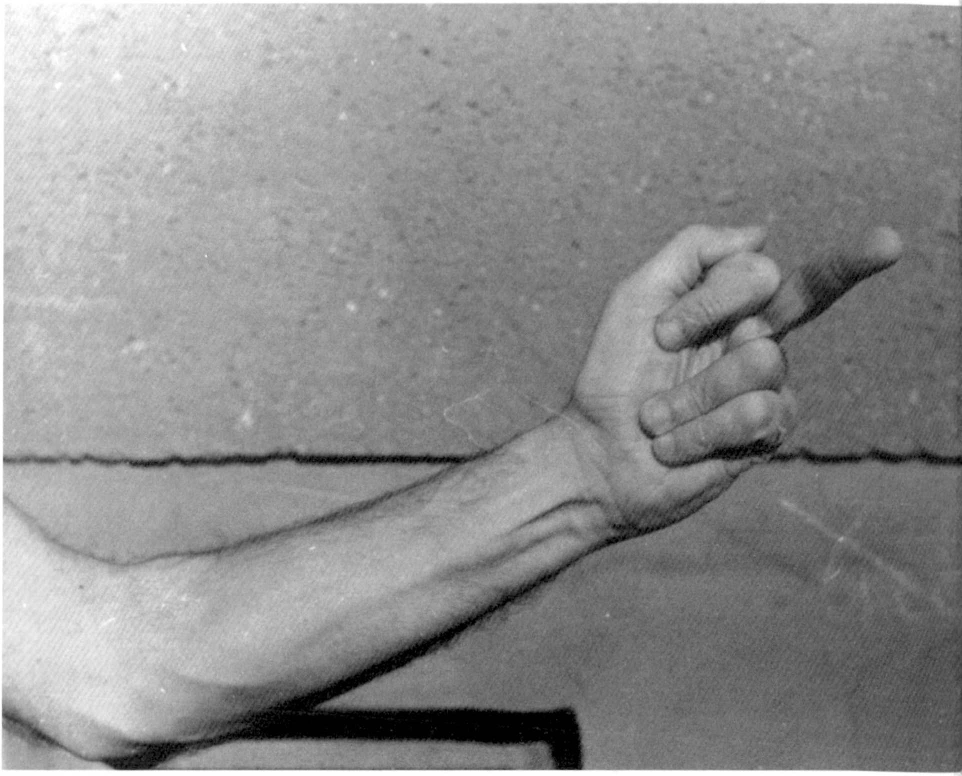

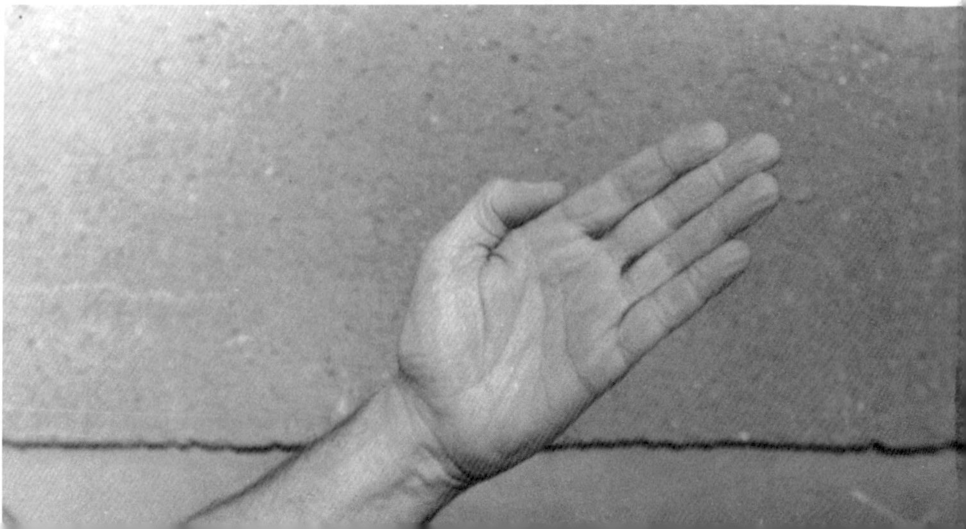

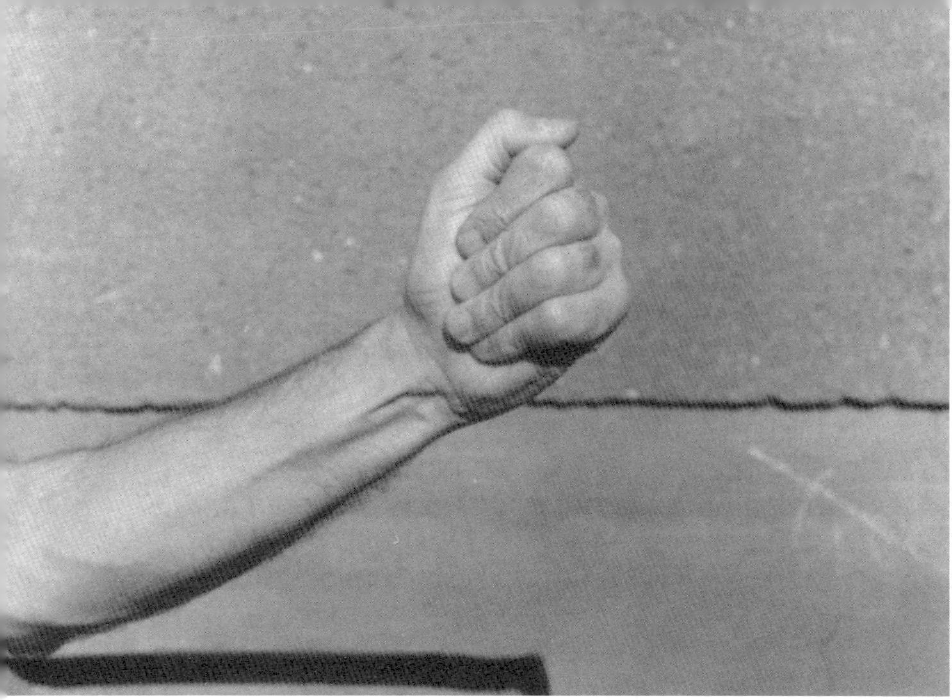

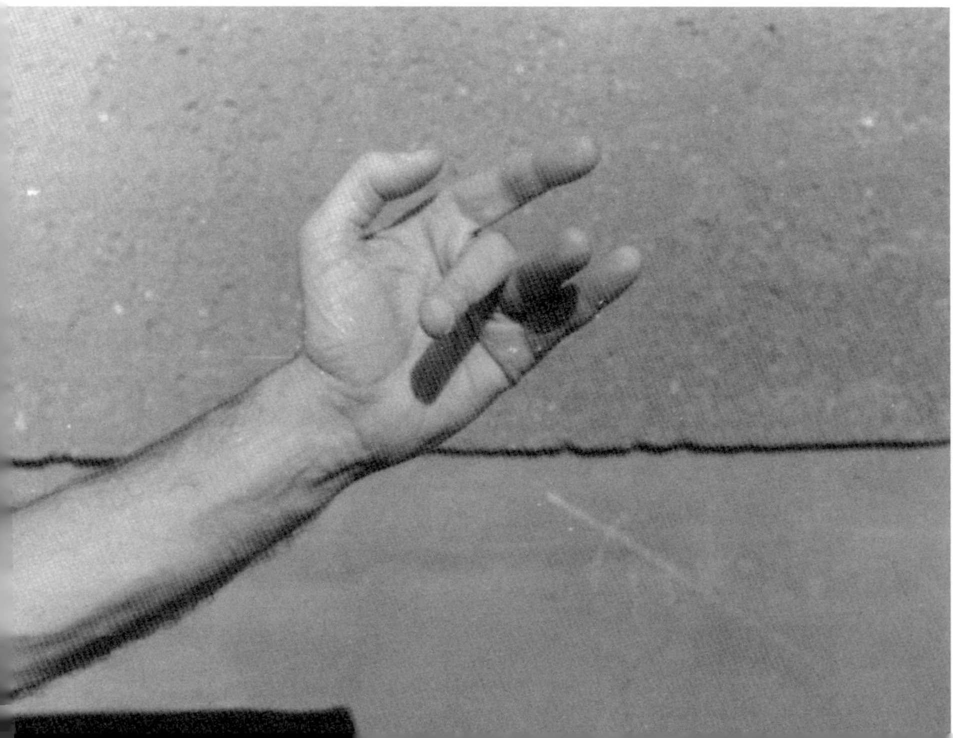

Table of Contents

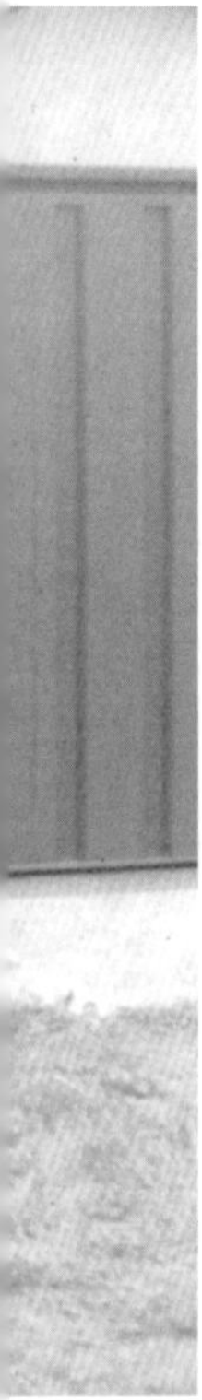

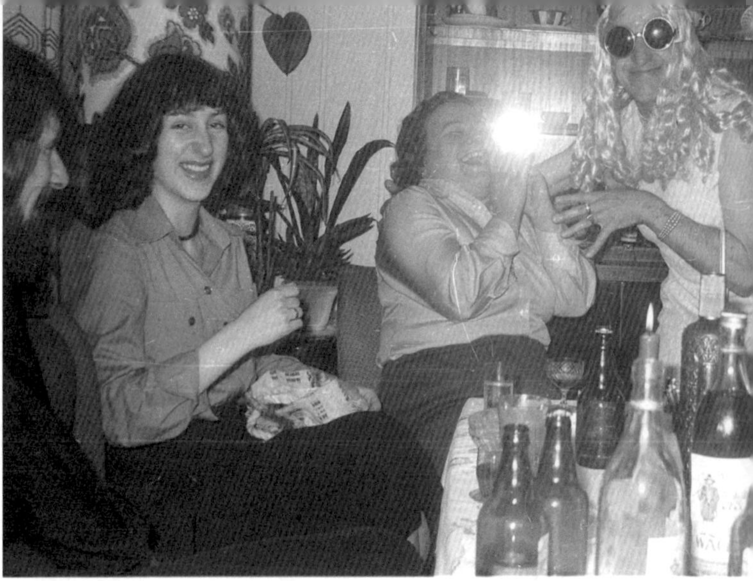

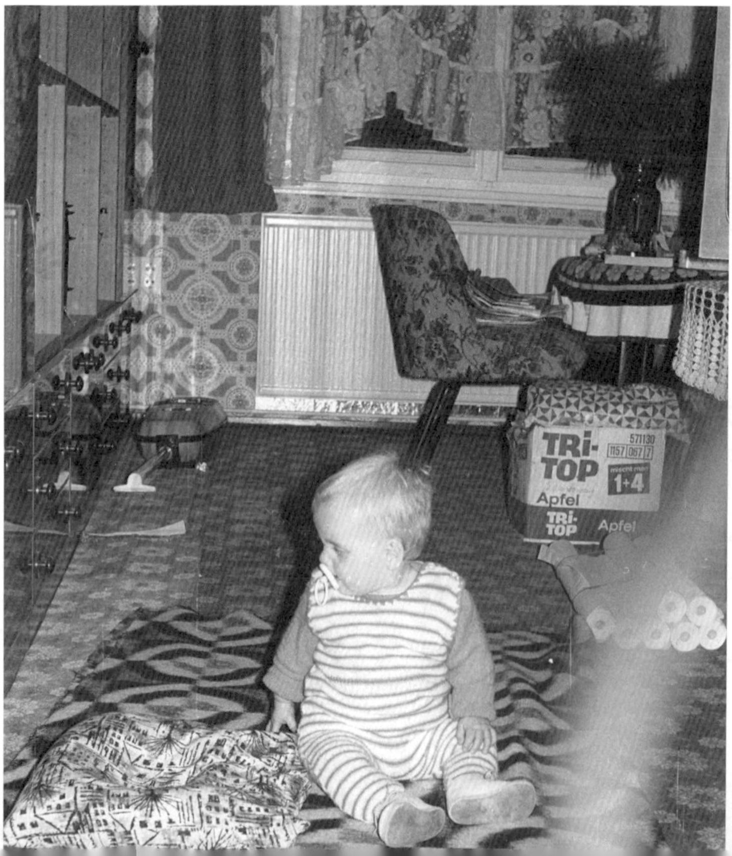
TRI-TOP
1+4
Apfel
TRI-TOP
Apfel

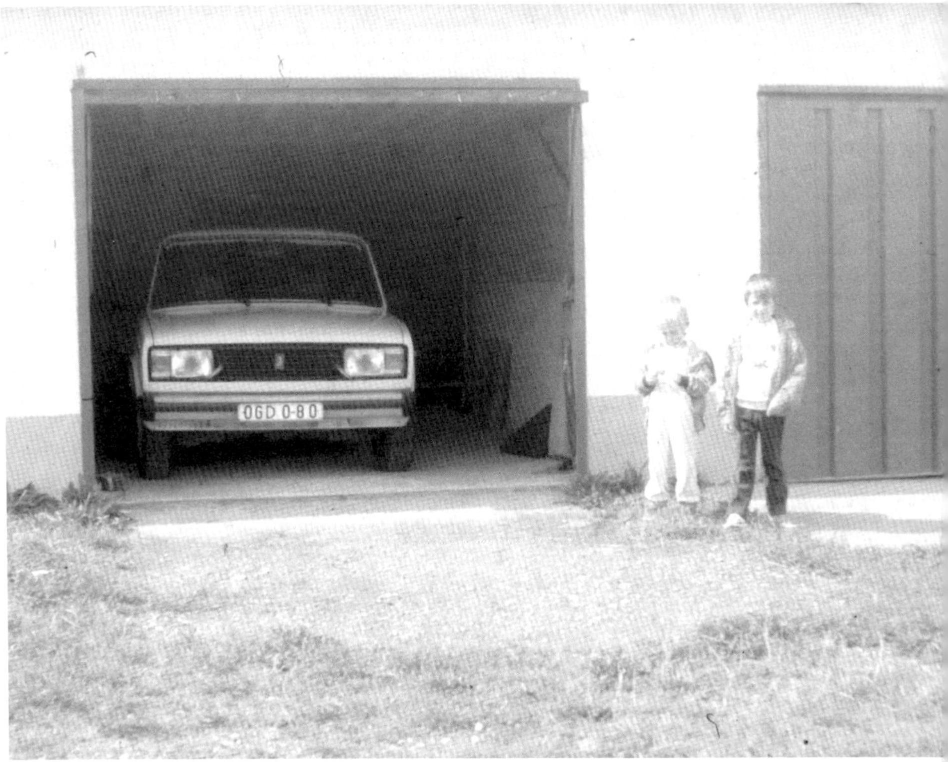
OGD 0-80

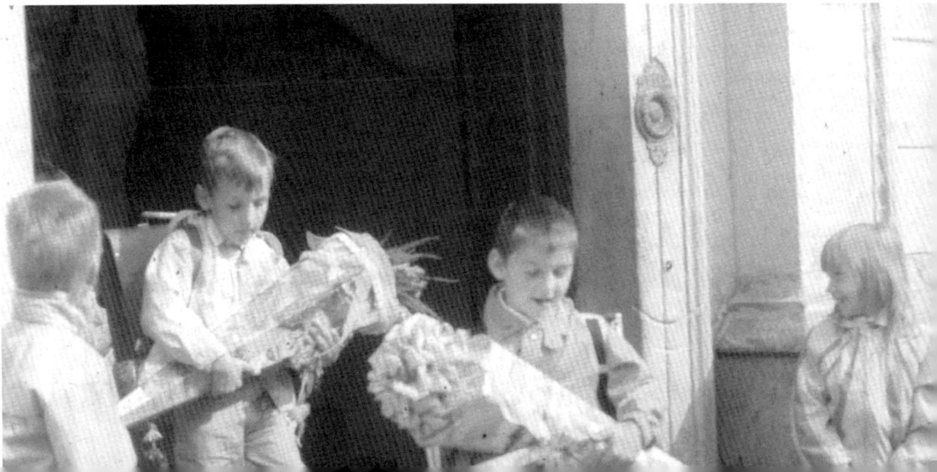

"... someone always had a camera ..."
Private Photography in East Germany, 1980–2000

Edited by:
Friedrich Tietjen
Project assistant:
Stephanie Wuntke
Authors:
Marie Egger,
Marit Lena Herrmann,
Judith Riemer,
Friedrich Tietjen
Translation:
Steven Lindberg,
Christina Oberstebrink
Copyediting:
Stephanie Wuntke
Proofreading:
Marie Egger,
Candice M. Hamelin,
Aloisia Moser,
Friedrich Tietjen
Graphic design:
Natasha Agapova
Videostills:
Sophia Uckmann
Lithography:
Falk Messerschmidt
Printing:
Kerschoffset, Zagreb

The Stiftung Reinbeckhallen sincerely thanks the album owners, photographers, contributors and supporters.

Reinbeckhallen
Reinbeckstr. 11
D-12459 Berlin

Published by:
Spector Books
Harkortstraße 10
04107 Leipzig
www.spectorbooks.com

Distribution:
Germany, Austria: GVA, Gemeinsame Verlagsauslieferung Göttingen GmbH&Co. KG, www.gva-verlage.de
Switzerland: AVA Verlagsauslieferung AG, www.ava.ch
France, Belgium: Interart Paris, www.interart.fr
UK: Central Books Ltd, www.centralbooks.com
USA, Canada, Central and South America, Africa: ARTBOOK/D.A.P., www.artbook.com
South Korea: The Book Society, www.thebooksociety.org
Japan: twelvebooks, www.twelve-books.com
Australia, New Zealand: Perimeter Distribution, www.perimeterdistribution.com

All images printed on the inner pages of this book are taken from the archives of Friedrich Tietjen, Martin Siebert and Karen and Andreas Koven.

Die deutsche Ausgabe des Buches mit dem Titel »... irgendwer hat immer fotografiert ...« Private Fotografie in Ostdeutschland 1980–2000 ist unter der ISBN 978-3-95905-699-1 erschienen.

First edition 2024
ISBN 978-3-95905-700-4

Supported with funds of the Federal Foundation for the Study of the Communist Dictatorship in Eastern Germany (Bundesstiftung Aufarbeitung)

BUNDESSTIFTUNG AUFARBEITUNG

Album Collections

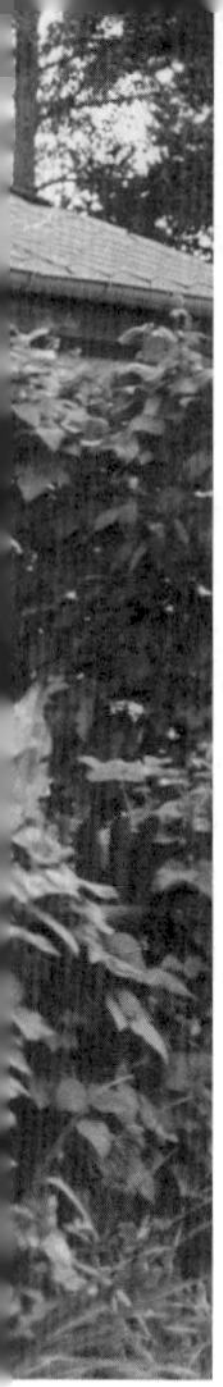

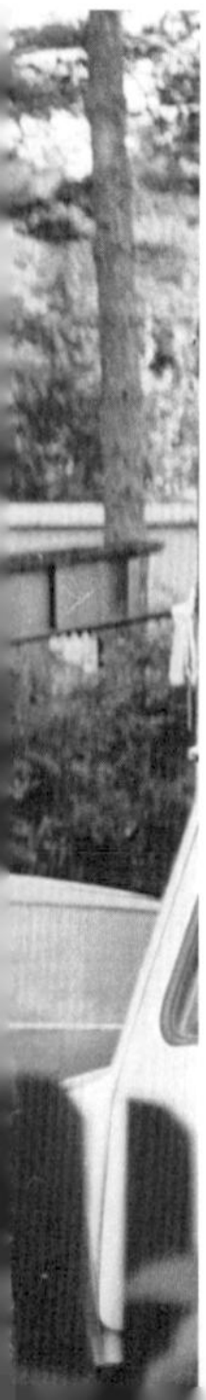

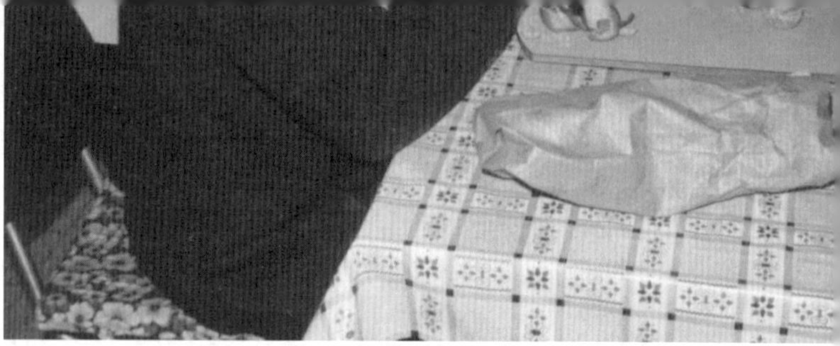

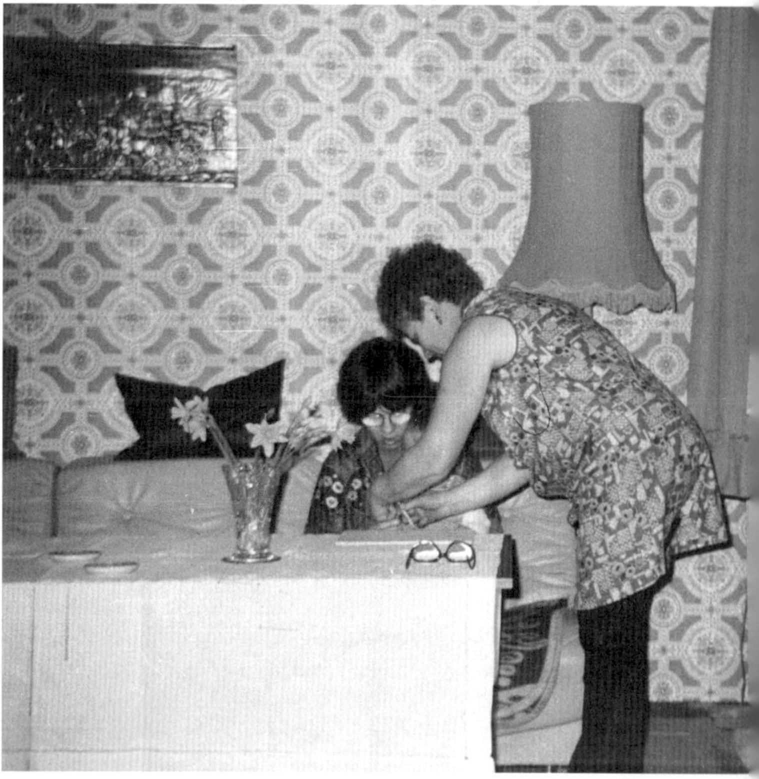

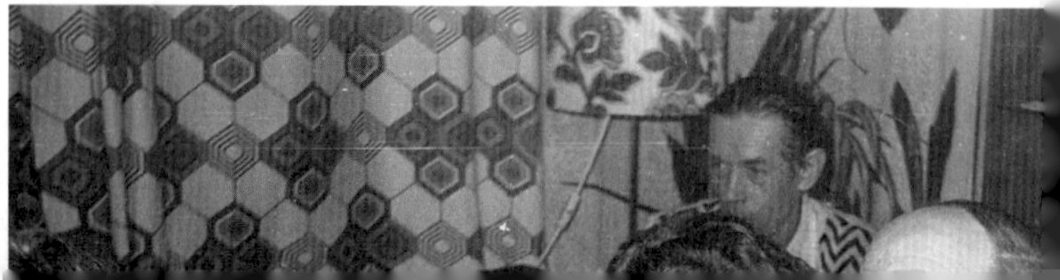

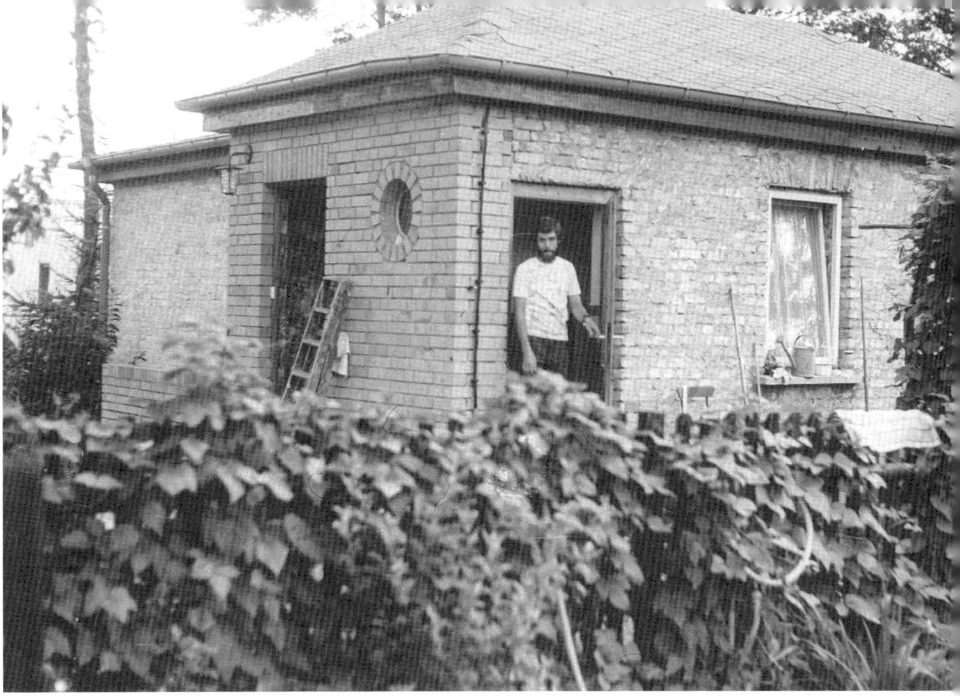

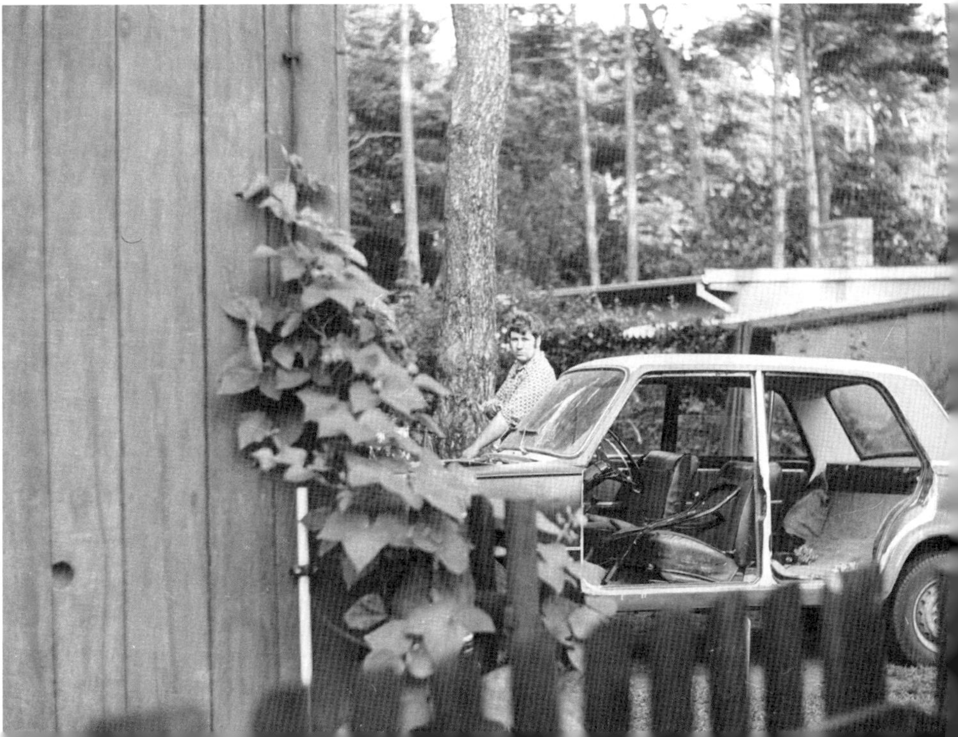

Private Photography in East Germany, 1980–2000

Friedrich Tietjen

"And in the summer of '89, we were in the Soviet Union for two weeks, on vacation visiting Olya and Sergei. And we come back, and people are standing at the embassy in Prague and want out of this country. And we thought, oh God, what's going on ... and the parties continued."(1) The discrepancy between the upheaval of the international political situation and the uniformity of private life that Beate Göldner formulated so casually in conversation also permeates the photo album through which she leafed as she told her story: on the pages are photos from vacations, happy garden parties, bicycle tours, visits to and from relatives. That around the same time the first inner-German border fell and then later the German Democratic Republic (GDR) went down in a long agony can be seen in her albums in little more than individual pictures and details—in two women reading an issue of the *Sputnik* magazine together, in a pasted-in ad for the cigarette brand *West*, and in a banner stretched above the street between two trees: "Kohlhasenbruck welcomes its neighbors from Babelsberg."

In the way they tell stories with images, the albums of the Göldner family are not an isolated case—only in the sense that the historical events of 1989/90 left even fewer visible traces in many other private photographers' collections. For the images of private photography often tell of political events and upheavals only ambiguously and in passing—different cars are driving on the streets, clothing changes, and the body of water in the background of a holiday snapshot could be the Lake Balaton in Hungary or the Mediterranean. Of the great demonstrations in the fall of 1989, of the opening of the border and the first

1 Album conversation with Beate Göldner, Potsdam, July 24, 2020, 2:14:20.

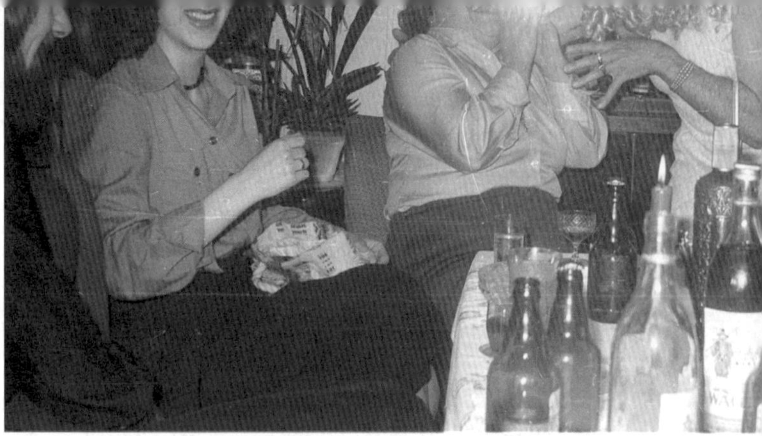

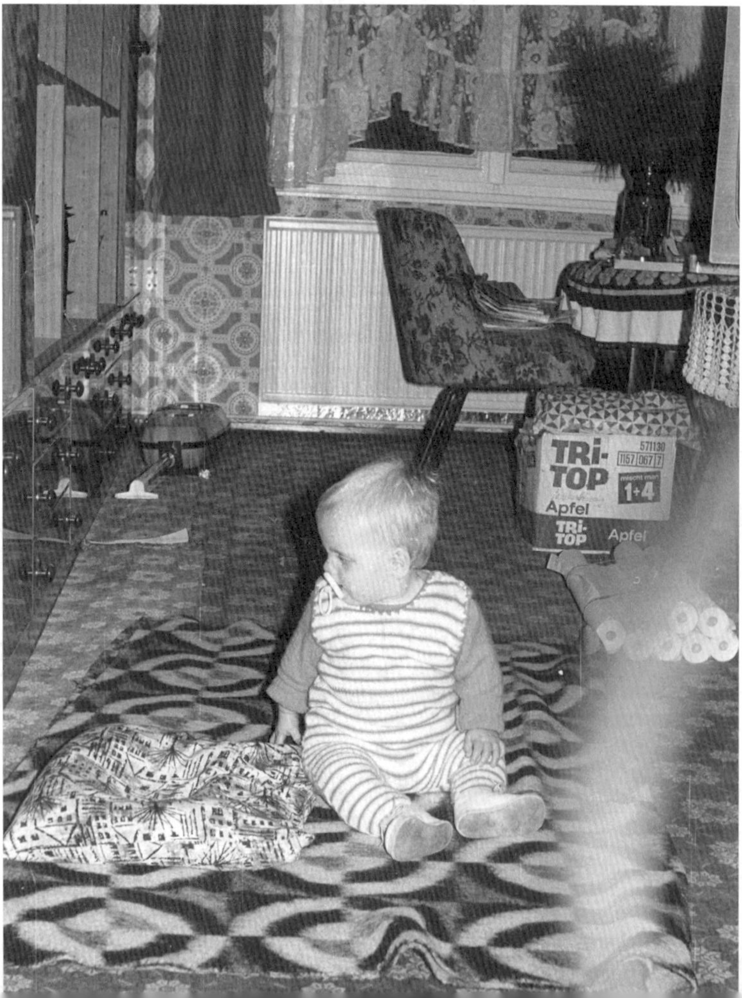
TRI-TOP
Apfel
TRI-TOP
Apfel

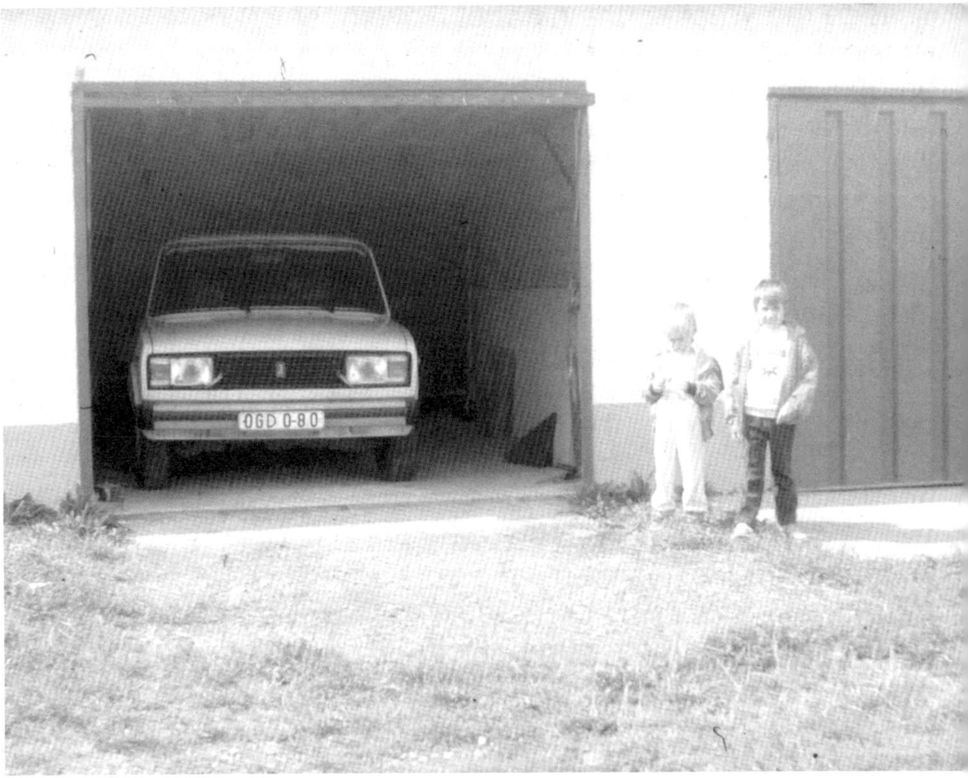
OGD 0-80

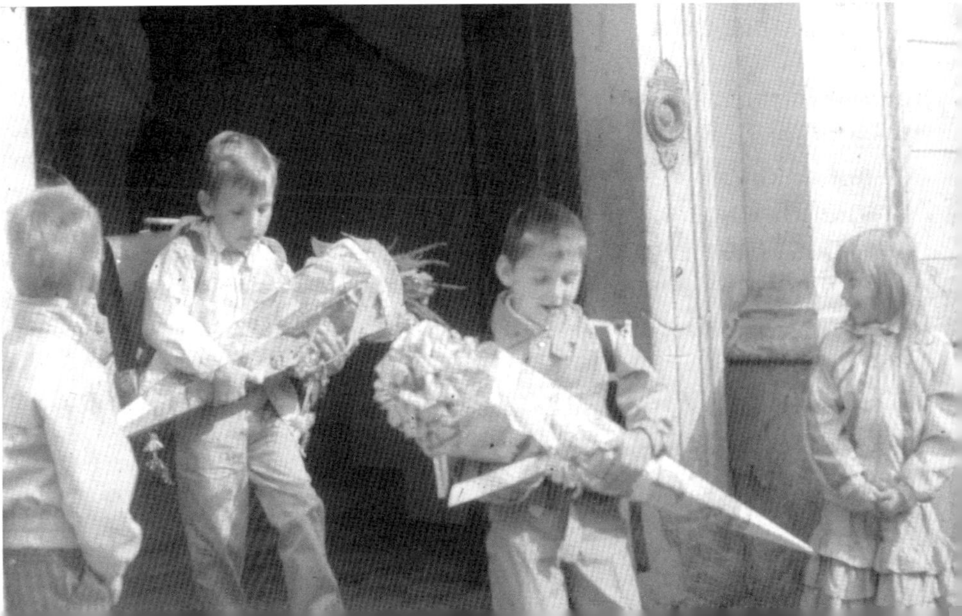

visits to the West on the night of November 9, and later of the mass layoffs, the violence of right-wing groups, and the decay of landscapes whose residents had been promised with amply false pathos that they would flourish—these photographs show little to nothing of all of this. If the images from private photo albums were the only source for East Germany's history between 1980 and 2000, then these years must have been, for its population, a series of vacations, parties, and happy days in allotment gardens.

Yet without question, they were not. The people who came to the conversations about private photo albums for the research project *Biography and History. Private Photography in East Germany, 1980–2000* included a woman who fell in love with a man from West Germany and applied to emigrate, for which she was harassed until she was allowed to leave the country as a stateless person; a couple who had been living in a prefabricated building in Berlin-Marzahn since the 1980s and lament how quickly the close and friendly connections between neighbors in the building fell apart after 1989; and the mayor of a small town in Saxony who was crowded out of office in the spring of 1990 despite her committed work.(2) We spoke with a former animal keeper from the state circus of the GDR, with husband-and-wife furriers, with a rowing coach, with a passionate bicycle racer, with a writer who moved from West to East Germany in 1993, and with a former officer of the Nationale Volksarmee (NVA; National People's Army) and his wife. They and many others spoke not only about their photographs, but also sometimes about what their photographs do *not* show: that the cheerful family photo with the children in the new apartment was a façade and the marriage fell apart shortly thereafter; that the man smiling so nicely in the photograph was later identified as an informant

2 See also https://stiftung-reinbeckhallen.de/privatefotografie/ (accessed November 21, 2022).

for the Staatssicherheit (GDR Secret Police); and how arduous it was for a single mother with a poorly paid job to dress her children decently in the 1990s.

The *Albengespräche* (album conversations) with these and many other people confirm an observation from which the entire project had evolved: namely, that private photography was, as a rule, barely affected by political events and upheavals even when they had an impact that extended into the private sphere. Regardless of time and place, this dissonance appears to be specific to private photography.(3) And it does not only affect the spheres of the political or historical, for private photography usually overlooked the rifts in private life as well. As a rule, it does not show everyday life, but rather the exceptions to it: not the shopping but the festive meal, not the work but the hobby, not the marital quarrel but the harmonious Christmas next to the tree, even if these Christmases were anything but harmonious away from the camera. Although they record specific events, private photographs are not a comprehensive documentation of private life. Rather, they present realities that often appear better, richer, and happier than they were in the contexts in which the photographs were taken. Private photography ensures that these realities can be staged and thus, be produced in the first place. The image that private photographs convey of life does not show a somehow true or authentic *good life* but rather, notions about it.

Thus, private photography is by no means the comprehensive medium of memory that it often appears to be when memory is understood as first and foremost a way of making people aware of, illustrating, and repeating the past. The fact that it is essentially limited to special events outside of everyday

3 It is also found, for example, in private photography in Austria between 1930 and 1950, as Herbert Justnik and I have demonstrated in the methodologically similar exhibition project *"Everybody line up! It's time to snap!" Private Photography in Austria 1930–1950* at the Volkskundemuseum in Vienna in 2018. See https://www.volkskundemuseum.at/privatefotografie (accessed November 9, 2022).

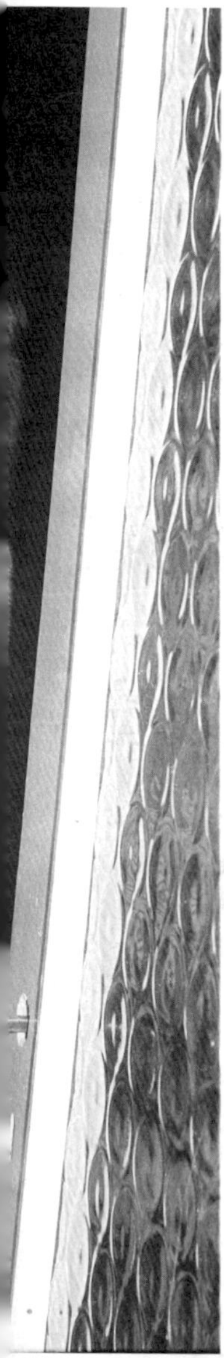

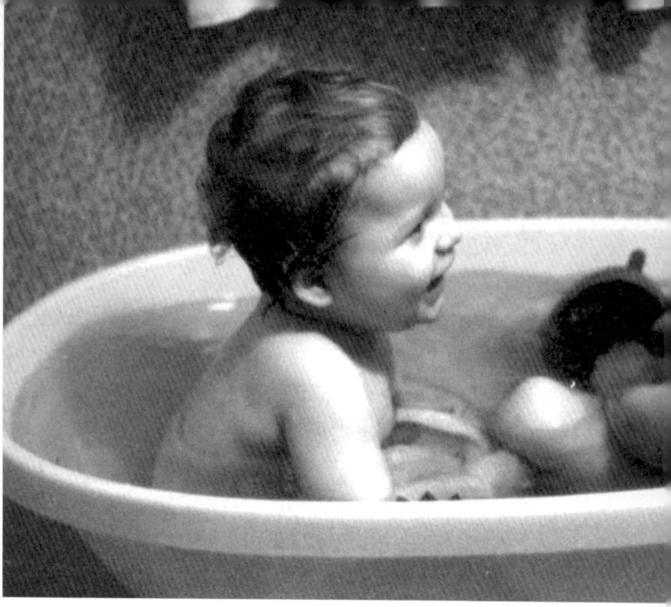

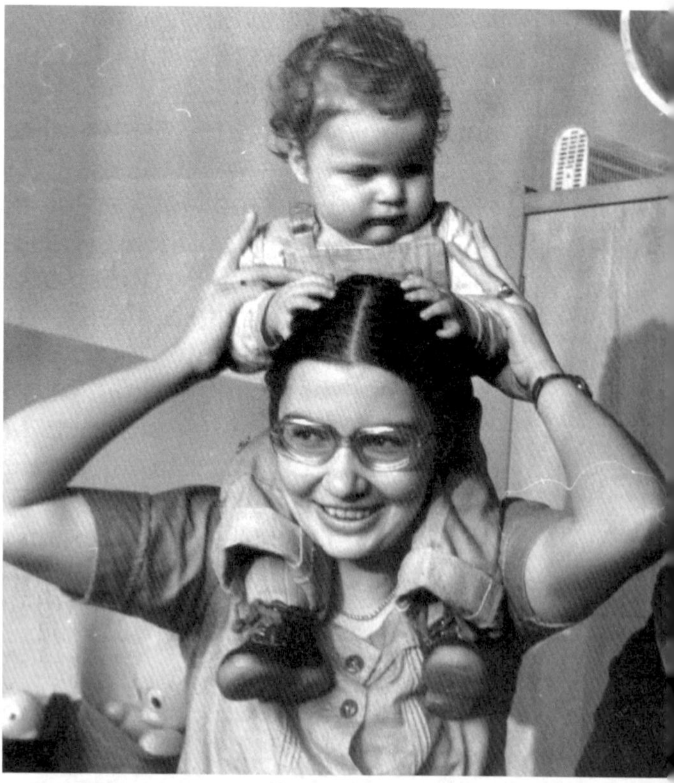

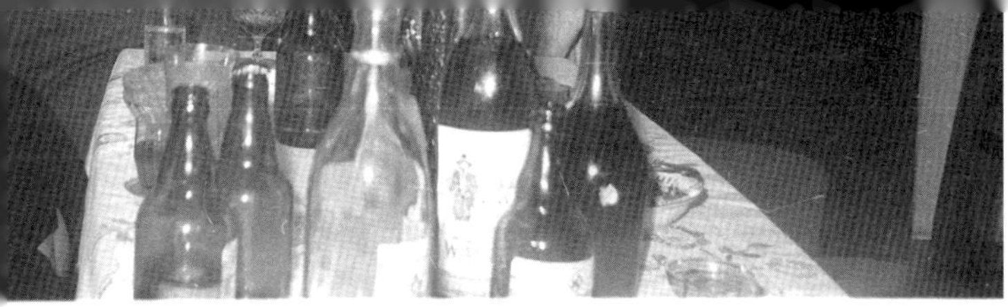

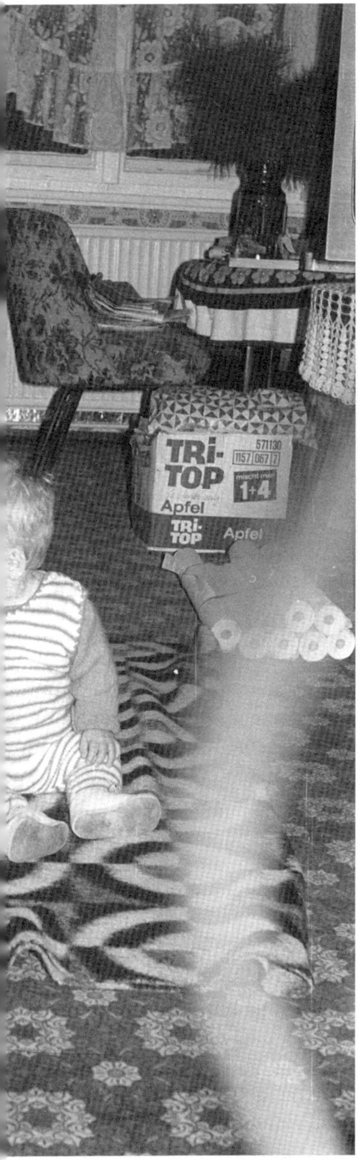
TRI-TOP
571130
1157 067 7
1+4
Apfel
TRI-TOP
Apfel

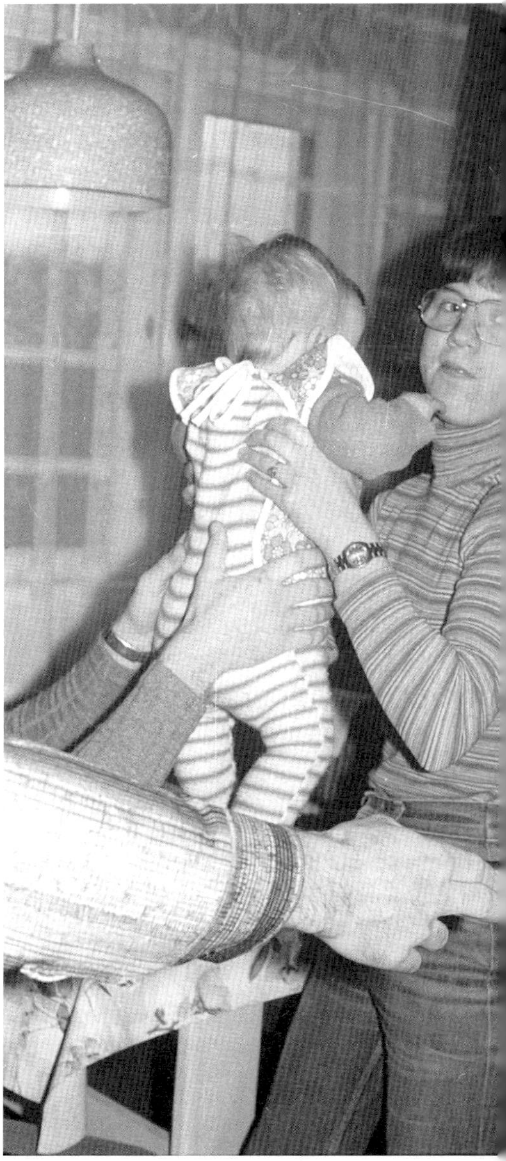

life is, after all, not simply an expression of a need for memory. Rather, the images of private photography also reflect hopes, wishes, and dreams of how wonderful an idle life with happy children would be, with travel and all sorts of parties in pleasant company, a life free of conflicts, violence, hunger, and work. Such a carefree life is, of course, not to be had, but private photography can at least potentially block out and ward off disturbances to these fantasies.(4) The desire for this pervades and structures the entire process of private photography. Anything that could be disturbing is not photographed in the first place, and already during the shooting, the subject can be optimized by the perspective, the cropping and the background, or by the arrangement of the people. And from the photographs that are taken, the appropriate ones can be selected later and others discarded if need be. Private photographs and their meta-media such as slide shows, photo albums, and photo books are thus always also media of non-memory, of avoidance, of disinterest in and erasure of memory.(5) Memory and forgetting are not opposed in private photography—they condition each other.

This becomes clear especially from the fact that private photography in East Germany between 1980 and 2000 consisted not solely of the image as object, but was—as it is today—primarily a social practice. Cameras were bought or given as presents;

4 See also the entry “Erinnerung” (Memory) in the glossary of the eponymous exhibition in: Friedrich Tietjen (ed.), *Private Fotografie in Ostdeutschland, 1989–2000: Glossar*, Berlin: Druckerei der Humboldt-Universität zu Berlin 2021, p. 15. And this apotropaic quality of the private photography is also found when the people in the photographs are outside the private sphere in a kind of state of exception: the photographs taken by German soldiers in World War II are dominated by motifs that are similar to those of albums from more peaceful decades, recording joyful comradery, Christmas celebrations, and sights of all kinds.

5 Experiments have shown many times that photography can also generate false memories. See, for example, Linda A. Henkel, “Photograph-Induced Memory Errors: When Photographs Make People Claim They Have Done Things They Have Not,” in: *Applied Cognitive Psychology* 25, no. 1, 2011: pp. 78–86.

some photographers spent hours in the darkroom; photos were exchanged after joint vacations; albums were arranged on long winter evenings; pretzels and soda helped getting through a boring slideshow; sitting on the sofa, people told—and still tell—stories about the pictures; and the album taken from the shelf of the grandmother who has passed away shows nothing but unfamiliar people who no longer mean anything—just throw it away!

For all the monotony of its motifs, private photography is a complex web of actions that differ for each person and in every family. The collections of photographs and albums that were examined for this project were all organized differently; each album looked like no other. Some of them are revised and supplemented again and again even today, while others were created at the end of a year and then never changed. The captions sometimes address the viewers of the albums directly or are—especially popular with children's albums—written in the first-person singular: "Now I'm already one year old!" Often the albums contain a mixture of image sources, with photographs of friends or from photo booths or with ephemera such as tickets, postcards, leaflets, and dried plants pasted in addition to the viewer's own photographs. Not every photographic practice necessarily generates albums: in some cases, the photographs were stored in boxes or existed only as negatives from which prints were or still are produced as needed. In several families, the albums are a living archive that is consulted again and again when discussing events and experiences, and the individual volumes show more or less obvious signs of use. Other albums were produced and put on the shelf where they remained until this project on private photography in East Germany offered an occasion to take them down again.

The size of some collections was striking. A considerable number of the interviewees arrived with suitcases, bags, or boxes full of albums, and

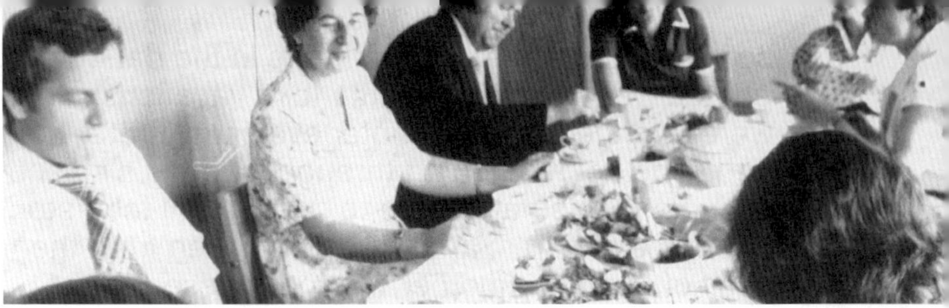

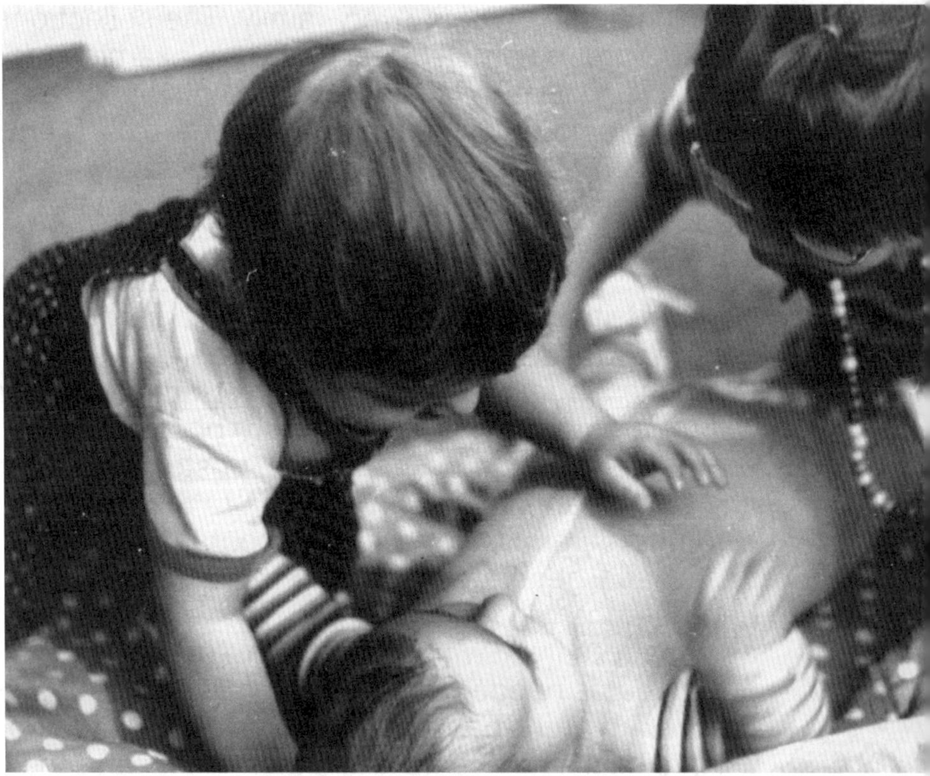

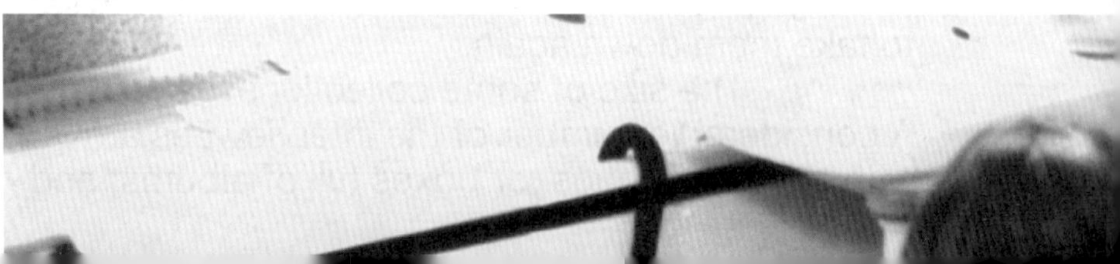

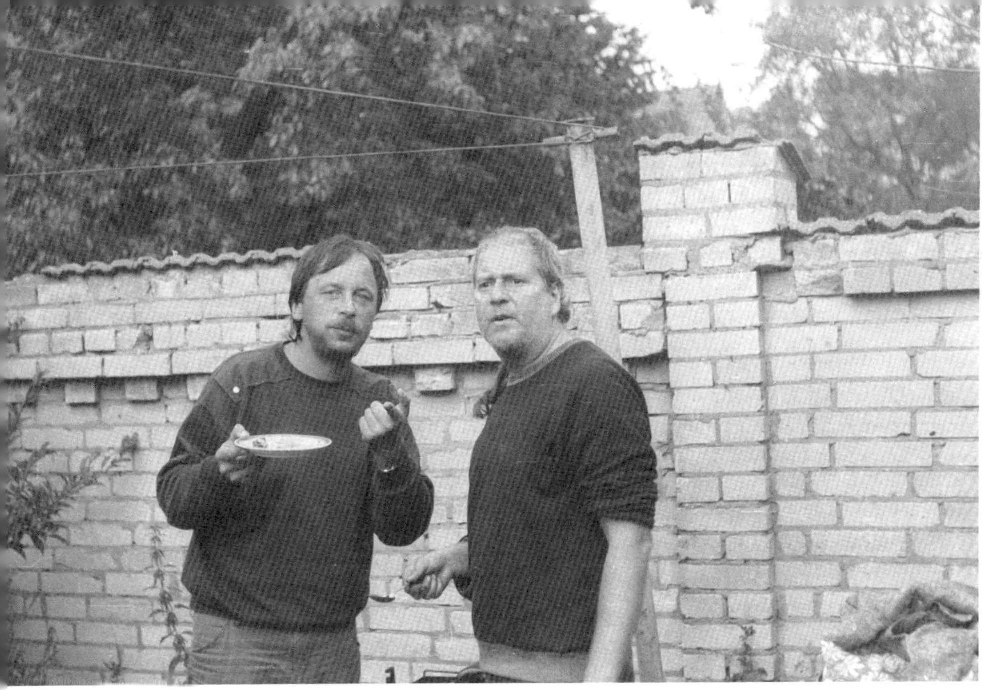

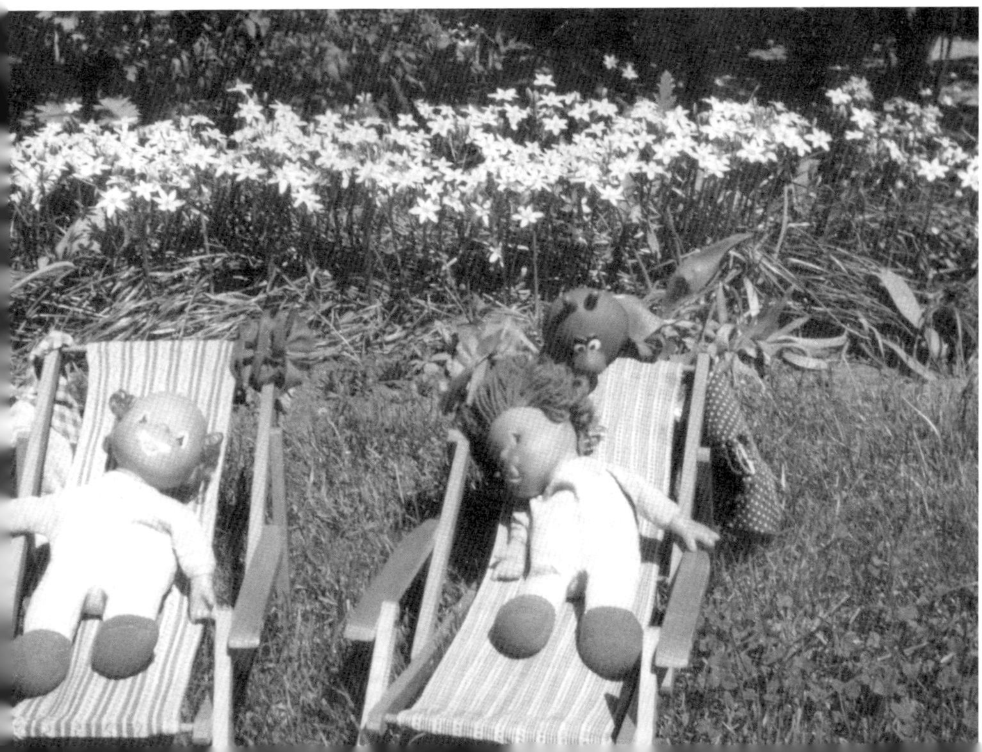

during home visits the albums or folders with negatives sometimes occupied a meter or more of shelf space. Whether this finding can be generalized is open to question, since with a total of 53 conversations, our sample was vanishingly small. In any case, the necessary prerequisites for mass private photography existed in the GDR and also later in reunified Germany: with almost ten thousand workers, the Pentacon Kombinat (collective combine) was, until 1990, the largest producer of single-lens reflex cameras in Europe. As many as 450,000 cameras were produced annually, of which eighty percent—and sometimes more—were exported, especially to the West, to bring in foreign currency.(6) While they were relatively inexpensive there, they could easily cost more than a month's wages in the GDR. A Praktica Super TL 1000, for instance, was around 460 Deutschmarks in the Federal Republic of Germany (FRG) in the 1980s. In the GDR, however, the same camera was around 750 marks at the time.(7) Moreover, these cameras were not always available in stores in the GDR. More readily available and significantly cheaper were simple viewfinder cameras such as the Pouva Start, which had been produced in huge numbers since the 1950s and sold as a "camera for millions" for 16.50 marks, making it a popular gift at *Jugendweihen* (coming-of-age ceremonies at fourteen in the GDR).(8) In total, almost 11 million cameras were produced in the GDR between 1960 and 1989 alone.(9) Given that cameras

6 On these numbers, see Doris Cornelsen / Andreas Koch / Horst Lambrecht / Angela Scherzinger (ed.), *Konsumgüterversorgung in der DDR und Wechselwirkungen zum innerdeutschen Handel*, Berlin: Duncker & Humblot 1985, pp. 99–100.

7 On this, see https://www.digicamclub.de/showthread.php?t=19799 (accessed November 11, 2022).

8 A total of 1.7 million Pouva Start cameras were produced. See https://zeissikonveb.de/start/kameras/pouva-start.html (accessed November 11, 2022).

9 On this, see Susanne Müller, *Von der Mangel- zur Marktwirtschaft. Analyse der Konsumbedingungen und des Konsumverhaltens in der DDR (Teilprojekt 1)*, Leipzig: Institut für Marktforschung 2000, appendix 52.

from the 1930s continued to be used, it can be assumed that, with a population of sixteen to eighteen million in the GDR, there was approximately one camera in every household. We can only speculate about how intensely they were used, but even estimating cautiously it can be assumed that at least three million photo albums were produced in East Germany between 1980 and 2000.(10) And this consideration even ignores that the production of private albums was and is not dependent on owning a camera. Changing formats, different photographic papers, and other indications in the albums suggest that photographs circulated to a considerable extent in familial and social contexts not only within the GDR, but also with relatives and friends in the FRG.

The conditions of private photography practices changed with the demise of the GDR. Since the available color film were not just of rather mediocre quality (color balance and the chemical stability of prints were especially criticized) but also comparatively expensive (a seven-by-ten-centimeter print cost about 1.50 marks) private photographs were predominantly black-and-white until 1989. The film stock and baryta paper required for them were of high quality and yet relatively inexpensive. And because developing, fixing, and enlarging black-and-white photographs was comparatively easy, many photographers simply did it themselves in temporary darkrooms installed in bathrooms or kitchens. And anyone who did not want to or could not do that, could also have film developed and enlarged inexpensively at a photo store. With the liquidation of the ORWO photo film factory in 1990 and the drastic cutbacks in production, its black-and-white films and

10 This estimate is based on the assumption that around four million cameras were in private hands, of which I assume that half of them were never used at all. Of the other half, photographs were taken for at least one album; one fourth of the cameras produced at least one more album. With reasonable certainty, however, these numbers are clearly too low.

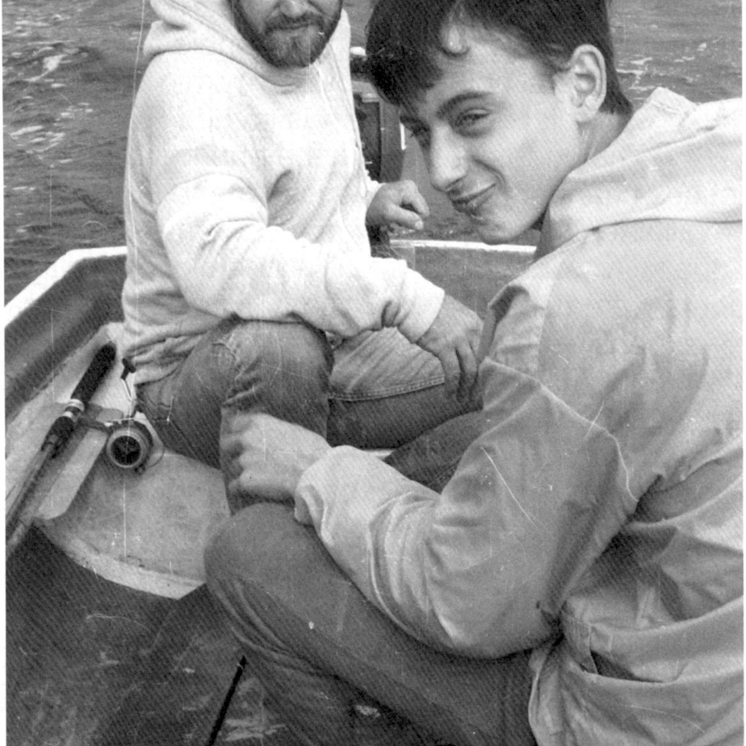

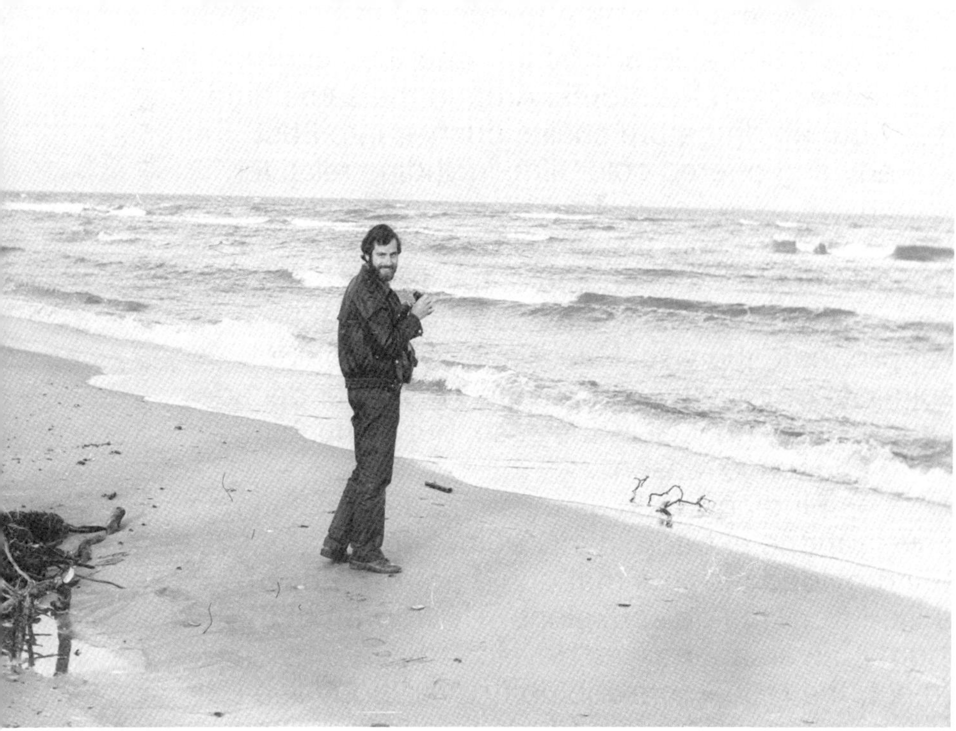

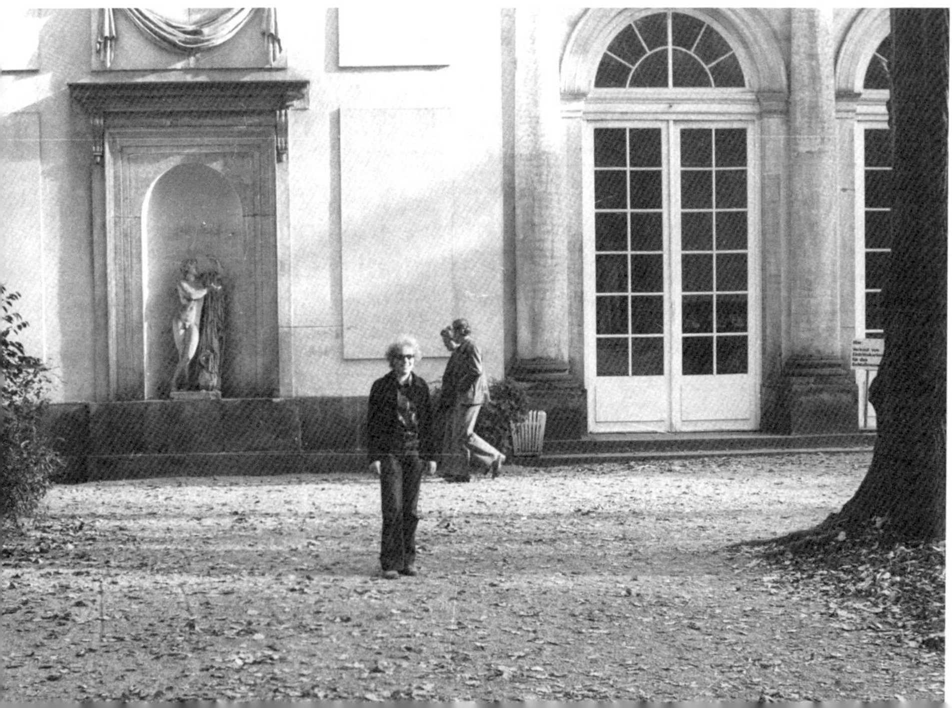

papers were first sold off cheaply and then largely disappeared from the stores. Around the same time, West German drugstore chains pushed into East Germany and offered color film, including relatively inexpensive developing. That black-and-white photography was rapidly displaced by color photography in many albums in the course of the 1990s thus has less to do with East Germans now finally wanting to appropriate the visual blessings of the colorful capitalist commodity world of the West after decades of supposedly gray GDR tristesse, but is much more due to economic reasons.

Findings such as these made the album conversations extraordinarily fruitful and instructive. They provided insights that could not have been derived from the objects alone. The format of these album conversations was developed in a previous project, the research exhibition *"Everybody line up! It's time to snap!" Private Photography in Austria 1930–1950* at the Volkskundemuseum in Vienna, developed by Herbert Justnik and myself. The temporal framework for both projects was defined on the basis of the question of whether, and if so, how, private photography reacts to historical ruptures—in the case of the project about private photography in East Germany, these are above all the demonstrations in the fall of 1989 and the demise of the GDR as an independent state the following year. At its core, the album conversations involve inviting individuals, usually through calls in the media, to show their family albums and other photographs and to talk about both these images and their private photographic practices. Thanks to generous financial support from the Bundesstiftung zur Aufarbeitung der SED-Diktatur (Federal Foundation for the Study of the Communist Dictatorship in East Germany), it was possible, despite the Corona pandemic, to view nearly sixty collections of private photographs in 2020 and 2021 and to hold conversations with their owners, who had often been the producers of the images and albums themselves. These conversations were recorded with an overhead camera and dictaphones. Over the course of the project, nearly seventy hours of recordings were made, which, once the project was completed, will be transferred, along with several donations, to the photography collection of the Deutsches Historisches Museum in Berlin, where they will be made available to interested researchers.

This volume evaluates the results obtained in the course of the project through the album conversations. This is done first through four essays. Starting from Jürgen Jabs' (Berlin) archive of negatives and contact prints, Marie Egger studies how his private photography practices evolved and how his training as an exploratory geologist played a key role in this evolution. Using the example of the albums of the Göldner family (Potsdam), Judith Riemer discusses how the different temporal layers in private photography are reflected in the design of albums. The collection of albums and photographs of the Specht family (Magdeburg) are unusual insofar as the couple developed and enlarged color film at home. In her essay, Marit Lena Herrmann examines the processes inside and outside of the darkroom and derives several insights and questions from them. My own contribution sets out from several photographs by Martin Siebert (Ilmenau) and Georg Mohr (Rostock) and two flea-market finds in an effort to understand how the West was visually present in the East. We very much hope that the study and examination of these extensive materials does not end with these four essays. In order to make it easier for other scholars to begin working on it, to the end of the volume holdings of private photographs are also presented in a concise form, whose owners are happy to make their pictures and albums accessible and are also willing to engage in further discussions.

The book also contributes to the increasingly intense discussions that have emerged in recent years about the significance of private photographs

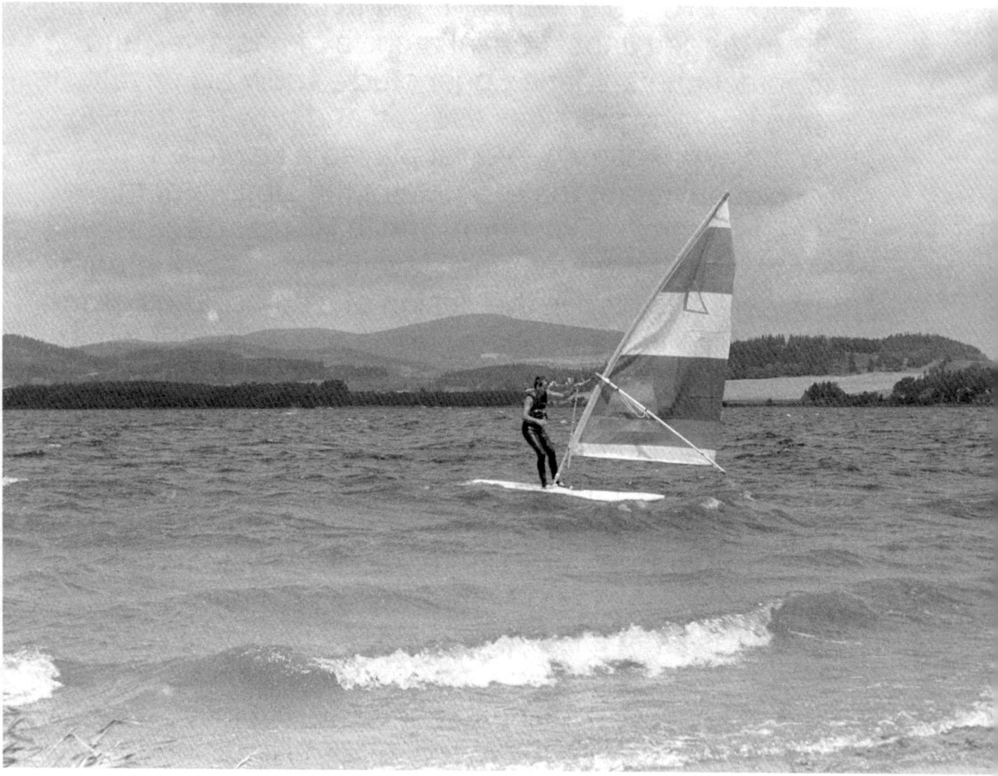

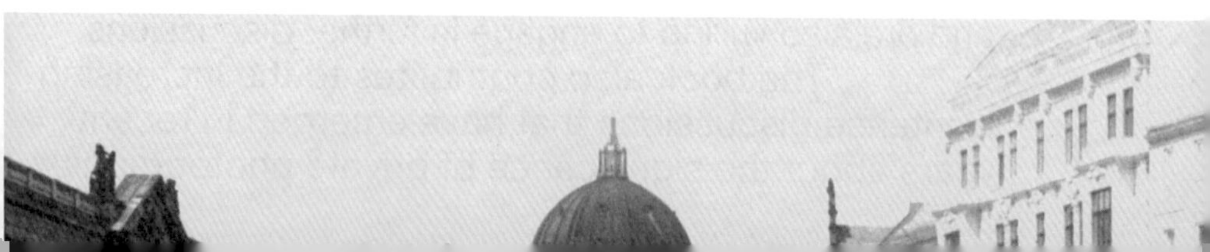

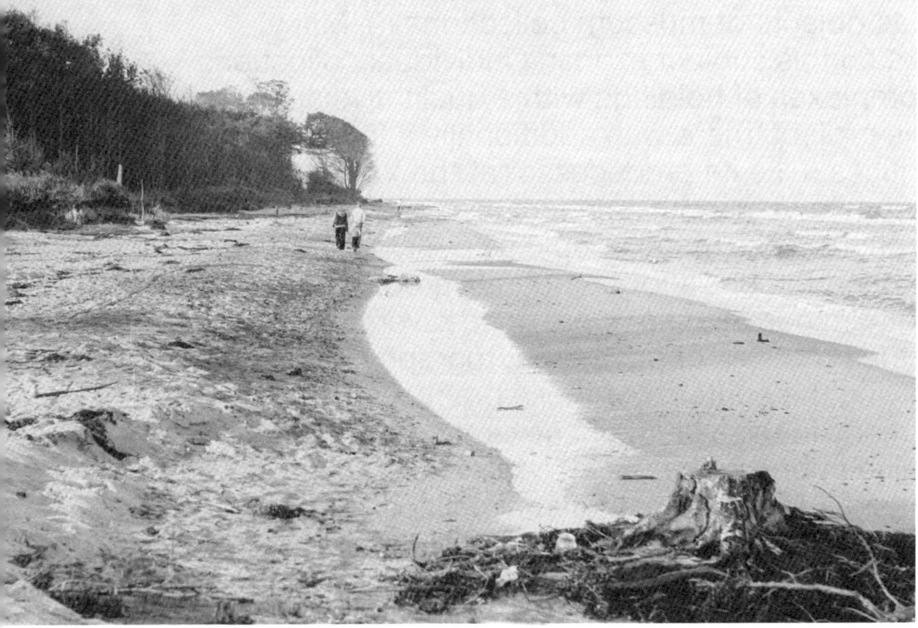

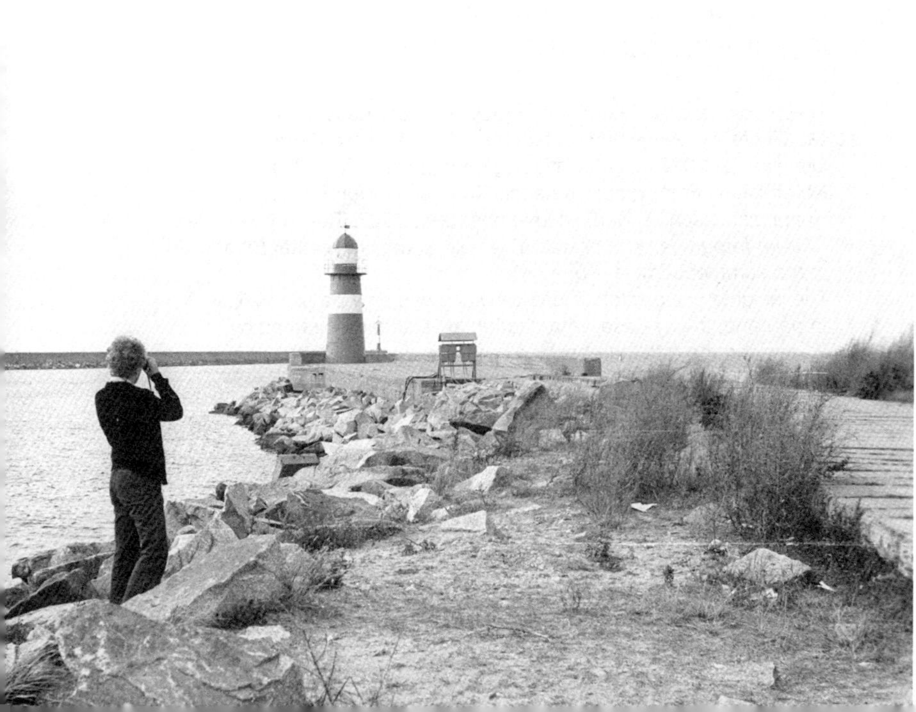

and photo albums as objects of scholarly research and as objects of museum collections.(11) Many works on this subject examine individual collections or complexes of holdings with a qualitative approach; in this project, there was additionally a focus on their quantities. Like its predecessor at the Volkskundemuseum in Vienna, this project also examined the collections of as many people as possible in order to expand the basis for comparative observations.(12) The album conversations provided diverse insights into the practices of private photography, thus also archiving the contexts of these practices. The descriptions in this volume of several collections remaining in private hands also represent an effort to reconsider forms of institutional collecting and the archiving of such collections. From the perspective of conservation, it might seem problematic to leave the objects in home shelves and cabinets. The advantage of such an approach, however, is that large holdings of materials can be examined without burdening the scarce storage space of museums and archives. In private hands, moreover, the albums and photographs remain in place where they can continue to be organized, shown, narrated, and remem-

11 In 2022 alone, there were two conferences on these themes: *Die Geste des Zeigens: Fotoalben im Archiv*, Photoszene Köln, October 22, 2022, and *Kuratierte Erinnerungen: Das Fotoalbum*, Kommission Fotografie, Deutsche Gesellschaft für Empirische Kulturwissenschaft, Berlin, November 3–4, 2022. The lecture series *Warum fotografieren wir?* was also held at the Universität Siegen in the summer semester of 2022.

12 The insights gained from these viewings can only be generalized in part and, in any case, with caution as is already dictated by comparing the total number of albums produced with the vanishingly small sampling. Moreover, even though we tried to reach people who were as different as possible for our album conversations, organizing appointments in small towns as well as large ones, for all their biographical, professional, and political differences, our conversation partners were almost without exception well educated and, though they had not gotten through the years between 1980 and 2000 without a few scratches, they at least do not face any existential threats at present. And despite some efforts, we did not manage to win over any former *VertragsarbeiterInnen* (contractual employees from abroad) or their descendants for our album conversations.

bered and thus exposed to the social practices and changes that make them the living objects that they were produced to be in the first place.

With this volume, the project on private photography in East Germany between 1980 and 2000 comes, after three years, to a conclusion. Like its subject, the project itself has had not just one author but owes its success to the ideas and work of many. As the editor of this book, I am pleased to be able to express gratitude for the fruitful collaboration. I would like to thank my colleagues Marit Lena Herrmann, Solange Lingnau, Stephanie Wuntke, and Sophie Schulz, with whom I was able to realize this project. Franziska Kuschel supervised the project on the part of the Bundesstiftung Aufarbeitung for three years with a patience, friendliness, and willingness to improvise without which we could hardly have brought the project through the pandemic and inflation in one piece. Carola Jüllig from the Deutsches Historisches Museum was a great project and conversation partner at all times. Together with Katja Müller-Helle, I was able to offer two seminars at the Humboldt-Universität zu Berlin in 2021: the exhibition *"… someone always had a camera …" Private Photography in East Germany, 1980–2000* at the Stiftung Reinbeckhallen (Berlin) and this book owe decisive impulses and insights to the students and to her. And my greatest gratitude goes to those who contacted us, showed us their albums and photographs, and told us their stories. Like my colleagues, I have learned a tremendous amount from these conversations—as a historian of photography, as a West German who has now lived in East Germany for many years, and as someone who takes the same photographs as everyone else.

Friedrich Tietjen
Leipzig, November 2022

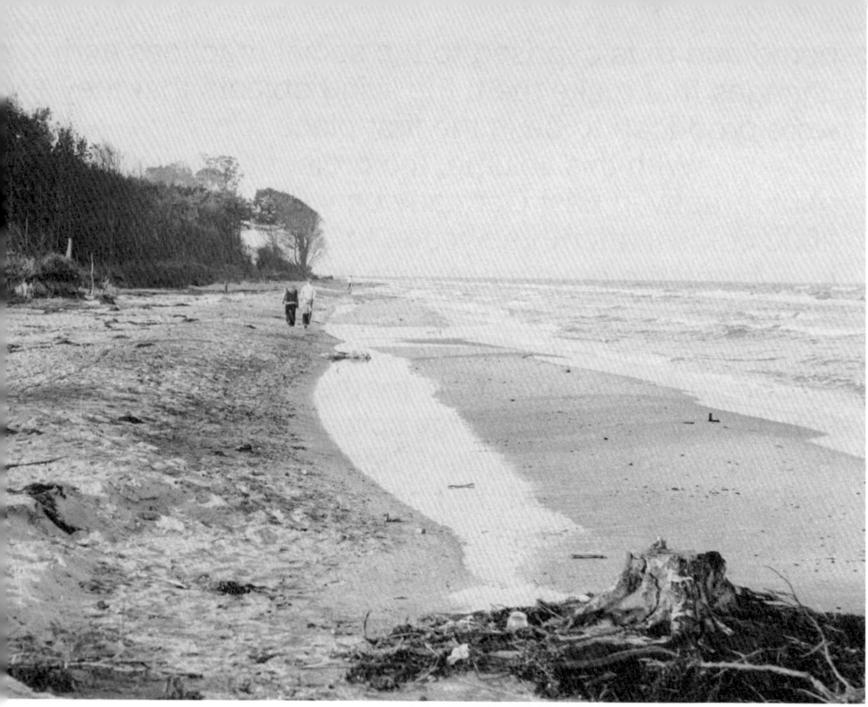

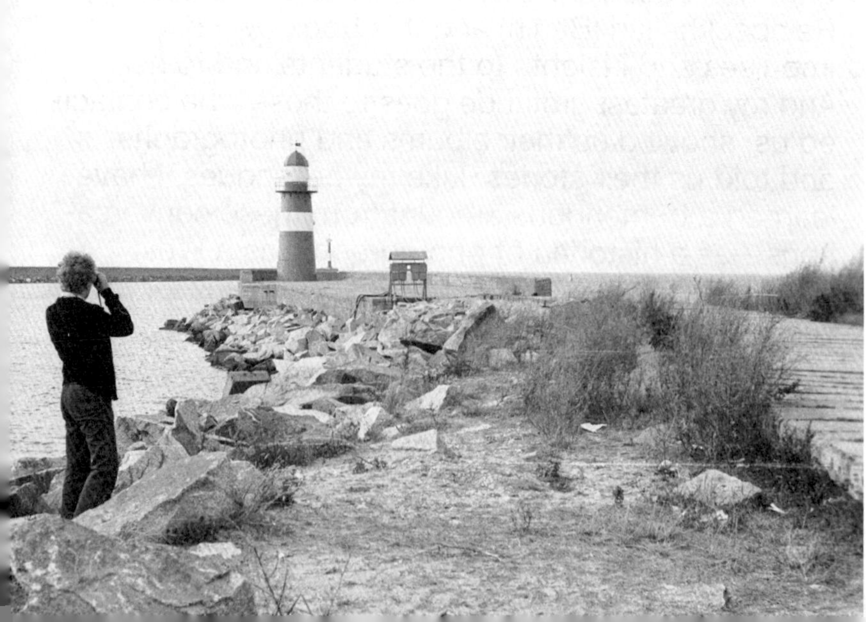

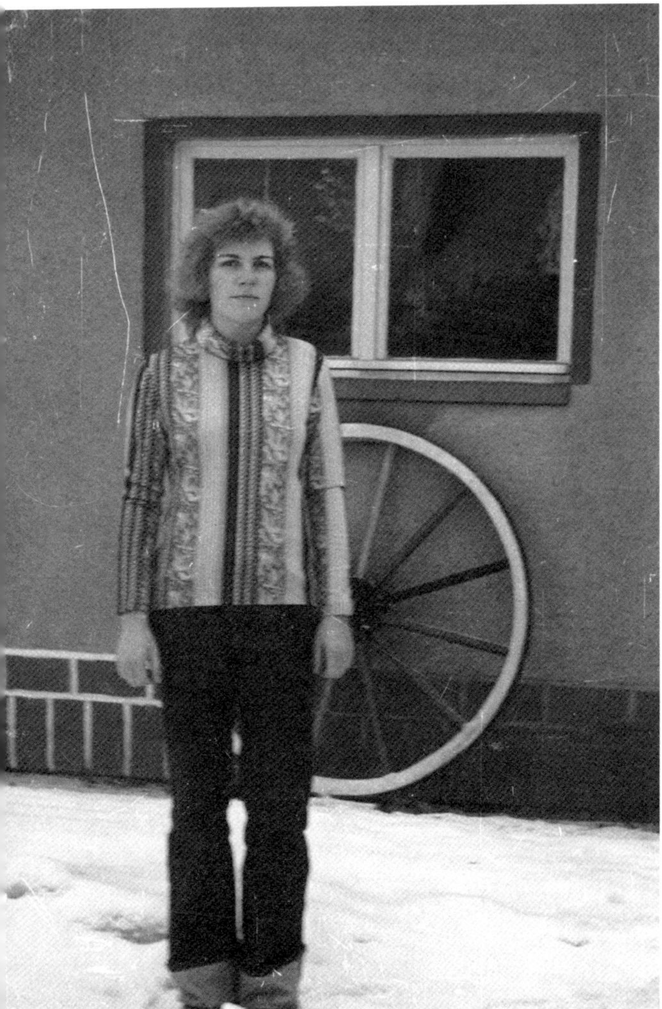
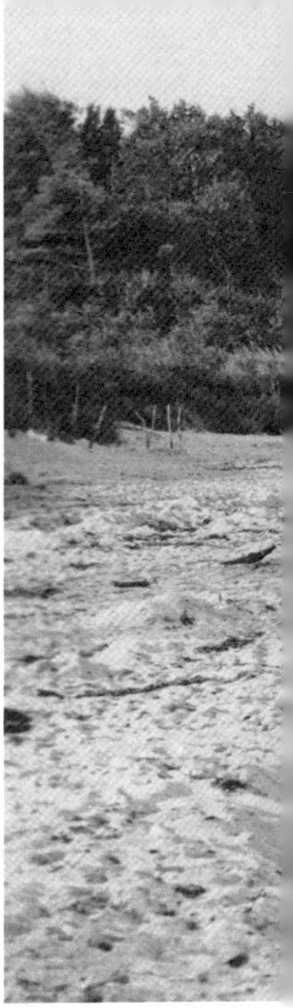

1968

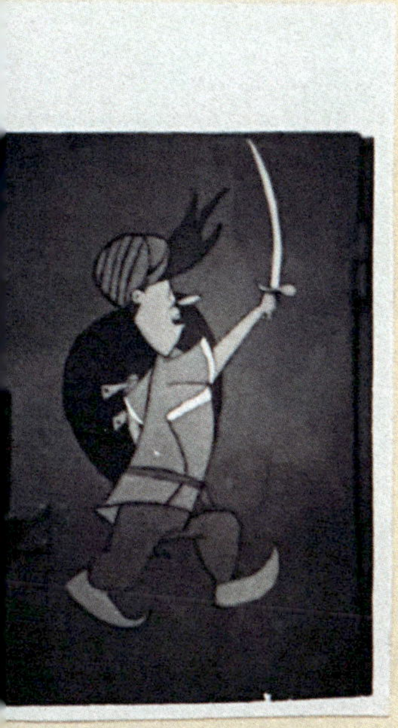

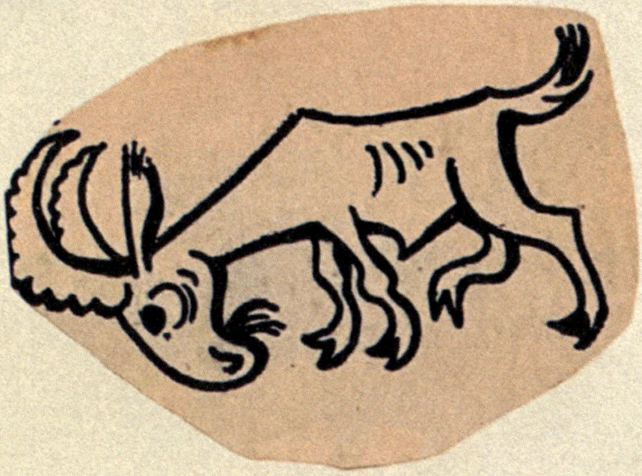

Jetzt kommt es darauf an:

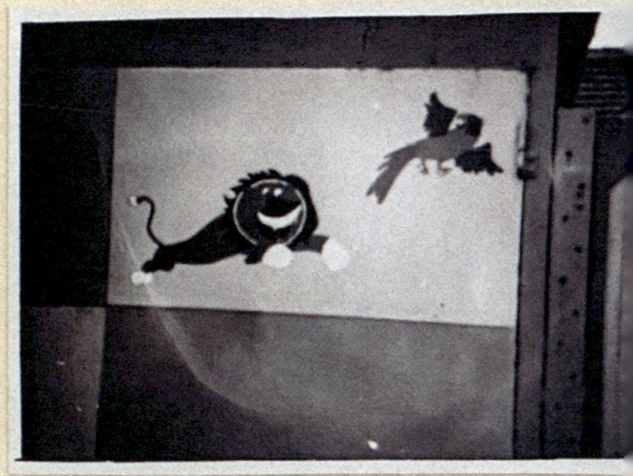

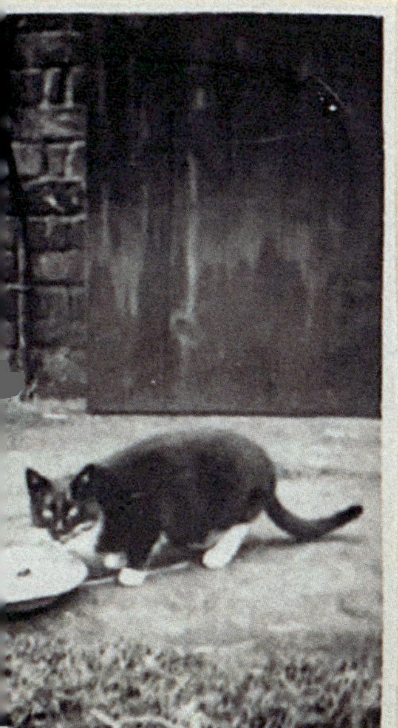

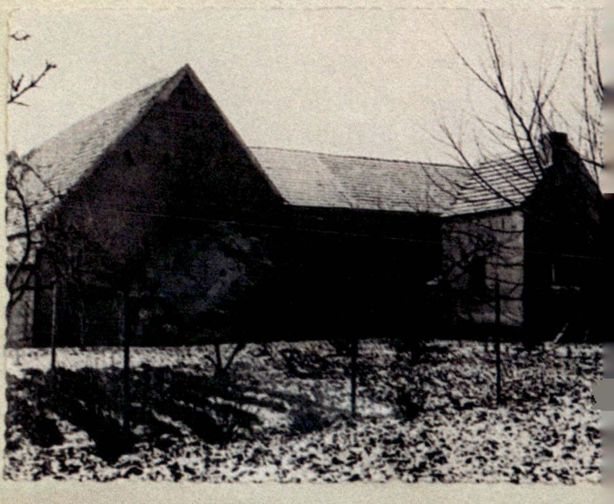

Margrit and Burghard Specht

Margrit and Burghard Specht

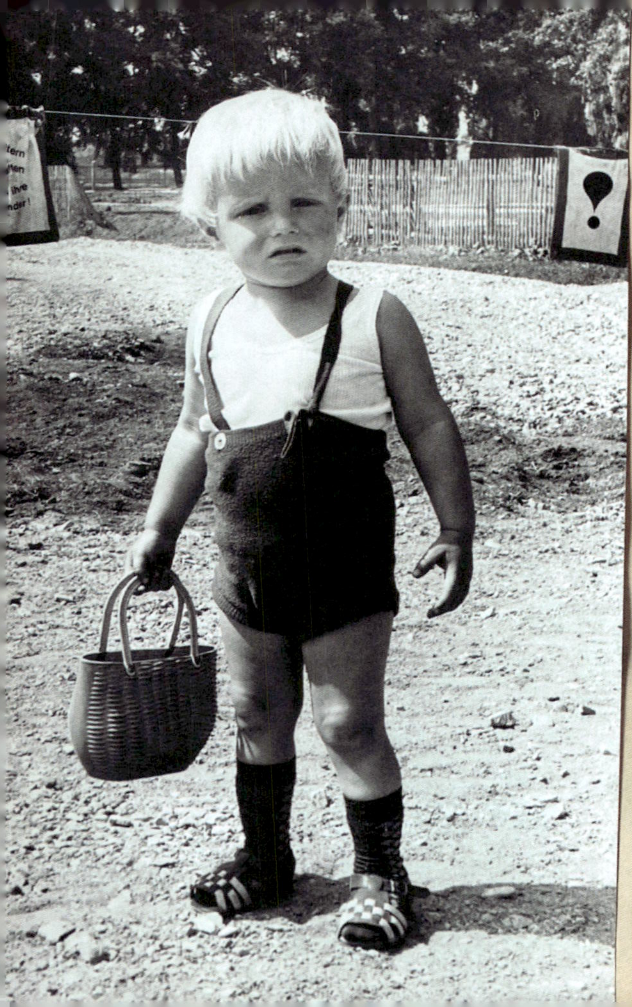

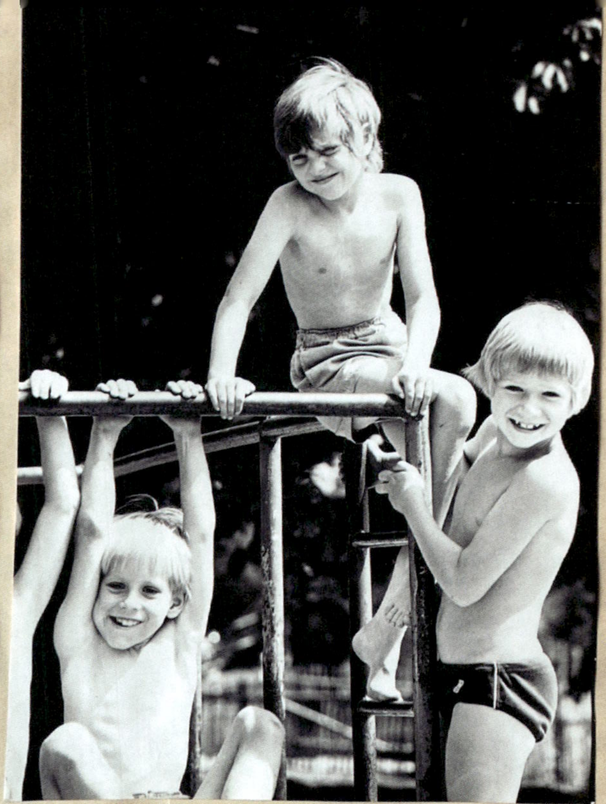

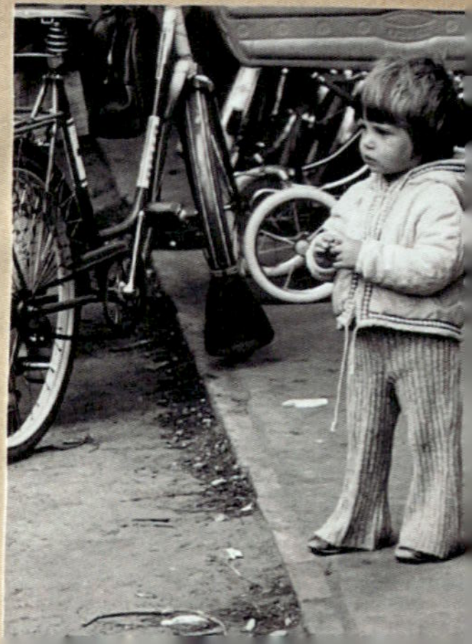

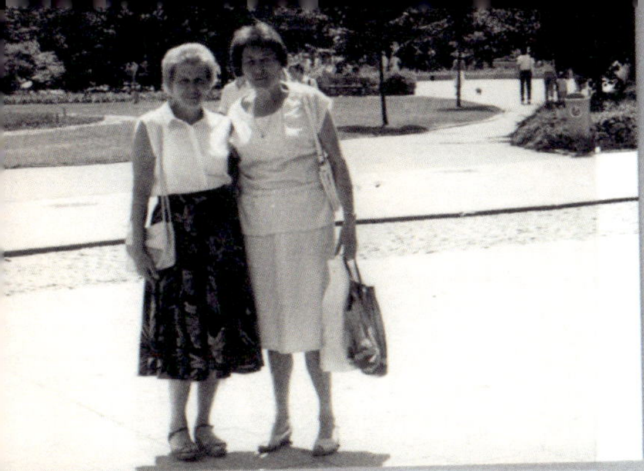

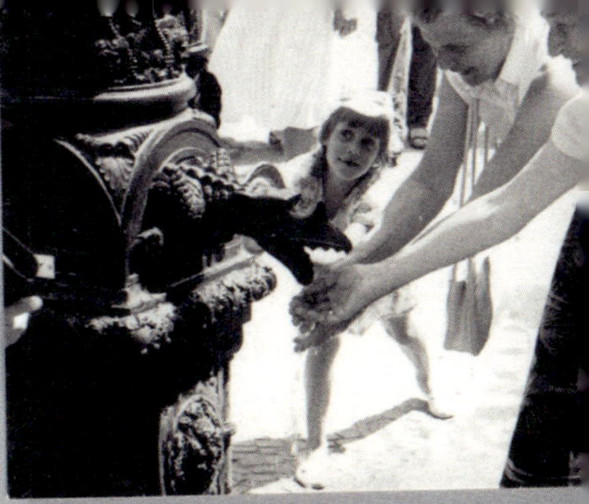

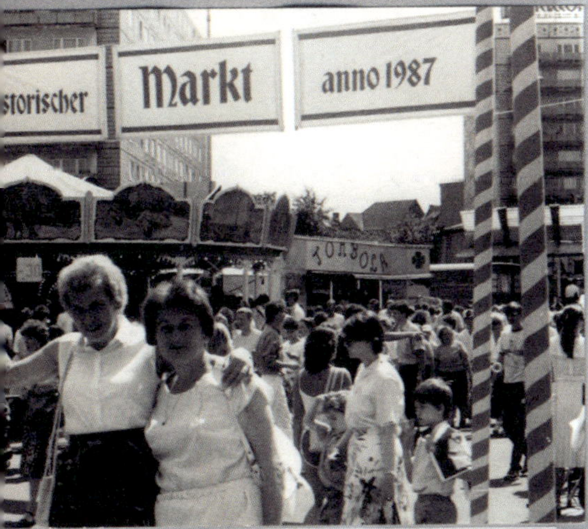
storischer
Markt
anno 1987

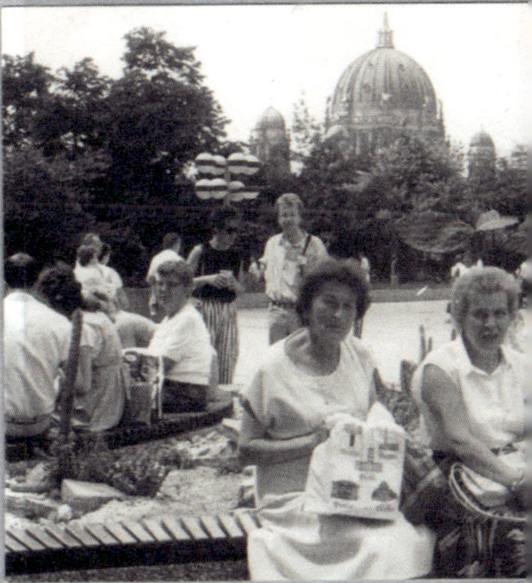

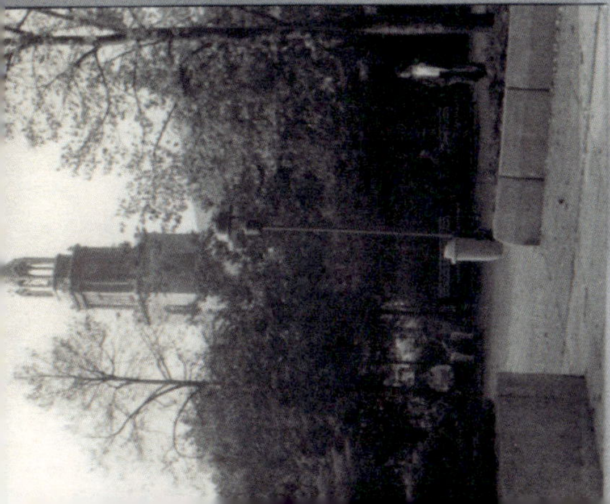

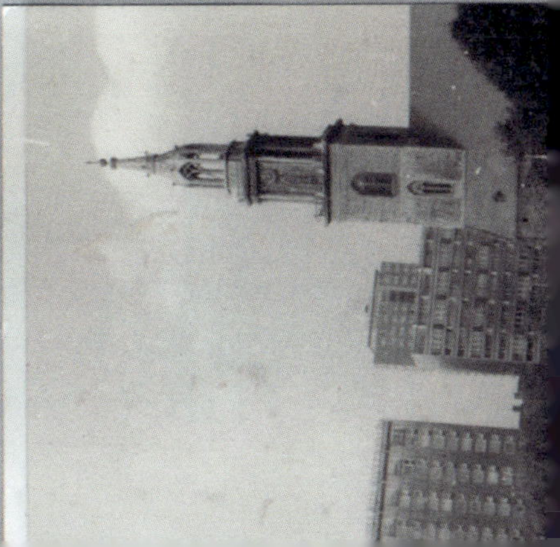

Archive Tietjen

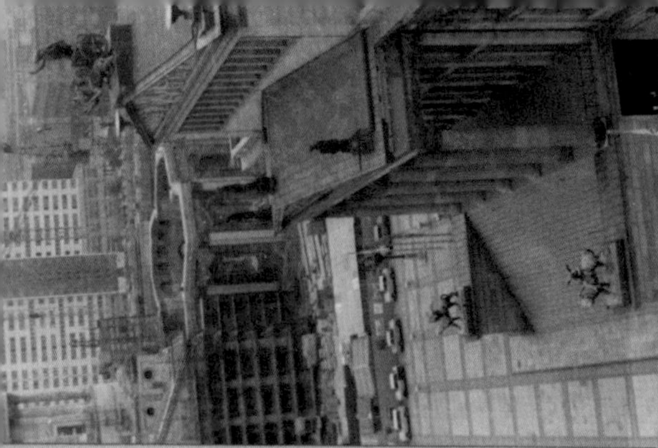

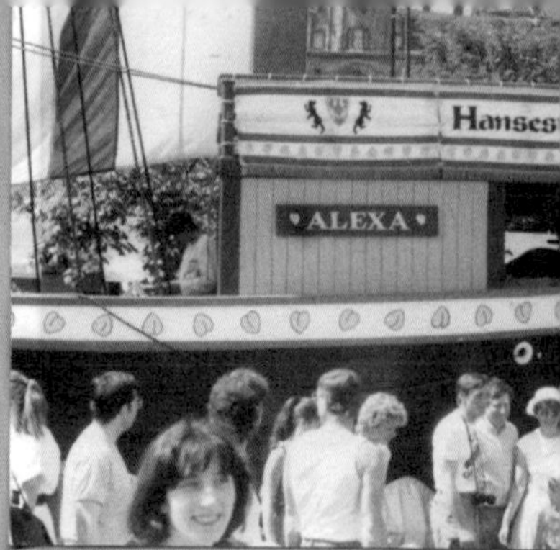
ALEXA

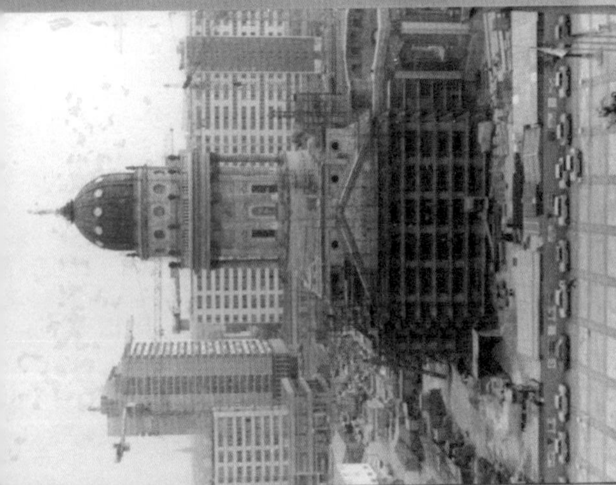

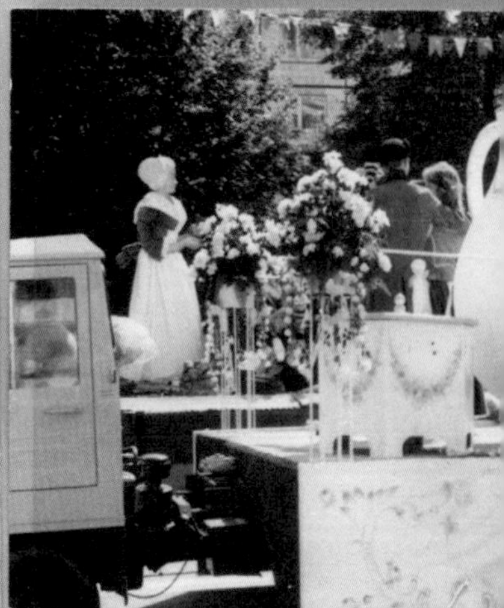

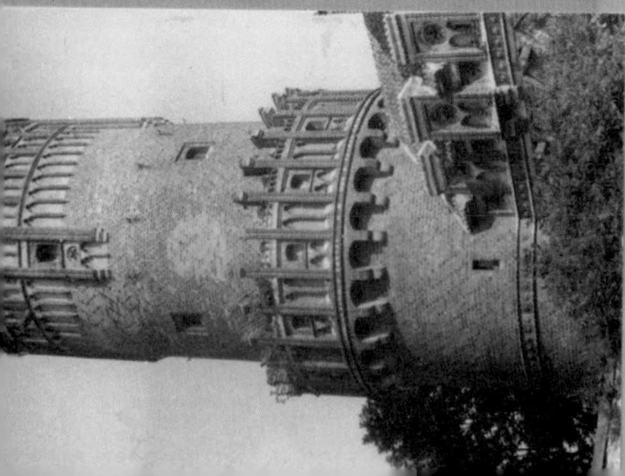

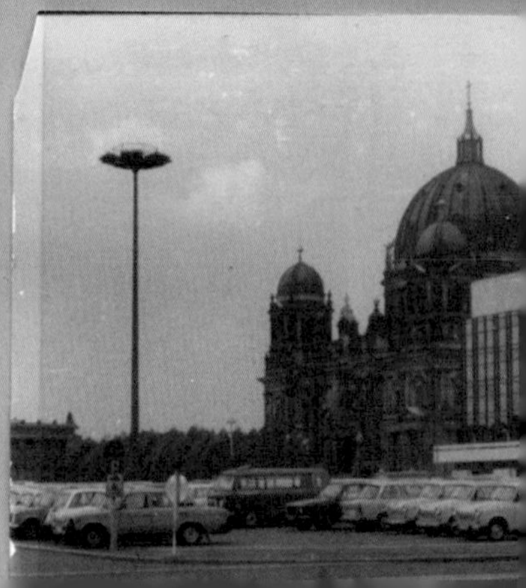

Winter 1969/70
im Treptow

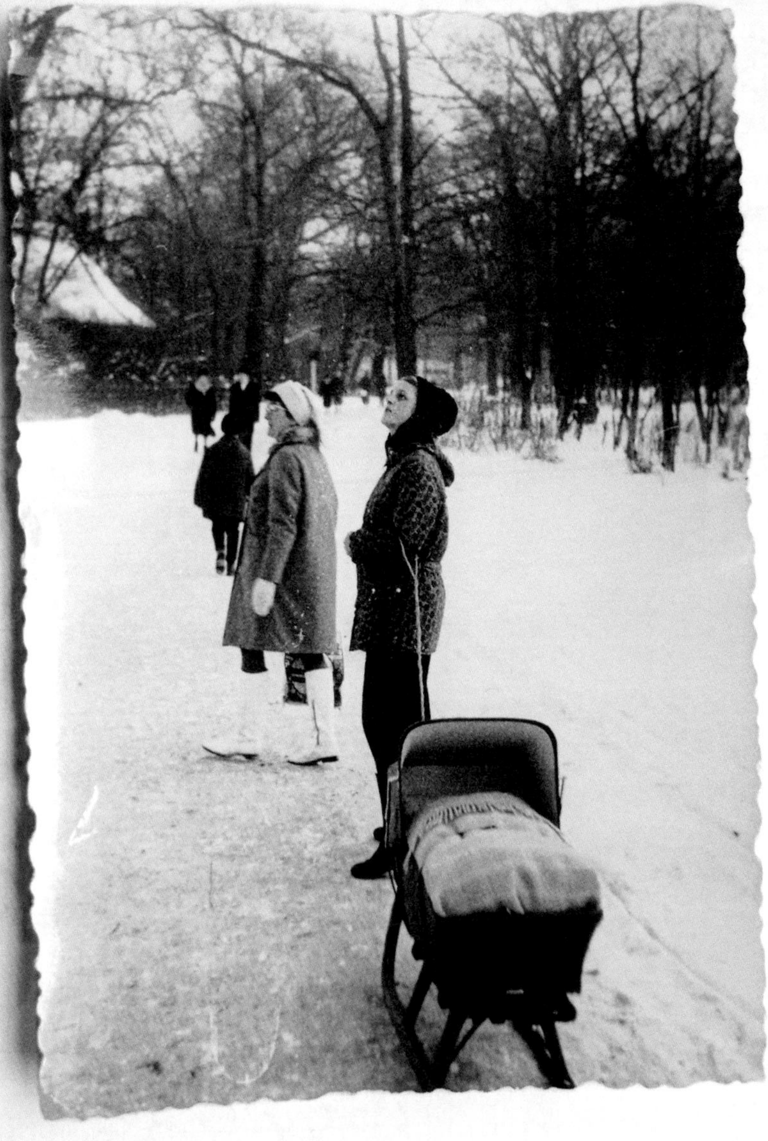

Borghild Carus

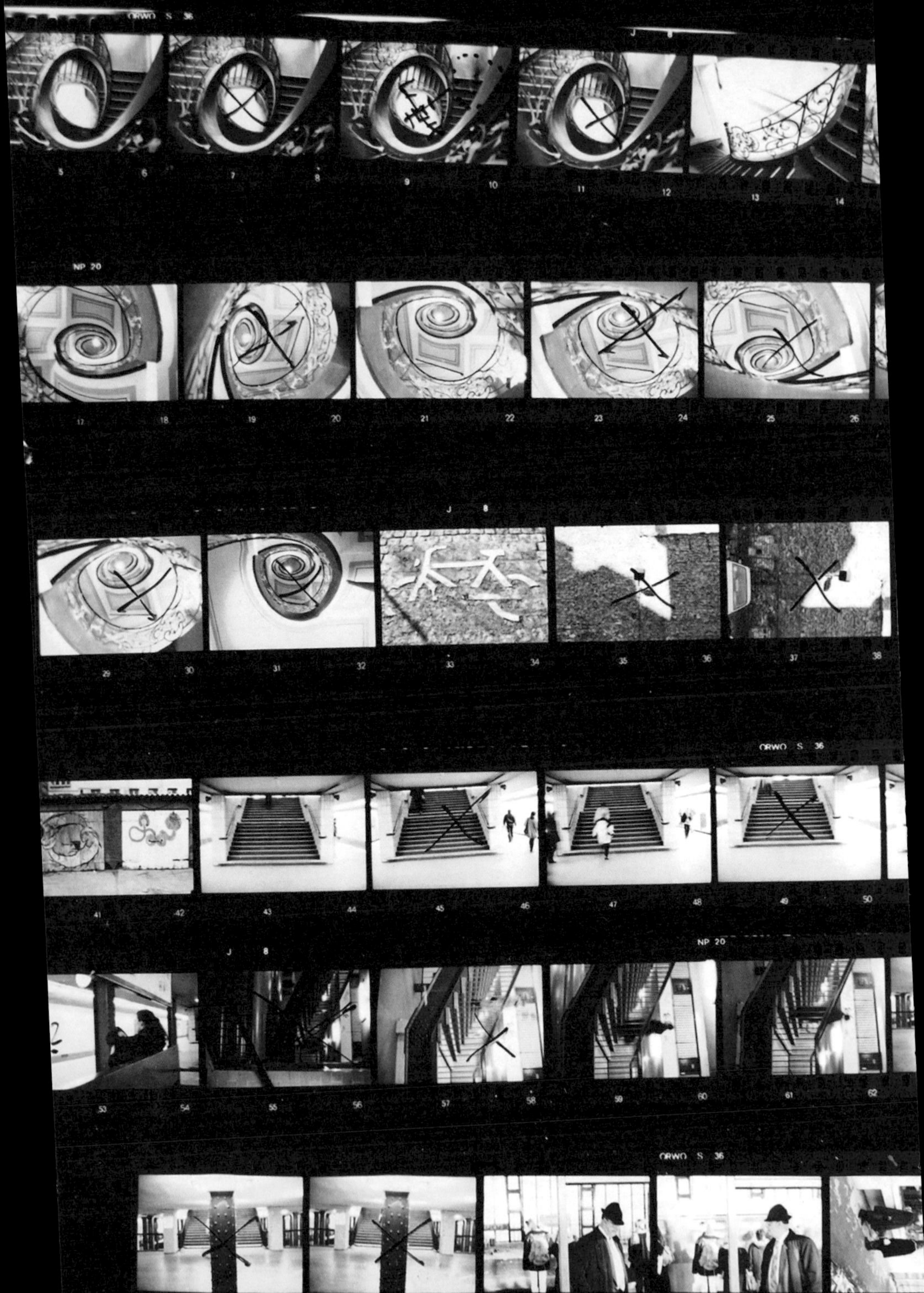
ORWO S 36
NP 20
J 8

Searching for the Right Image. A Geologist's Private Contact Sheets

Marie Egger

Jürgen Jabs began taking analog photographs with an EXA1 camera in 1975 while studying geology in Greifswald. During an internship, he took numerous sample and reference photos of fossils, stones, landscapes, and geological situations on field trips to Pomerania, Brandenburg, and Armenia, which he then developed in the laboratory of the university's institute. Jabs reports that he made the prints of the negatives himself in the darkroom and that he felt proud when he "could finally remove a photo from the fixer that was correctly exposed."(1) Although he then experienced for the first time the "magic of photography" as a "great art," today he stores these photos in the basement of his flat in Berlin and not in his study like all his other pictures. Nowadays he sees his excursion shots only as his first steps in the field of photography and quickly became interested in other motifs: events, book readings, rock concerts, sports competitions for the university newspaper, and the birth of his first son in 1978, among "the obligatory family photos." Since then, Jabs has always carried a camera on him: on the way to work, to soccer practice, when exploring the streets and backyards of his residential district Prenzlauer Berg, on excursions to his rural hometown in Brandenburg, at family celebrations, and on vacation. Alongside his work as a collection conservator for fossil invertebrates at the Museum für Naturkunde in Berlin, Jabs always took photography seriously "with the vehemence and athletic ambition of an Uckermärker." Even today, he seeks meaning in his photos and hopes to take

1 Album conversation with Jürgen Jabs, Berlin, June 13, 2021. This is the source for all of Jabs's comments cited in the chapter. I would like to thank Jürgen Jabs for the very stimulating and open discussion about his work as well as for his support, cooperation, and trust in providing research material.

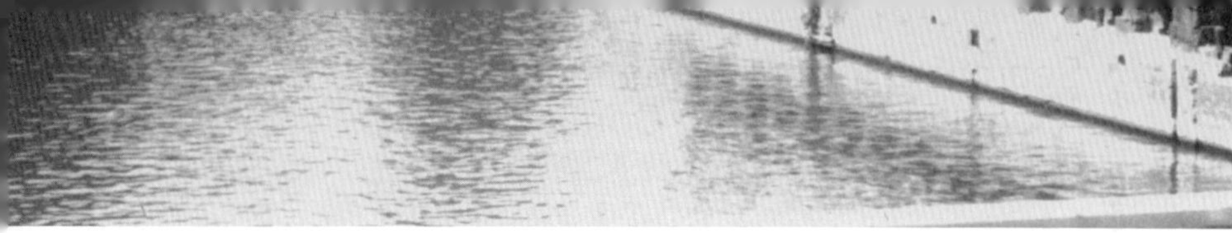

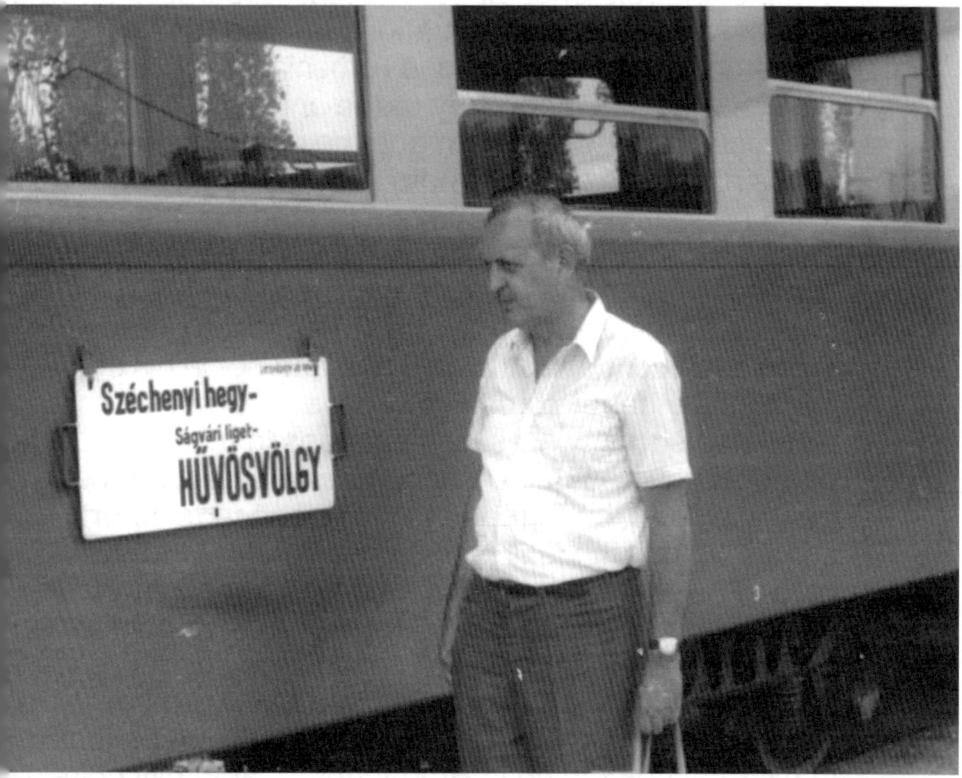
Széchenyi hegy-
Ságvári liget-
HŰVÖSVÖLGY

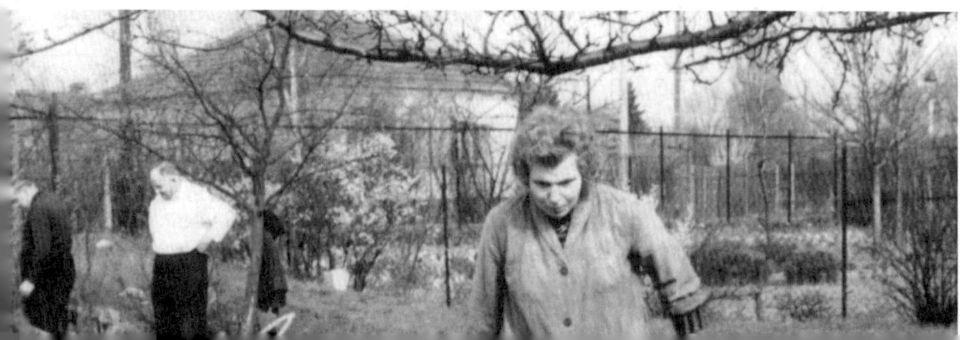

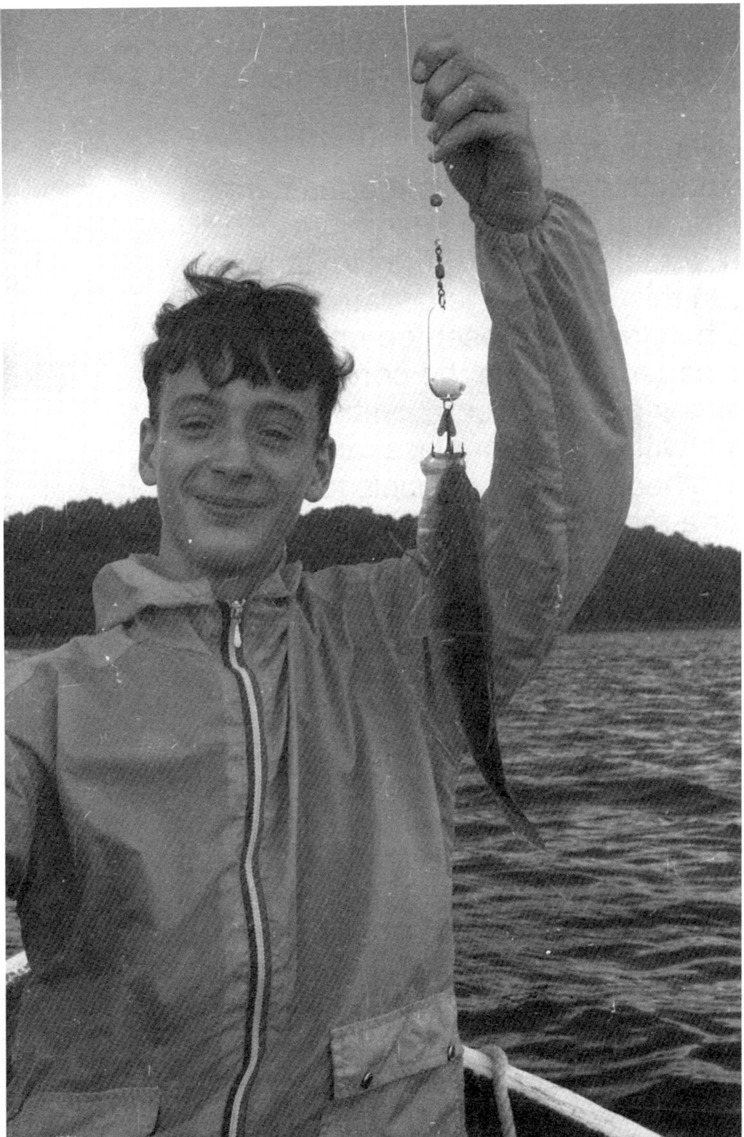

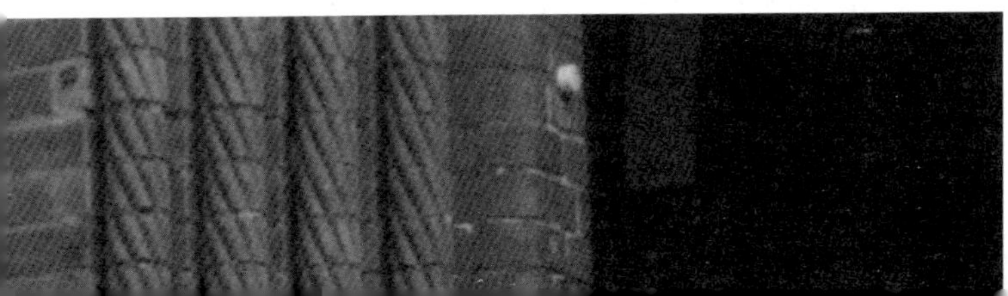

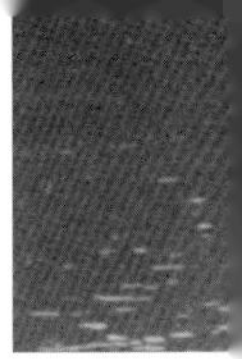

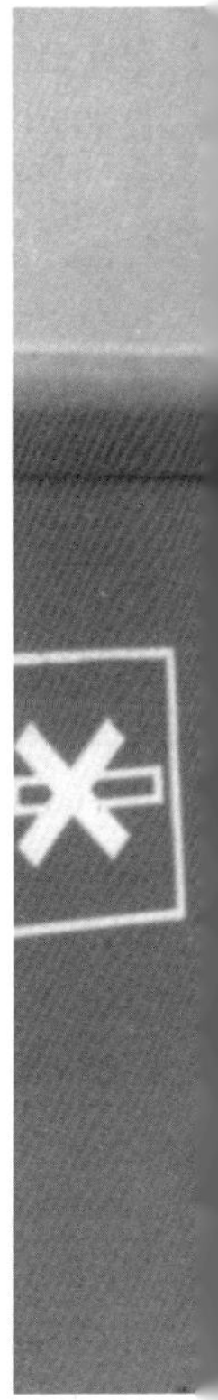

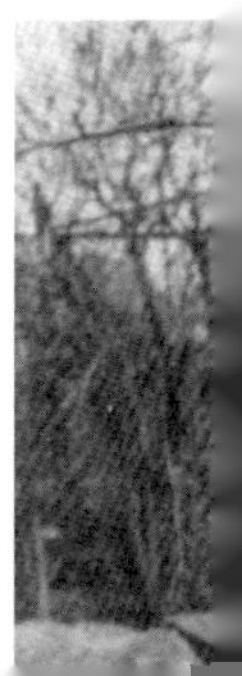

viewers "a step further." His contact sheets provide the answer to what he means by this and how he ensures that his pictures meet these requirements.

Visual Diaries of a Flaneur

A standard film for a thirty-five-millimeter camera provided space for about thirty-six exposures. Cut into six pieces that make six rows, the film fit roughly on an A4 sheet. In this way, all the negatives on a roll of film can be clearly represented on a sheet of photographic paper. To make the contact sheet, the developed film is placed directly on the paper, pressed against it with a plate of glass, and then exposed. Contact sheets make it possible to compare the photos under a magnifying glass without first making an enlargement of each image.

An undated sheet by Jabs shows the sequence of thirty-six photographs numbered consecutively through the film (fig. 1): on the upper left, a mural of two indigenous horsemen in front of a United States flag; to the right, a photo of a house wall taken from around the corner; then a wall with the slogan "Damn it, Sarah, I love you! Fuck your neurodermatitis!" and three oblique views of passers-by. A pensive figure sitting on a park bench opens the second row of images, which includes two shots of bicycles and two of a soccer goal in front of a wooded area. This is followed by several views of another soccer goal with a boat behind it, yet another soccer goal in a different location, and two photos of a naive-style mural of a goalkeeper with a ball going into the net. The lower half of the sheet continues with shots of an overturned goal frame, a bench overgrown with plants, and a rickety gate. Then the photographer seems to have changed locations again to capture a wide landscape, an overcast sky, and a field after harvesting seen from different angles. Returning to urban space, the film ends with two photos of bicycles, a portrait of a sleeping person, and four views of artworks in public spaces.

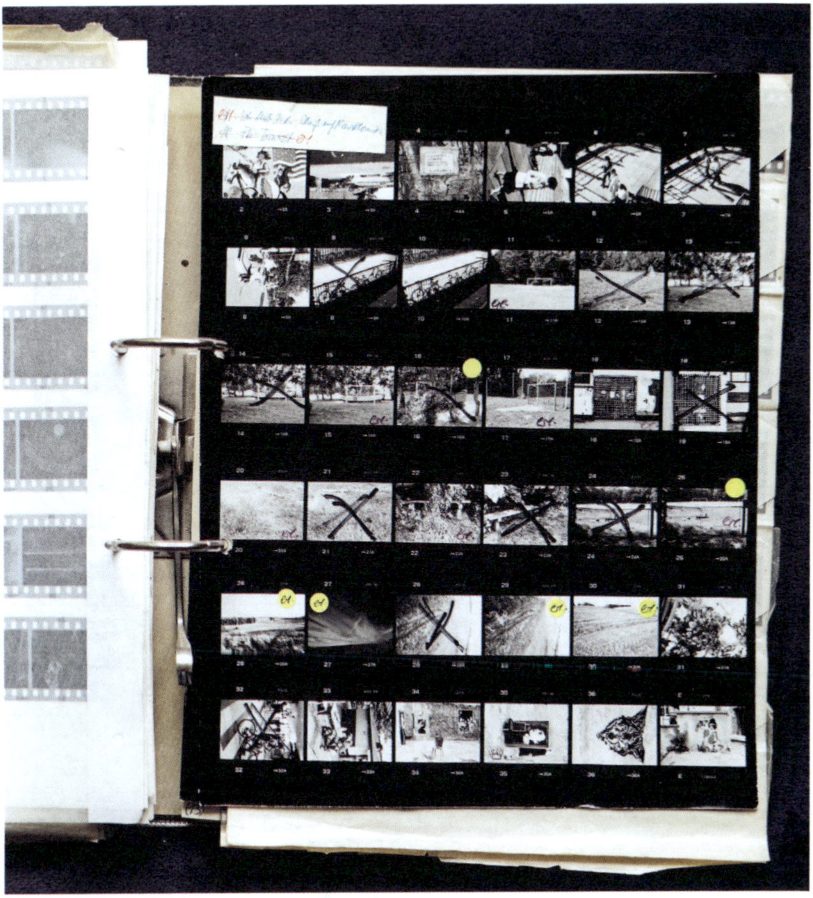

Fig. 1: Opened file folder with undated contact sheet from the private archive of Jürgen Jabs. Photo: Jürgen Jabs.

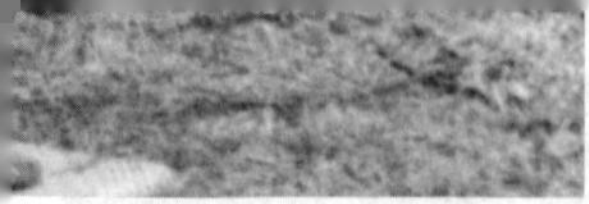

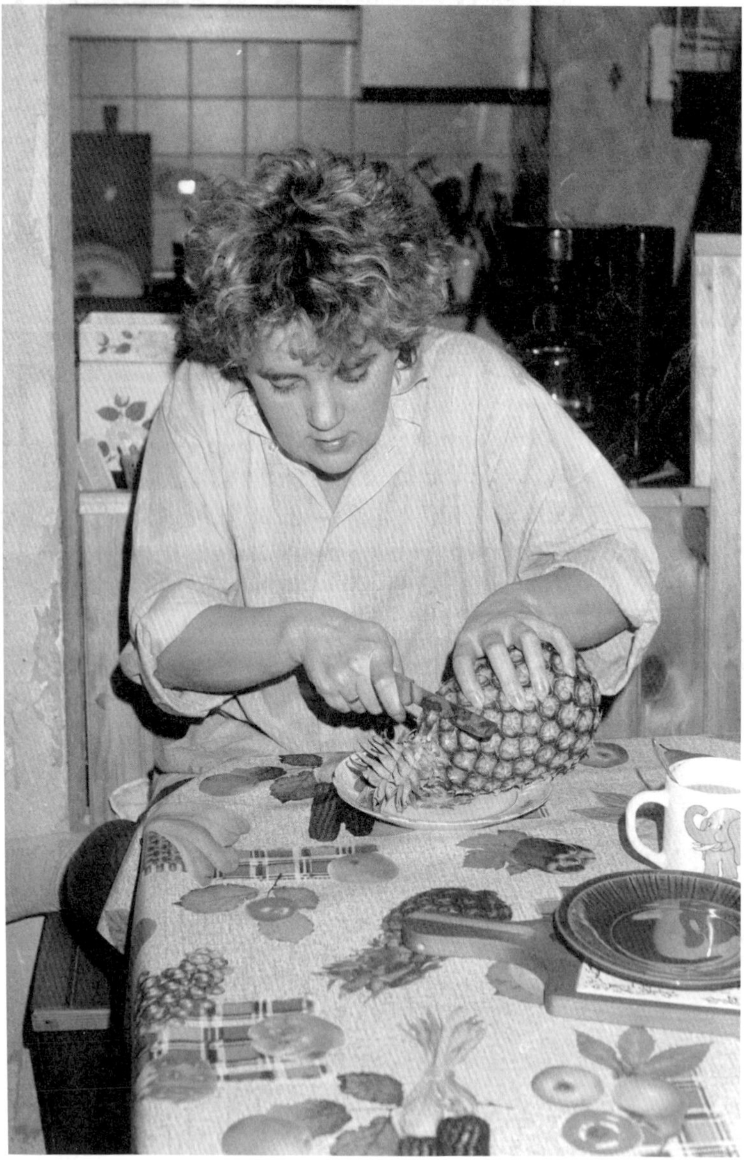

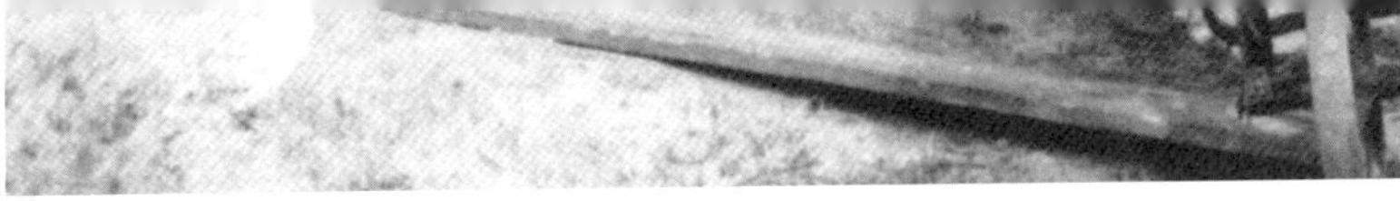

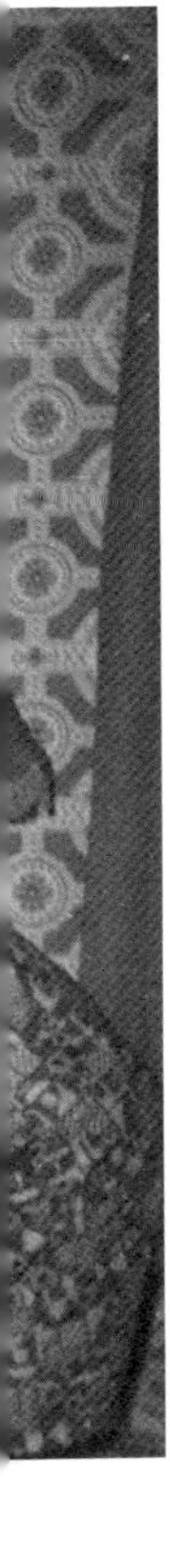

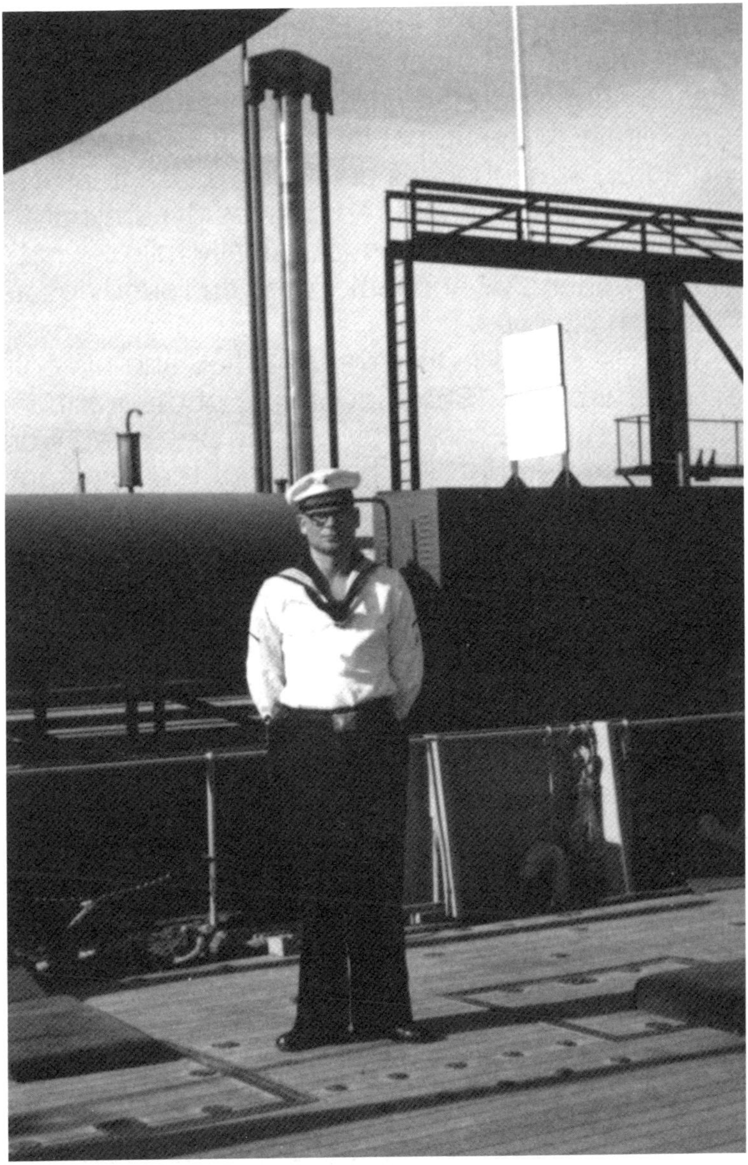

Jabs was apparently out and about, armed with his camera in fine weather during the summer. Like a diary entry written over several weeks, the contact sheet records when and where he strolled photographically through the world, how quickly or slowly, and how Jabs photographed the objects he observed from different angles. From the second to the second-to-last image, the sheet shows a before and after of each shot, so that different events are represented episodically in the strips. In this way, Jabs created photographic sequences on film en passant, as it were, which the contact sheet reproduces dynamically, so that viewers can almost physically follow what the photographer saw and look at the surroundings as if through his eyes.

Sociologist Pierre Bourdieu and his colleagues wrote in 1965 that private photographers like Jabs capture "aspects ... of the perceived world" that are "imperceptible" because of their "instantaneousness."(2) They also argued that releasing the shutter at a particular moment was a highly individual decision and sometimes difficult for outsiders to grasp, so that photographers sometimes could not explain it themselves. In order to describe successful chance shots and other aesthetic phenomena in private photography, which only become visible on the film after being developed or on the enlargements of images, Bourdieu and others adopted the concept of the "optical unconscious" from the philosopher and flaneur Walter Benjamin.(3) By assuming this effect to be a characteristic typical in private photography, they attributed not only a decidedly

2 See Pierre Bourdieu, "The Cult of Unity and Cultivated Differences," in: Pierre Bourdieu/Luc Boltanski/Robert Castel/et al (eds.), *Photography: A Middle-Brow Art*, trans. Shaun Whiteside, Stanford, CA: Stanford University Press 1990, p. 76.

3 See Walter Benjamin, "The Work of Art in the Age of Its Technological Reproducibility" (second version), trans. Edmund Jephcott/Harry Zohn, in: Benjamin, *Selected Writings*, vol. 3 (1935–1938), Howard Eiland and Michael W. Jennings (eds.) Benjamin. Selected Writings, vol. 3 (1935–1938), Cambridge, MA: Belknap Press of Harvard University Press 2002, pp. 101–22, esp. p. 117.

subjective perspective, but also a lower artistic competence to private photographers—and a certain analytical inability to comprehend their own motifs.

Jabs's contact sheet contradicts such an interpretation of private photographic seeing in that the markings recognizable on it add another layer to the photographic one: the subsequent evaluation of the contact sheet. Jabs has crossed out almost a third of his pictures in black and flagged just as many with a pen, a sticky note, and yellow adhesive dots with the abbreviation "erl."—*erledigt*, that is, "done." He thus tagged as "done" the images that had already been processed in one or more of his projects; for example, in the form of self-printed postcards or framed enlargements that he gave away to friends. The handwritten markings date from the 1980s and the adhesive dots from the 2000s. They show how Jabs successively selected photographs anew over the years. He sees the unmarked photographs as neither sorted nor "done," but apparently as promising enough to possibly do something with later. What exactly, he leaves up to his work with the images in the future. In the meantime, they are put into his private image archive in the shape of contact sheets—with the photos that have already been used and those that have been crossed out.

The image archive contains all the motifs he has photographed: family photos, street photographs, pictures of façade inscriptions and urban courtyard paintings, portraits of friends and strangers, soccer photos, travel pictures, landscape panoramas, and nature shots.

A Photo Agency for the Personal Sphere

Unlike other private photographers, who sometimes even dispose of their negatives after they have printed photos from them, Jabs always worked with the reproducibility of the negative with the help of his contact sheets. To this day, he can potentially use any of his images for something. By making contact sheets of all his films between 1984 and 2014, Jabs

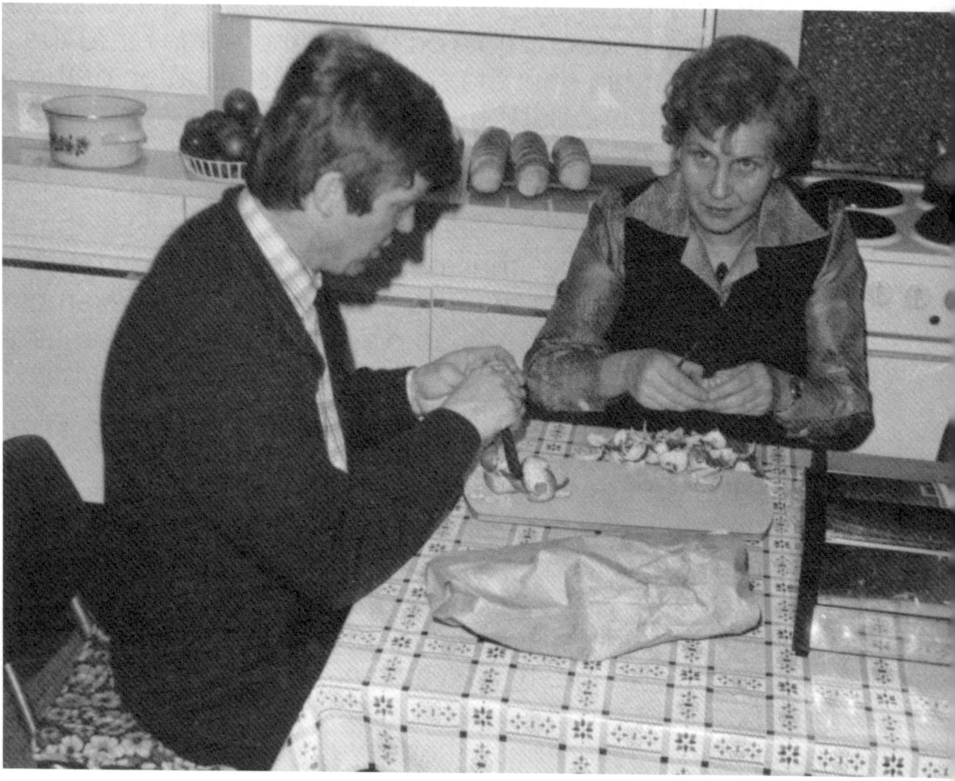

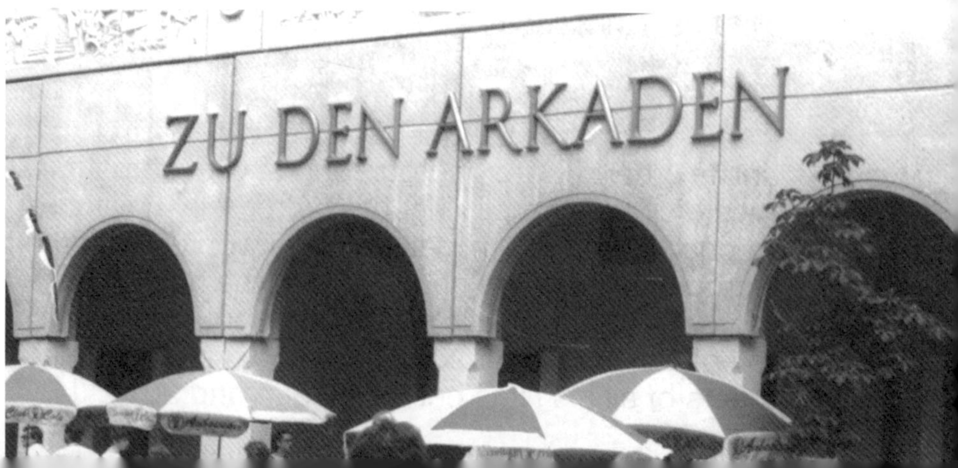
ZU DEN ARKADEN

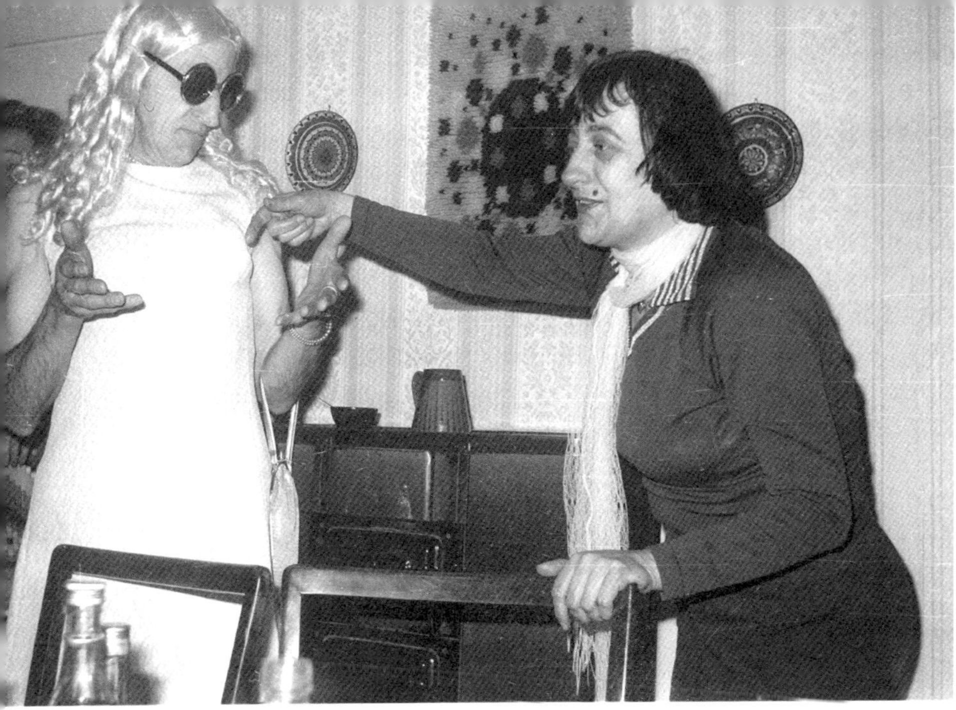

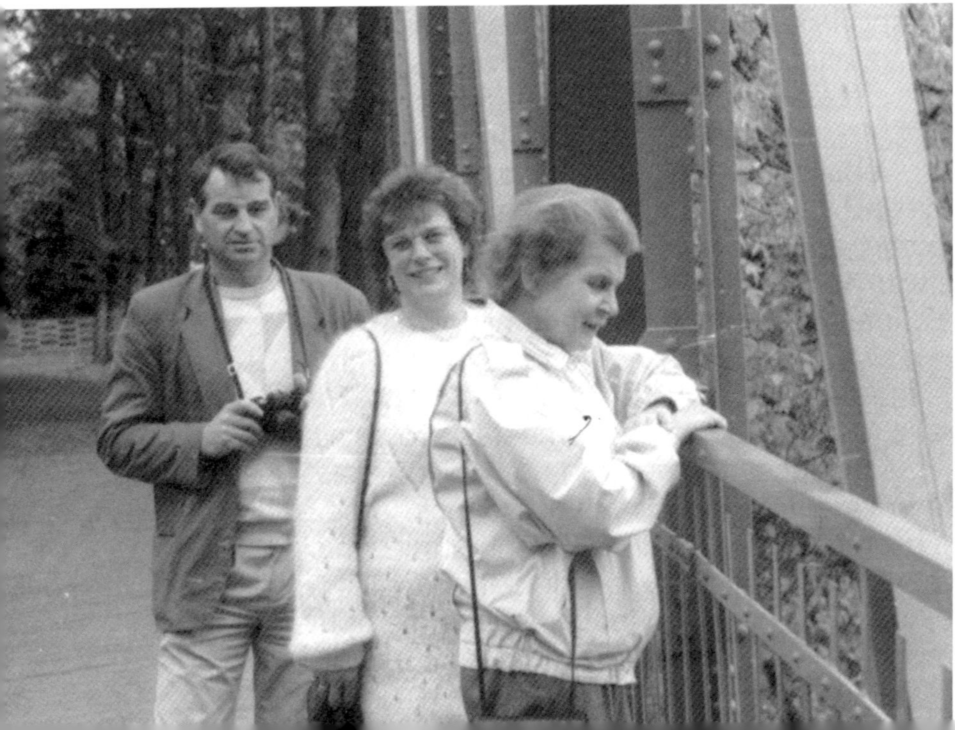

accumulated a private image archive of approximately 2,000 sheets in about twenty binders, which he keeps in his study and still uses today (fig. 2). In the meantime, he sorts the archive thematically and no longer chronologically. It includes more than 72,000 black-and-white photos, from which the self-taught photographer repeatedly selects individual ones for projects of various sizes. For example, as recently as 2013, he designed his annual calendar under the title Haus Hoffnung (House of Hope) with his photos of house walls in East Berlin from the 1980s (fig. 3). Jabs uses his contact sheets for selecting from his multitude of images, regardless of when they were taken, the most suitable ones for a specific project and for deciding which image is most fitting for his current needs.

Although his photographs are often devoted to everyday public urban space in terms of motifs, the way Jabs works with them on a practical level remains largely private. In order to take the viewers of his pictures "a step further," he conceives gifts for his family, friends, acquaintances, work colleagues, and sports comrades by selecting a single image or several images that fit the current situation and interests of the recipients, enlarging the appropriate motif, and making a print of it for them. In a similar vein, Jabs makes his own Christmas, New Year, birthday, and vacation postcards, calendars, posters, albums, and booklets—sometimes by the hundreds—as well as more unusual projects such as monthly calendars on matchboxes and his own Panini albums for his soccer buddies (fig. 4). They intentionally resemble the products sold in stationery shops. Partly ironic, partly serious, Jabs imitates professional media designs, meandering between the public and the private. His images are personal photographic reflections on the public environment in which he lives, thematically transcending the familial while being beheld mainly in private. Jabs distributed them amongst his social circles in the form of self-created

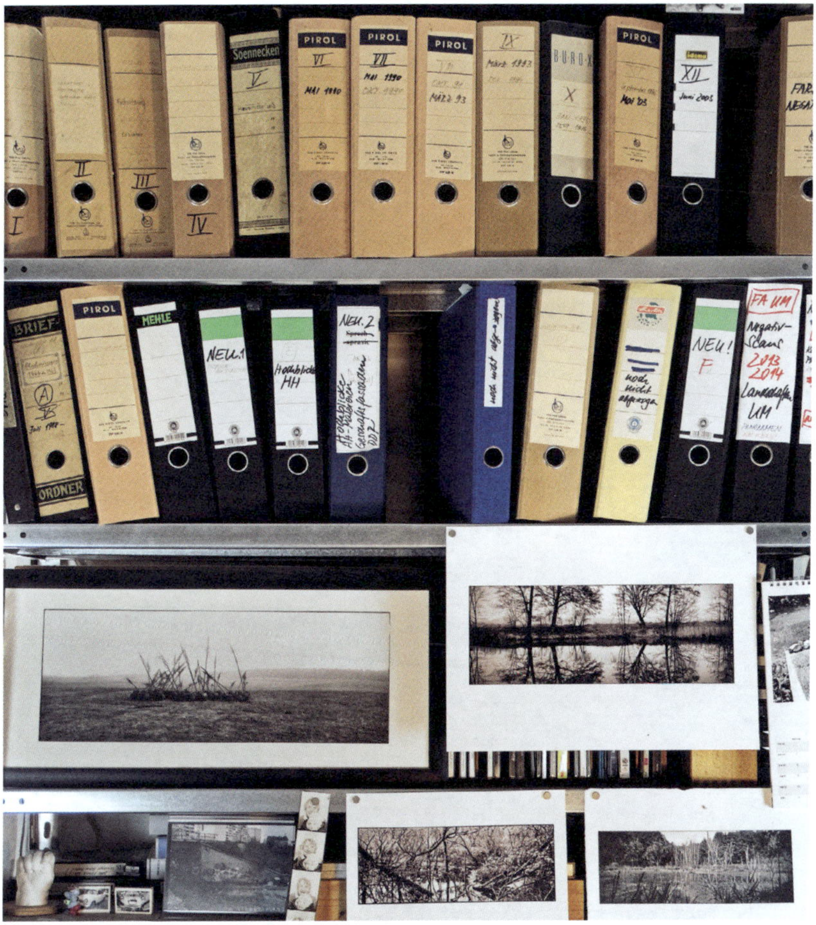

Fig. 2 Filing cabinet with the files of the photographer Jürgen Jabs in the study of his Berlin apartment. Photo: Project Archive.

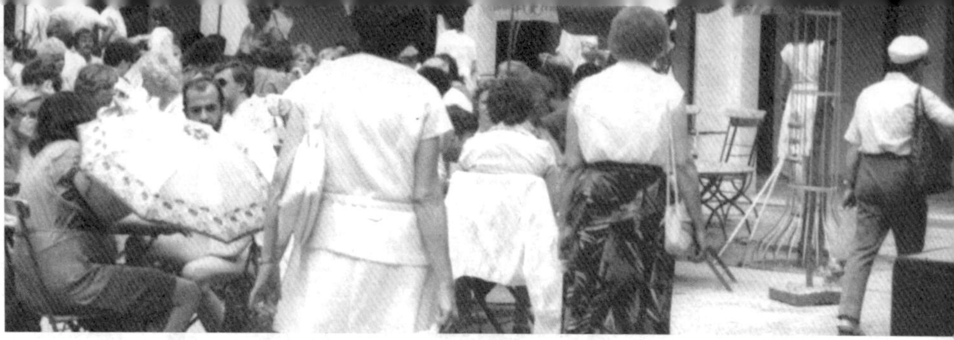

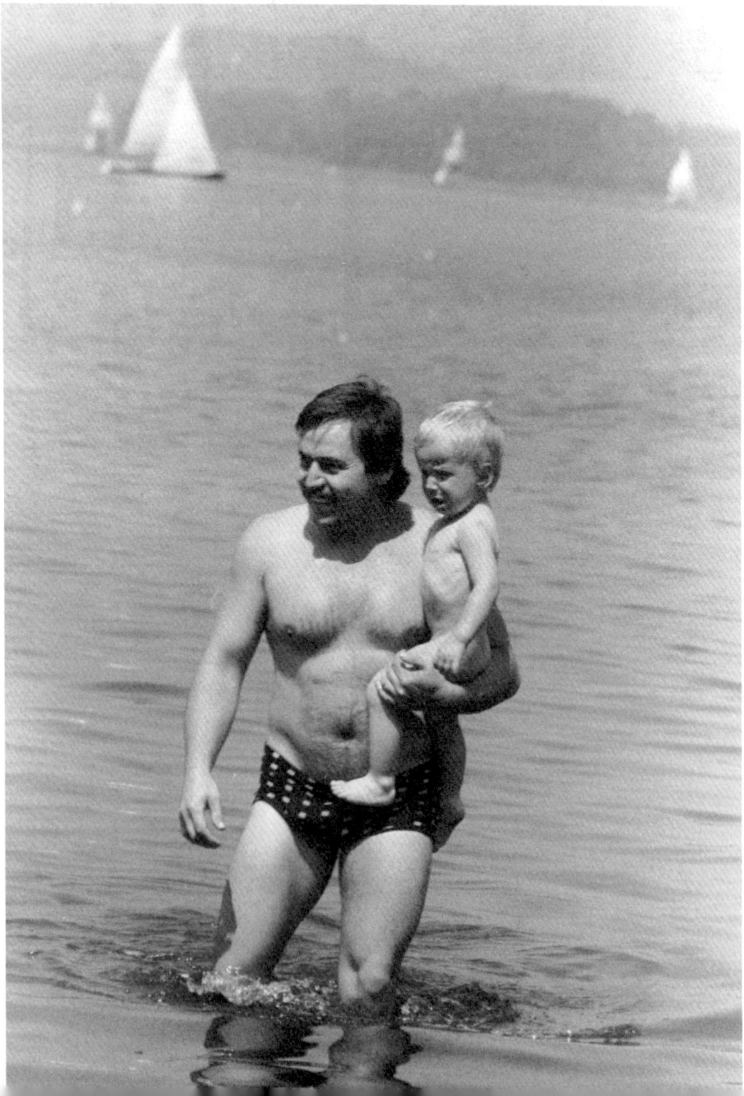

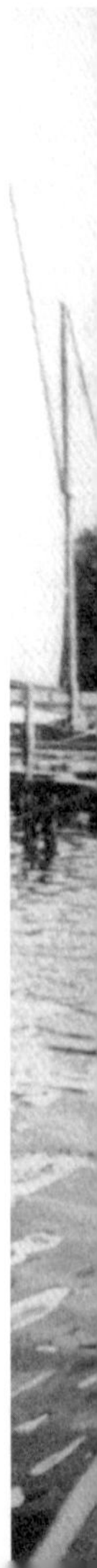

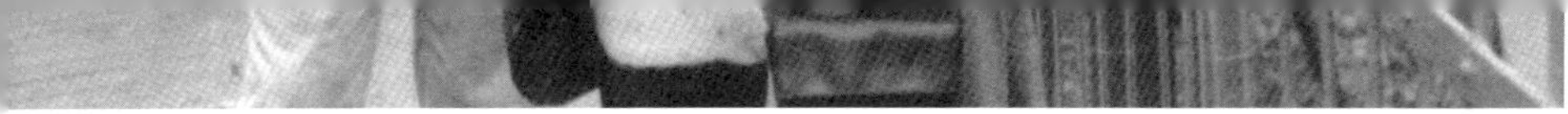

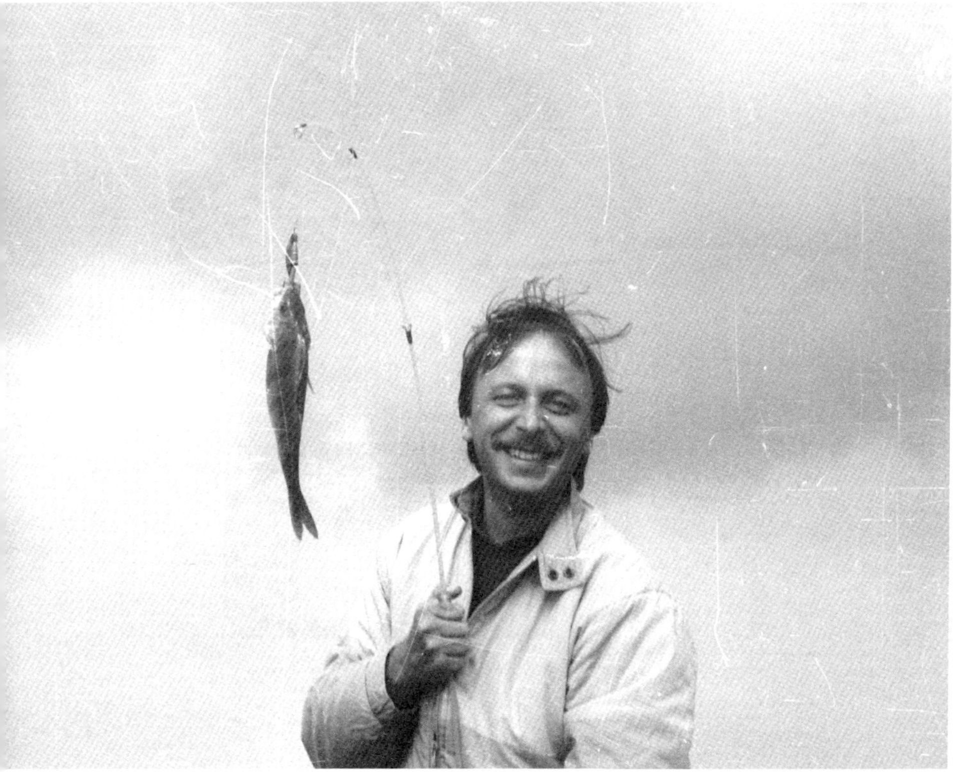

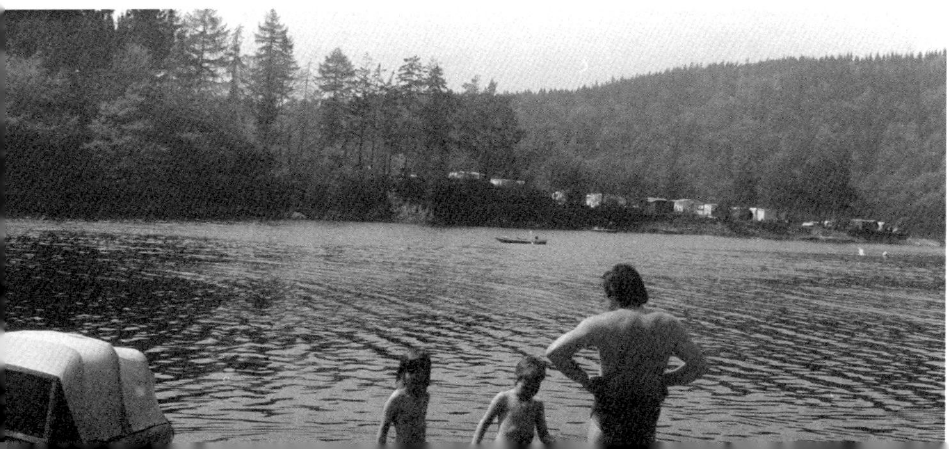

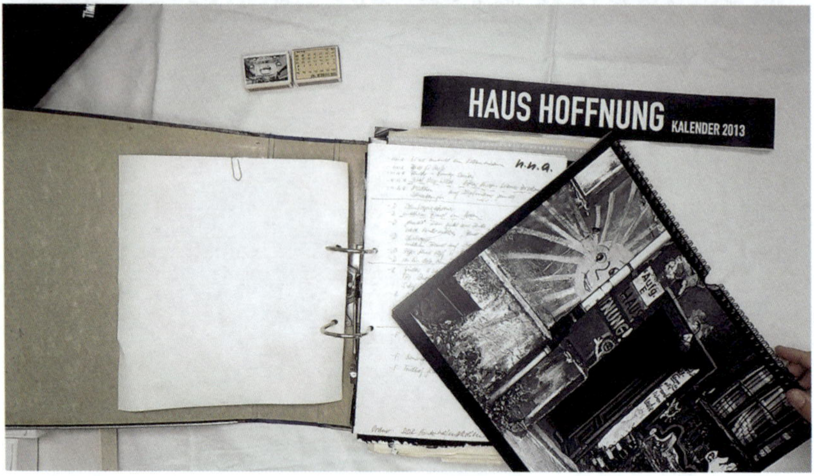

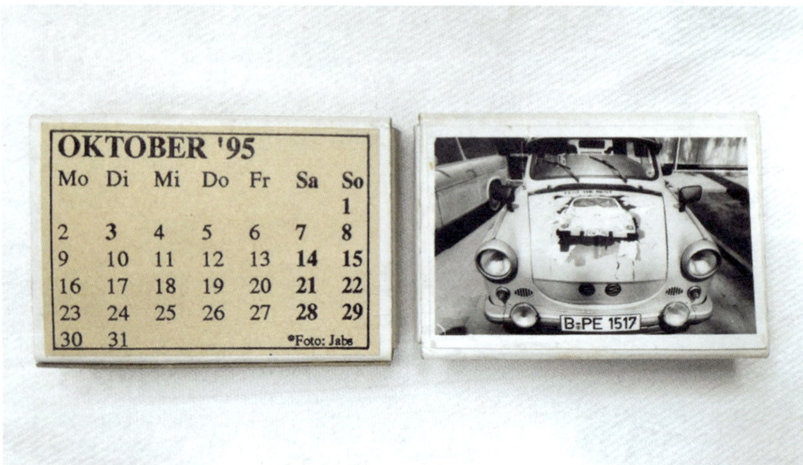

Fig. 3 Album conversation with Jürgen Jabs, Berlin, June 13, 2021. Videostill, 00:38:06.

Fig. 4 Matchboxes with a page from a calendar and a photo, photographed by Friedrich Tietjen during documentation of the Jabs collection, June 13, 2021. Photo: Project Archive.

designs. These he had created himself at considerable cost in terms of time and money, sometimes without identifying himself as the artist.

In contrast to private photographers who primarily focus on motifs related to their inner circle, in order to situate themselves and their loved ones within their social contexts, Jabs decidedly goes further afield in search of his motifs. From today's perspective, his image archive represents a long-standing observation of everyday urban life; for example, in numerous photos of overlapping layers of text on façades in Berlin. Looking back, these photos give an impression of how Jabs explored his life and reality through the lens of his camera from 1984 to 2014. In the beginning, his expeditions on the streets and in the backyards of Berlin were an open-ended pastime on weekends; today, they represent an impressive empirical long-term documentation of public space that also spans German reunification, which Jabs witnessed about halfway through his photographic career. Like many other private photographers from East Germany at the time, he did not take pictures of the political events of 1989/90. Rather, his image archive shows what it looked like in and around Prenzlauer Berg, Berlin, and the Uckermark, Brandenburg, fifteen years before and after reunification. Jabs's photos depict the changing urban space and the coexistence of different people in it. With remarkable perseverance and patience—and possibly not always aware of it himself—Jabs observed contemporary social life around him and, at home, devoted himself to evaluating what he saw. His photographic practice can therefore be understood as an ongoing experiment with his own ways of seeing. For this purpose, he records his own sensual and physical experience of his surroundings to subsequently think through and evaluate them creatively with calendars and photo books.

It is no coincidence that his archive and the way he uses it are reminiscent of Magnum Photos, the photo agency founded in 1947 by photographers

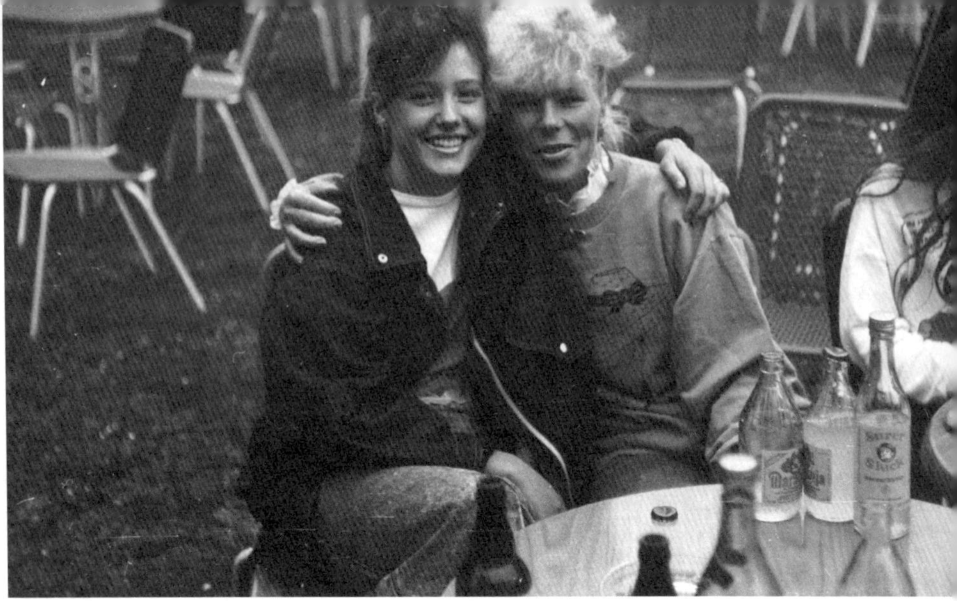

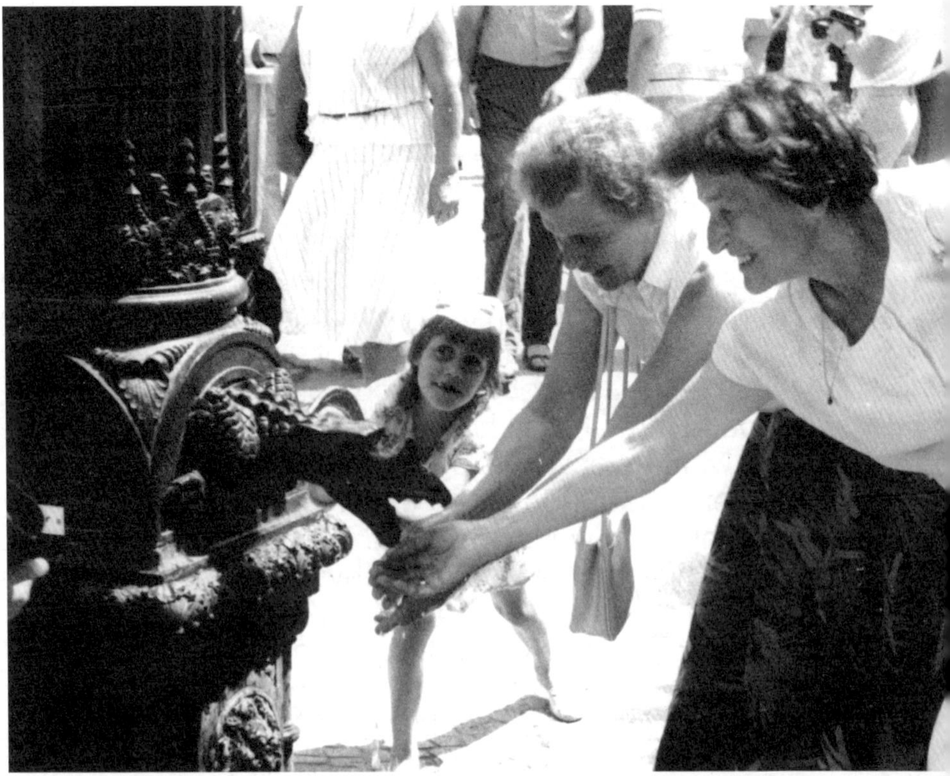

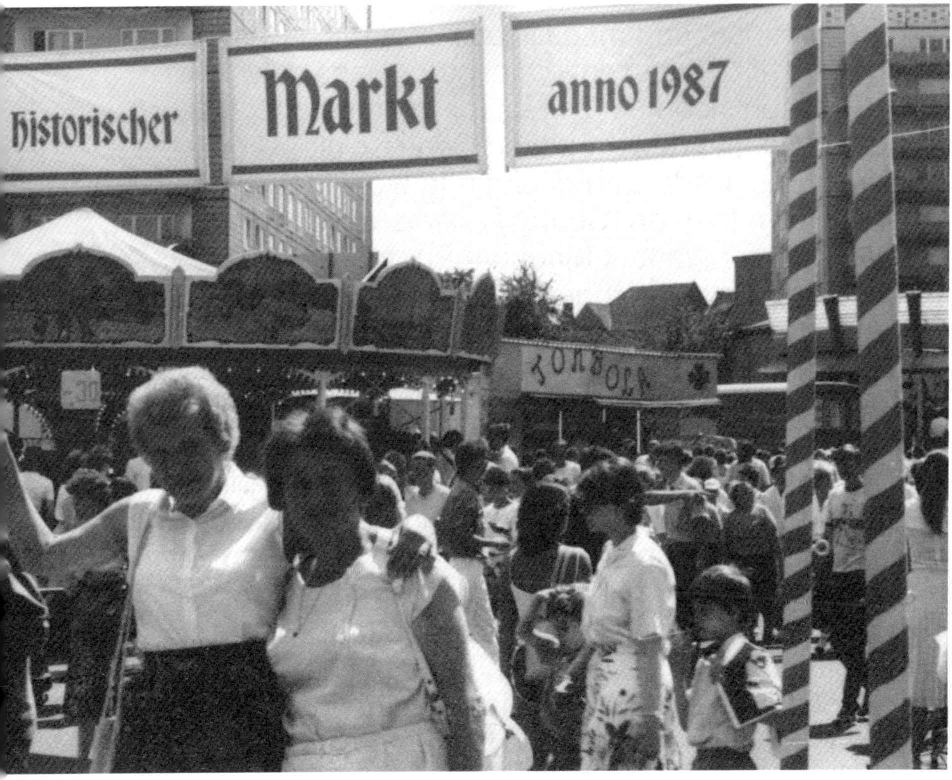
Historischer
Markt
anno 1987
TOMBOLA

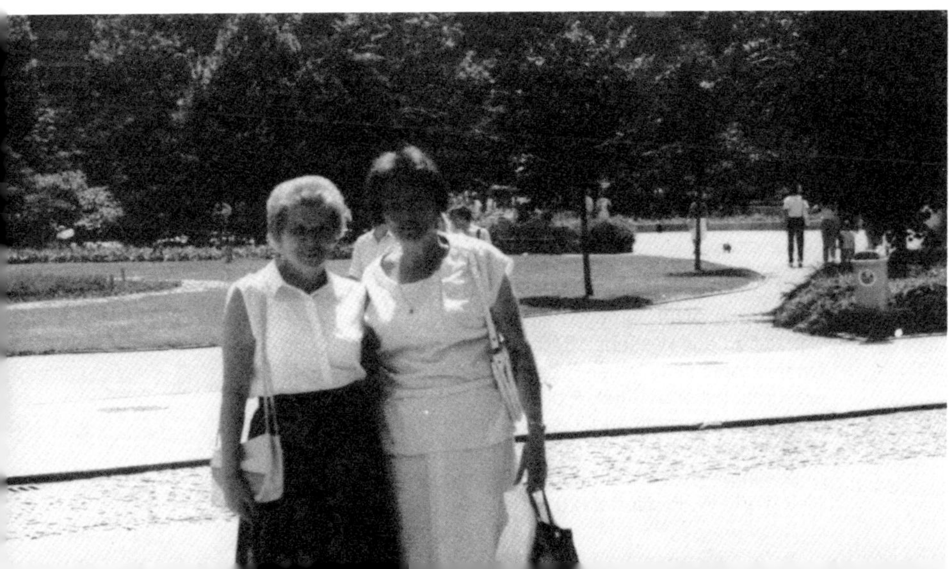

Robert Capa, Henri Cartier-Bresson, George Rodger, and David Seymour, whose images dominated illustrated newspapers and magazines in the West during the second half of the twentieth century. Jabs saw Cartier-Bresson's contact sheets for the first time around 1984 in the newly opened Centre Culturel Français in East Berlin and decided to work in the same way from then on. Contact sheets were the most important tool for work at Magnum Photos. Because they showed how a photographer worked, anyone who wanted to join the agency had to submit their contact sheets. Whether in the case of Jabs or of Magnum, the sheets reenact photographic activity—physically experienced and recorded with the camera—as a process of seeing a particular person, in a particular place, at a particular time. Additionally, the notes, deletions, and crop marks inscribed on them document those subsequent decision-making processes that led to the selection and editing of certain photographs and disregarding of others. Moreover, contact sheets now have historical value because it is not only photographers who use them to evaluate their images. As "museum artifacts," contact sheets provide historians of photography with information about the context of individual photographs; for example, whether they were actually a spontaneous snapshot taken at the "decisive moment" (Cartier-Bresson) or a staged image that involved many failed attempts and devoured immense resources.(4) Therefore, contact sheets are always private photographic documents because they record not only the successful but the invisible and failed attempts of a photographer.(5)

4 See Marie Egger/Raphael Hoffmann/Marlene Militz/et al., "Bildtableau," in: Nina Samuel/Felix Sattler (eds.), *Museale Reste*, Bildwelten des Wissens 18, Berlin: De Gruyter, 2022, pp. 4–5.

5 On this topic see Cartier-Bresson, "A contact sheet is full of erasures, full of detritus. A photo exhibition or a book is an invitation to a meal, and it is not customary to make guests poke their noses into the pots and pans, and even less into the buckets of peelings." Kristen Lubben (ed.), *Magnum: Contact Sheets*, New York: W. W. Norton 2017, p. 18.

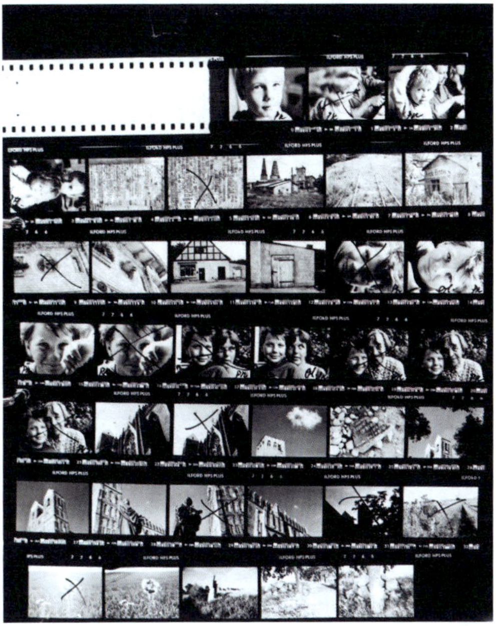

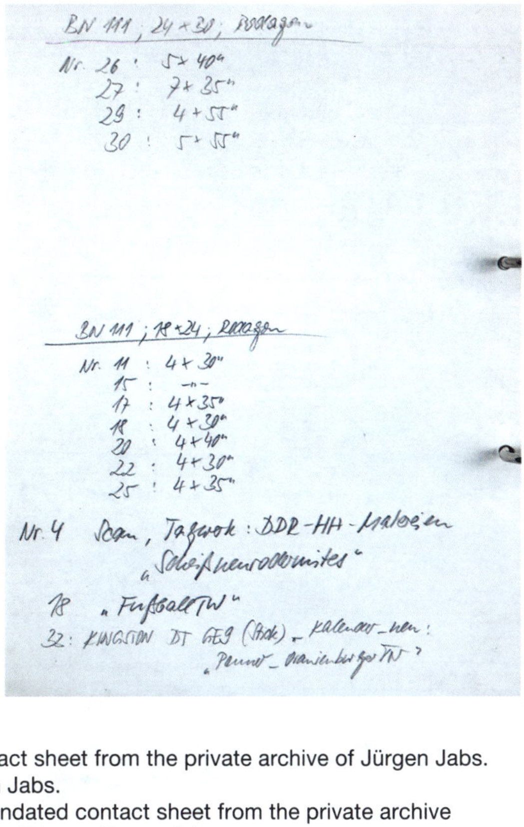

BN 111 ; 24×30 ;

Nr. 26 : 5+40"
27 : 7+35"
29 : 4+55"
30 : 5+55"

BN 111 ; 18×24 ;

Nr. 11 : 4+30"
15 : –"–
17 : 4+35"
18 : 4+30"
20 : 4+40"
22 : 4+30"
25 : 4+35"

Nr. 4 Scan, Tagwerk : DDR-HH-Malereien
„Schleifkneurodomites“

18 „FußballTW“

32: KINGSTON DT GE9 (Stick) – Kalender–neu :
„Panner – OranienburgerTW“?

Fig. 5: Undated contact sheet from the private archive of Jürgen Jabs. Photo: Jürgen Jabs.

Fig. 6: Verso of the undated contact sheet from the private archive of Jürgen Jabs. Photo: Jürgen Jabs.

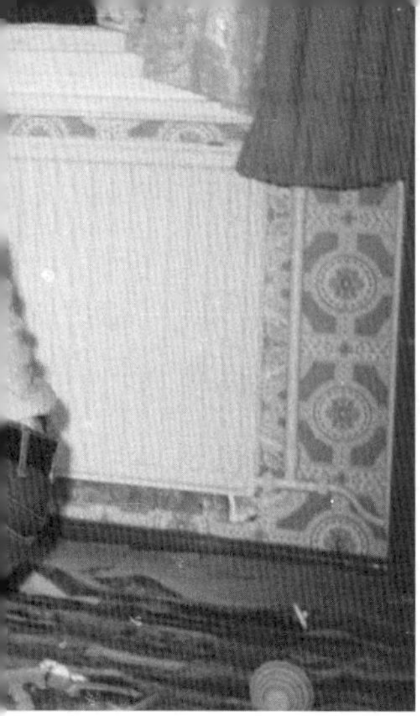

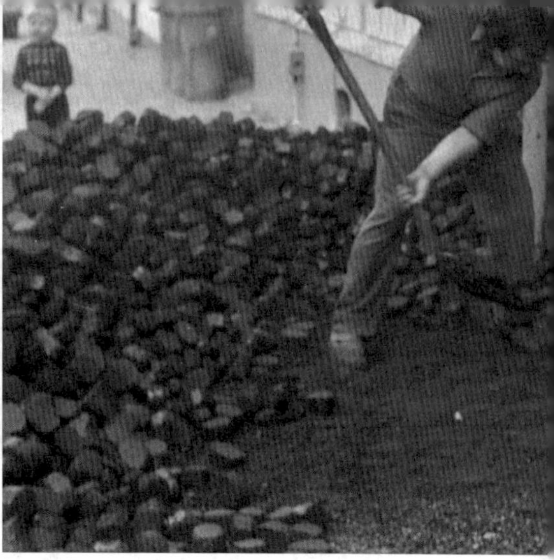

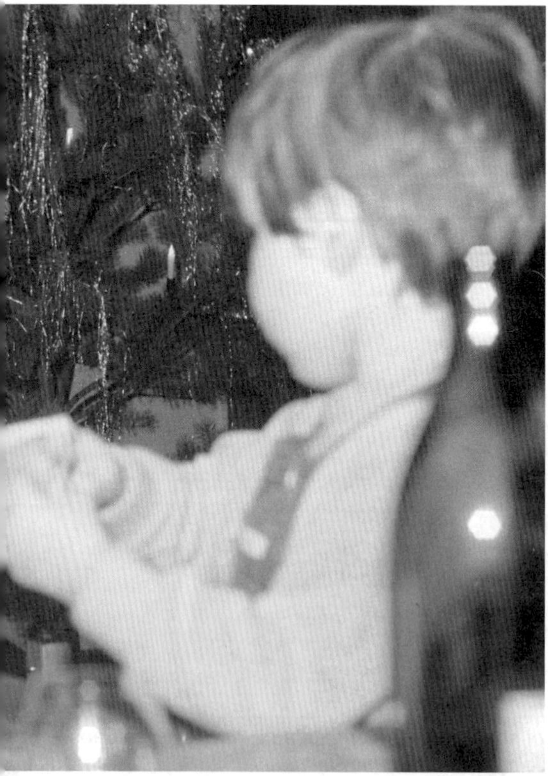

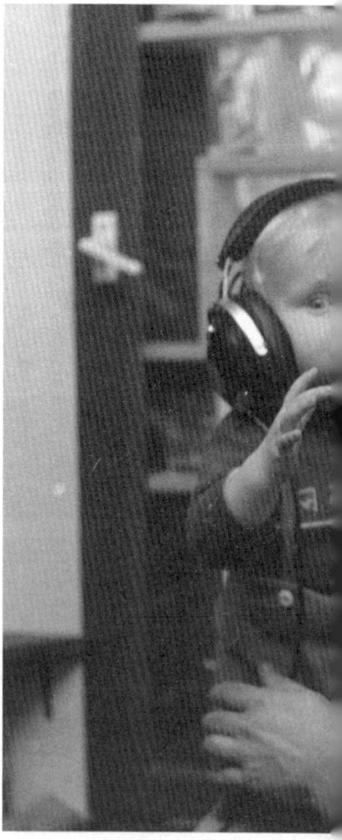

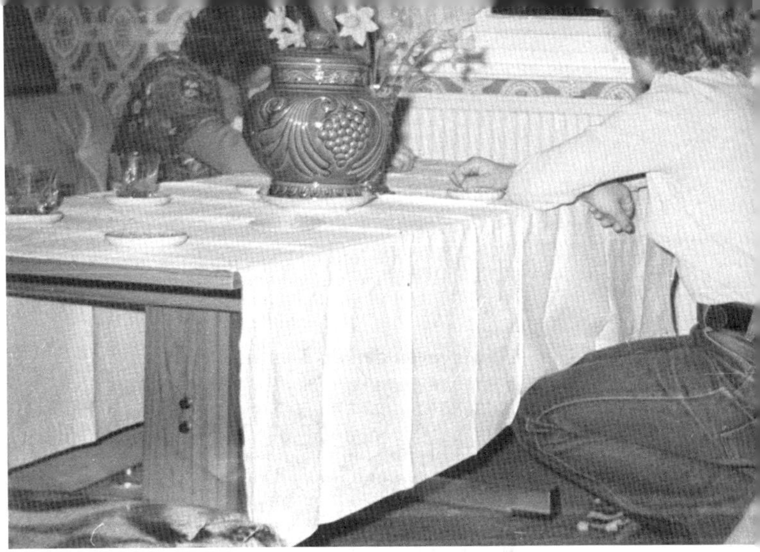

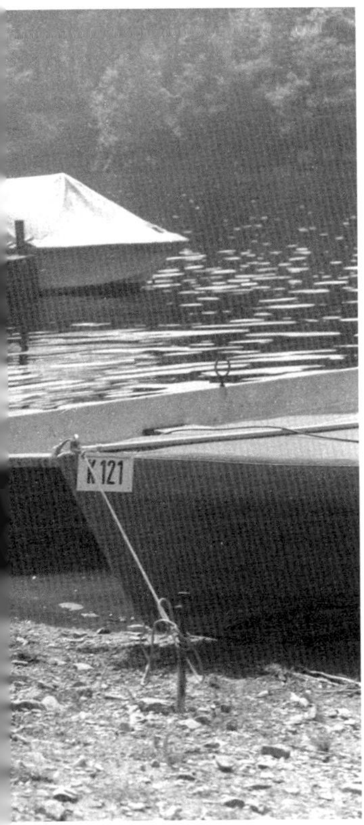
K 121

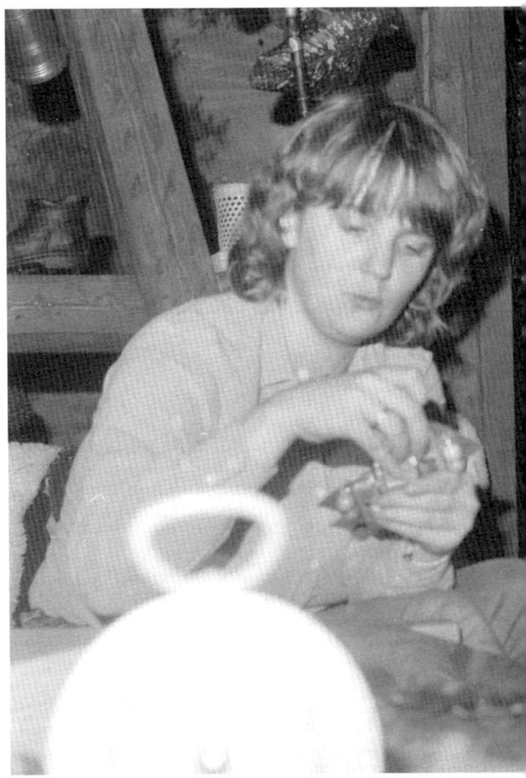

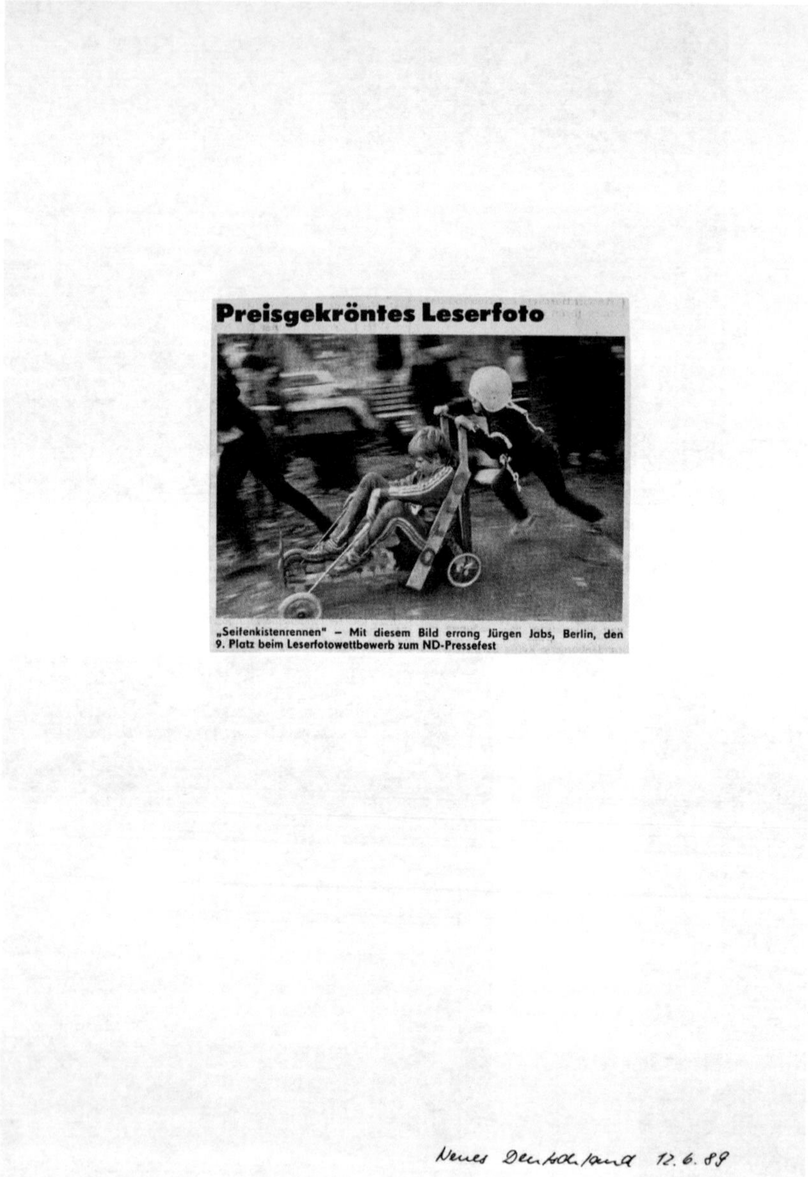

Preisgekröntes Leserfoto

„Seifenkistenrennen" – Mit diesem Bild errang Jürgen Jabs, Berlin, den 9. Platz beim Leserfotowettbewerb zum ND-Pressefest

Neues Deutschland 12.6.89

Fig. 7: Opened file folder with press clippings from the private archive of Jürgen Jabs. Photo: Jürgen Jabs.

Jabs's Private Photographic Activity

Jabs's contact sheets also contain occasional attempts to get close to getting the "right" picture by pressing the shutter release several times (fig. 5). On the whole, however, they show that the photographer preferred single shots, possibly also for economic reasons. His observations over many years seem open-ended and in no hurry; his visual rambles bear witness to seeing various subjects in parallel ways, which he still today retrospectively reworks in a creative manner. This practice, like the systematic structure of his archive, favors subject matter over chronology and is expressed in the notes on the sheets as an analytical search for signs in the sediments of his own photographic work (fig. 6). Jabs meticulously notes on the back of each contact sheet which motifs it contains on which subject and which images were already used and for what. The thematic reappraisal is an evaluation of one's own biography in terms of seeing, with more or less of a temporal distance, from the respective photograph. With "public time" and "personal time," this evaluation mixes the two spheres put forward by sociologist Andrew Walker and photographer Rosalind Moulton in 1989 to distinguish sophisticated photos from private ones. They see sophisticated photographs as devoted to the "public time" of a nation, a society, or nature, and private photographs to the "personal time" of one's own family memories and impressions.(6)

Jabs is able to meld the two spheres not only because visual culture has evolved since Walker and Moulton's assessment and eroded this division, but also because of his earnestness about the demands he placed on his photography naturally links the two levels. Clearly, he sees them as intertwined and does not distinguish between

6 See Andrew L. Walker/Rosalind K. Moulton, "Photo Albums: Images of Time and Reflections of Self", in: *Qualitative Sociology* 12 no. 2, June 1989, p. 157.

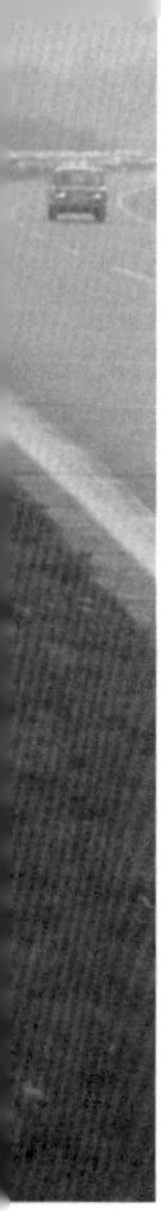

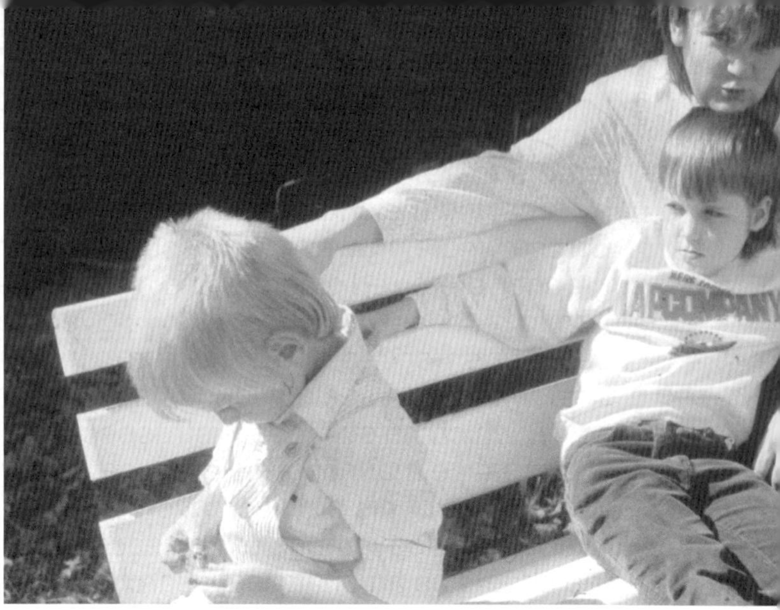

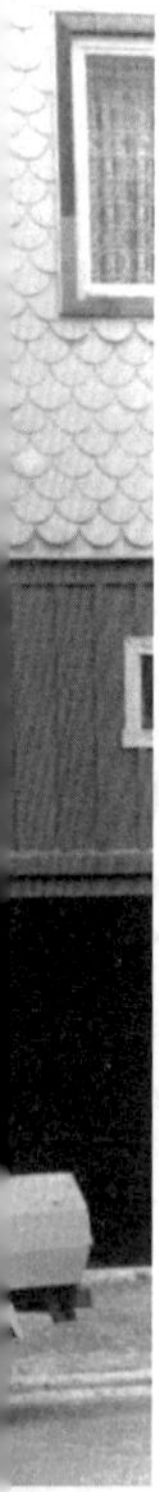

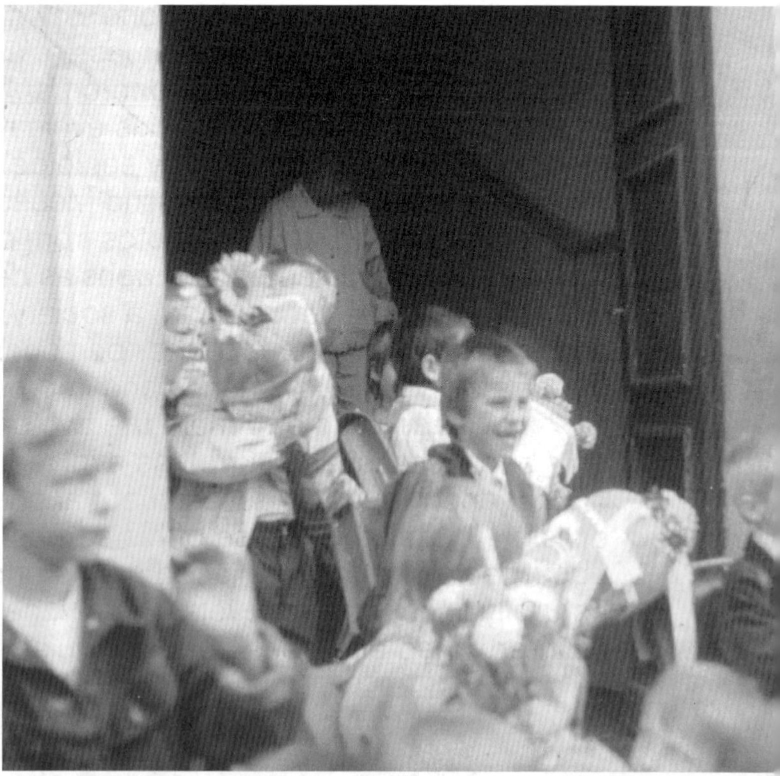

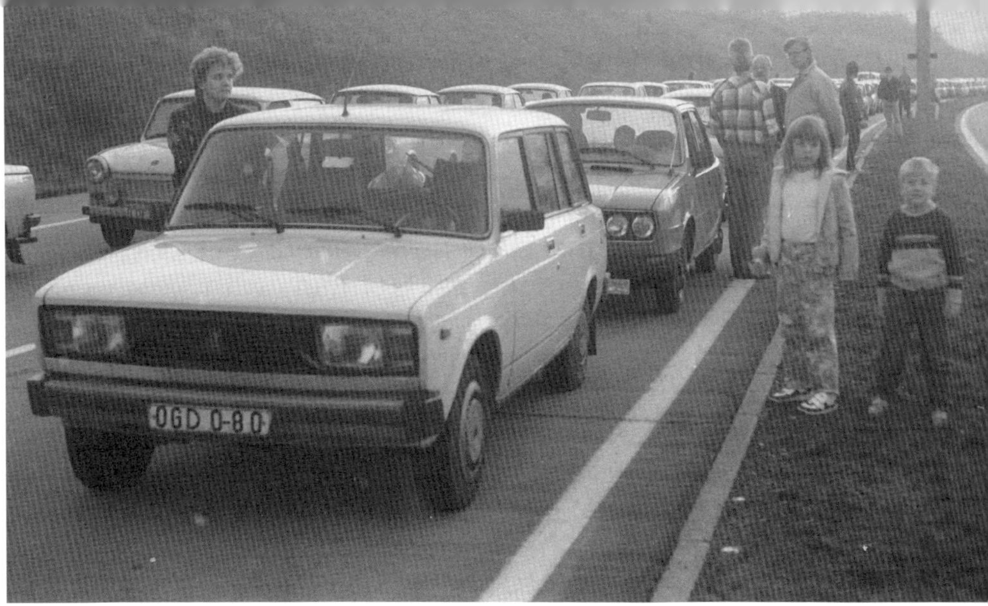
OGD 0-80

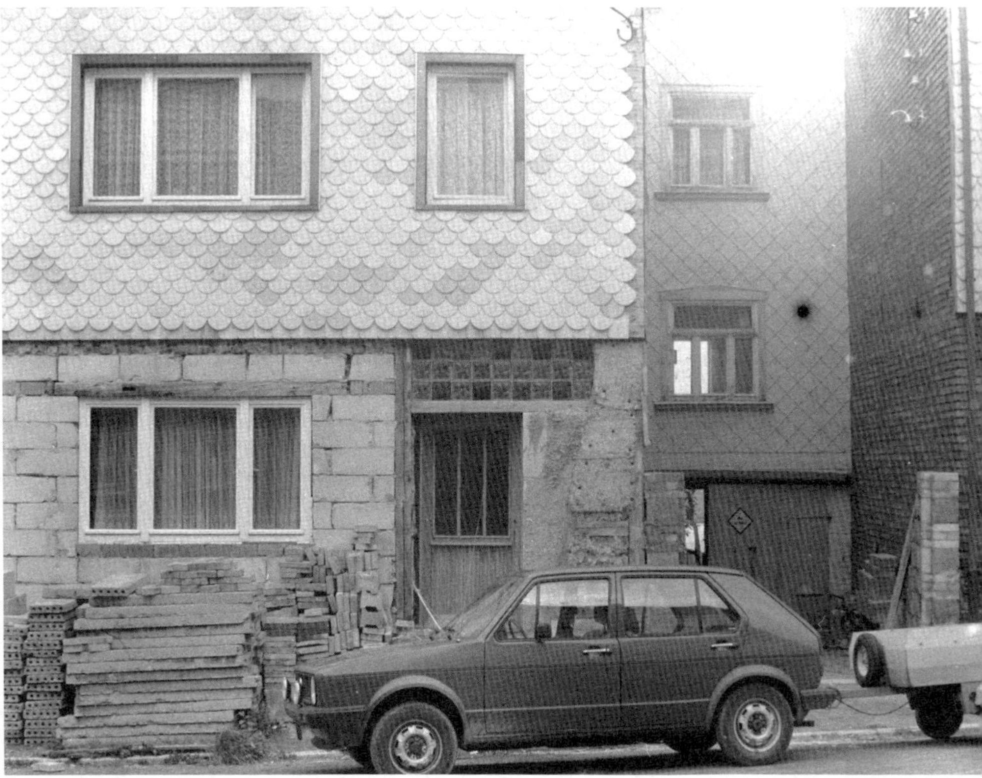

public and personal time. This is evidenced by the projects for his personal environment as well as by hundreds of records of items from his holdings being published in the press (fig. 7). Jabs took part in competitions and regularly supplied the editorial offices of local and regional daily newspapers and the church newspapers in East Germany with a selection of his pictures. Although they are presented as "readers' photos" or "private shots," the fact that they have been printed in the media, where they illustrate articles and contributions by journalists, brings their status more in line with the photos of professional photo agencies, so that in them the boundary between private and public or amateur and professional photography becomes blurred.

This praxeological complexity finds its pictorial counterpart in Jabs's contact sheets. The flaneur's view of his own private and social environment, his umpteen selection processes, his subsequent processing of the pictorial material in projects, the publication of his images in the media, and the archiving of all of this is documented by the contact sheet, which bundles together on the front and back several references to Jabs's various modes of action associated with the images. It bears traces of Jabs's practice of private photographic image-making in which images are linked to different practices and purposes.(7) Jabs aspires

7 This is based on Annette Vowinkel's characterization of the journalistic use of photos in the media as "photographic pictorial action." This she defines as "forms of communication" that implement images as a medium in a targeted way. Photographic action presents a "special form," which, by means of mass reproduction, develops the full impact of its social relevance and power to influence. Annette Vowinckel, *Agenten der Bilder: fotographisches Handeln im 20. Jahrhundert*, Visual History, Göttingen: Wallstein 2016, p. 14; see also Klaus Sachs-Hombach, *Das Bild als kommunikatives Medium: Elemente einer allgemeinen Bildwissenschaft*, Cologne: Herbert von Halem 2021, p. 19, and Goda Plaum / Klaus Sachs-Hombach (eds.), "Bildhandeln," in: *IMAGE. Zeitschrift für Interdisziplinäre Bildwissenschaft,* 32, 2022.

to actively engage with the sociopolitical present in response to his private surroundings, and, if possible, to influence this present at a later date.

His published images can be seen as a vigilant engagement with society and a proactive participation in shaping it—for which the contact sheet is instrumental. The photographer finds his method already in his first steps in photography: Jabs's approach is scientific. It involves a private photographic inventory in the form of his visual sociocultural explorations, which he then analyzes and transforms, both in terms of media design and as a recipient of the media, into creative projects for his private environment and into suggestions for the press. His photographs are not exclusively private. They are personal confrontations with the private and public realities of life, for which the photographer seeks his own forms of expression and both a familiar and public audience. Although not ostensibly for Jabs, this practice also shapes the experience of the change of political system in 1989/90; after all, it marks the transition between a time when Jabs glued his calendars together from cardboard and bicycle tape and a time when he commissioned his calendars to be printed (fig. 3).

In sum, his photographic observations also speak of the geologist who documents the layers and overlying strata—in the case of his images of painted-over façades—that his eyes are sensitized to see. Jabs gets to the heart of them with the meticulousness of his geological excursion reports of the 1970s, in which he described the observations made on site, illustrated them with a selection of four to five photos, and pasted them on paper. He has learned to empirically evaluate and analytically review a conglomerate of images in order to use them to illustrate certain scientific contexts. His photographs are the observations of an exploration geologist in a big city, stored in a photographic archive that has grown over decades and is gradually being unearthed. They

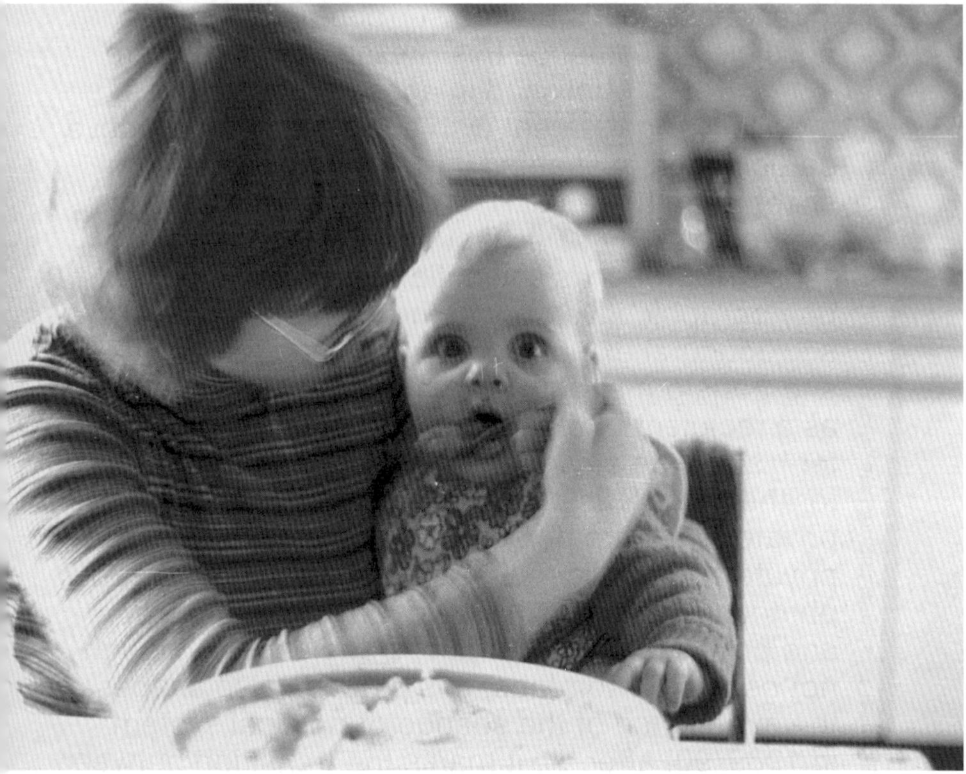

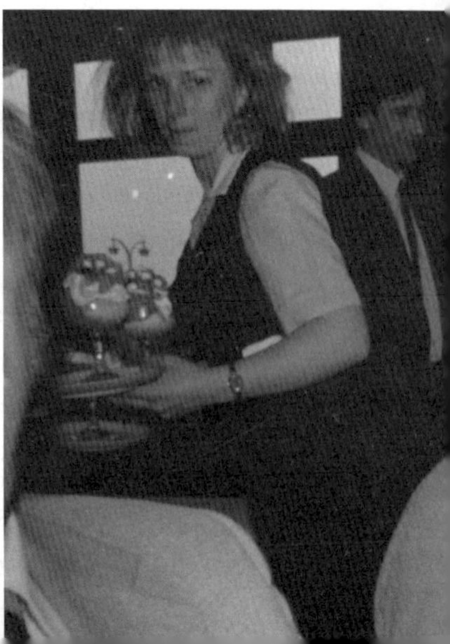

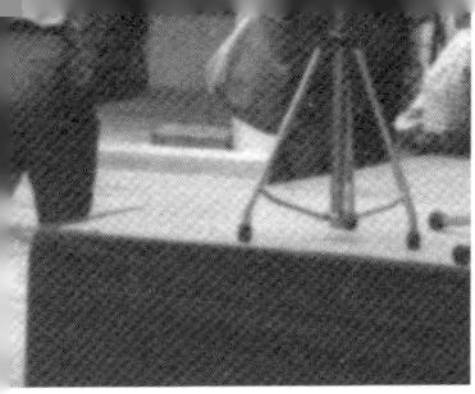

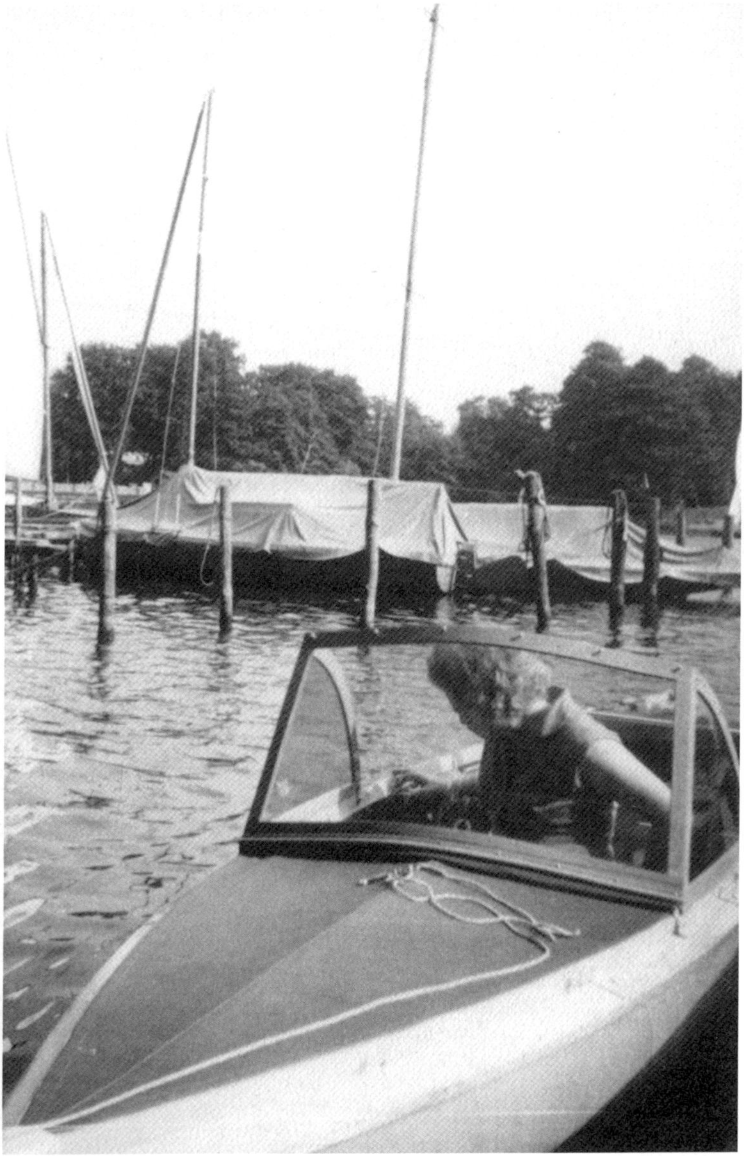

resemble the fossils to which Jabs devoted his entire professional life and which today serve as paper weights on his project piles, keeping them from getting mixed up. They help geologists precisely classify and accurately date their findings. But in order to uncover the knowledge preserved in them, they must find out how they are interconnected by means of comparison, sequencing, and contrast. What results is a picture of the past that reaches into the present from constantly shifting perspectives.

BN 111 ; 24 × 30 ; Rodagon

Nr. 26 : 5 + 40"
27 : 7 + 35"
29 : 4 + 55"
30 : 5 + 55"

BN 111 ; 18 × 24 ; Rodagon

Nr. 11 : 4 + 30"
15 : – " –
17 : 4 + 35"
18 : 4 + 30"
20 : 4 + 40"
22 : 4 + 30"
25 : 4 + 35"

4 Scan, Tagwerk : DDR-HH-Malereien
„Scheißhausrollenmuster"

18 „FußballTW"

32: KINGSTON DT GE9 (Stick) „Kalender_neu:
„Penner_OranienburgerTW"

Jürgen Jabs

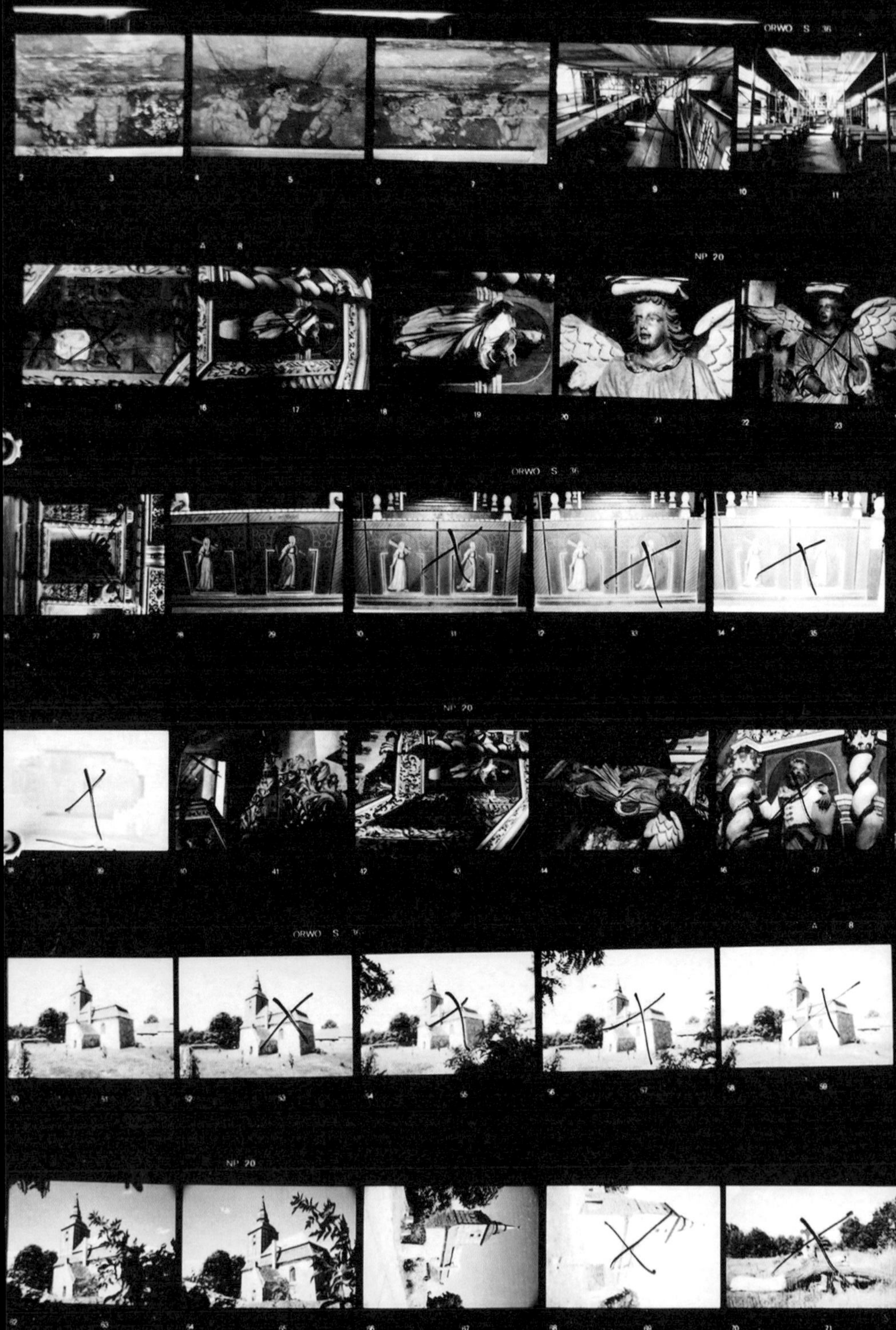
ORWO S 36
A 8
NP 20
ORWO S 36
NP 20
ORWO S 36
A 8
NP 20

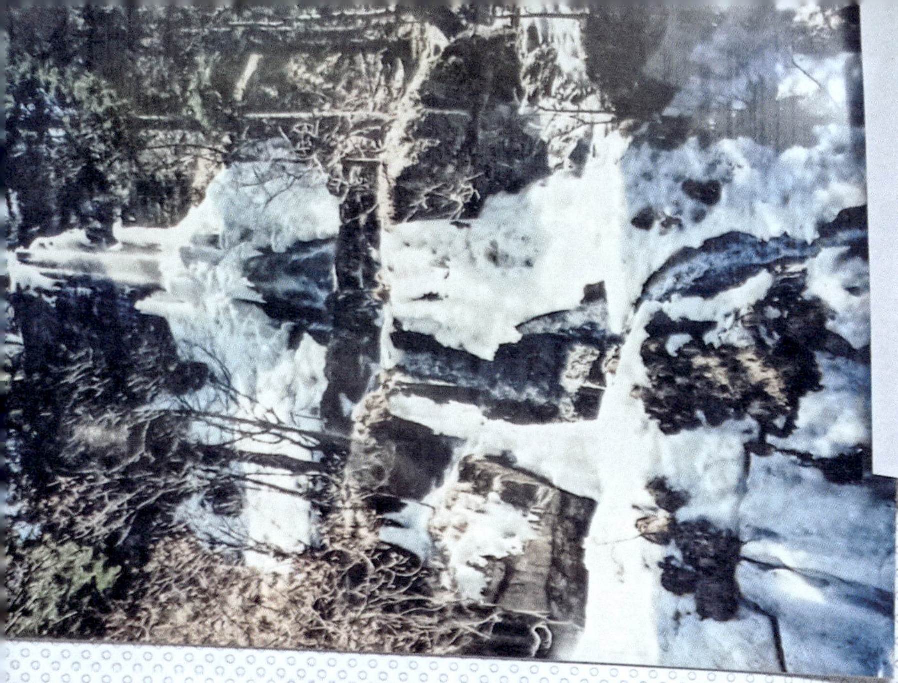

MEMO Das kleinste König

MEMO

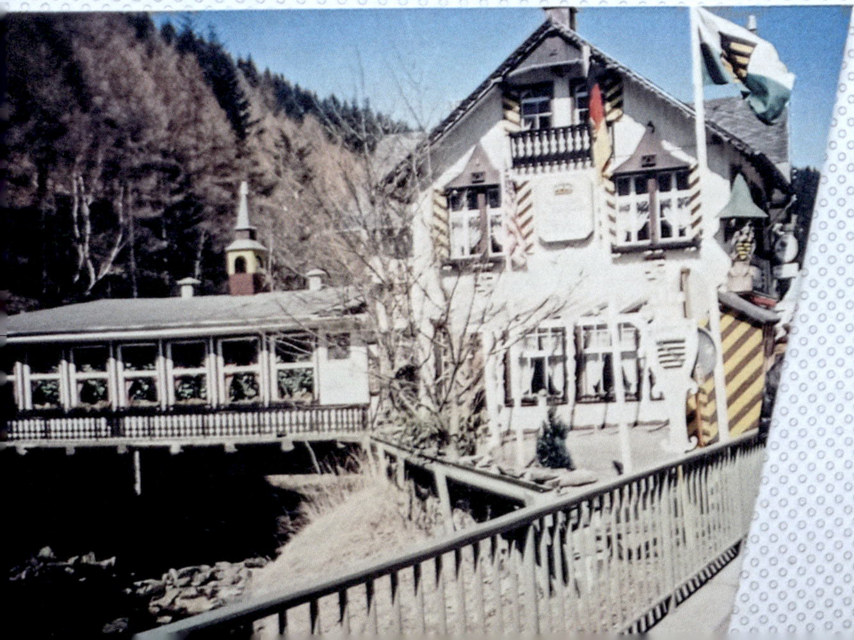

Borghild Carus

Borghild Carus

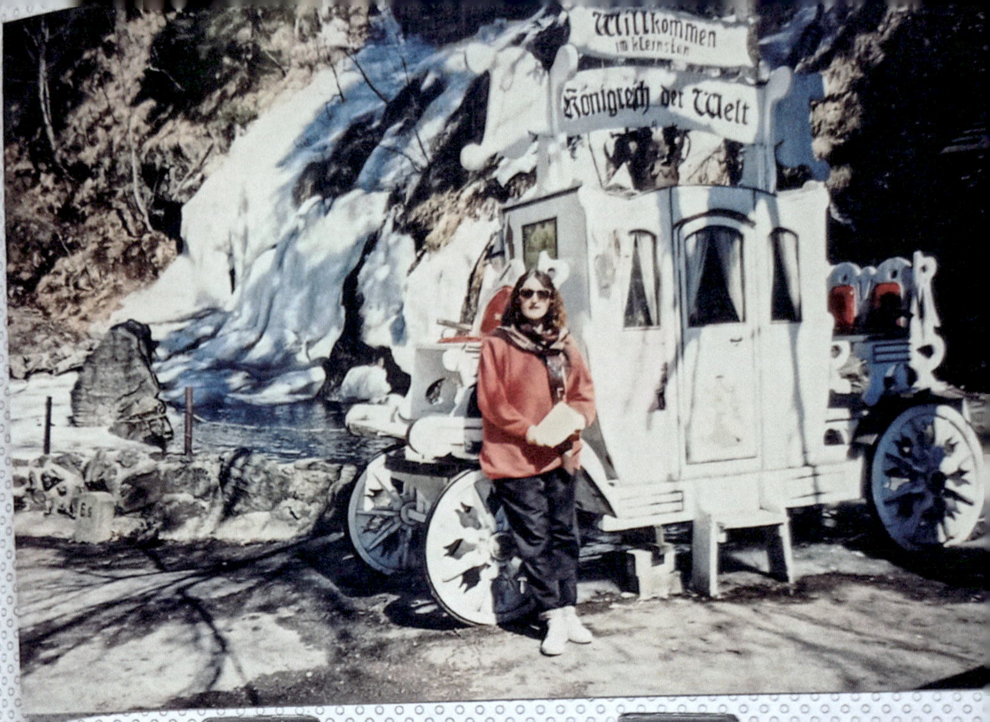
Willkommen
im kleinsten
Königreich der Welt

n der Welt

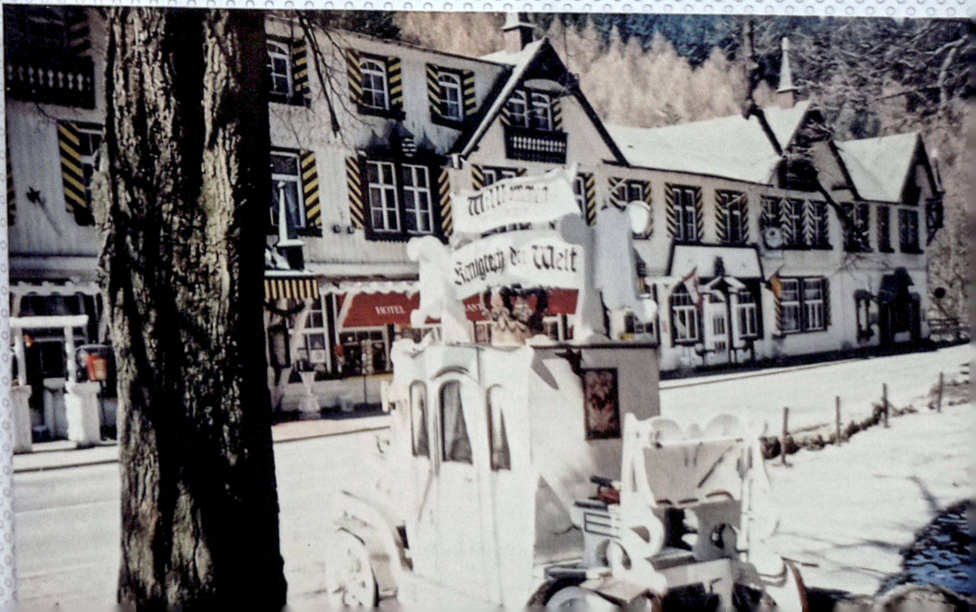
Willkommen
Königreich der Welt
HOTEL

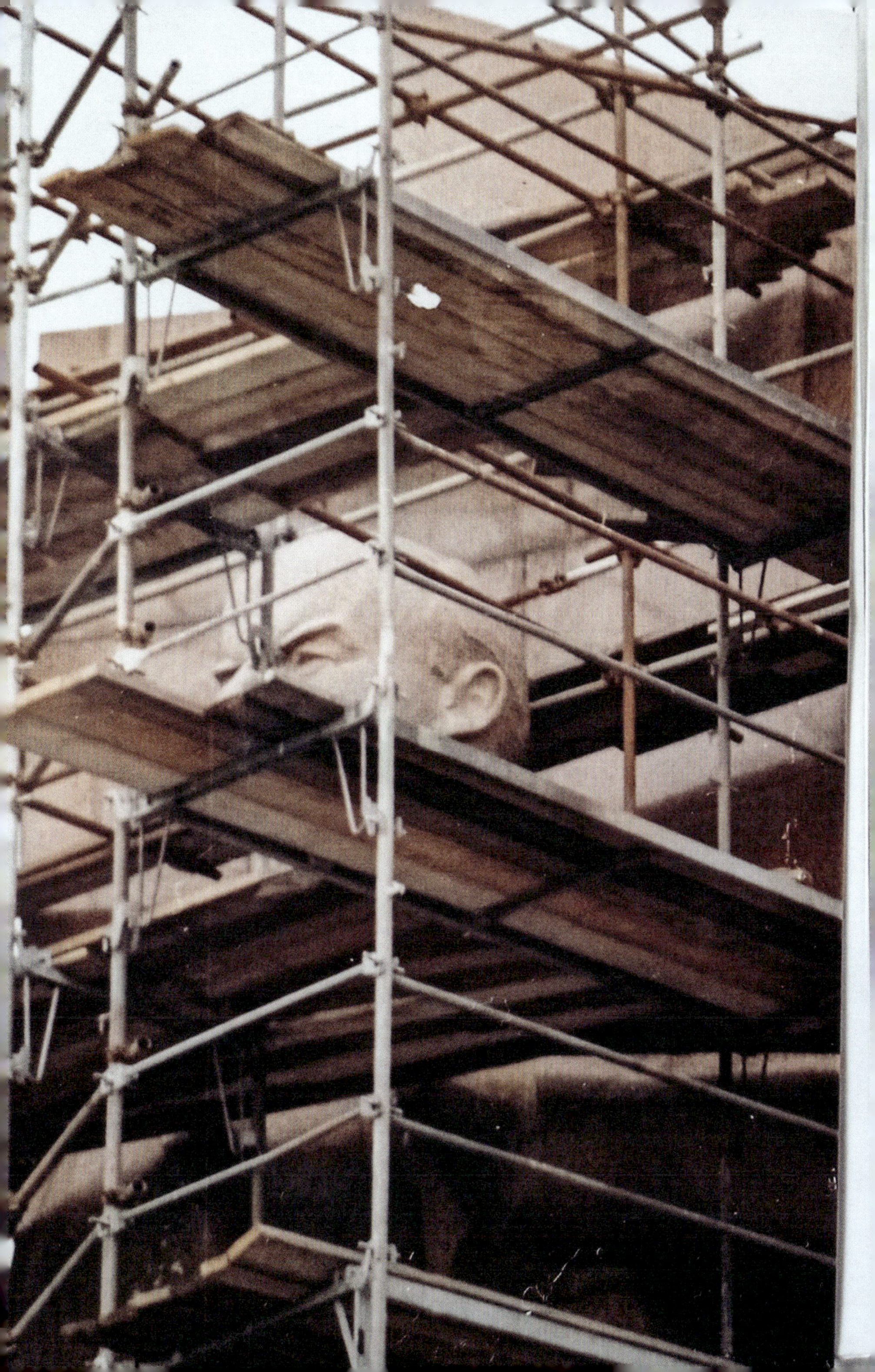

Borghild Carus

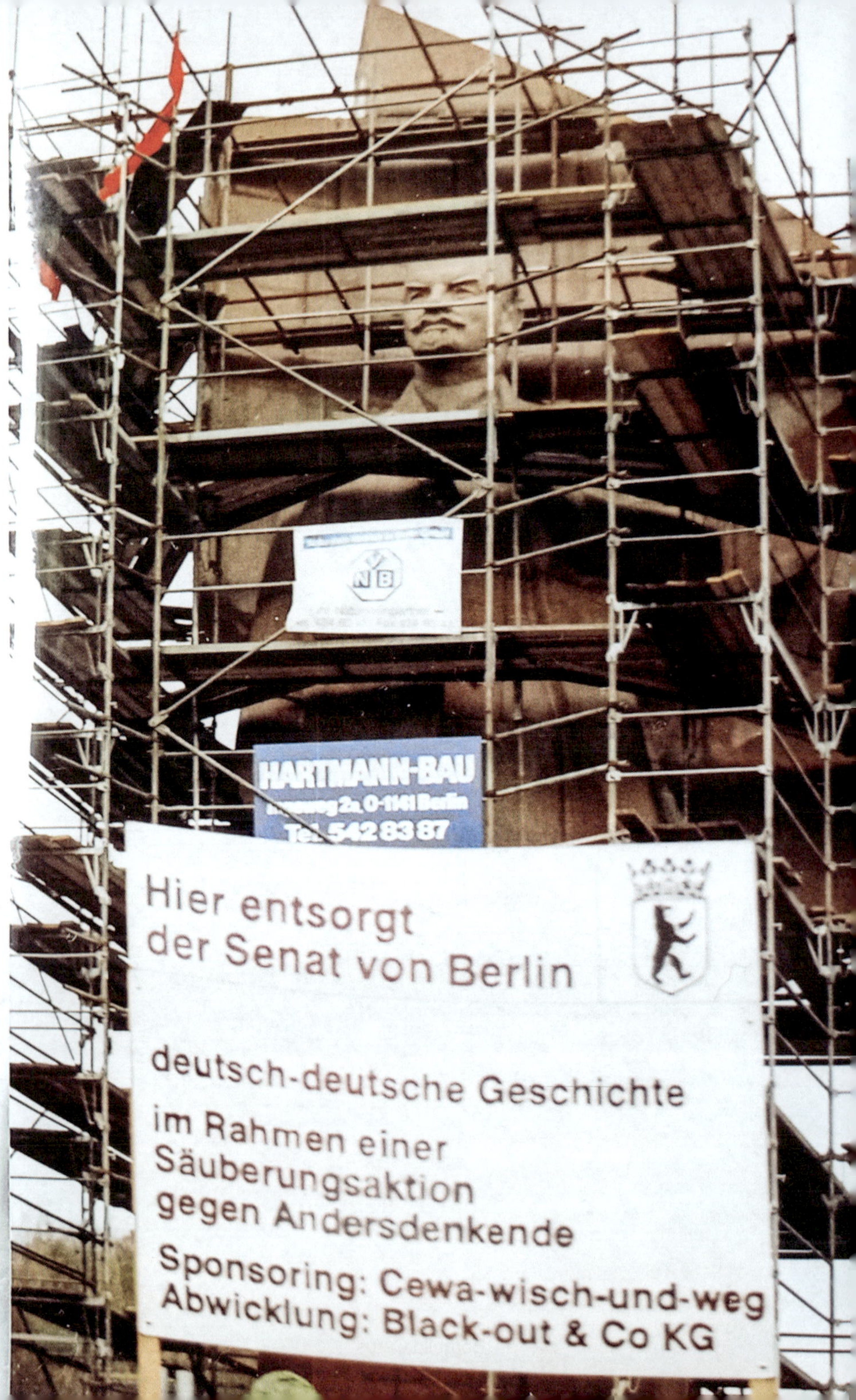
HARTMANN-BAU
542 83 87
Hier entsorgt
der Senat von Berlin
deutsch-deutsche Geschichte
im Rahmen einer
Säuberungsaktion
gegen Andersdenkende
Sponsoring: Cewa-wisch-und-weg
Abwicklung: Black-out & Co KG

"Things were already changing in this country, but somehow life went on as normal for the time being." Material and Temporal Stratification in an East German Family Photo Album

Judith Riemer

The way the Göldner family photo album was put together has an intriguing history. Jürgen Göldner is the family's principal photographer and up until a few years ago he mainly took pictures with slide film. The slide show—today in digital format—is also the Göldners' preferred medium for viewing and showing pictures. Especially during the dark months, they spend sociable evenings watching slide shows with other family members and friends.

The family's slide collection grew and grew, while their living space remained the same. It was eventually necessary for the family to reduce its collection to make room for new slides. Photographs that were not well-made in their eyes were particularly in danger of being discarded. However, many of the motifs were too good to throw away, so prints were made from the slides. But where to put the prints? Some were added to already existing photo albums. Some were added to new albums; in particular to a West German product purchased in the early 1990s that stands out on account of its impressive format of 30×30 centimeters next to the smaller East German albums owned by the family. The new album was to replace an existing one. This too was purchased after 1989 in the same format and was already filled from beginning to end with photographs. According to Beate Göldner, a caption was the trigger. It was carelessly written, so the album could not remain as it was. Instead of revising the page, however, the whole thing had to be redone. Some of the photographs were removed from the original album and put into the new one, along with newer prints from slides and older black-and-white prints. Photographs from different contexts were combined in the album, and the

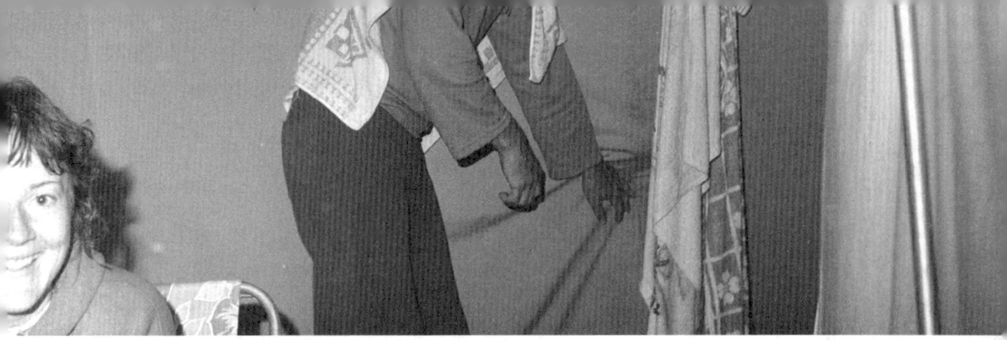

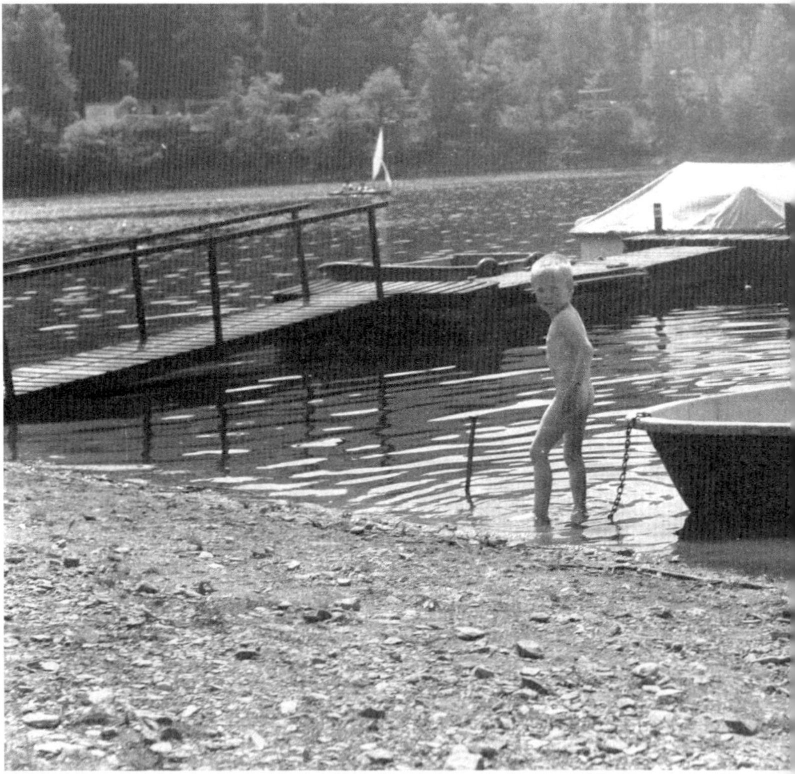

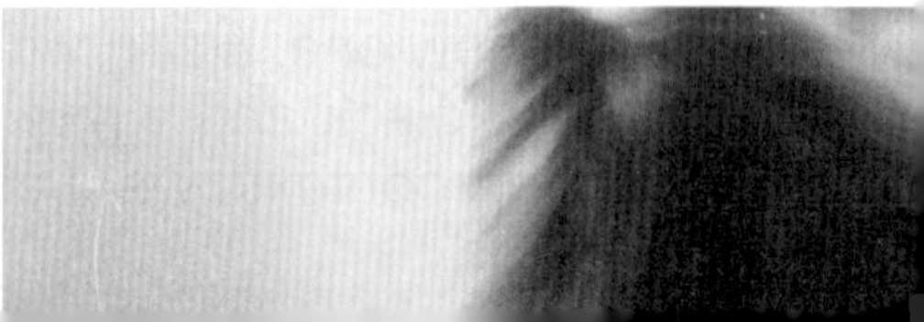

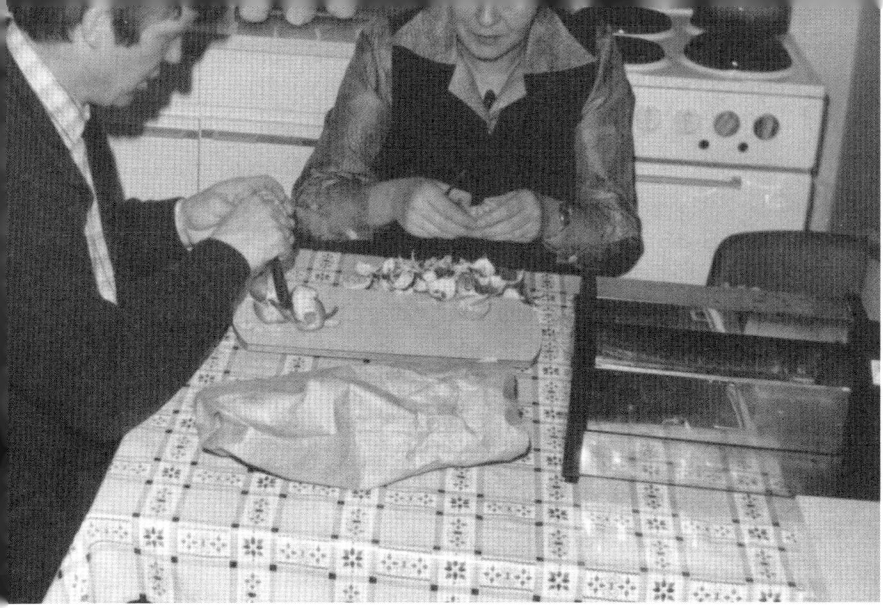

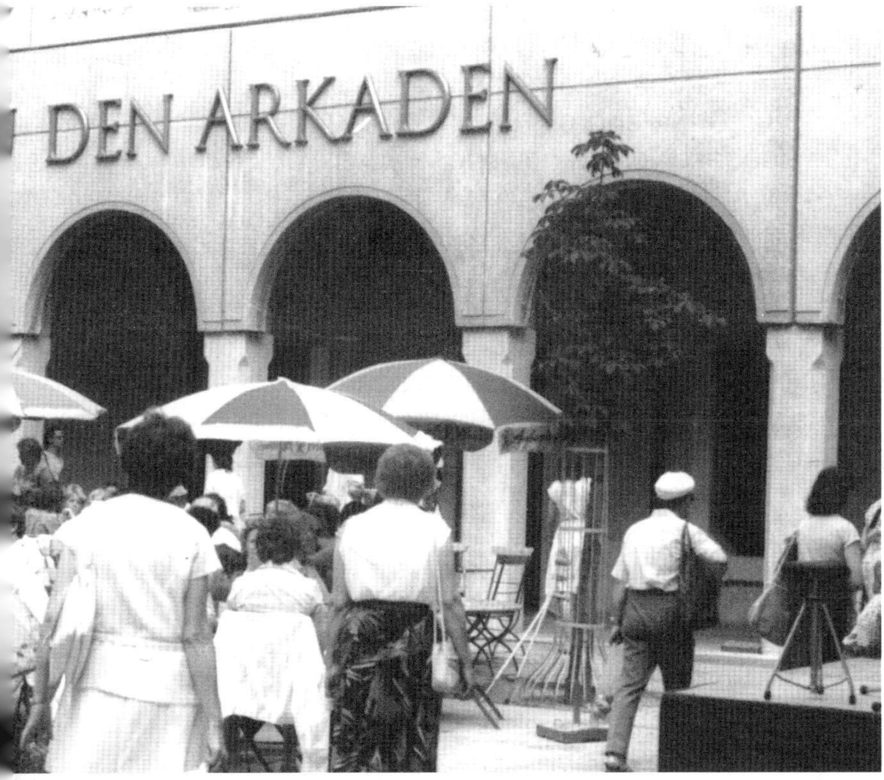
DEN ARKADEN

period from 1984 to 1990 was subjected to a renewal. But work on the album did not end there. Until the end of the 1990s, the described procedure was repeated: slides were sorted out, prints were made from them, and they were inserted into the album.

It comes as no surprise then that its pages are packed. Even the cover is concealed by photographs, some are even fastened one over the other; the photographs cover the front and back endpapers almost without a gap, and even in between hardly a spot has been overlooked and instead has been filled by a picture, an inscription, or an admission ticket (fig. 1). Very little white space is left; the photographs often extend to the edge of the page. Photographs of different formats have been arranged together and pasted, sometimes cropped to fit into tight spaces, sometimes overlapping one another. In general, the images are given priority, the captions have to find a space. In many cases the writing seems squeezed in and becomes increasingly smaller.

The temporal strata in the album are complex. Although the overarching narrative runs chronologically from 1984 to the end of 1990, the album was not created successively during those years, but was edited after 1990. The prints too stem from different times. Some are contemporaneous and were printed relatively soon after they were taken. These include black-and-white prints and a few color prints that have the brown tint typical of the German Democratic Republic (GDR). The prints from the discarded slides from various years were commissioned in batches throughout the 1990s. How does the design reflect the process of making the album as well as the temporal and material strata?

They are particularly visible when looking at the glassine sheets, which as dividers between album pages are not intended for inscriptions and images. These were only filled when there was no more space left on the album page itself. Above all, the prints made later from sorted-out slides found their place there. Many ephemera such as postcards, letters, and documents were also pasted onto the fragile paper pages. The protective function of glassine sheets is all but ignored, and instead they are utilized as additional space, as intermediate pages that the album provides. This opens new creative spaces between the album pages proper. The basic approach seems to have been as follows: individual photographs were mounted centrally on the glassine so that they are well placed even if no other photographs are added. Several photographs at a time are frequently arranged in rows that are oriented vertically or horizontally.

Now and then, series that have already begun on the album pages are continued on the glassine sheets. The added photographs migrate to the glassine sheets, such as those of Beate Göldner's study group celebrating the commencement of their studies (fig. 1). Many small-format black-and-white photographs are arranged on one half of the page. The arrangement is casual in keeping with the character of the social gathering. On the glassine sheet there is a little more order: arranged in a vertical row, the free-floating photographs acquire a kind of framework and structure that knits them together. This can be found in a similar manner on other pages too, sometimes as a horizontal strip that starts at a photograph and runs to the right across the glassine. In terms of both design and content, the series on the album pages are continued on the glassine sheets with the aim of welding the photographs from different contexts and times together.

On other glassine sheets, the supplemented materials add new small narratives and episodes (fig. 2). Postcards find a grateful recipient in the glassine. On it both front and back can be shown as the transparent glassine leaves the text legible. A postcard from the son to his parents reads: "I like it here. I like the food." According to Beate Göldner, however, this was not true. The grandparents, with whom he was on vacation, put a veto on the first, blunter version of

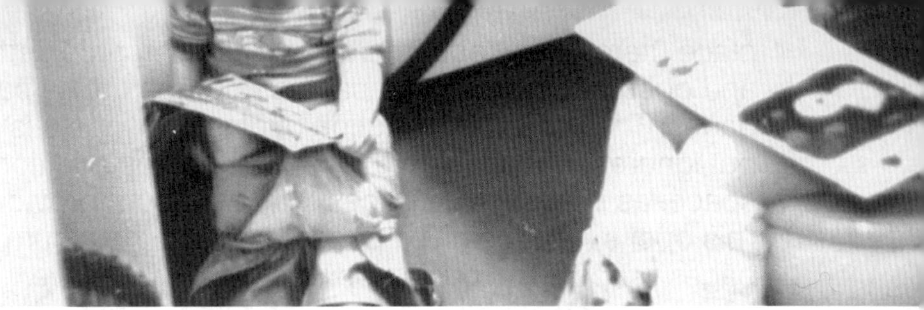

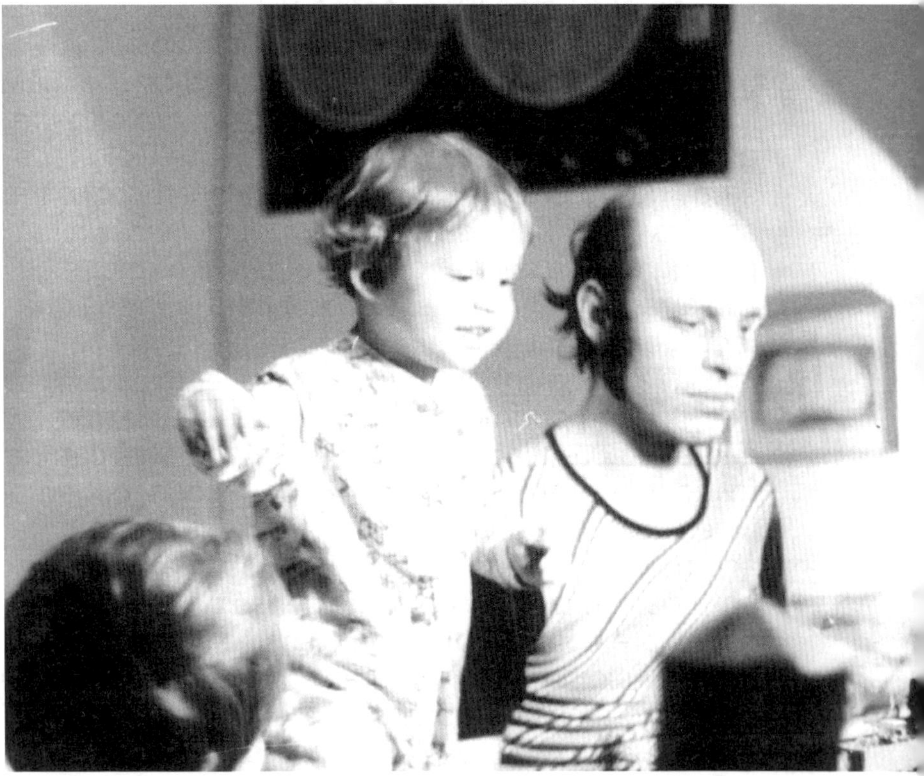

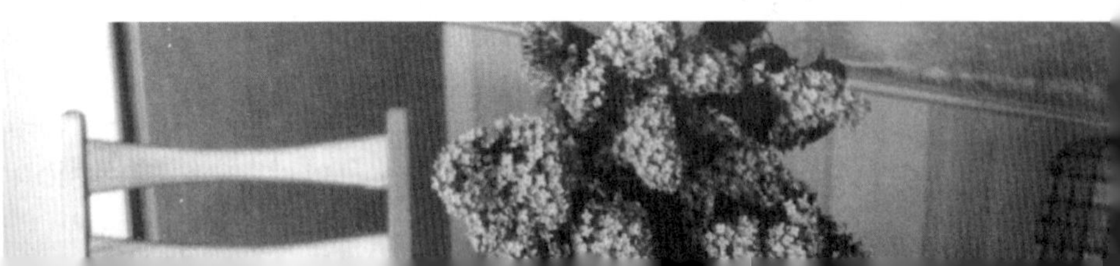

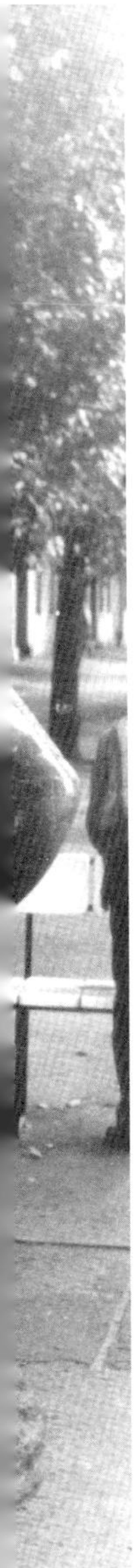

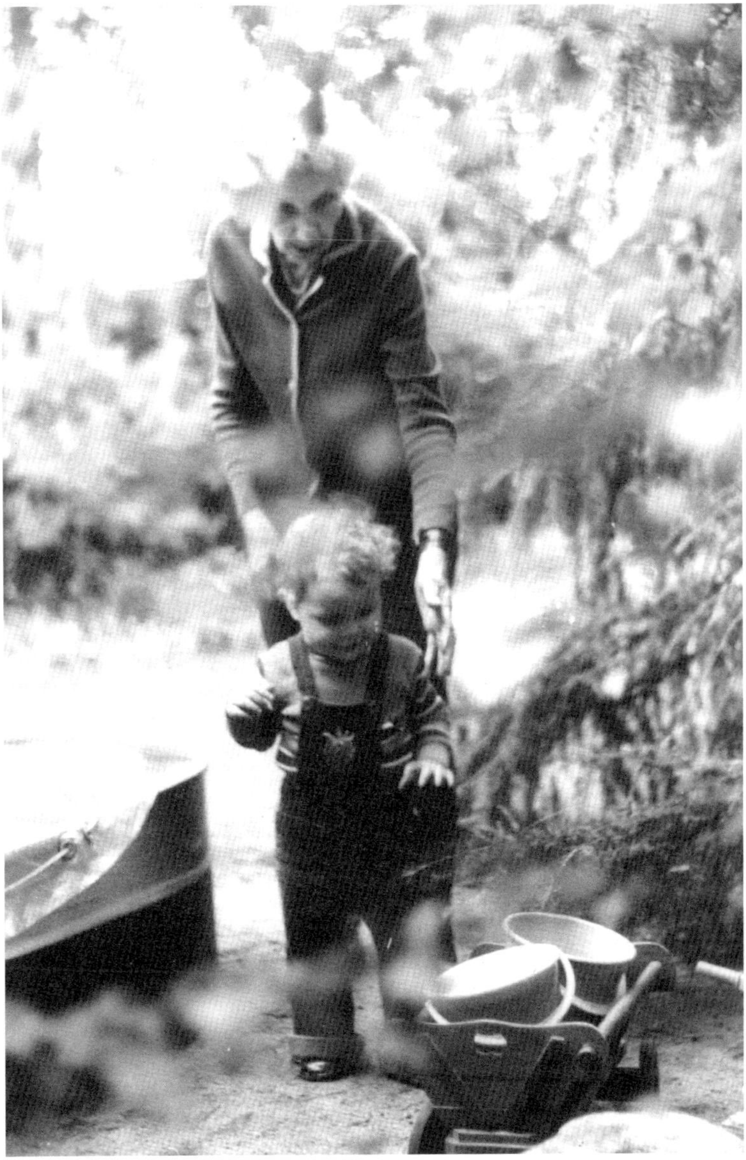

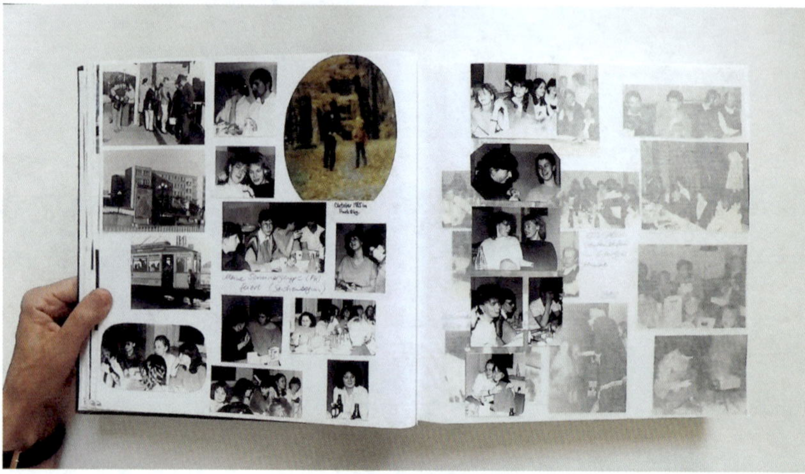

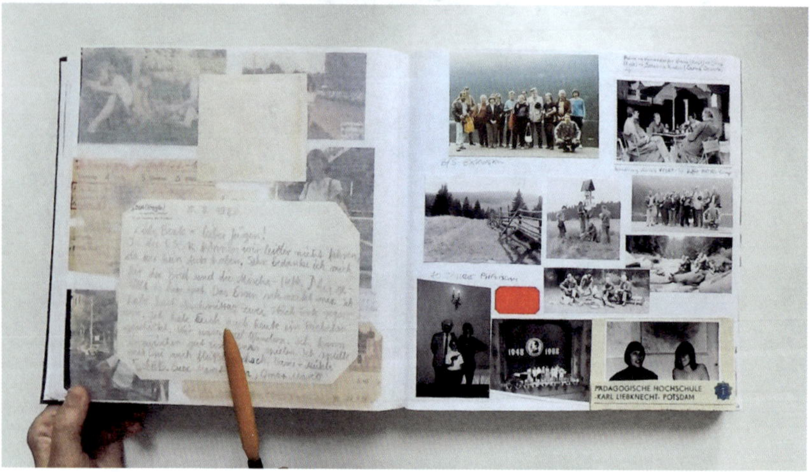

Fig. 1: Album conversation with Beate Göldner, Potsdam, July 24, 2020. Videostill, 1:27:00.

Fig. 2: Album conversation with Beate Göldner, Potsdam, July 24, 2020. Videostill, 2:01:55.

the card. Her son had to reformulate it anew, and now it reads as very distanced and polite. But you only learn about this other side of the story in conversation with Beate Göldner, nothing else points to it. It reminds us of how we write postcards, sometimes in a more superficial or honest way depending on the addressee. The postcard also demonstrates how fragile a thing interpreting biographical documents and artifacts is for scholars. Outsiders can hardly decipher what these objects mean to the members of the family. One can hardly guess what hidden levels of meaning there must have been to justify pasting them into the album. Besides the captions, ephemera of this kind add another textual stratum to the pictorial representation of the family. The persons depicted are given an additional voice in the shape of text additions. They offer the opportunity to insert minor episodes in the album. These narrative additions supplement what could not be represented in the photographs alone. In conversation with Beate Göldner, she explained that the pages in between were used to tell "fill-in stories."(1) They build a second stratum in the album, which complements, follows up, and elaborates. In this way, a photo album expands into a family archive that preserves not only pictorial, but also written accounts.

When you open the album, one cannot see all the photographs on a double page at first glance. Comments and protruding edges indicate that there is another layer hiding underneath. But for what reason is the album stratified, why are photographs mounted one over the other? For one, it was the limited space. The book form of the album has its limits with only a certain number of pages and a predefined format. The Göldners only reluctantly throw photos away, no matter how poor in quality they may be. This is not uncommon among amateurs.

But although the new album offered a lot of space, it was hardly adequate for the Göldners.

1 Author's conversation with Beate Göldner, Potsdam, June 3, 2022.

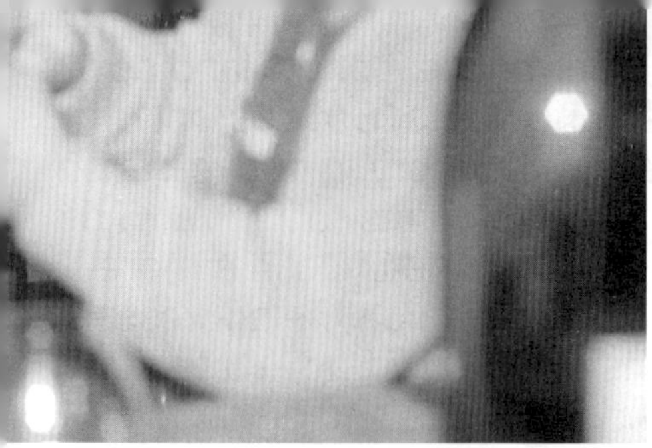

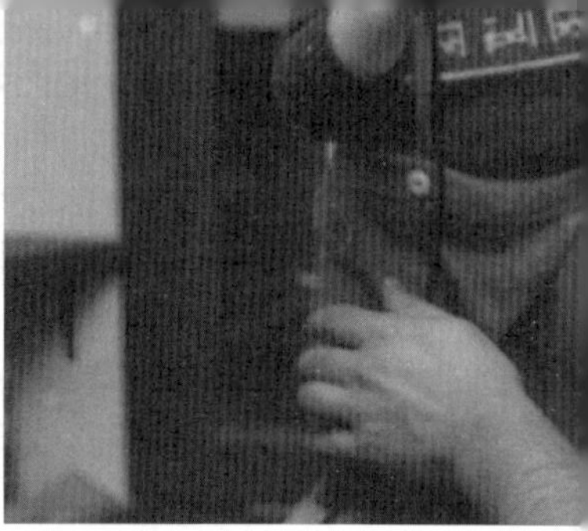

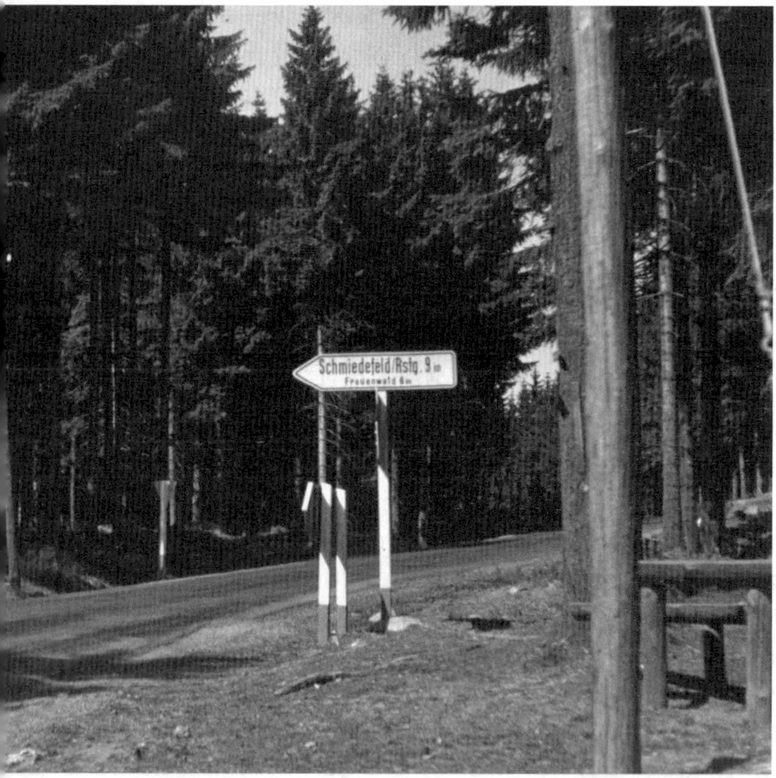
Schmiedefeld/Rstg. 9
Frauenwald

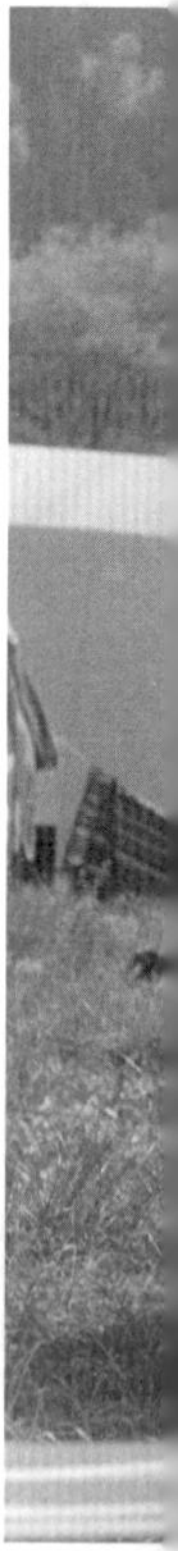

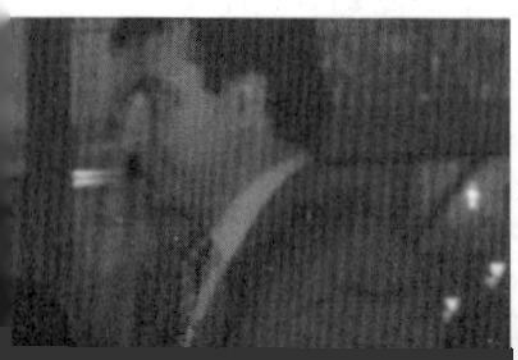

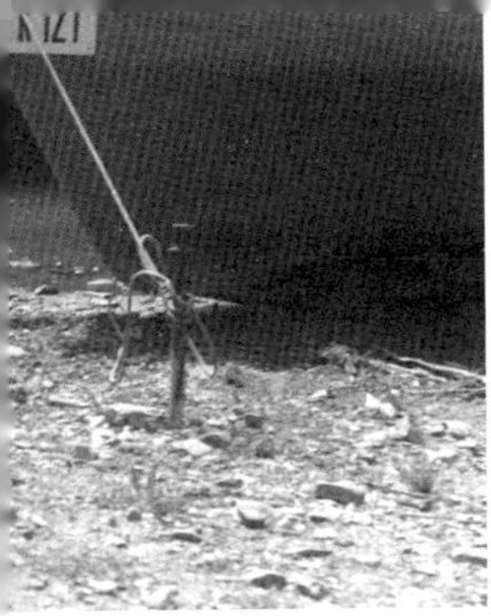
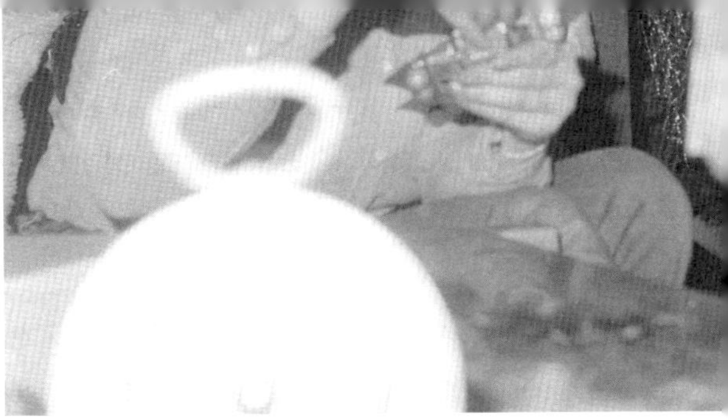
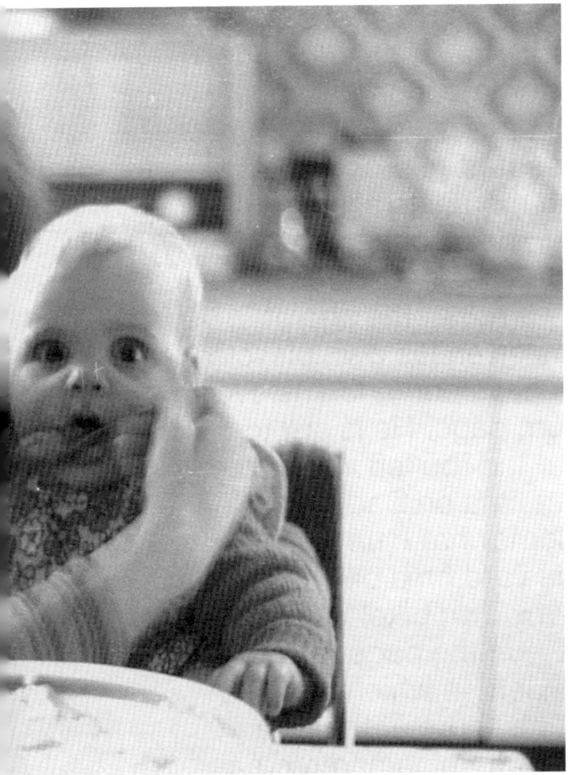
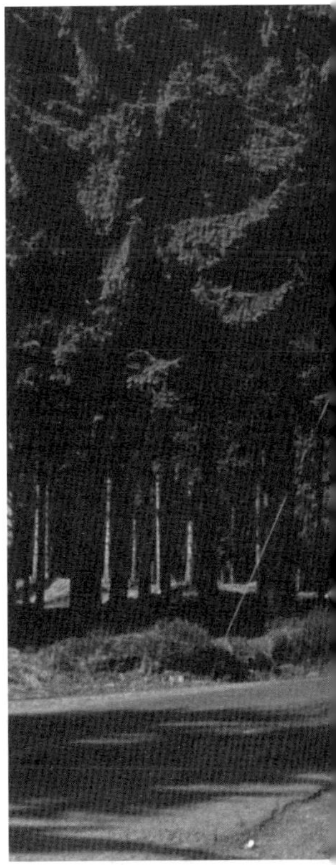
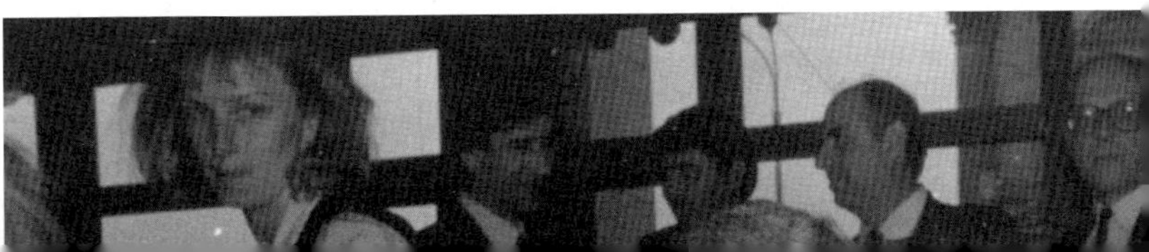

An additional kind of page design compresses together similar motifs and images from a series. An example from the summer of 1989 illustrates this (fig. 3). The photograph shows people sunbathing at the Babelsberg municipal swimming and recreational area. At first glance, it is neither noticeable that the photograph folds out at the bottom left nor is there an arrow or label referring to it. There is also no photograph pasted in underneath, but the photo paper can be folded out to the side like a fanfold, revealing a very similar photograph. A panoramic view of sorts can thus be unfolded and subsequently be refolded again to save space.

The second reason for the stratification of the material includes the aforementioned aspect while also adding another—the narrative dimension. In addition to the openly presented photographs, brief narrative punch lines and moments arise now and then while exploring the folded prints. Again at the Babelsberg city bath, a small episode took place two years earlier in April 1987 (fig. 4). At the age of 8, the Göldners' son Marcel was given his own bicycle, an important step in a child's development. The event is built up over the entire album page. He is still to be seen on his father's bike at the top left with the caption announcing: "The last time on Dad's bike!" Small and in the center is a somewhat blurred shot with a child whizzing by in the yard on a bike, with the comment: "From now on my own bike!" An arrow and the instruction "(fold out)" on the page refer to the photograph at the bottom left, in which two people on horseback ride along the shore of the lake of the Babelsberg city public swimming and recreational area. A bike leans against a tree. In our conversation about the album, Beate Göldner points out what the viewer cannot know: "The new bicycle is already standing there."(2) On folding back the print,

2 Album conversation with Beate Göldner, Potsdam, July 24, 2020, 1:45:07.

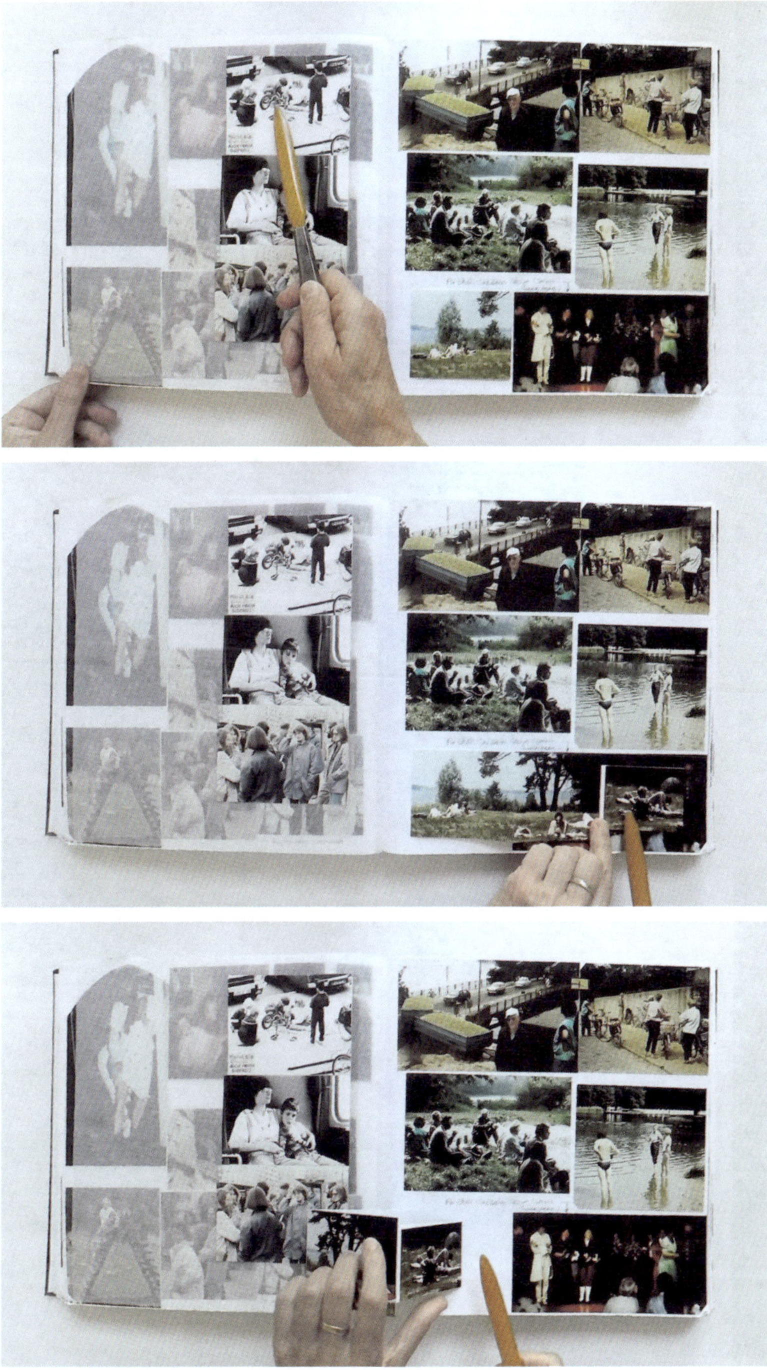

Fig. 3: Album conversation with Beate Göldner, Potsdam, July 24, 2020. Videostill, 2:11:23 / 2:11:33 / 2:11:38.

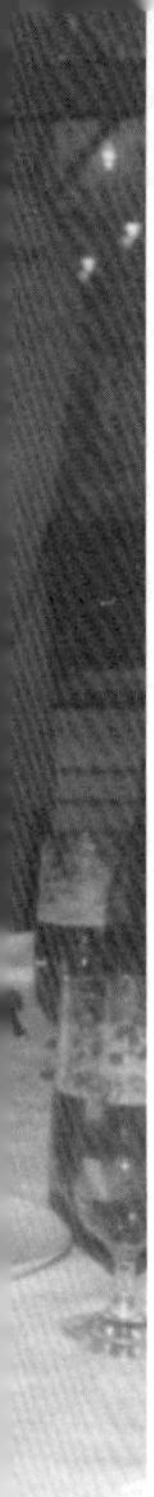

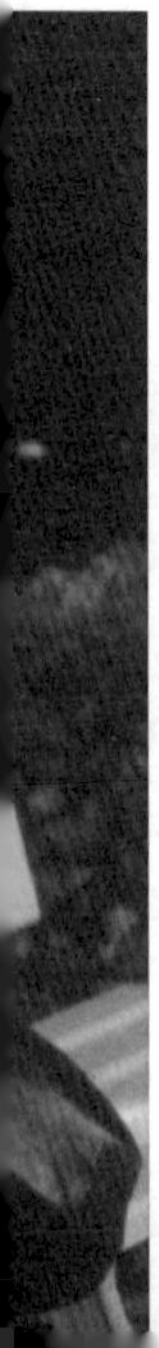

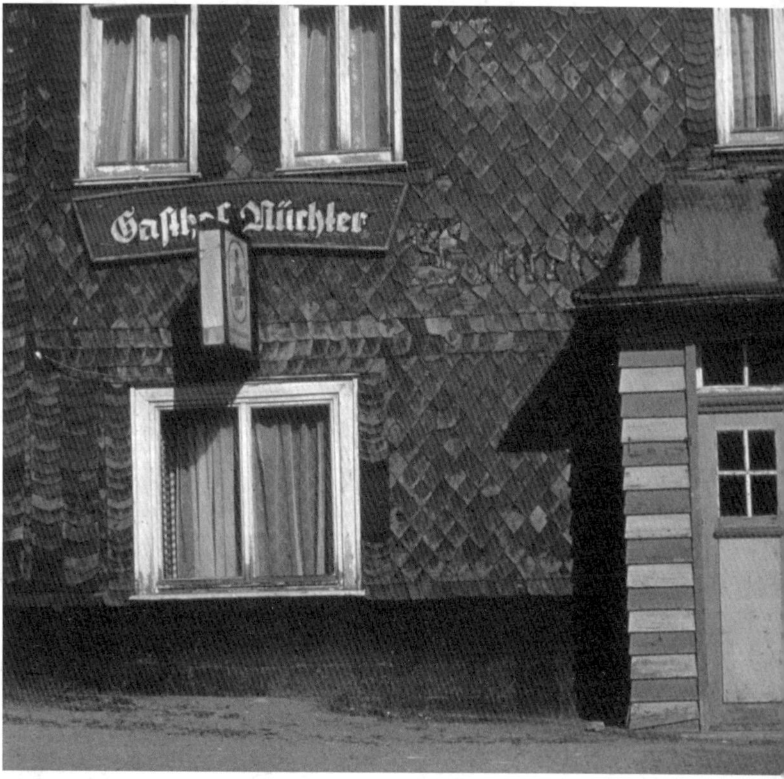
Nüchter

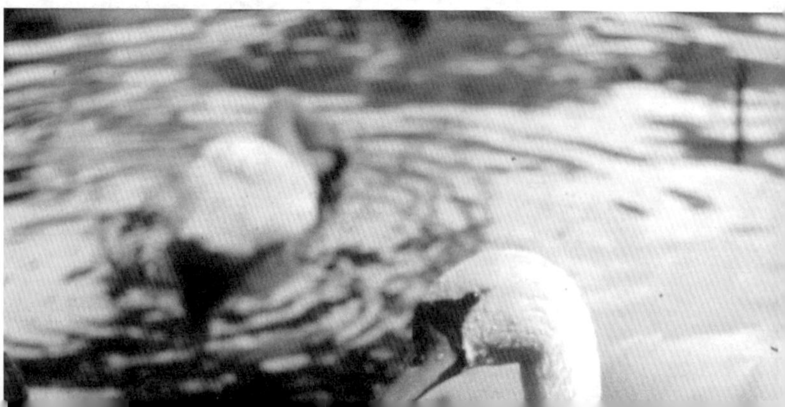

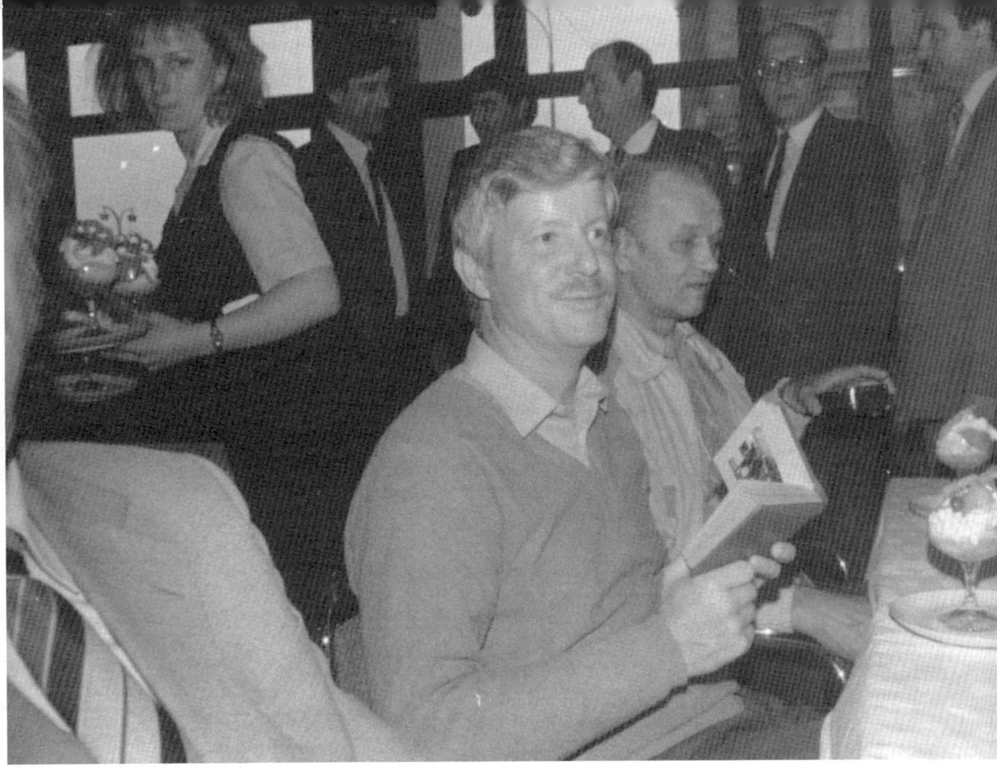

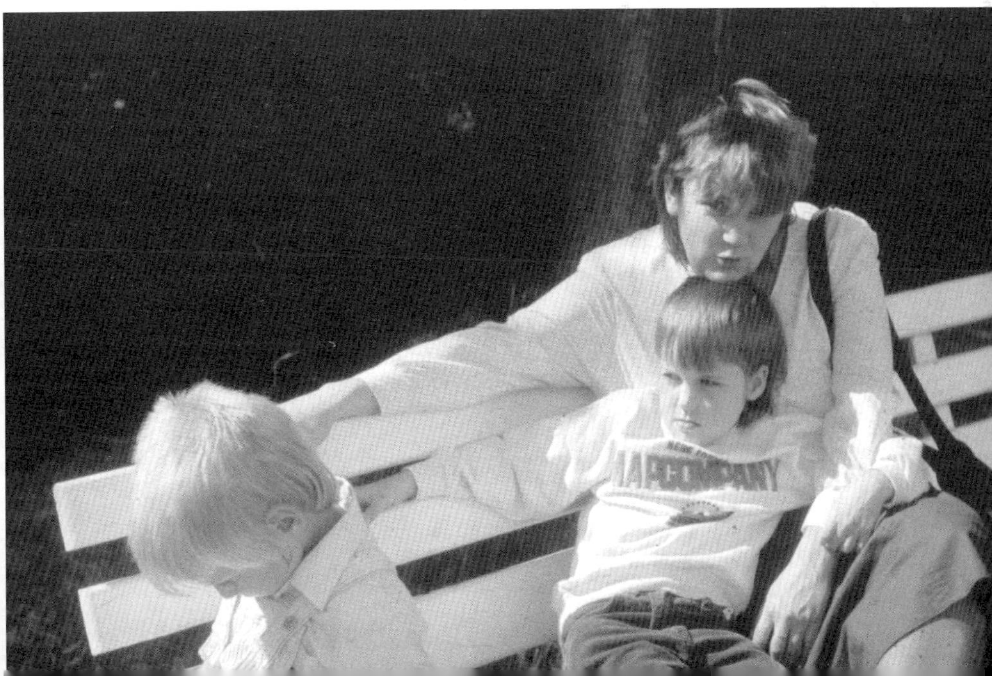

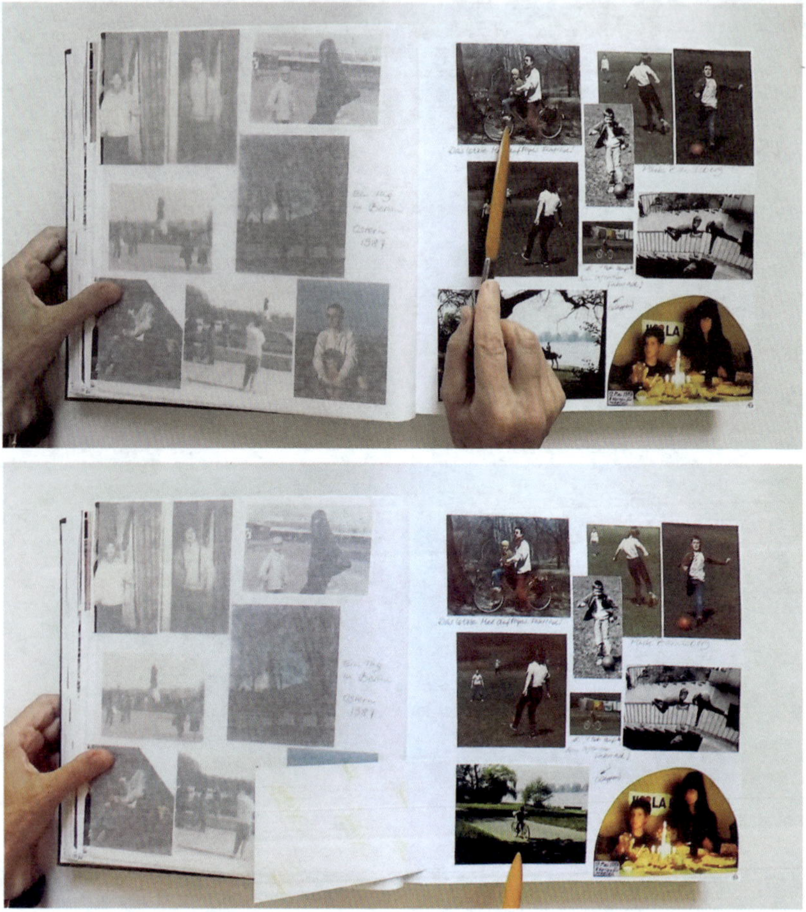

Fig. 4: Album conversation with Beate Göldner, Potsdam, July 24, 2020. Videostill, 1:45:01 / 1:45:10.

the climax of this little tale follows. “His first solo bicycle tour,”(3) Beate Göldner explains, on which her son rides his own bike along the shores of the lake. The act of folding out builds up the suspense; the highlight of the page must be revealed. It becomes evident that Beate Göldner’s comment on the page is closely interwoven with the design. Her narration whets anticipation in a way that would not be so intense without her remarks, despite the revelatory staging.

A kind of stratified narration emerges by folding the photographs to mimic the sequential nature of the album pages. It is not the juxtaposition of the images on the album page that generates the narrative, but rather the sequence that they build. Jürgen Göldner might have been thinking of the slide shows in which images are projected one after the other. The photographs placed one over the other are interlinked quite differently. Sometimes micronarratives arise, or series and motifs are compacted. Some constellations play with the idea of hide-and-seek. Above the caption “FKK am Baggersee” (Nudist beach at the quarry pond) sticks the shot of a woman dressed in a towel toga. At the top edge of the print, her face peeks out a second time. Here it is not concealed that another photograph is hidden underneath, but rather played with the voyeuristic moment of revelation when the prints are folded over. The interrelationships are not clear in some cases. How do black-and-white shots of dreary-looking streets fit in with the underlying snapshots of a coffee table? In discussing the album together, Beate Göldner does not link the situations and instead talks about them one after the other. Hence, the design does not always establish interrelationships and pursues more arbitrary goals—or is more concerned about finding space-saving solutions, with design ambitions taking a back seat.

3 Album conversation with Beate Göldner, Potsdam, July 24, 2020, 1:45:12.

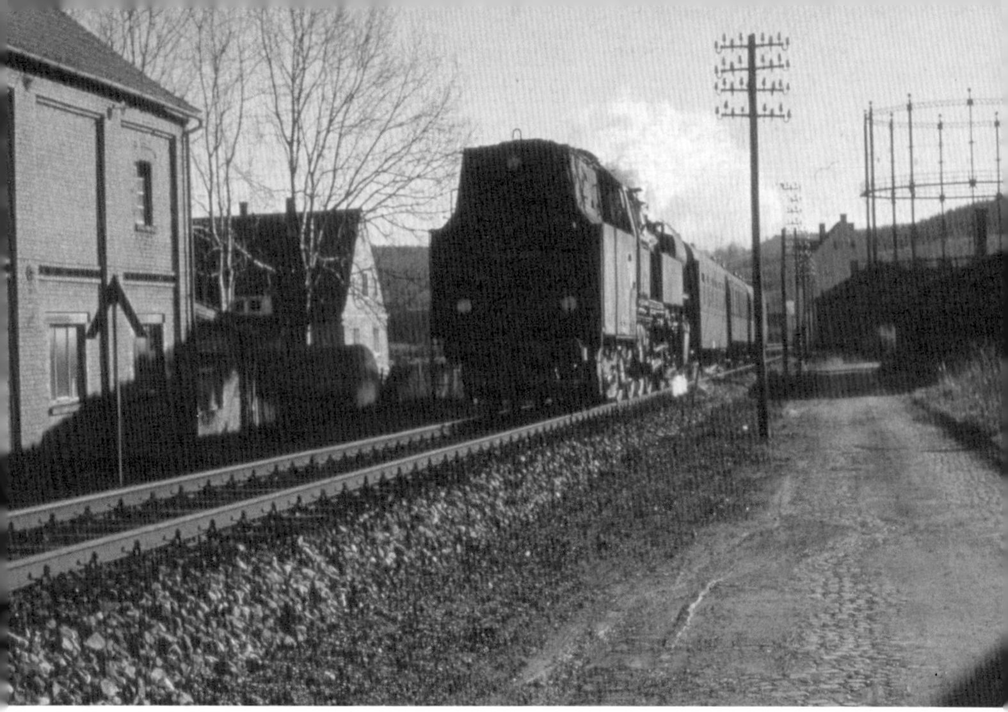

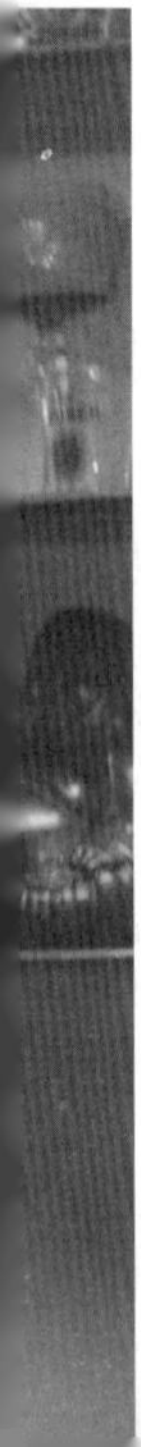

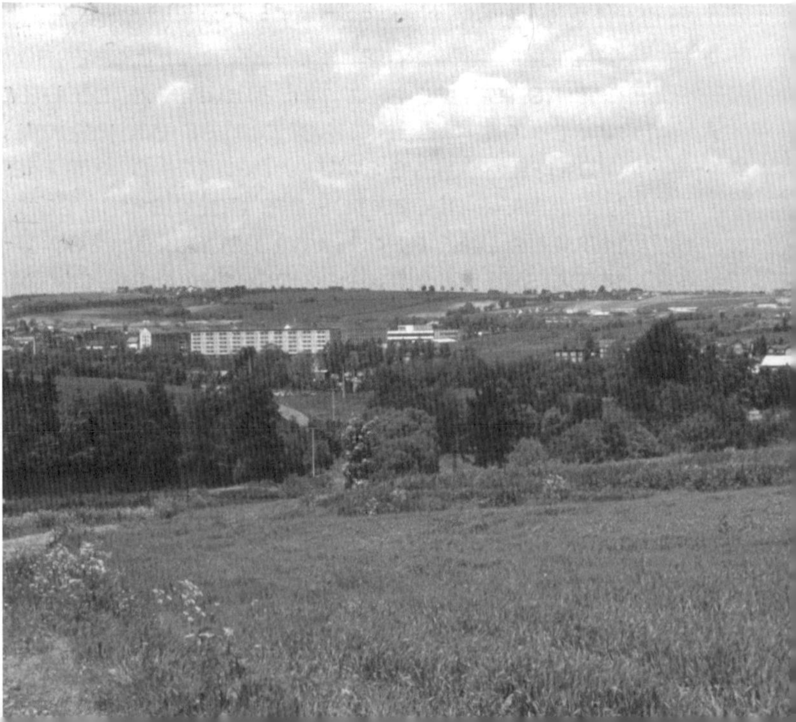

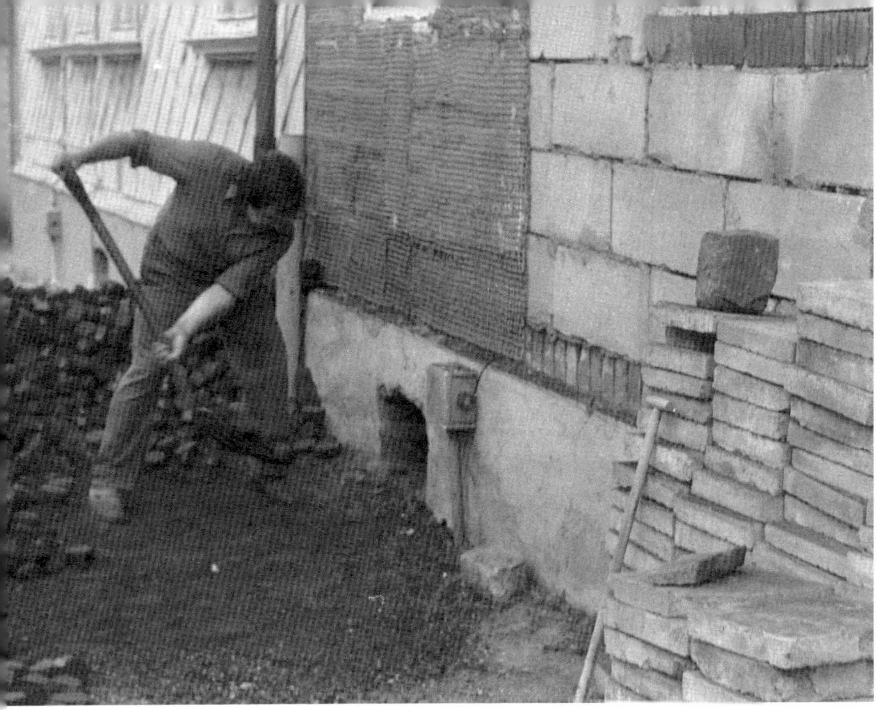

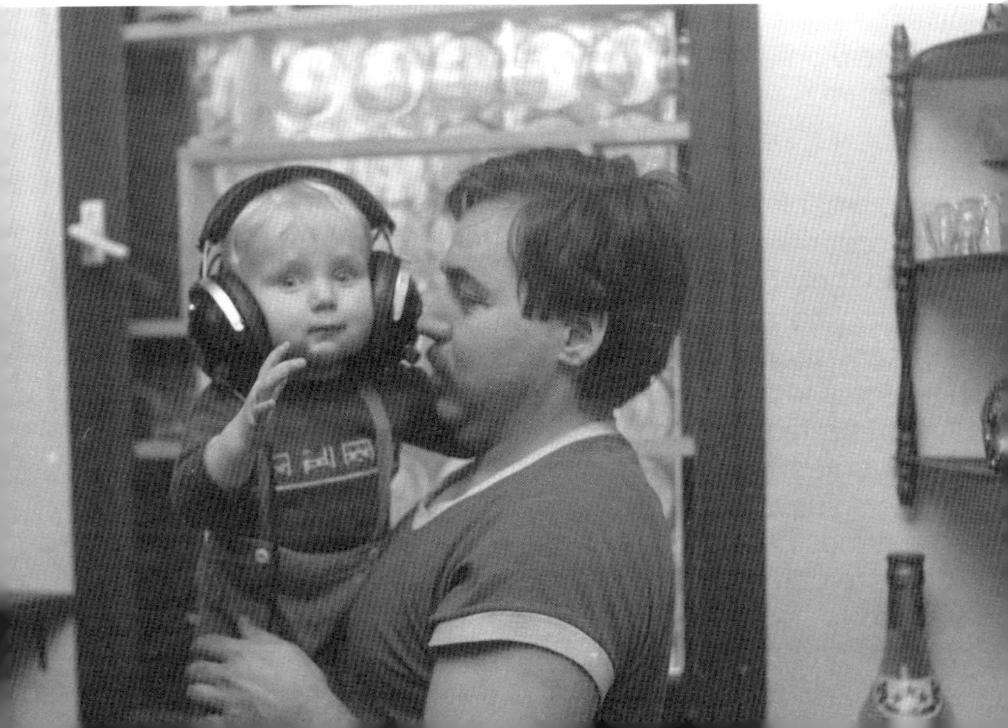

The foldable prints make viewers inclined to see a haptic dimension in the album. Not only do the album and glassine pages have to be turned, but prints must also be folded back by hand so that all the photographs can be seen. The written instructions literally ask the viewers to both look at and proactively explore the material. However, as a guest in the lives of strangers, looking through their albums with them, as in the album discussions, one inevitably slips into a more passive role. You don't turn the pages yourself; you leave that to the authors of the album. In addition, objects that we have become accustomed to as scholars must be handled with care. Therefore, people like myself can but look and point and not experience the album haptically. The authors of the album and the circles for which the album was created are certainly more relaxed about the way they handle it. In the video, however, Beate Göldner herself often uses a letter opener instead of her fingers to fold out parts of the album as if she were an archivist. With this device, she can in fact slide under the prints more easily. It would not be all that easy in many places to grip the edges of the prints with your fingers. What is ultimately left of the haptics offered by the album?

It is hardly possible to reconstruct which photographs and materials were added to the album when, what it looked like in its early stages, and in what order things were added. We can only say for certain that the photographs on the glassine paper and the fold-over prints were later additions. The constant additions probably also led to each album page having a different appearance—and no generic design patterns are discernible. In many cases, the arrangements appear associative, and events are shown in several views as frayed clusters. These can sometimes be read horizontally, sometimes vertically. The gaze can hardly be said to be guided, having instead to find its way unaided through the densely packed compilations. The cycle of taking photo-

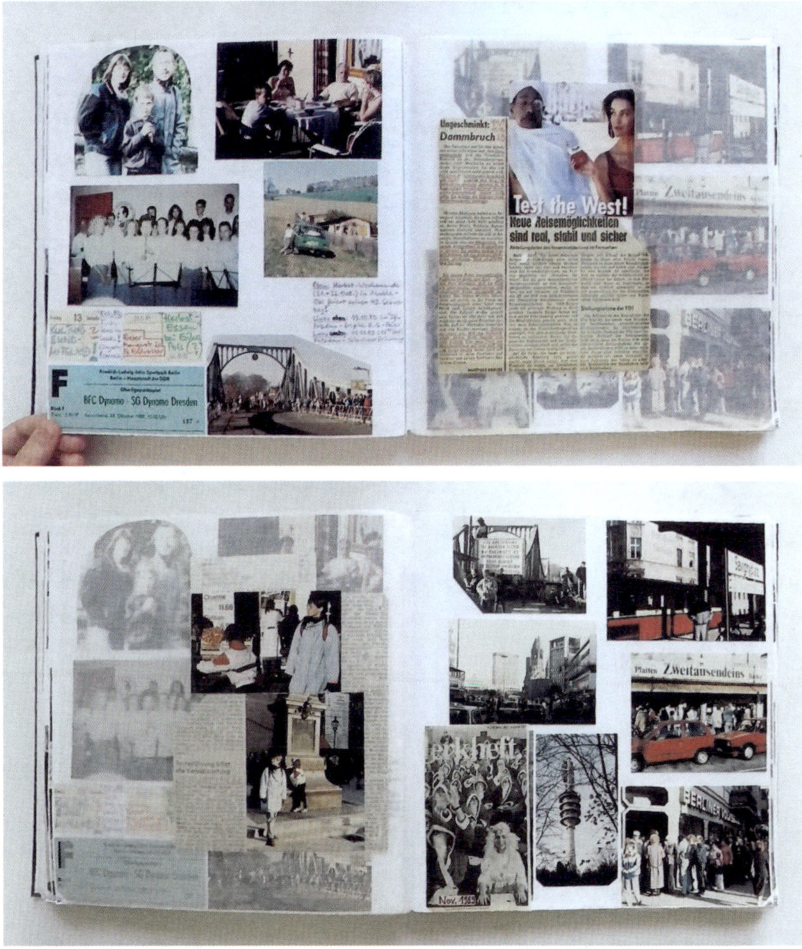

Fig. 5: Album conversation with Beate Göldner, Potsdam, July 24, 2020. Videostill, 2:16:25/2:17:00.

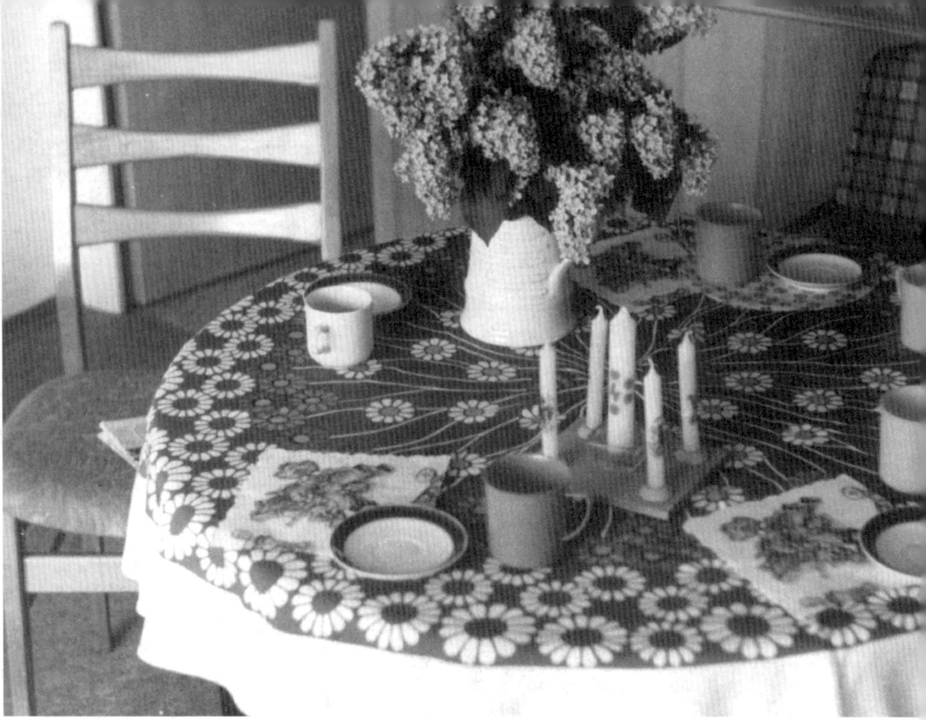

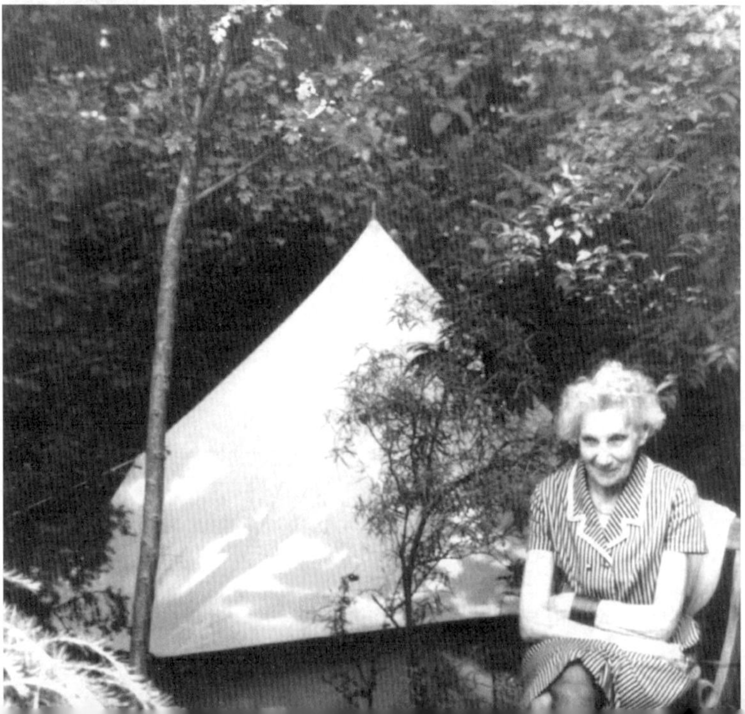

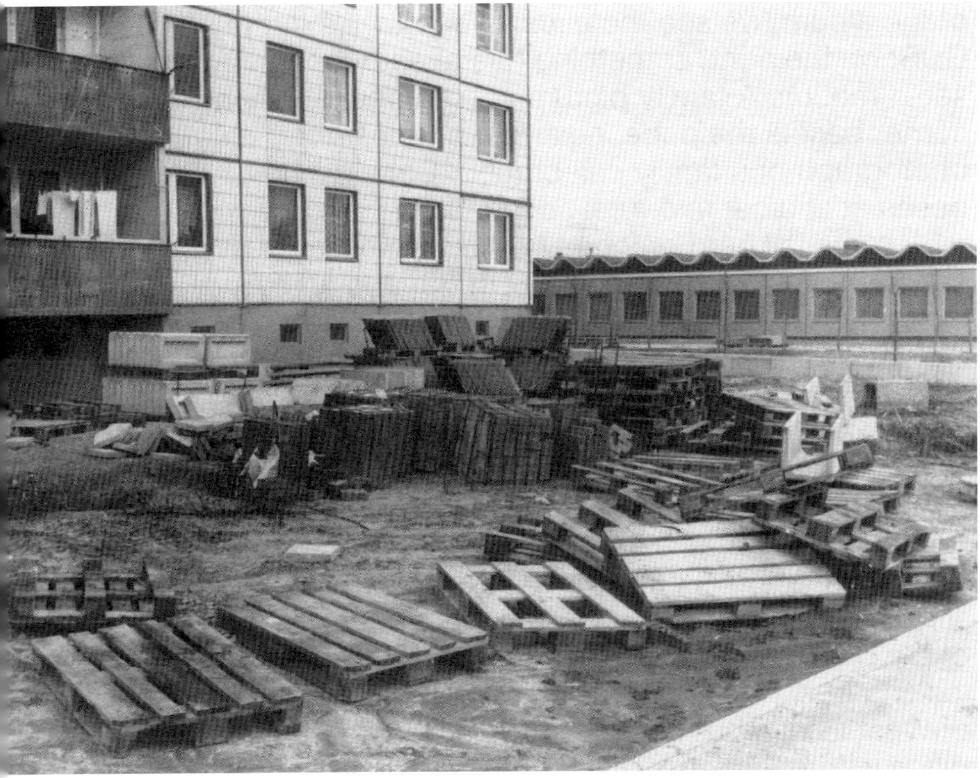

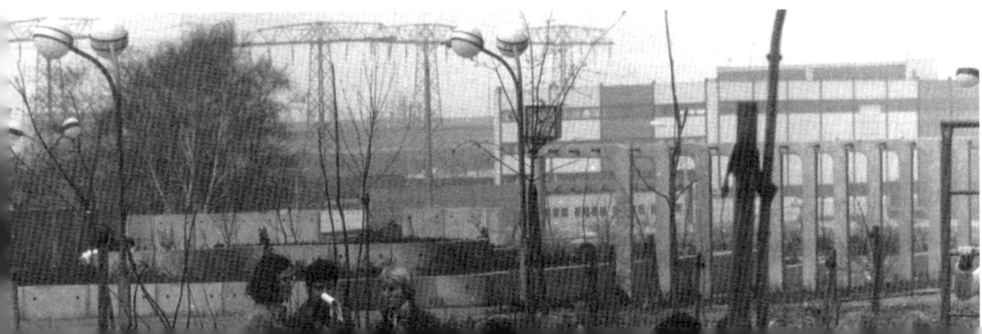

graphs, sorting them, having prints made, and pasting in testifies to a continuous engagement with the photographic images.

The album was put together barely two years after the end of the GDR. The dramatic events of that time seem to be swallowed up by the rest. It is easy to inadvertently flip over the decisive album page. It is the autumn of 1989 (fig. 5). On the left side of the album, we see the usual everyday life in the GDR; on the right, something has already been set in motion. A family picture in the upper left-hand corner begins the page, next to it on the right is a photograph of a family celebration. Below, a boy poses near a car in a rural scenery. Further down, the events fall hard on one another: the ticket of a soccer match from October 28, 1989; above that excerpts from a calendar in which several dates in October have been highlighted. Then rather inconspicuously on the lower right is a picture of the Glienicker Bridge in Potsdam taken on November 11, 1989 at 11:11 PM, as noted in the caption. The border crossing had been opened the day before. There is a hustle and bustle, people are pushing their way ahead, yet there is still ample space on the street. Jürgen Göldner is also standing there, in the middle of the bridge between the two still existing states, looking back. He is not taking pictures in the direction of West Berlin, but back towards Potsdam, to the place where the family lived until the fall of the Berlin Wall and afterwards. The left album page is still completely related to the GDR, even if the state border has already been crossed. To the right of it on the glassine paper, a newspaper clipping from the *Märkische Volksstimme* from November 11, 1989 has been pasted in at a later date together with the advertising slogan "Test the West!" Under these two items of printed matter, some photographs on the next page, which can be located in the "West," already shimmer through the glassine paper. The walk that crossed the border continues on the right-hand page.

On the lower left, they are just leaving the territory of the GDR and are already on the other side of the bridge. The first visit to West Berlin takes them mainly to Charlottenburg. Later, two shots were added on the glassine that show Beate Göldner and her son, Marcel, roaming through West Berlin. They are moving about in the photos and not posing in front of landmarks. She doesn't look at the camera; instead, she walks around with a concentrated gaze. During this time, Jürgen Göldner seems to be the only one in the family to have viewed the new world through the camera; he is not to be seen in any of the photos. The Göldners move like tourists in an unknown country. They don't do this in an unconcerned, curious way but with a reserved, observant gaze. If you turn the page, you take a small leap in time to New Year's Eve in 1989. Suddenly you are in the private realm again, photos of the celebration and skating follow. Normal life with its celebrations and events continues. The political may encroach on the private sphere but seems kept at a distance in the album.

All of this was laid out in retrospect, not as a break with the past, but as a flowing transition. In the album talk, Beate Göldner explains, "and now suddenly the Wall is no more. And the album continues as normal."(4) She presents the album as if it had been created parallel to the events, not afterwards and shaped by years of revising it. She gets completely absorbed in the self-made logic of the album. Events were not perceived as breaking with the past in the early 1990s because "somehow, for now, life went on as normal."(5) Viewing the situation as an event that initially had no major impact on the family also influences the design of the album.

The temporal and material strata are presented on this page as follows: first, the photo-

4 Album conversation with Beate Göldner, Potsdam, July 24, 2020, 2:32:34.

5 Album conversation with Beate Göldner, Potsdam, July 24, 2020, 2:32:24.

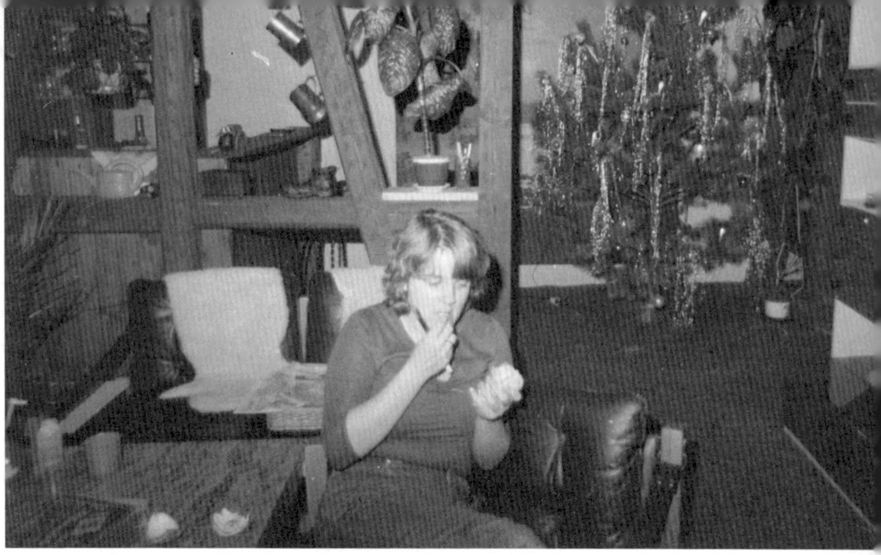

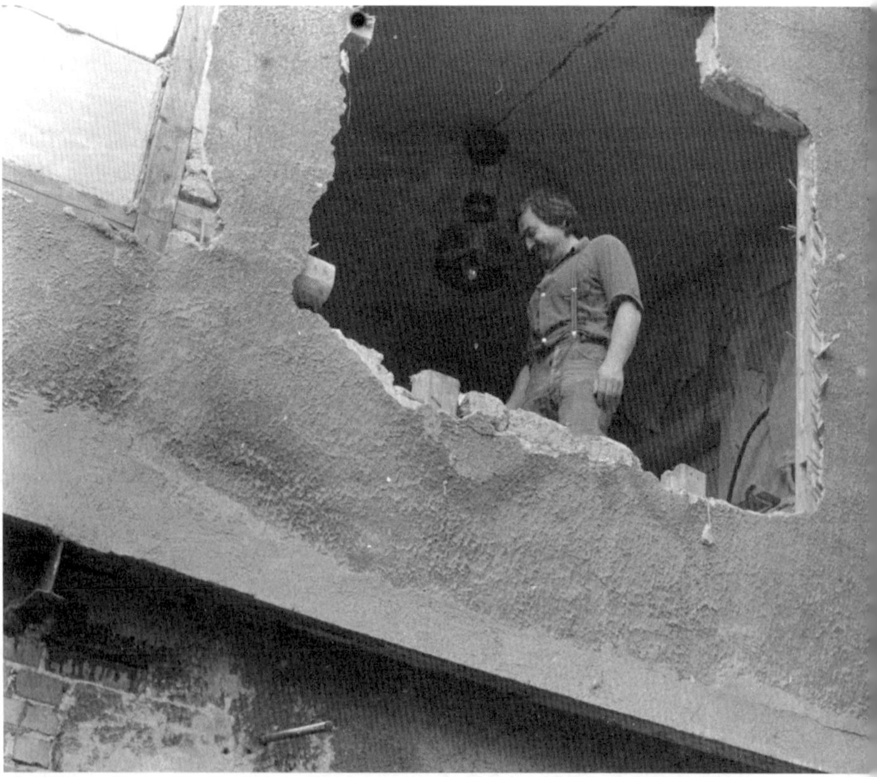

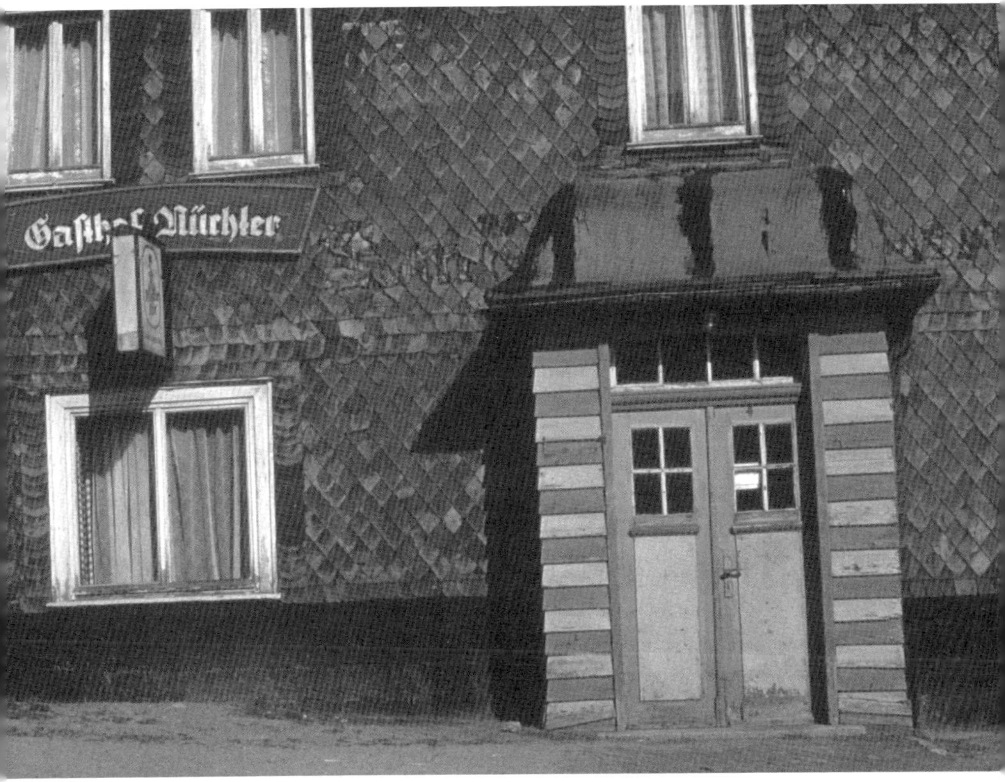
Nüchler

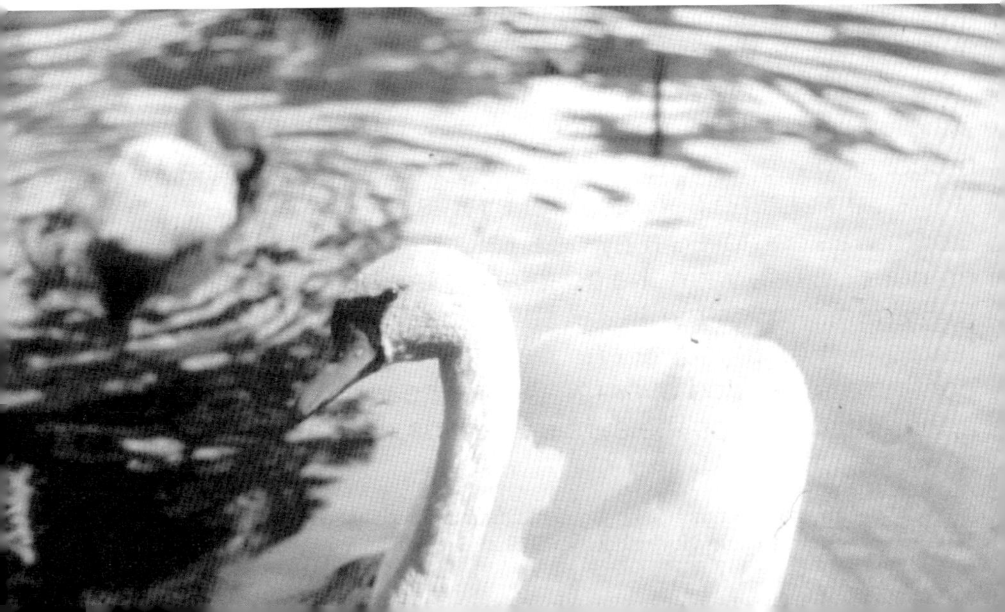

graphs were pasted in, possibly together with the ticket to the soccer game and the clippings from the calendar. Later, the photograph of the official celebration of Beate Göldner's promotion was added and mounted over another print. An important private and professional event. Two pieces of paper were added last. One is an addition to the calendar reading "Oct '89: Turbulence in the country! (Hungary/ Austria)," the other contains explanations for the pictures. The combination of newspaper clipping and advertising slogan on the glassine paper is probably the most obvious reference to the fall of the Wall. The article titled "New travel options are real, stable, and safe" reveals that the government is still trying to downplay the significance of opening the borders. The Göldners have added another headline to the text in the form of the advertising slogan—"Test the West!"—from the West cigarette brand. The similarity of the statements here is ironically emphasized: the advertising slogan, somewhat coincidentally its slogan at that time, calls for testing the "West," while the party leadership hopes that the citizens really only want to test the "known unknown"(6) and then return. GDR reporting and the West German advertising campaign are combined in such a way that they convey the conflicting/diverse feelings about the present as well as the future.

They are contemporary documents that suggest a parallelism between historical events and processing them in the album, which was not the case. The length of time between the events and when the album was compiled may be a reason why the pages do not disclose what the opening of the border meant to the family, whether the events made them hope, fear, or left them indifferent. Despite the album being continuously edited over the years, the view of events apparently remains the same. Perhaps the key lies in

6 Matthias Krauss, "Ungeschminkt: Dammbruch," in: *Märkische Volksstimme*, November 11, 1989, p. 3.

this observation: the continuous editing is not an adaptation or update, but the consolidation of a family history and a view of things. The narrative in the album is a "personal construct … from which the contours of a person's self and world can be read." (7) They are shaped retrospectively with the awareness of the continuity that "normal" life goes on for the family members despite the political upheaval affecting their lives. The album forms and consolidates a present that is supposedly immediate—however, it has long since passed. The sense of immediacy nevertheless remains powerful to this day. Thus, the act of cutting and pasting creates order in life. It is a "narrative of stability."(8) It is the means by which the authors, in a time of change and uncertainty, regain the interpretative sovereignty over their lives. While at first glance the photo album of the Göldners appears to be a finalized project from a bygone era, it turns out to be the continuous, still ongoing work on the image of the past. Is this process ever completed? Beate Göldner comments in the video on still empty glassine pages in the album: "So who knows what this will look like in ten years? When we have to sort through the slides again?"(9)

7 Jürgen Straube, "Geschichten erzählen, Geschichte bilden: Grundzüge einer narrativen Psychologie historischer Sinnbildung", in: Jürgen Straube (ed.), op. cit., Frankfurt am Main: Suhrkamp 1998, pp. 81–169, esp. pp. 124–25.

8 Kenneth J. Gergen, "Erzählung, moralische Identität und historisches Bewußtsein. Eine sozialkonstruktivistische Darstellung", in Jürgen Straube (ed.), *Erzählung, Identität und historisches Bewußtsein. Die psychologische Konstruktion von Zeit und Geschichte*, Frankfurt am Main: Suhrkamp 1998, pp. 170–202, esp. pp. 178.

9 Album conversation with Beate Göldner, Potsdam, July 24, 2020, 1:19:45.

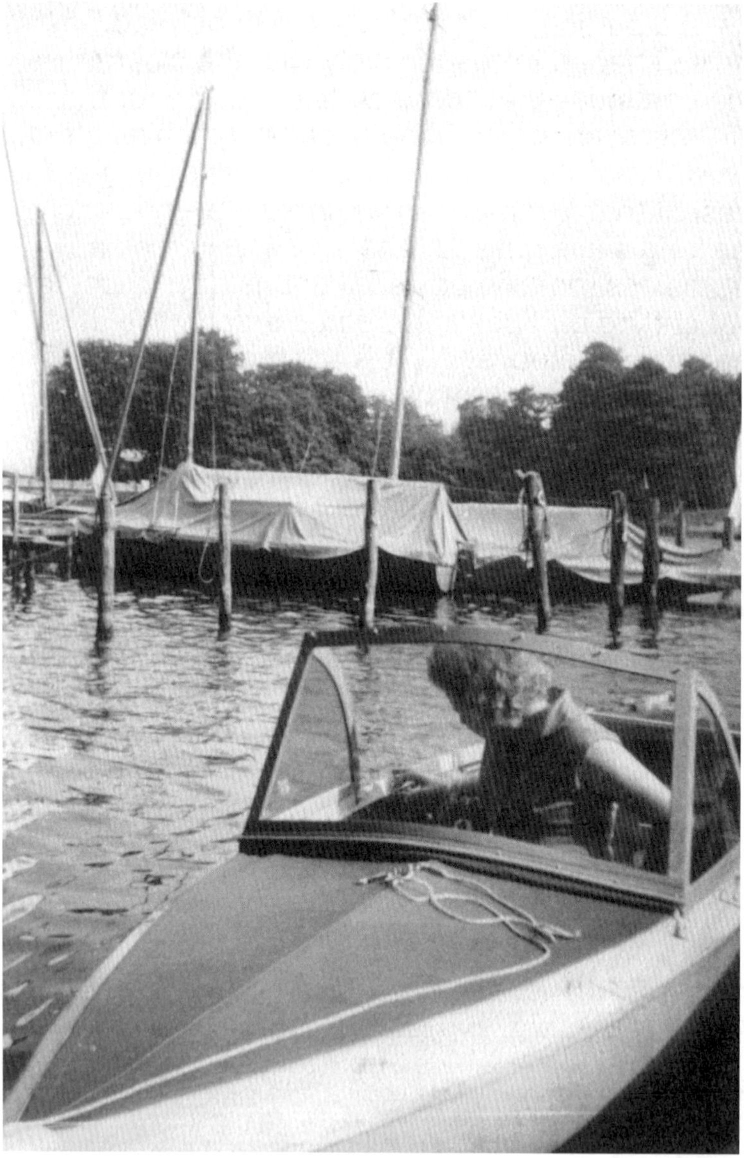

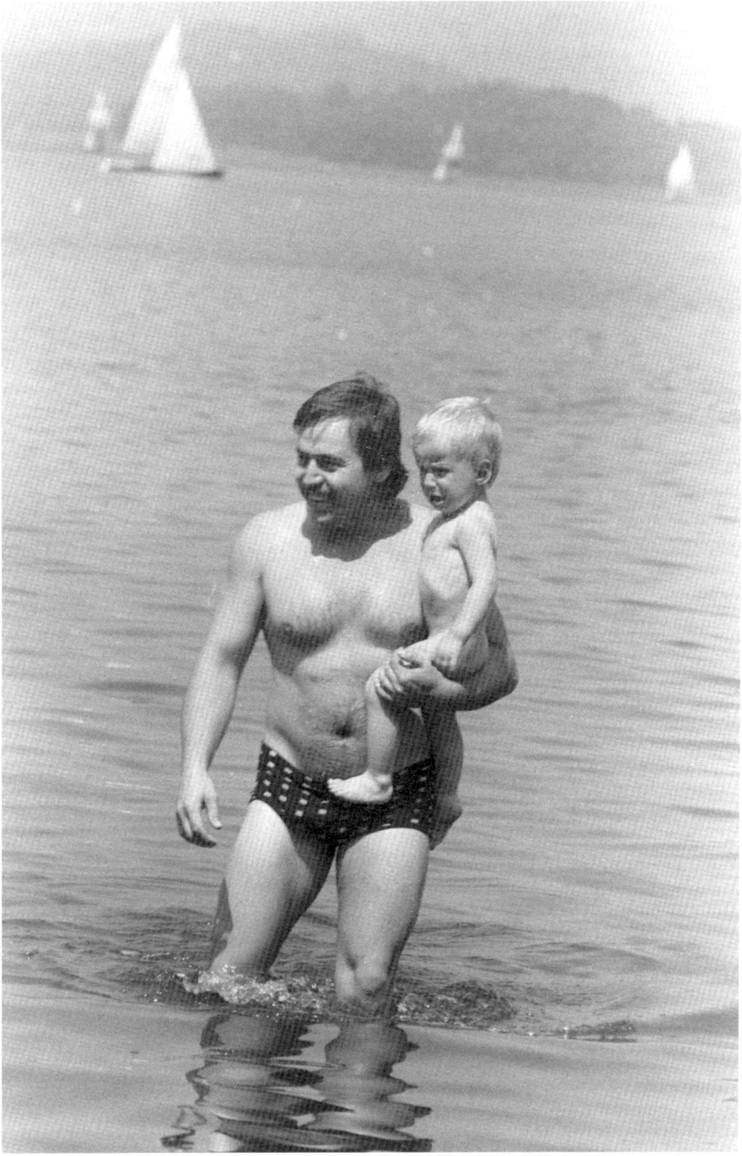

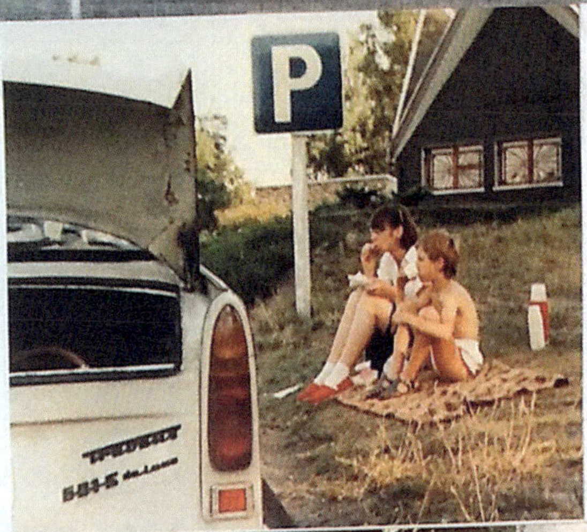

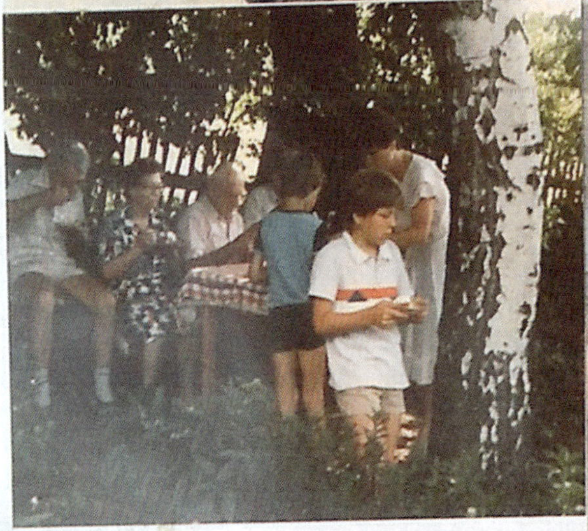

Oben & links:
Bei Lebart im Garten in GLINDOW

Unten und rechts:
Auf nach MILDA zur Geburtstagsfeier – Mutti wird 73! (7/89)

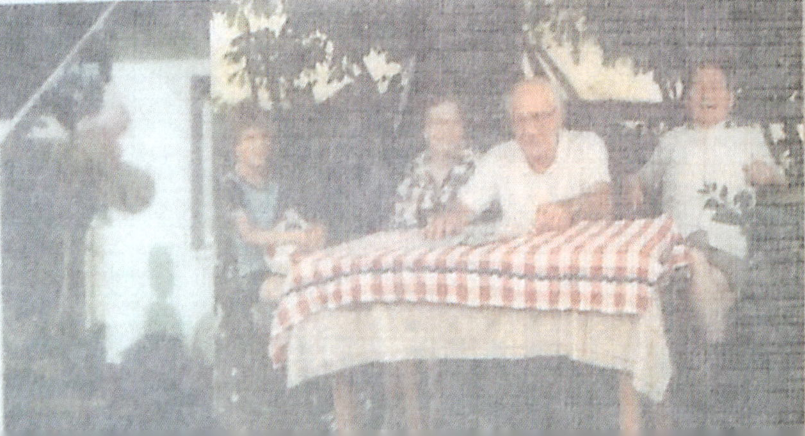

Beate and Jürgen Göldner

Beate and Jürgen Göldner

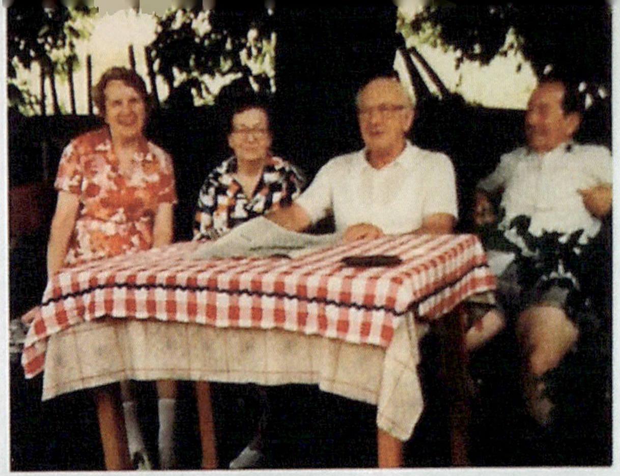
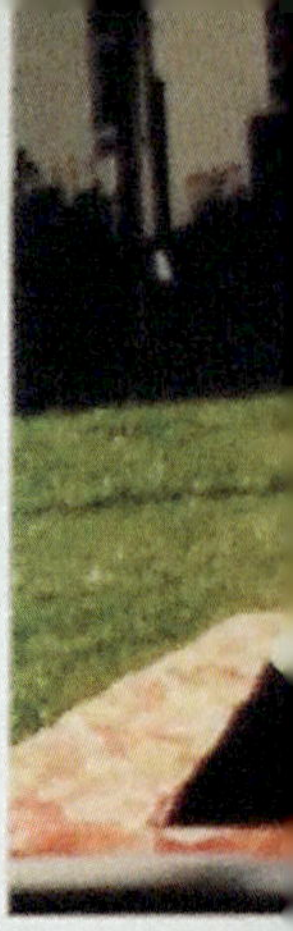
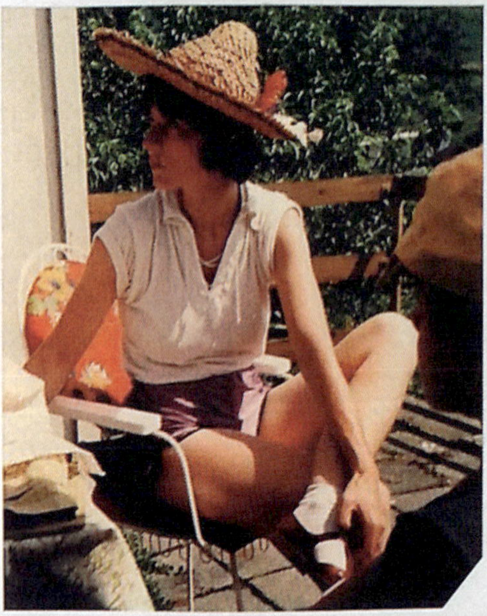
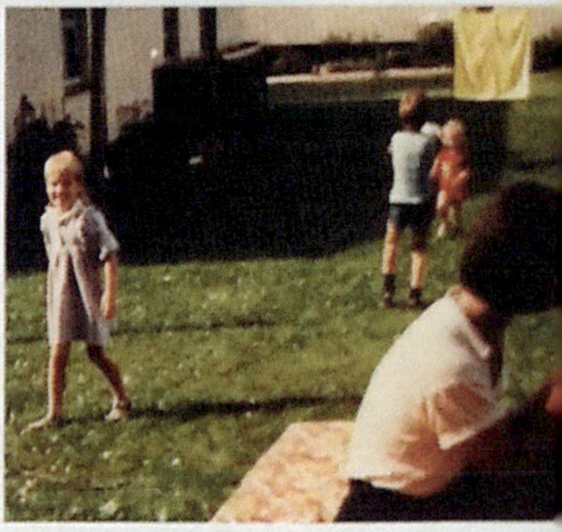

SOWJET-
UNION-Urlaub
bei Olya + Sergei

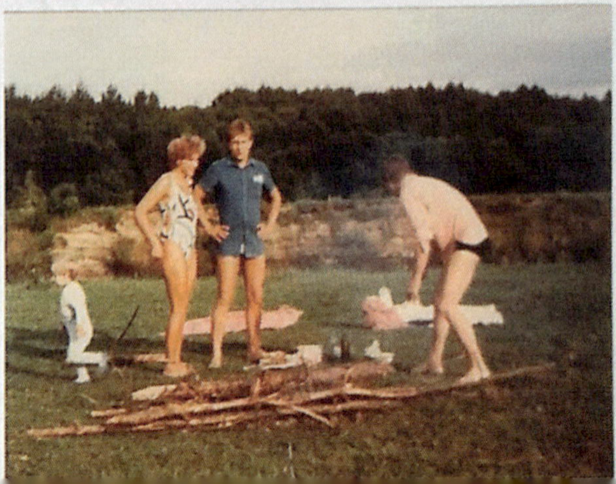
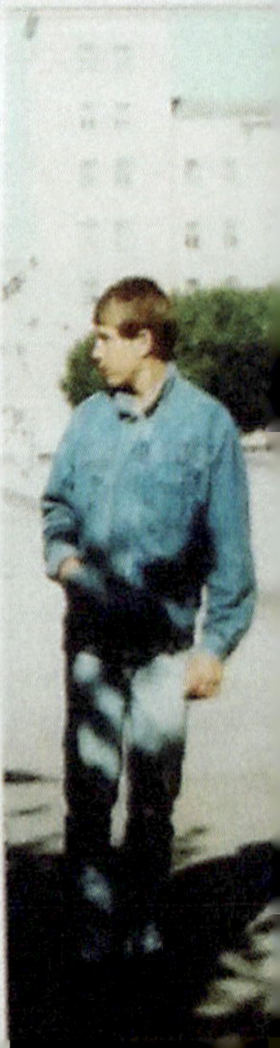

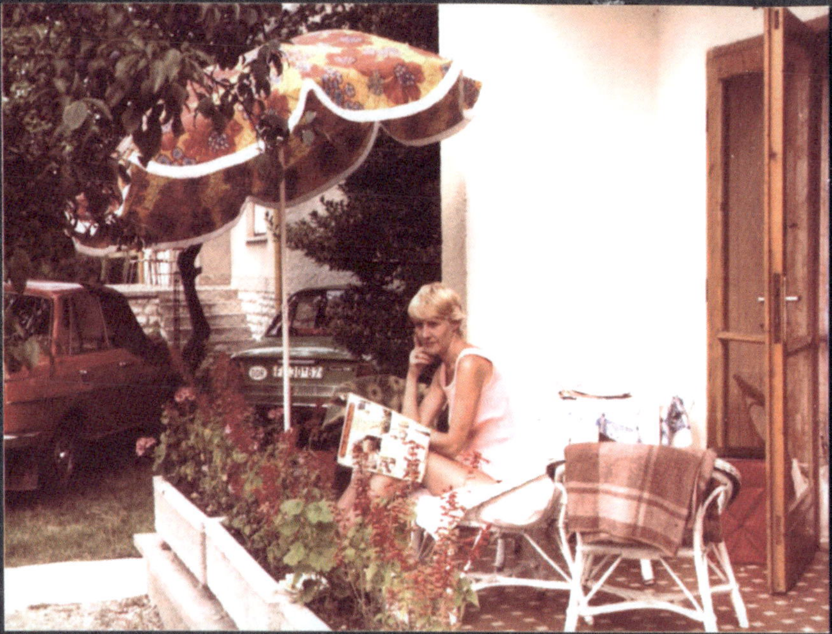

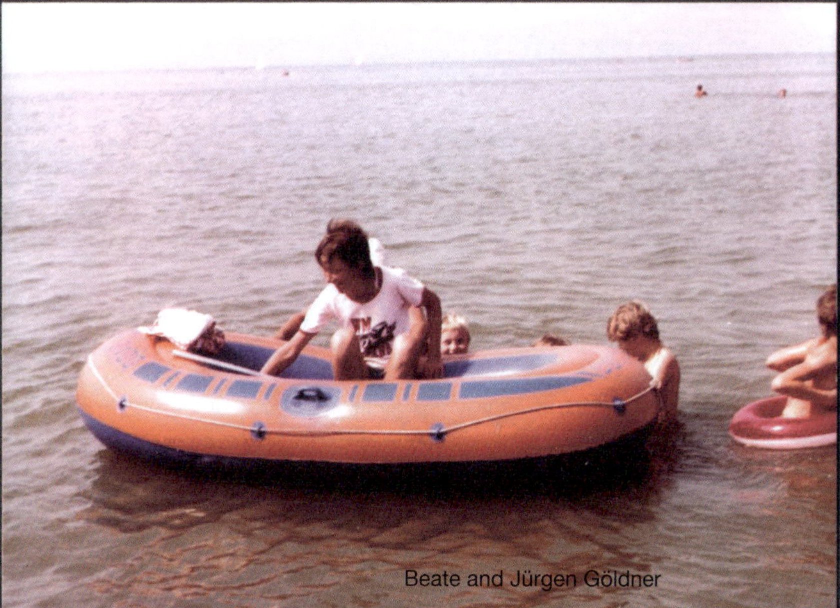

Beate and Jürgen Göldner

Bettina and Manfred Simon

...leine Exkursion in die Niederungen der deutschen Geschichte

...heutigen Olof-
...c-Platz stand
...l Eden, wo Rosa
...mburg und Karl
...knecht gefangen
...en.

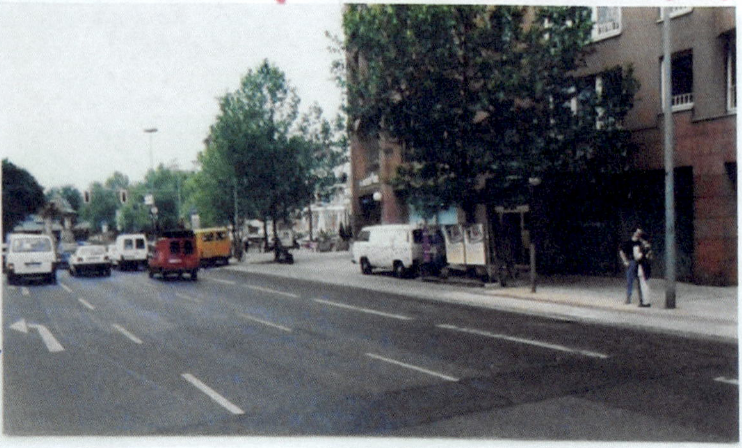

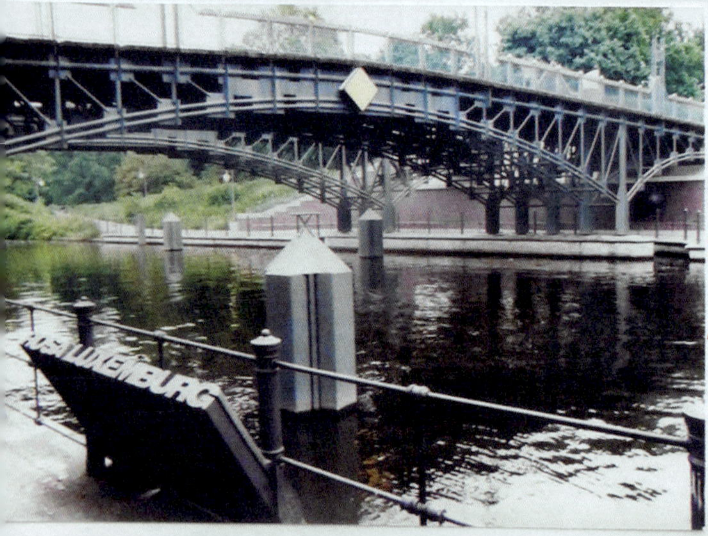

Unterhalb der Lichten-
steinbrücke wurde der
Leichnam Rosa Luxem-
burgs in den Landwehr-
kanal geworfen. Zuvor
war sie erschossen worden.

...er am Ufer des
...nen Sees im Tier-
...ten wurde Karl
...knecht aus
...hster Nähe von

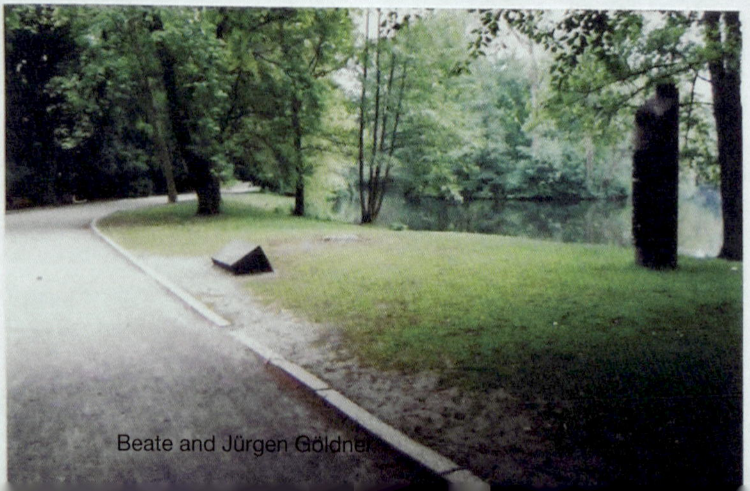

Beate and Jürgen Göldner

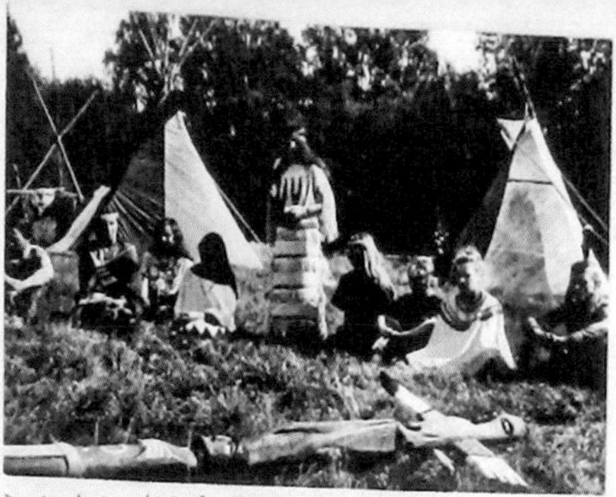

in der Mitte steht „Der Morgenstern" Taljana Elifterjewa

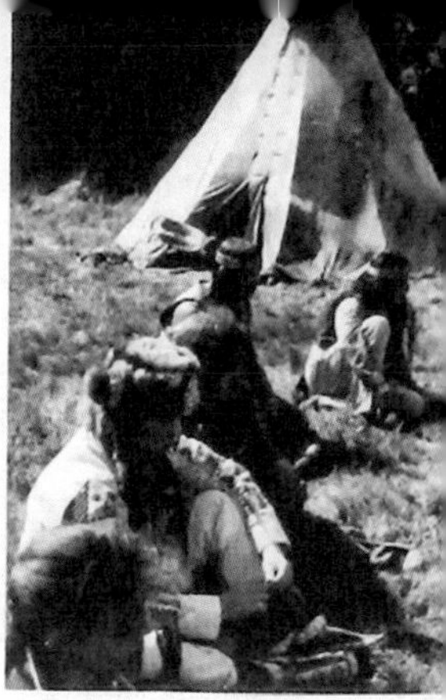

links die Frau von Roter Wolf, Großer Biber - Koslow, Adlerfeder, Bärentatze, Linkshand von der Apachen-Gruppe

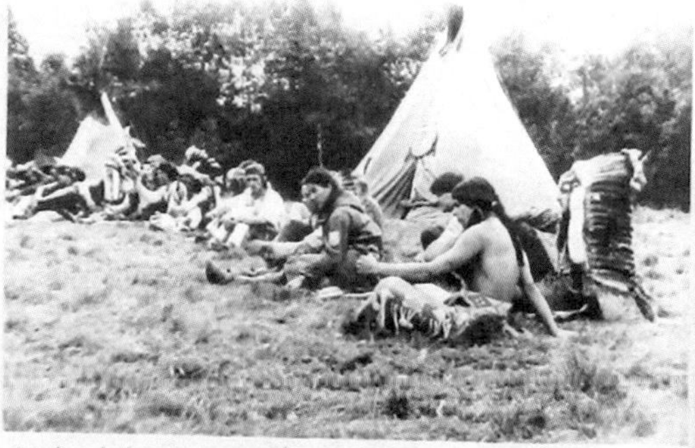

in der Mitte das Haupt-Tipi, Pow Wow 1982

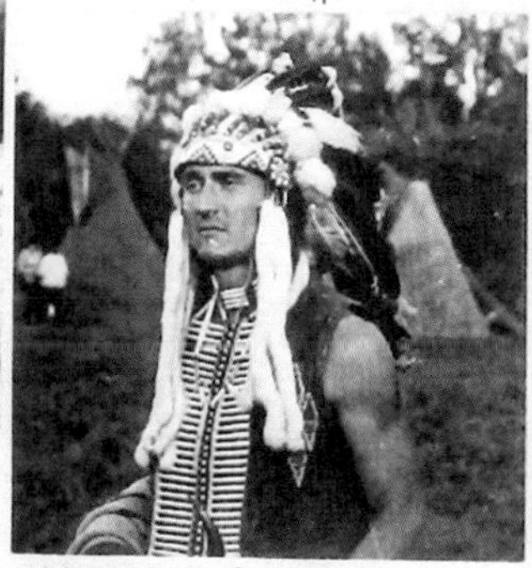

„Stehender Bär" - Sergei Nemkow von der Gruppe „Rote Pfeile" Nowosibirski

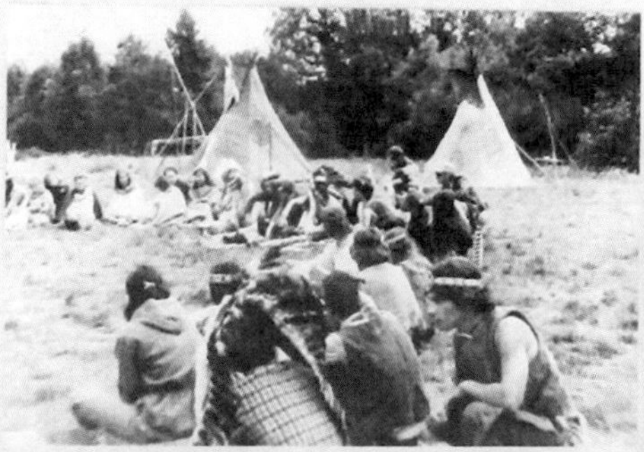

die Beratung läuft

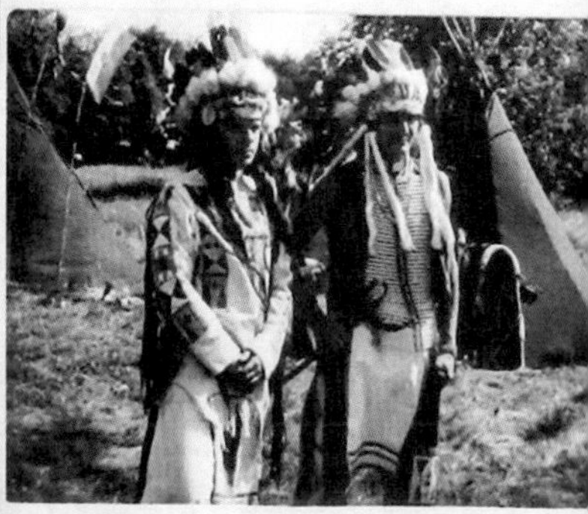

Sascha Koslow und Sergei Nemkow

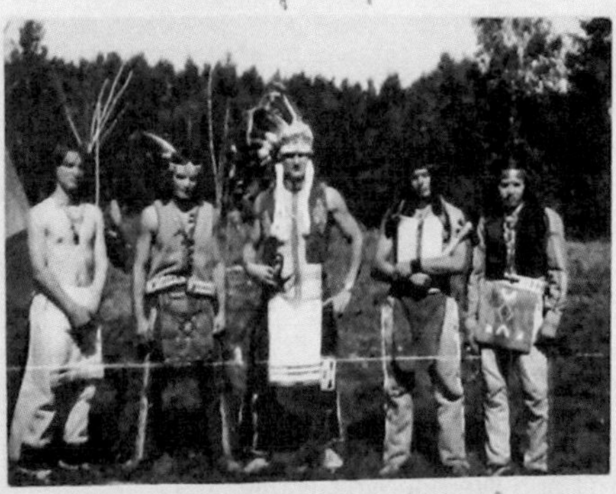

von links: Roter Wolf, Bärentatze, Stehender Bär, Blauer Adler, Linkshand (Apache)

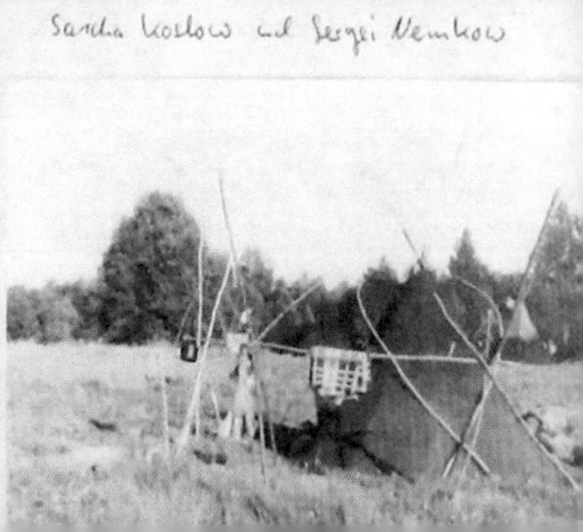

Birgit and Werner-Wolf Turski

Birgit and Werner-Wolf Turski

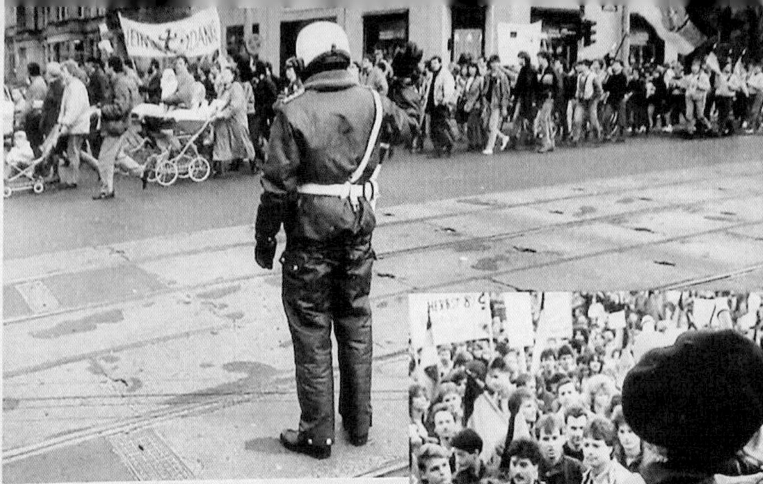

Bei der Kohl-Gegen-Demonstration in Cottbus vor den Wahlen am 18. März 1990

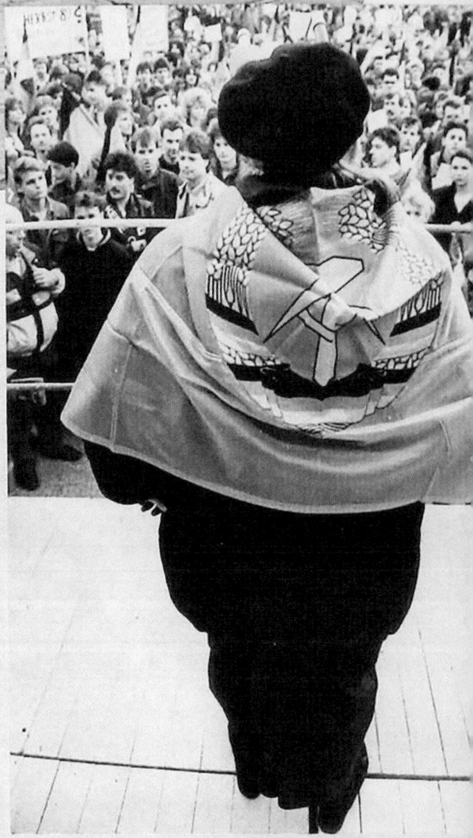

Gitti spricht auch

Teilnehmer des 1. Linken Runden Tisches Cottbus-Saarbrücken am 29.4.1990 bei einer Spreewaldfahrt

Frank Ramm
Torsten Löser

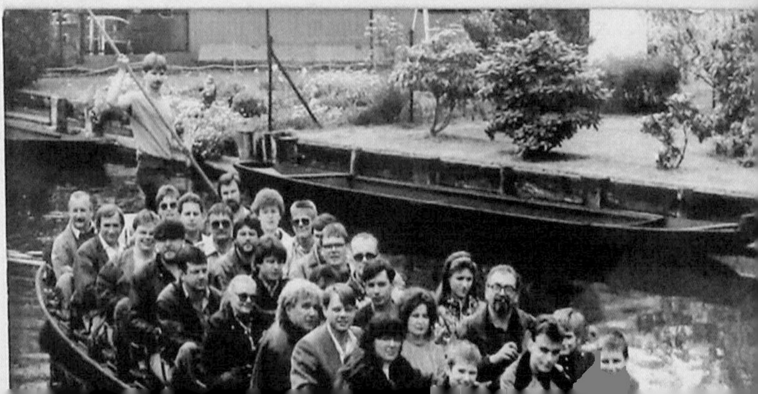

The Room Isn't That Dark: On the Question of the Visibility of a Private Darkroom Practice

Marit Lena Herrmann

Many East German homes were filled with photographs in the 1980s. They were pasted into albums, stored in ORWO sleeves, and mounted behind glass. Some households also stored equipment to produce photographic prints, such as plastic trays and bottles with liquid chemicals, enlargers, and tongs. For most residents, however, the darkroom existed only temporarily. An act of darkening transformed bathrooms, for instance, into what defines a darkroom: a place for the production of photographs.(1) This metamorphosis went hand in hand with the setting up of baths and the enlarger, mixing chemicals, and organizing the paper, tongs, stopwatch, and negatives. Meticulous darkening, including the keyhole, marked the end of a successful transformation.

In the Specht family's case, this conversion took place mostly at night and in winter. They moved into a 50-square-meter newly built apartment in Parey near Magdeburg at the end of the 1970s. There they lived as a foursome after the births of their daughters in 1976 and 1980, before moving to a larger apartment. With adapted add-ons, the bathtub became the base, and in it were prints that had been enlarged, developed, fixed, and rinsed that night. Margrit Specht commented on this intervention: "And when we had to go to work the next morning, the photos were still lying in it."(2) The prints were then

1 "No architect had intended that they exist one day, and when their use began to become commonplace, none bothered to include them in his plans." See Serge Tisseron, "The Chambers of Revelations: To the Memory of the Unknown Printers," in Michel Campeau, *Photographic Darkroom: Photogenic Obsolescence*, trans. James Mayor/Marcia Couelle, Heidelberg: Kehrer 2013, p. 131.

2 Author's conversation with Margrit Specht and Burghard Specht, Parey, September 5, 2022, 0:08:20.

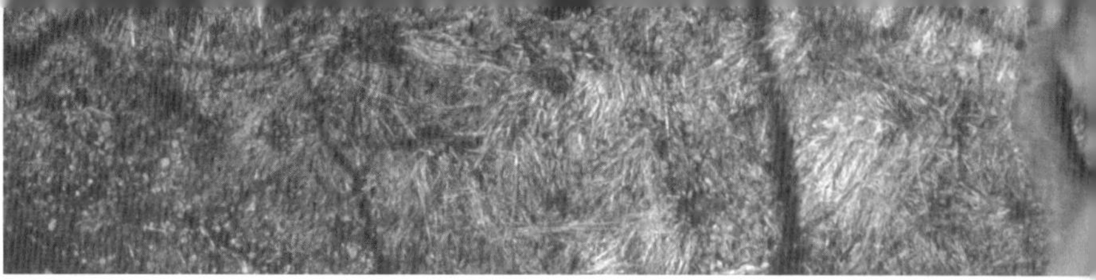

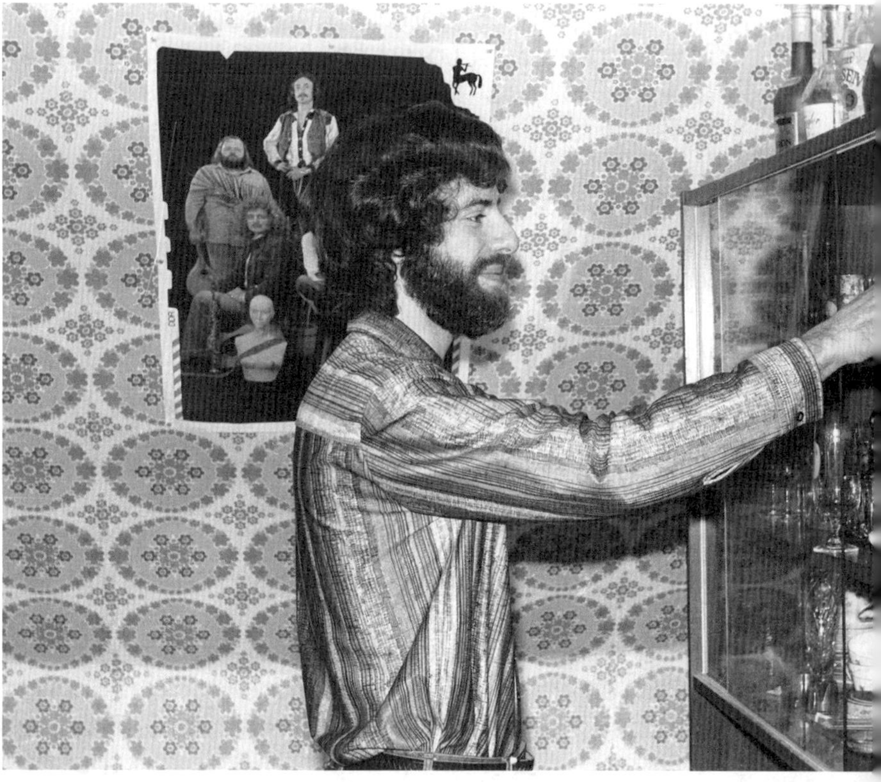

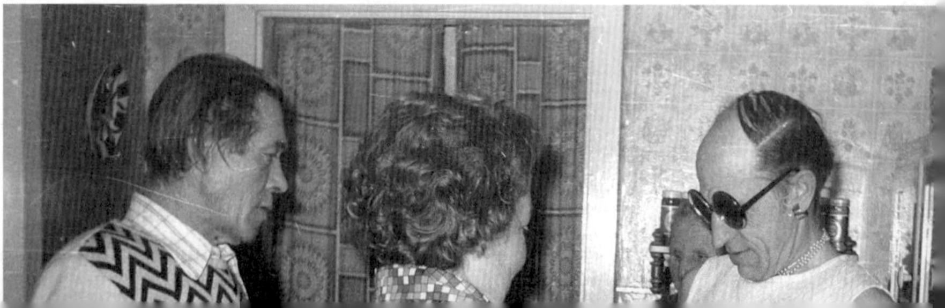

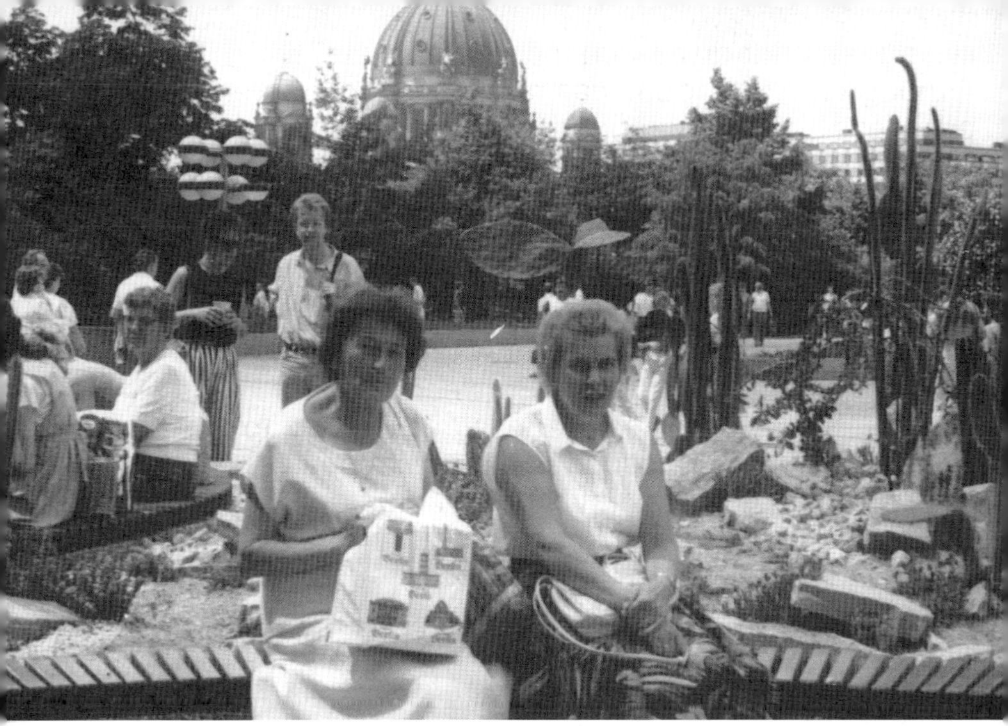

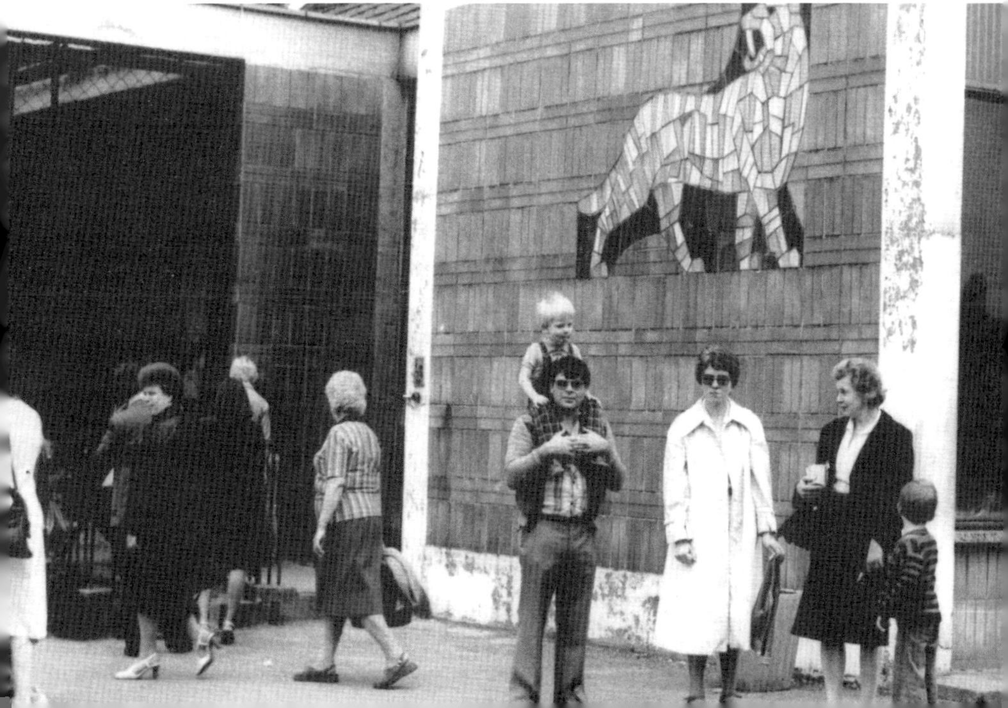

dried on a print dryer with a chromed plate.(3) Although the darkroom was rarely encountered and, even less so, photographed, it and the production of photographs at home played an essential role in the private photography of the German Democratic Republic (GDR). The far-reaching changes in 1989–90 have not stopped at the darkrooms either. In the 1990s their influence diminished, which also has a clear influence on how private pictures were handled. In her article "Between Life and Image. On the Biographical Handling of Photographs," Roswitha Breckner describes the use of private photographs as an essential part of biographical processes and refers to, among other things, the physical spaces where these processes took place. For her "there are many places where so-called private photographs are made, shown, exchanged, and preserved."(4) The verb "made" here refers to the practice of taking photographs. But taking photographs alone does not produce a photograph. Rather, in classical photography on negative film, making is an act that includes the camera and the darkroom. In a chain of sequential steps, both phases revolve around similar aspects of seeking out, framing, and designing: before the finger presses the camera's shutter release button and while the hands are producing prints in the darkroom. In these processes, the person tinkers, intervenes, and designs the final photograph. The photographs that are later viewed and stored in albums, ORWO sleeves, or frames are made in an additional step. And so, there is another place in the photographic process where these rhythmic, repeated actions take place: the darkroom.

3 The Specht family kept all the equipment for making prints in their private darkroom, such as the print dryer, the enlarger, the stopwatch, the pins, the developing reels, the trays, and other materials.

4 Roswitha Breckner, "Zwischen Leben und Bild. Zum biografischen Umgang mit Fotografien", in: Thomas S. Eberle (ed.) *Photographie und Gesellschaft. Phänomenologische und wissenssoziologische Perspektiven*, Bielefeld: Transcript 2017, p. 229.

For Breckner private photographs are always imbedded in a triad: "into the temporality and spatiality of the situation of the shoot, into the temporality and spatiality that is visible in the photograph itself, and in the temporal and spatial context of the situation of viewing it."(5) If the production of the photograph is extended to the processing in the darkroom, a new temporal and spatial situation arises. This includes the production of the prints as well as the corresponding preparation and post-processing. Using the example of the photographic practice of the Specht family in the 1980s, I will show how the private production of images, and specifically the use of the darkroom, becomes visible in the photograph, the album, and the story.(6)

Burghard and Margrit Specht incorporated the use of the darkroom into their photography practice from the outset. At the beginning of the first conversation, Burghard Specht spoke about the camera that he had purchased with the money from his *Jugendweihe*(7)—a Praktica Super TL 1000. He also explained his interest in photography, which had begun before 1968: "My father started it, having himself built an enlarger from a plate camera, and that was the source of the tradition of photography that my brother and I continued. That is how we came to get involved in photography ... and that's how the whole story got started."(8) The development of the photographs, from the negatives to the prints, was the focus of his interest. Burghard Specht does not mention his father's camera but the enlarger he built.

5 Breckner, 2017, p. 230.

6 I am very grateful to Margrit and Burghard Specht for their conversations and their stories. Our first conversation was supplemented by a second one on September 5, 2022. There is also a video recording of the first conversation.

7 A coming-of-age ceremony at fourteen in the GDR.

8 Album conversation with Margrit and Burghard Specht, Magdeburg, July 27, 2021, 0:02:40. This self-welded enlarger still exists. "It just stayed there."

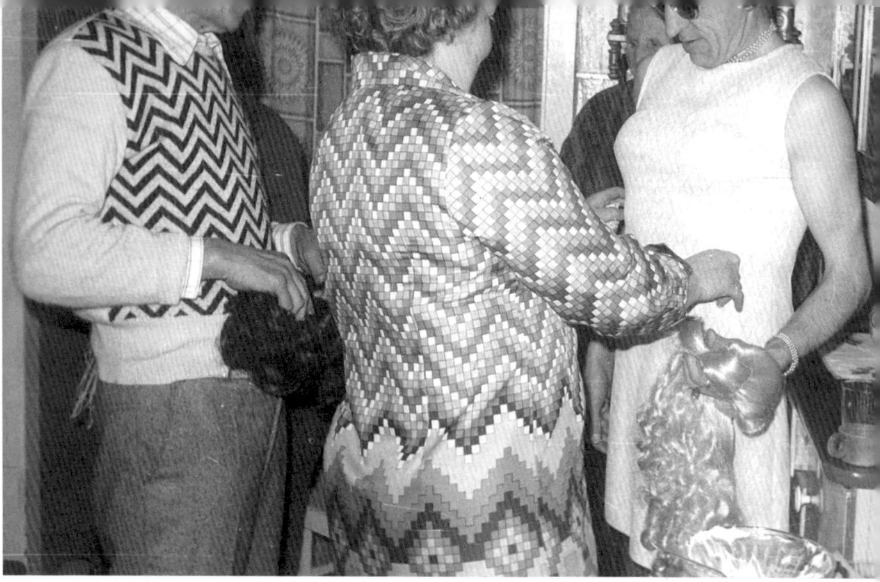

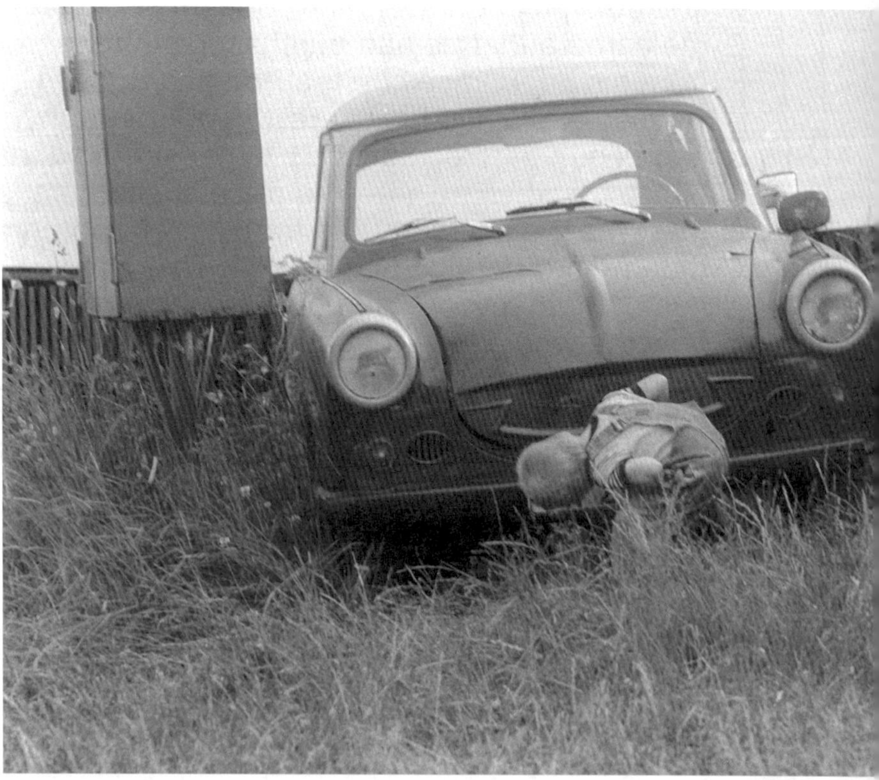

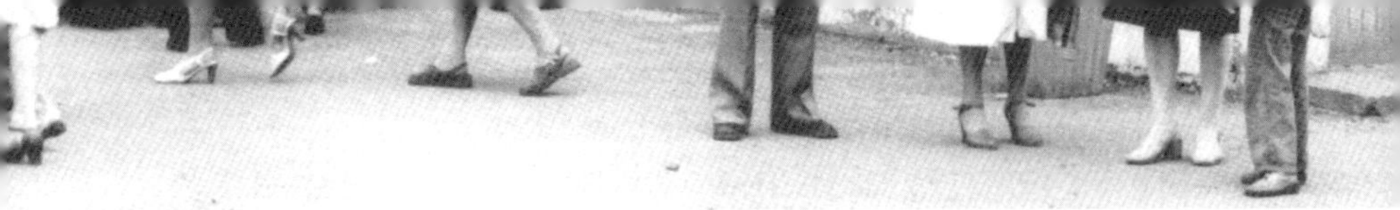

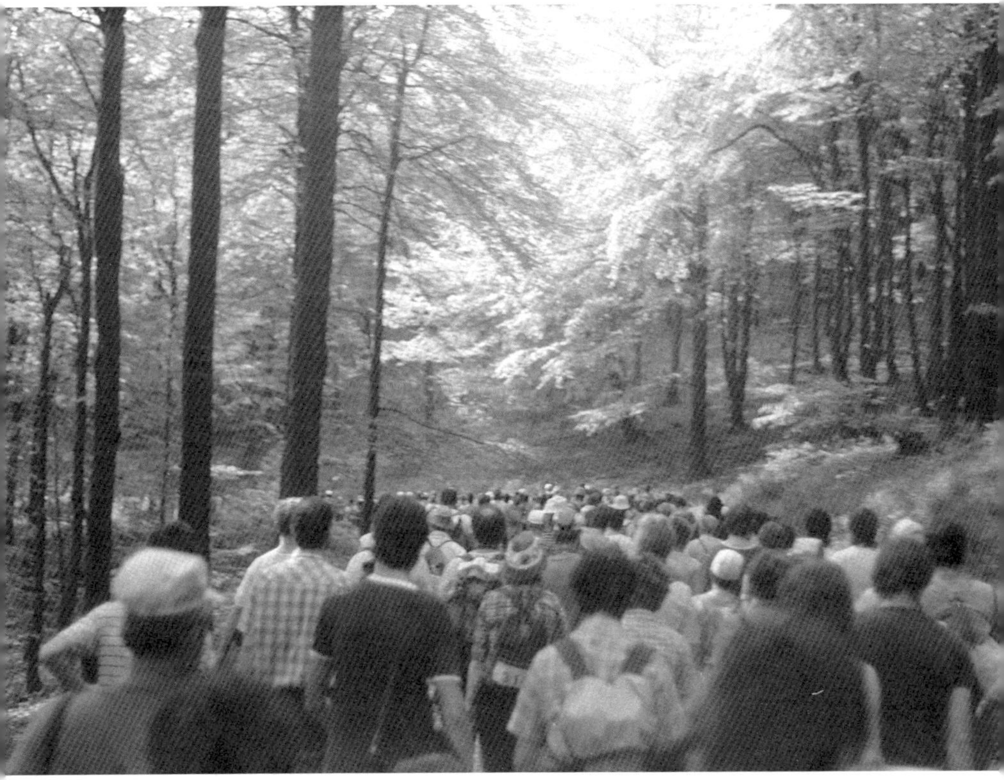

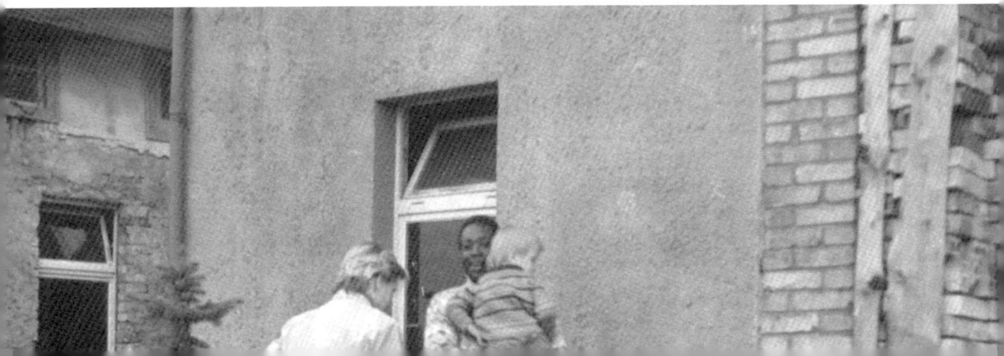

By 2022, Burghard and Margrit Specht have accumulated 75 photo albums and thirteen books of photographs that they have maintained together since they met. Each year and vacation are recorded in a separate album, to which Margrit Specht usually contributes short texts. Burghard Specht took, developed, enlarged, cropped, and pasted the photographs in the albums. In the 1980s, they were working on three albums at time, one for each of their two daughters and a family album. Burghard Specht still keeps the negatives in the basement. The numbered ORWO negative sleeves are in boxes and an index facilitates searches for specific negatives.

Whereas today they put together their books of photographs on a computer, in the 1980s Burghard Specht enlarged the assembled negatives in their narrow bathroom. At some suitable point (between working, gardening, and taking care of the children(9)), the non-simultaneity in the photographs from recent weeks lined up into a direct sequence. The developing of the negatives that preceded this was also done by Burghard Specht, and he rolled the small-format negatives—and occasionally 6×6 centimeter film rolls—in one of his two reels.

While enlarging the negatives in the glow of his darkroom lights, Burghard Specht became the first to witness his photographs; to see the faces of those portrayed; to retrace journeys to Binz and Romania; to discover previously unnoticed events in the background; and to spot technical details, such as blurriness. The motifs were enlarged either on small-format paper measuring 9×13 centimeters or large formats up 30×40 centimeters.(10)

9 Author's conversation with Margrit and Burghard Specht, Parey, September 5, 2022, 0:19:15.

10 Author's conversation with Margrit and Burghard Specht, Parey, September 5, 2022, 1:03:00. The large-format prints were not pasted into albums but mounted on cardboard and kept in a portfolio. Burghard Specht's enlarger was not adequate for horizontal large formats so he worked with paper mounted on the wall for vertical ones.

Burghard Specht selected the motifs by examining the film strips in the enlarger and then choosing one over the other based on the projected image. He always enlarged the complete negative. Only then did he decide for or against certain images and particular elements in the photograph. The detailed viewing of the prints, which also involved the critique of Margrit Specht, often resulted in the print being cropped to emphasize details and choosing highlights.

Especially in the early albums, it is evident that enlargement on different paper formats represents a separate design decision in addition to the subsequent cropping (fig. 1). On the first double-page spread in “Familienalbum I” (family album) by Burghard and Margrit Specht, the different formats of the prints are apparent. Each black-and-white photograph looks different on the black cardboard pages. On the left page a photograph has been placed parallel to the upper edge of the album page showing the ratio of a classic small-format-negative. One corner rises above a second photograph in an oval format that is showing a woman at a door. On the right side are three more photographs, cropped in different formats. Straight edges indicate the original ends of the negative. Margrit Specht is the subject of both the photographs and the page. With the cropping the context of every image was reduced. The original frame of the picture changed. The standardized ratio of the sides of the small-format negative is abandoned and altered to serve one's own needs. Margrit Specht articulates this by claiming: “With scissors he cut it out the way he really wanted it.”(11) The designing of the page is based on its format and Burghard and Margrit Specht used the photographic prints as transformable material.

11 Author's conversation with Margrit and Burghard Specht, Parey, September 5, 2022, 0:23:30.

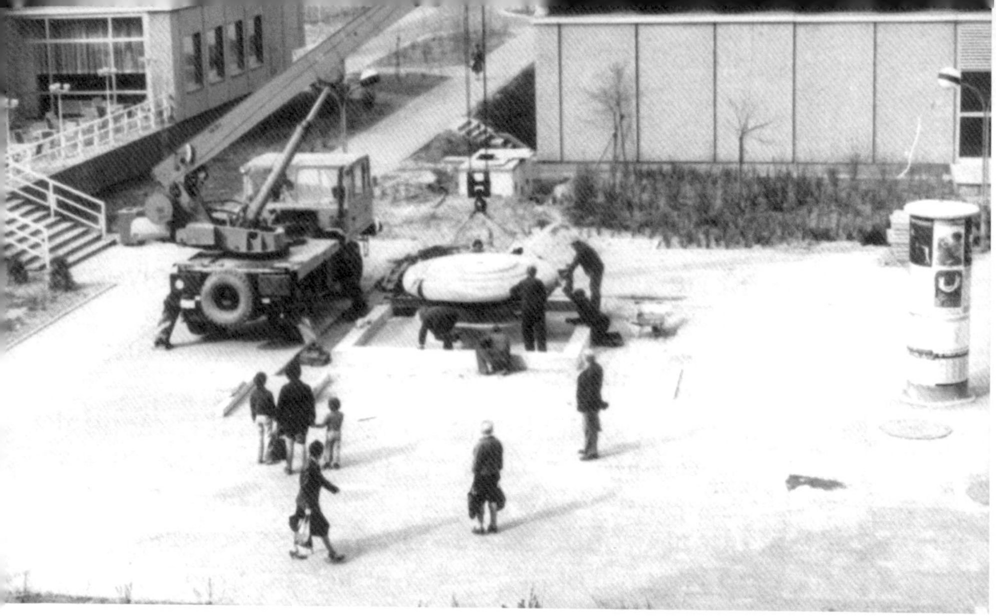

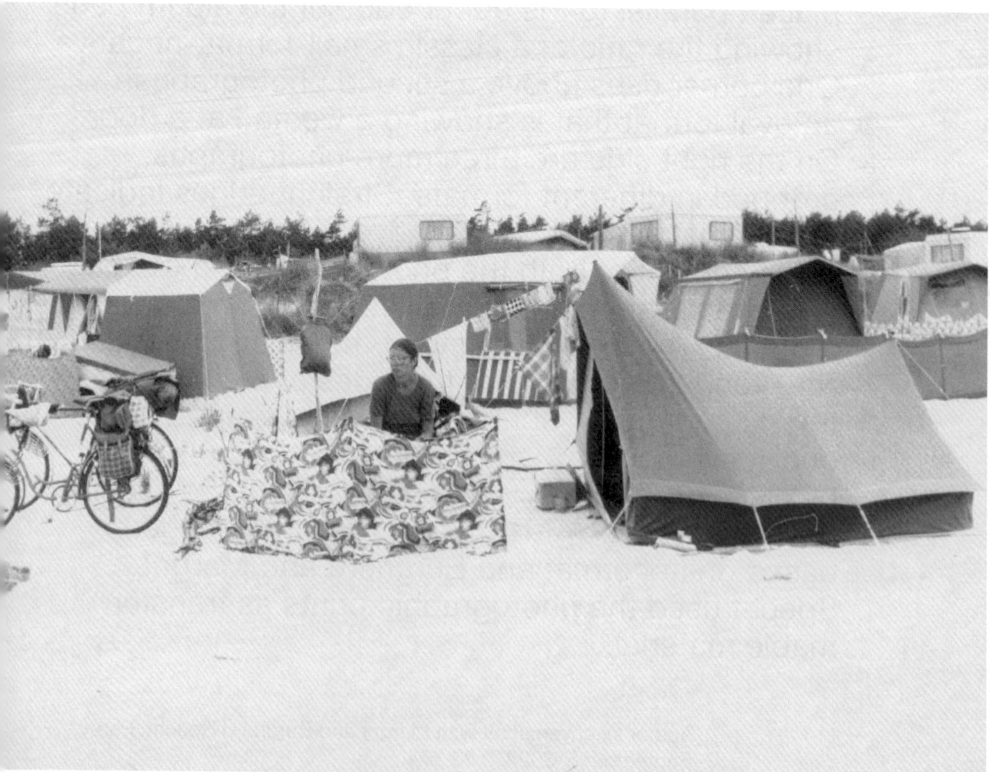

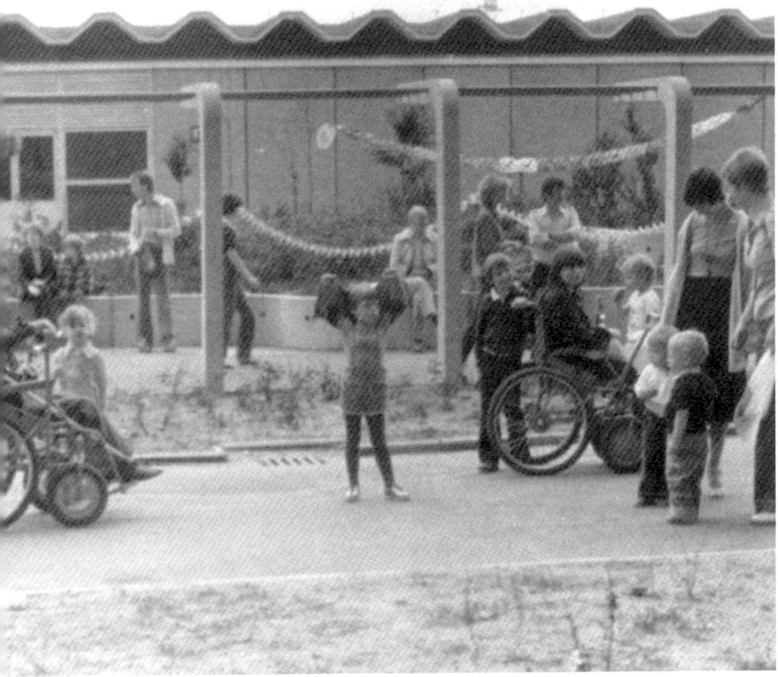

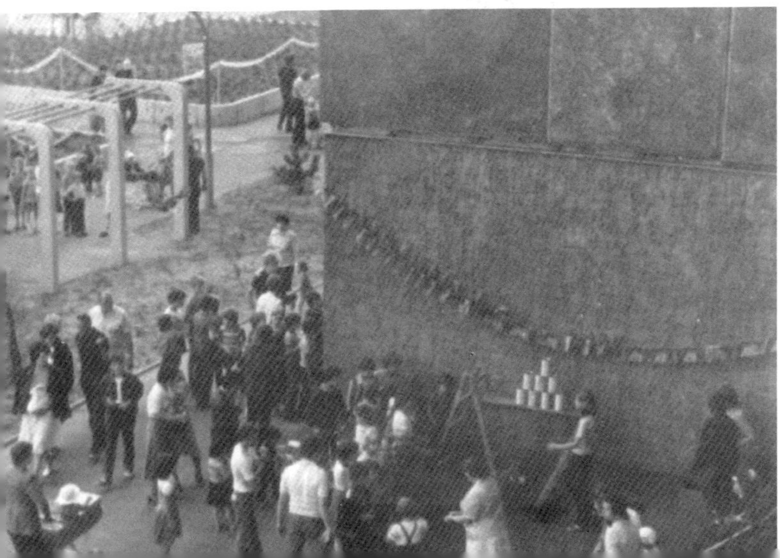

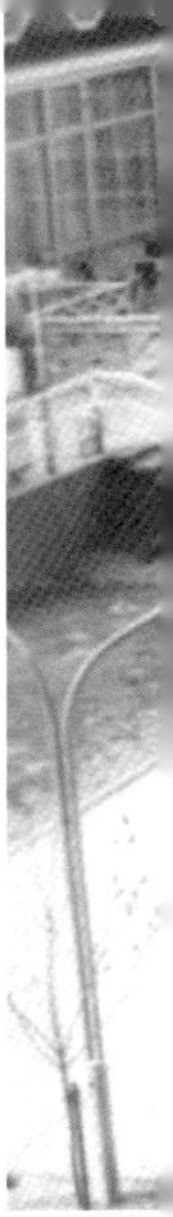

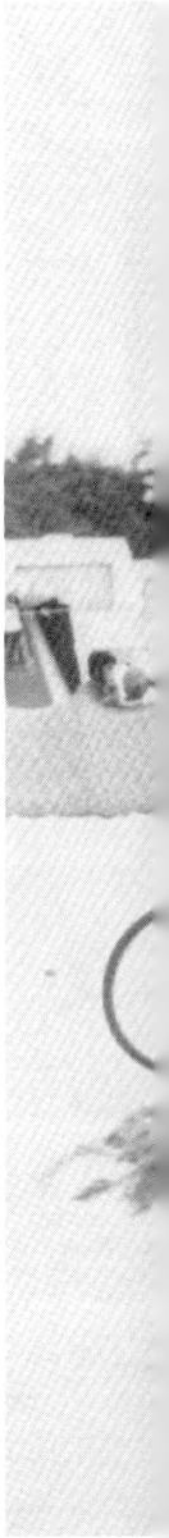

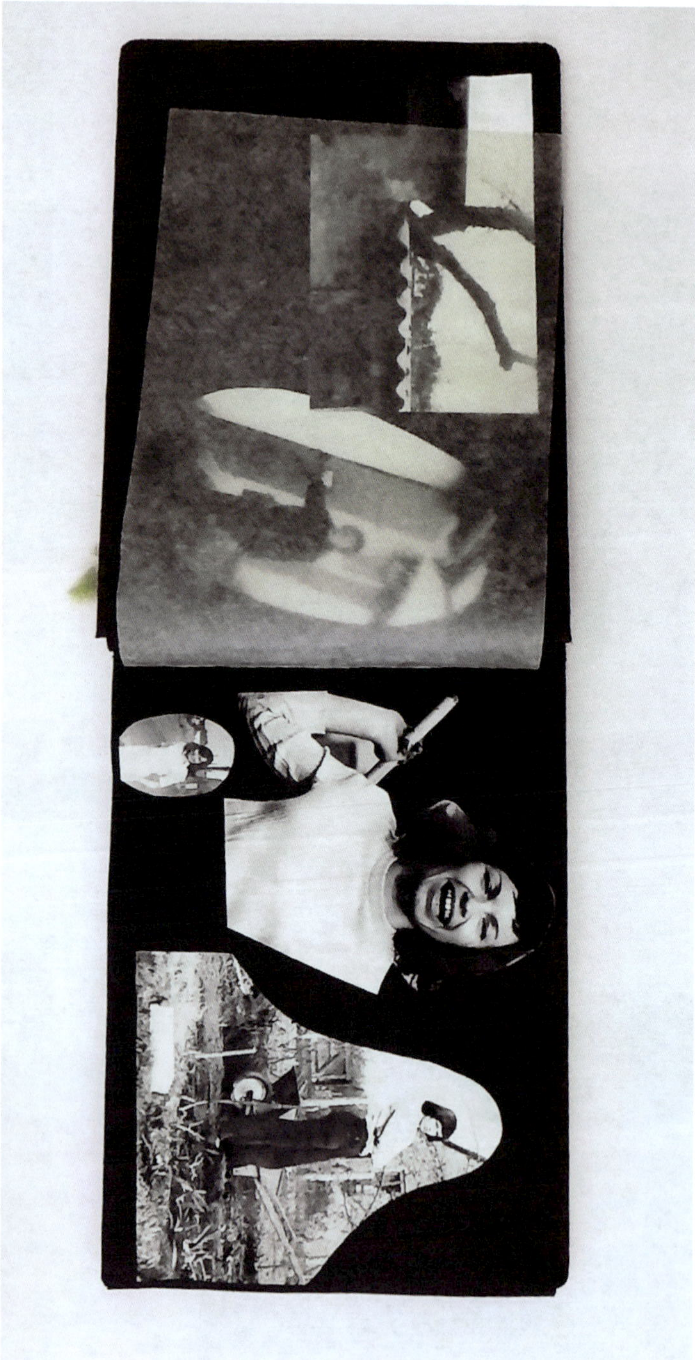

Fig. 1: Album conversation with Margrit and Burghard Specht, Magdeburg, July 27, 2021. Videostill, 0:03:29.

For Burghard Specht, the photos thrive from being cropped as well.(12)

For the Specht family, the value of a photograph does not primarily lie in its artistic composition but also in the possibility of emphasizing aspects through the size of the prints and their subsequent cropping and interweaving. Burghard Specht reports, for example, that he considered the choice of the negatives, the types and formats of the paper, the album page, and above all the relationship of the photos to one another. "That is what makes a photo album. If the photos are lying in a box, the way many people do it, then you just have a bunch of individual photos. I tried as best I could to relate the photos to one another."(13) The negatives he enlarged in his own darkroom provided him with a variety of materials with which he could tell his own stories. This is why Burghard Specht didn't enlarged all negatives from one film roll in the same format. Instead, he decided on specific sizes based on the motifs and the montage of the page he had in mind. The cropping of the photographs and their arrangement in the album were aspects influencing the size of the chosen paper format.

The album page then seems less like the "spatial organizing system for something preexisting"(14) than like the basis for something designed individually. For the Specht family, their own production of photographs meant that a first selection already happened in the darkroom and was continued by cropping the finished prints. Even after the positive had been produced, the sorting out

12 Album conversation with Margrit and Burghard Specht, Magdeburg, July 27, 2021, 0:14:20.

13 Author's conversation with Margrit and Burghard Specht, Parey, September 5, 2022, 0:22:00.

14 Matthias Bickenbach, »Die Enden der Alben. Über Ordnung und Unordnung eines Mediums am Beispiel von Rolf Dieter Brinkmanns *Schnitte*«, in: Anke Kramer/Annegret Pelz (eds.), *Album. Organisationsform narrativer Kohärenz*, Göttingen: Wallstein 2013, p. 107.

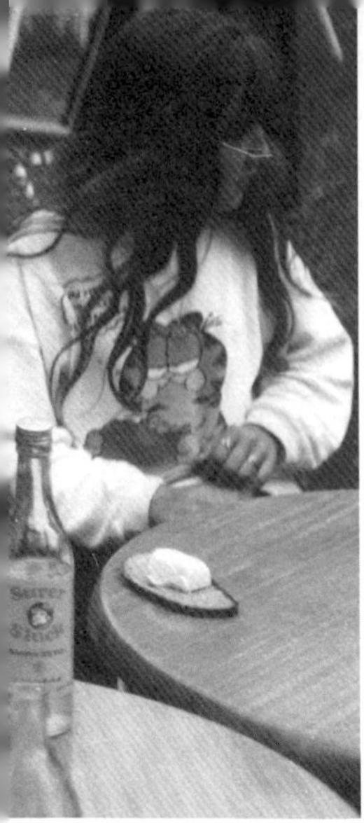

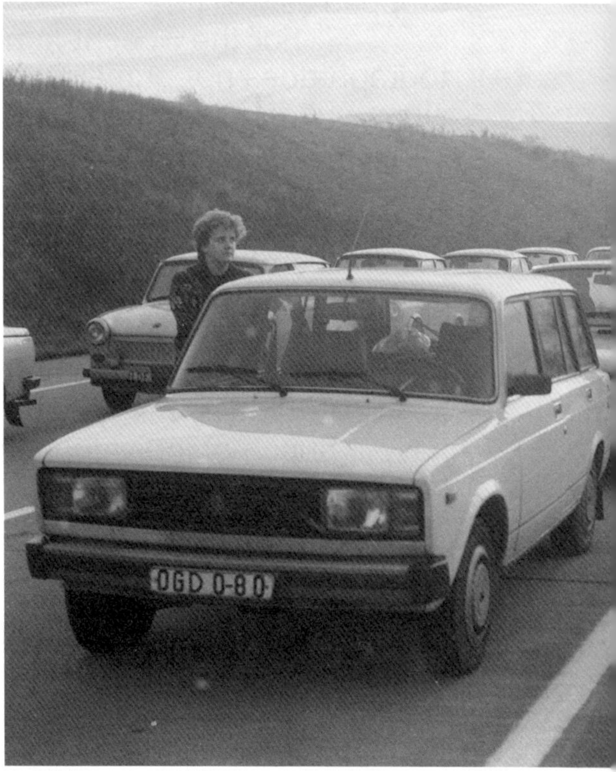
OGD 0-80

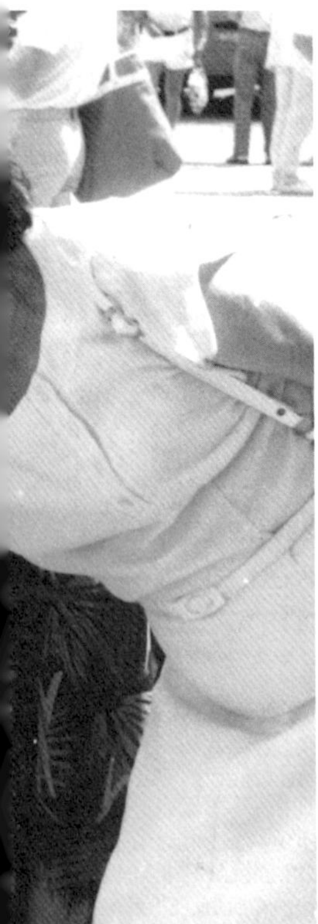

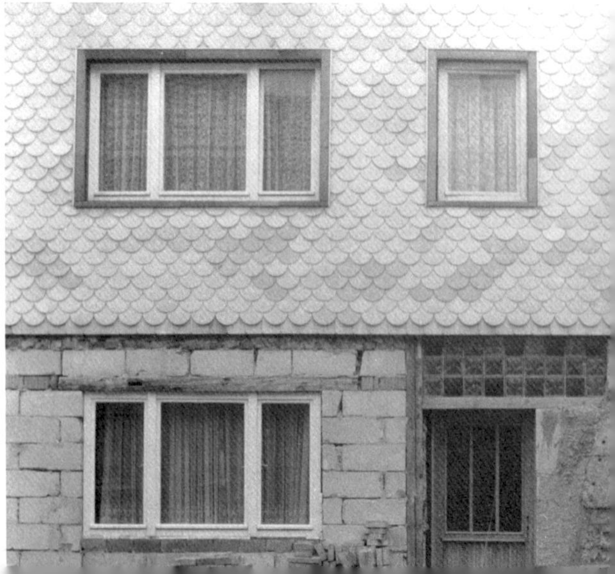

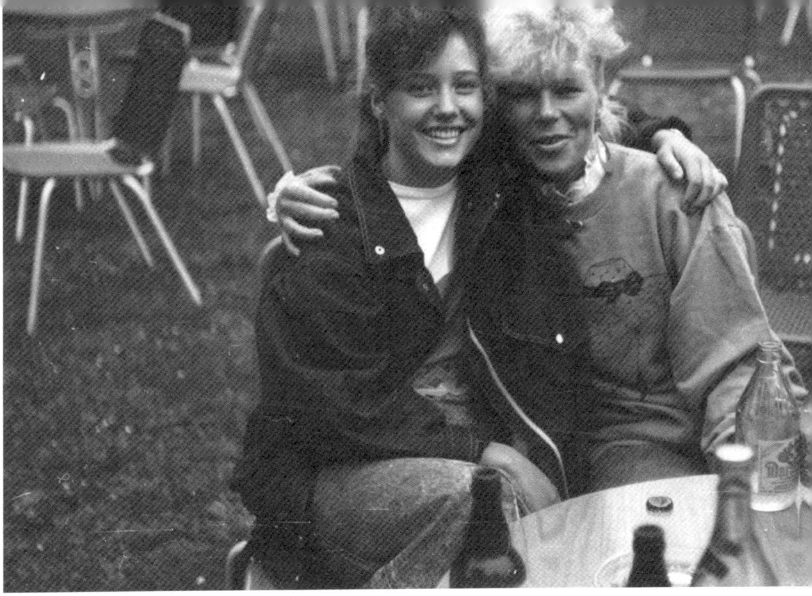

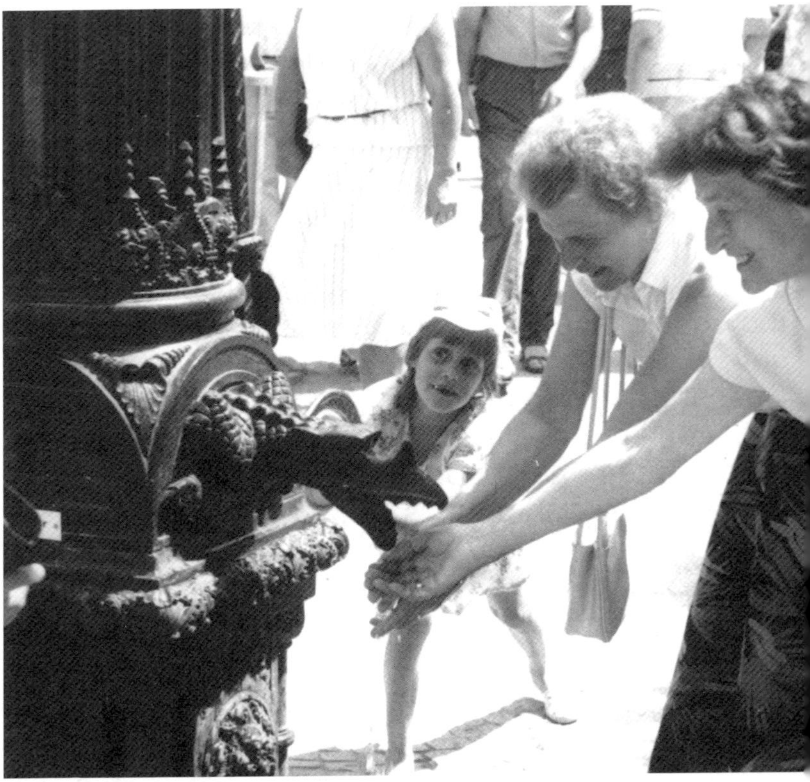

continued, as they admitted: "Yes, yes, we threw boxloads of them away or even made selections as soon as they had dried and took only the best ones."(15) This process in which one's own photographs are examined critically at several points considers the individual photograph and assigns it its own format, its own cropping, and finally a special place in the album.

The practice of having a private darkroom is reflected even in a given photograph, in the image itself and in the individual treatment of a print in the darkroom. This becomes particularly evident in the photograph on the first page of their wedding album (fig. 2).(16) It shows the newlyweds at the clerk's office in Elbe-Parey. The photograph is pasted on bright-blue cardboard next to the handwritten date of their wedding. In the photograph, Burghard Specht is looking at his wife. She is looking at the camera. In the background to his right, a portrait of Erich Honecker can be seen on the wall. When asked who "made" this photograph, Burghard Specht first responds: "My brother"—since, after all, he himself can be seen in the photograph. But his wife interrupts him: "no, but you developed it. [The brother] just took it." The question "who made the photograph" is ambiguous here. That may also be because the photograph is visibly designed: the couple, she in a white dress and he in a black suit, is surrounded by a sphere of light. Burghard Specht produced this effect by controlling the light in the darkroom. Similar to cropping but immanent to the image, the act of intervention and personal design in the darkroom is evident. By varying the exposure times, the area around the couple is overexposed. Everything is a blurry white, and only the couple in the center is clear. Vignetting

15 Author's conversation with Margrit and Burghard Specht, Parey, September 5, 2022, 0:11:40.

16 Author's conversation with Margrit and Burghard Specht, Parey, September 5, 2022, 0:16:30.

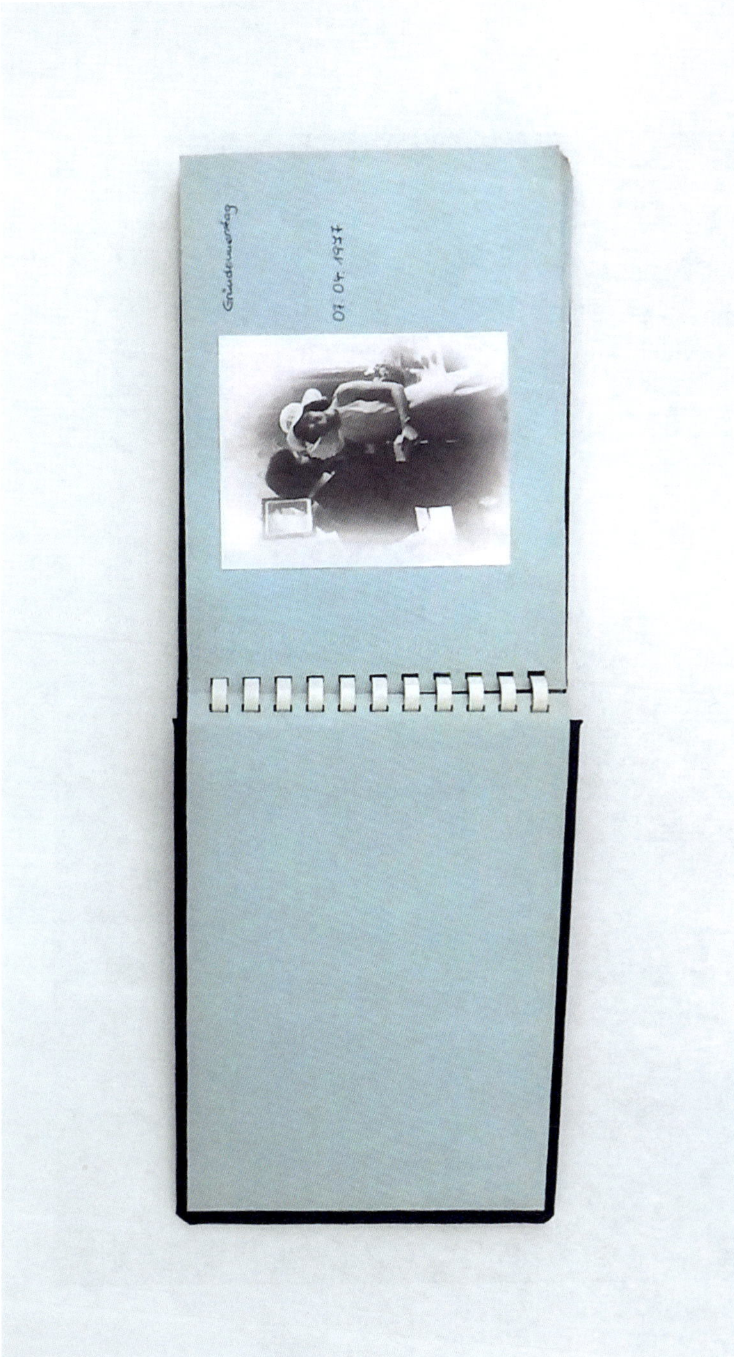

Fig. 2: Album conversation with Margrit and Burghard Specht, Magdeburg, July 27, 2021. Videostill, 0:16:53.

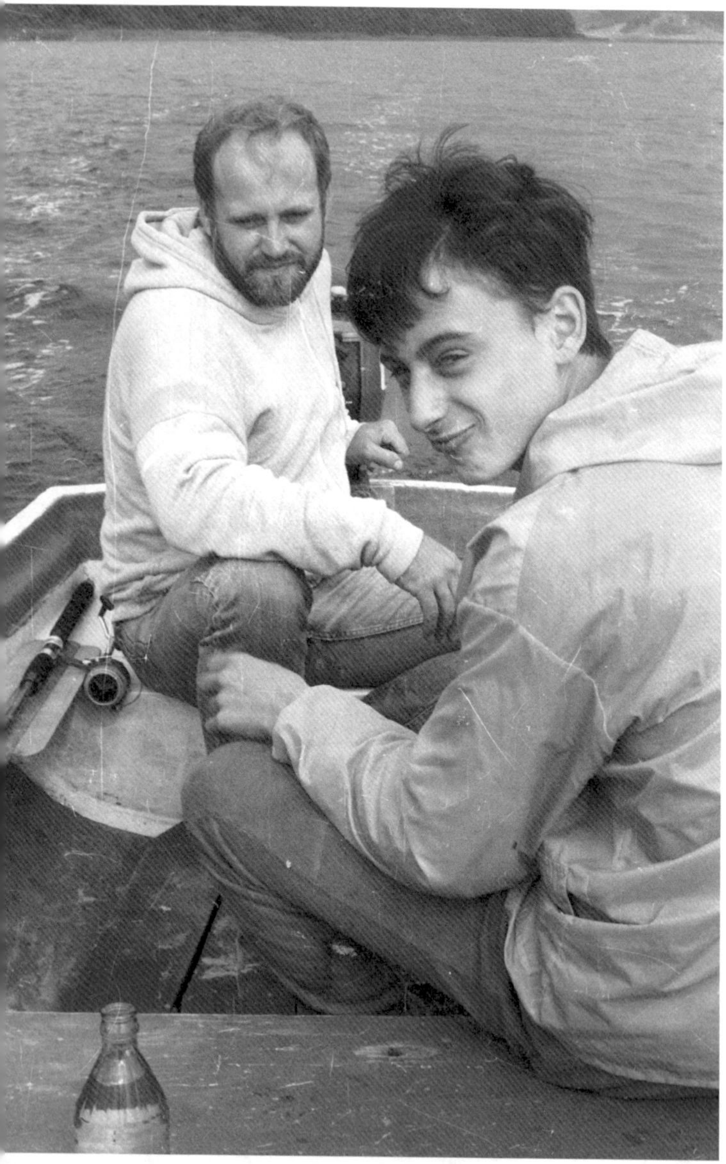

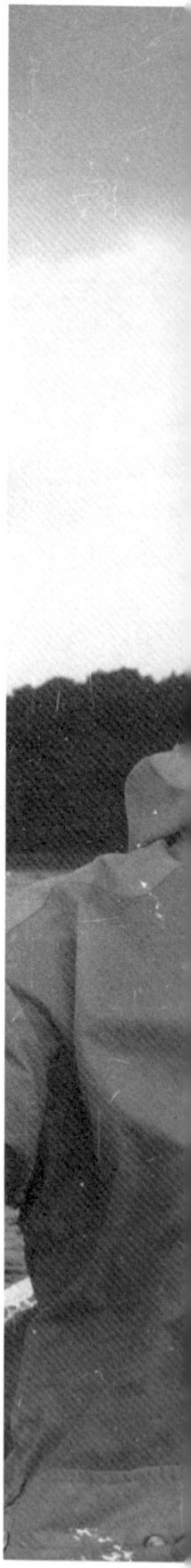

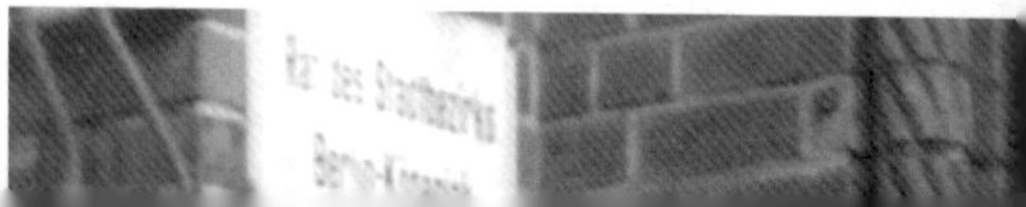
Rat des Stadtbezirks

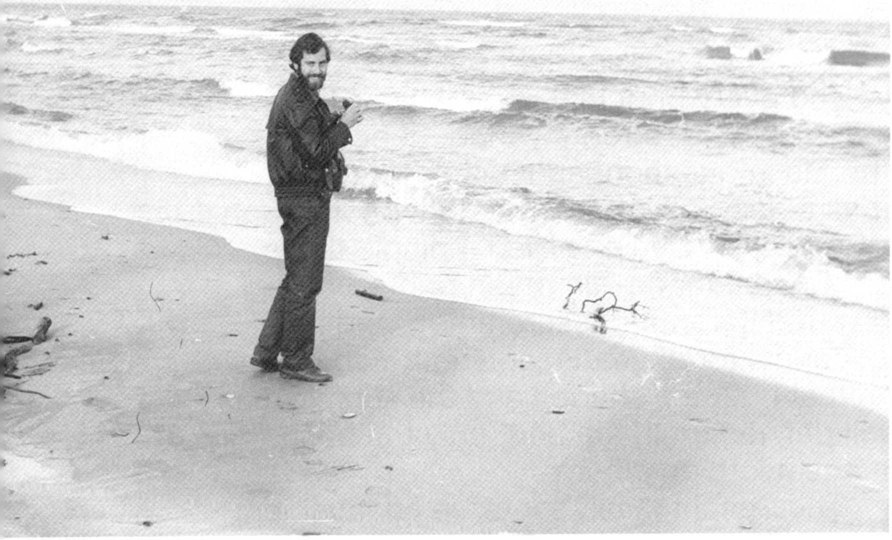

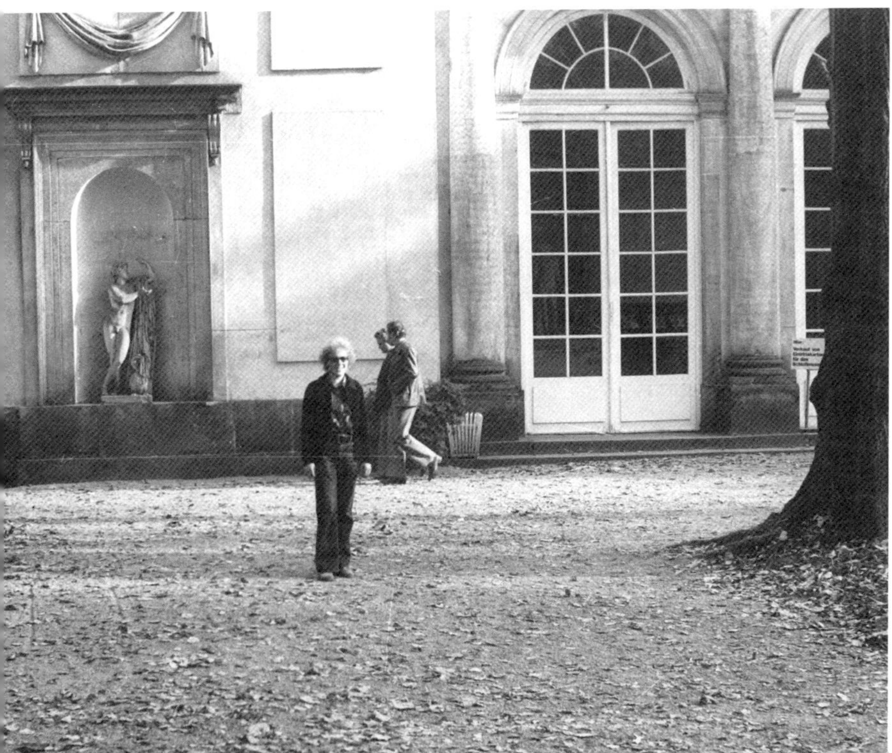

draws attention to the couple and focuses on their recent union. In parallel with cropping, this intervention too concentrates the gaze within the image.

Burghard Specht did not enlarge every negative and every print in the same way. His intervention in the darkroom varied, depending on the motifs in question, and it is decidedly present as a design feature in several photographs. Several negatives were enlarged multiple times. Burghard Specht made "umpteen prints," experimented with different exposure times, and in his landscapes, for example, concentrated on ensuring that both the shaded and the sunny areas were well defined.(17) In the end, only the best prints made it into an album.

The Specht family's intense engagement with the possibilities and limitations of photographic production was not restricted to black-and-white photographs. The considerably more complicated production of color photographs was not done in their apartment but in the more spacious home of Burghard Specht's parents. Since the enlargement of color prints required several baths in plastic trays, Burghard Specht used his grandmother's former kitchen, which offered him enough space. He was the only one in his circle of friends and family who enlarged color photographs.(18) "I developed my first photograph—that was the hard part—I developed mosaic prints and looked at them under the light to find the combination. Then I knew how to combine the filters in the filter drawer to get approximately

17 Author's conversation with Margrit and Burghard Specht, Parey, September 5, 2022, 0:23.00.

18 Another interview partner emphasized the complicated production: "Making color prints in your own laboratory in the GDR was crazy; the ORWO materials were a nightmare when it came to color accuracy; the filtering was a real art. Almost no one could do that privately: too expensive, too complicated, and the supplies were not as good as with black-and-white materials." Email from Martin Weinhold, May 21, 2022.

accurate colors."(19) Mosaic prints were combinations of many small prints that made it possible to evaluate different combinations of color filters. Nevertheless, producing color prints was already an intense experiment involving comparison, examining, testing, and assessing. The complete darkness necessary for their production further slowed the process. The black-and-white photographs in The Specht family's albums are repeatedly interrupted by color photographs they enlarged themselves. However, since they were so expensive, they are seen only occasionally in the albums and usually show important events such as vacations and Christmas celebrations. The Specht family's albums did not therefore undergo a fundamental change from black-and-white to color in the period around 1989/90, as was the case with many other families in East Germany. For many East Germans, a transformation in their albums went together with the fall of the Berlin Wall and all the profound changes that came along with it. The less-expensive color films of Kodak and Fuji and the drugstores that opened everywhere made color photography more and more common in the 1990s.

In the case of the Specht family, like many of the other participants in our conversations, the period just after the fall of the Berlin Wall was a time without photographs. "The last black-and-white photographs we have were taken just after the fall of the Wall. When we traveled to Hanover for the first time, we still took black-and-white photographs. And then time steamrolled us, more or less, and all of the political events, and during the fall of socialism we took almost no photographs at all. Then there were color photos everywhere, and people then [took them to the drugstore]." The much-used Praktica Super TL 1000 disappeared and with it the

19 Album conversation with Margrit and Burghard Specht, Magdeburg, July 27, 2021, 0:48:00.

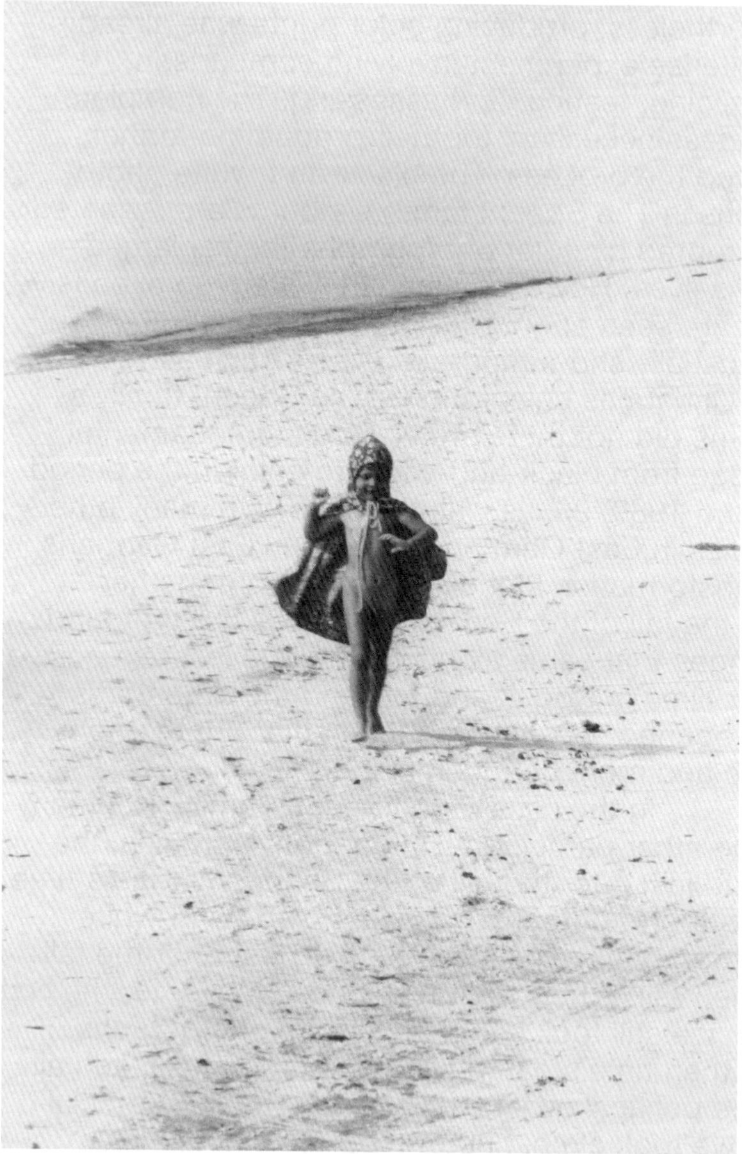

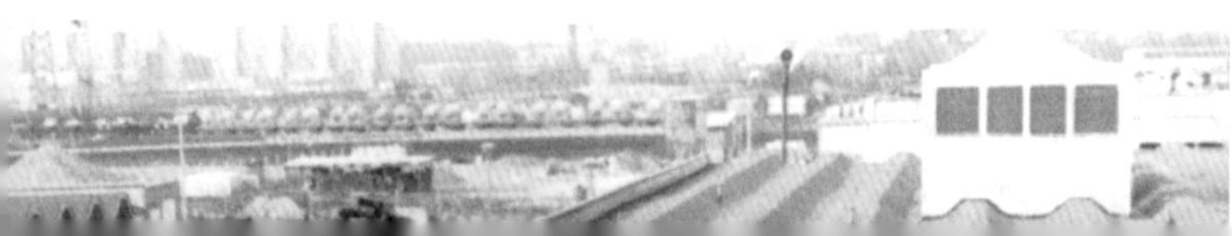

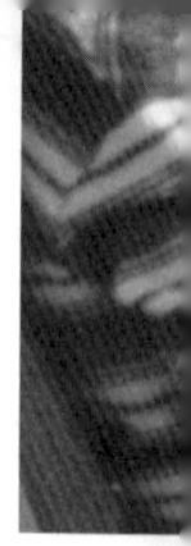

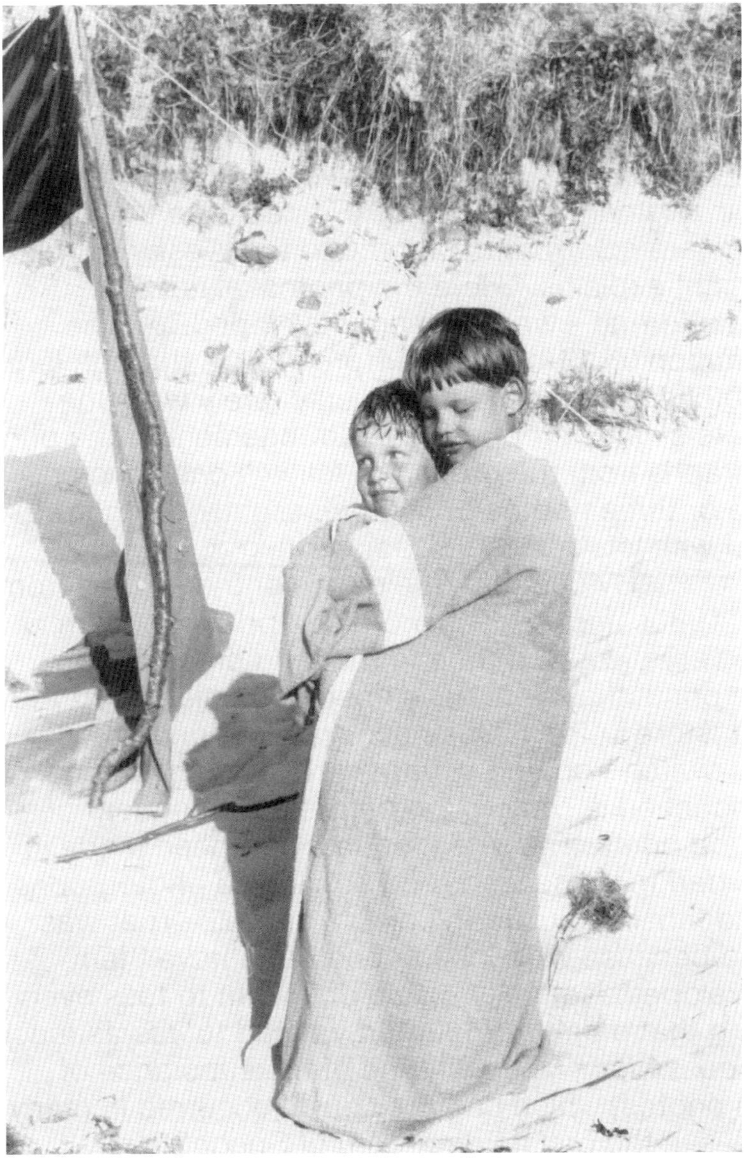

equipment for the darkroom in the early 1990s. "Yeah, for a long time you didn't have a good camera, and we did want to put out all that money for a new, expensive camera, because we weren't even sure whether we would keep our jobs, and whether the money might not be needed for other things."(20) The Specht family's first album after reunification was not assembled until 1991, and it shows changes in their photographic practice. Pasted onto the first page are color prints of a trip to the West. Burghard Specht explains: "Here the photos all have the same format—we had them developed."(21) The common 9×13-centimeter format runs through large stretches of the album, and only rarely were the prints slightly cropped. The arrangement of the photographs from the drugstore follows one schema: two or three photos on a page, slightly staggered, and with lots of white space for text (fig. 3).

By contrast, the pages of the albums from the 1980s and the self-produced prints on them are very diverse in their format and presentation. The prints that were developed and enlarged at the drugstore in the 1990s gave way to monotony. The switch from the private dark room to external production is clear in the consistent treatment of all the prints. The selection that had been made in the darkroom ceased. And so, flawed photographs made their way into the album as well: "That was also because we took the photos to have them developed. Naturally, you didn't want to toss everything that didn't turn out but wanted to use as much as possible."(22) The altering of the substance of the photos, which had previously occurred in many steps in the private darkroom of Specht family,

20 Author's conversation with Margrit and Burghard Specht, Parey, September 5, 2022, 0:15:30.

21 Album conversation with Margrit and Burghard Specht, Magdeburg, July 27, 2021, 1:38:00.

22 Album conversation with Margrit and Burghard Specht, Magdeburg, July 27, 2021, 1:46:00.

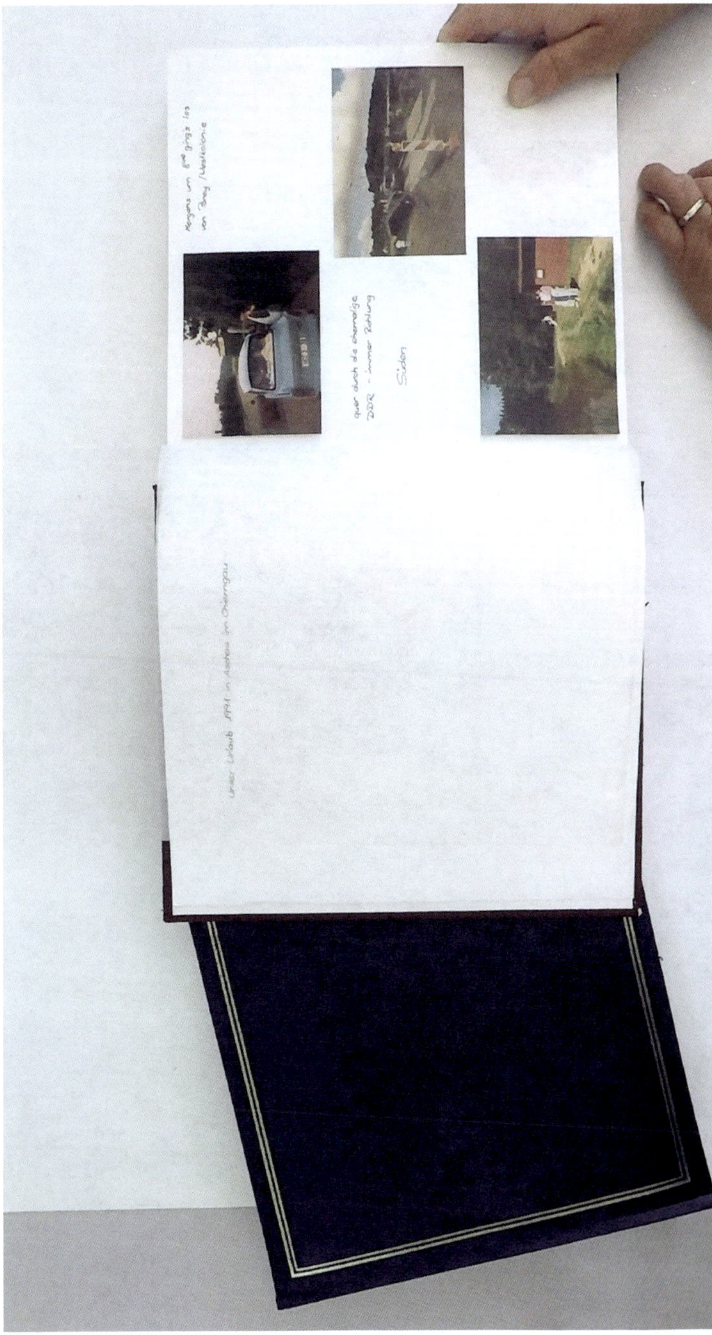

Fig. 3: Album conversation with Margrit and Burghard Specht, Magdeburg, July 27, 2021. Videostill, 1:37:23.

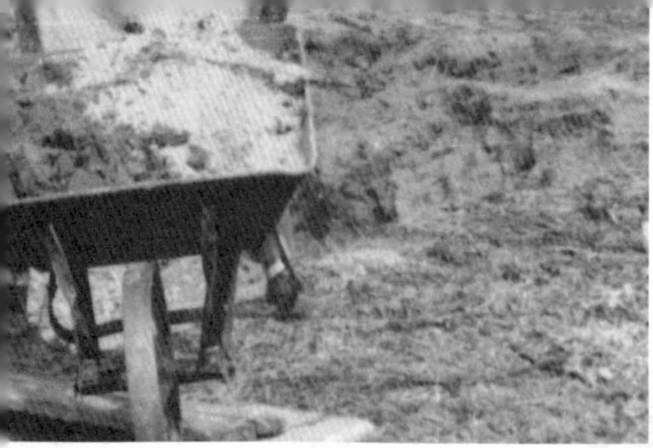

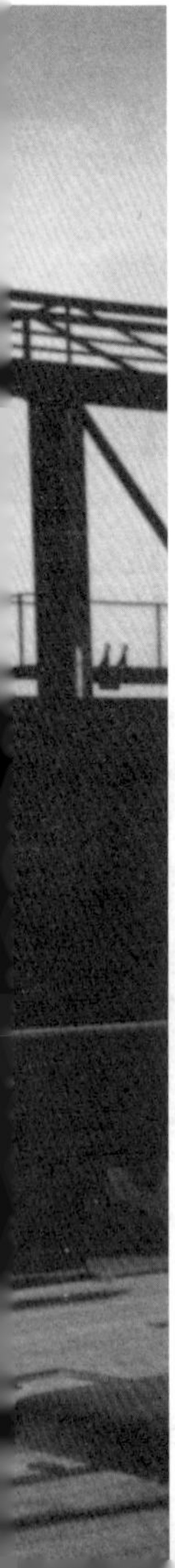

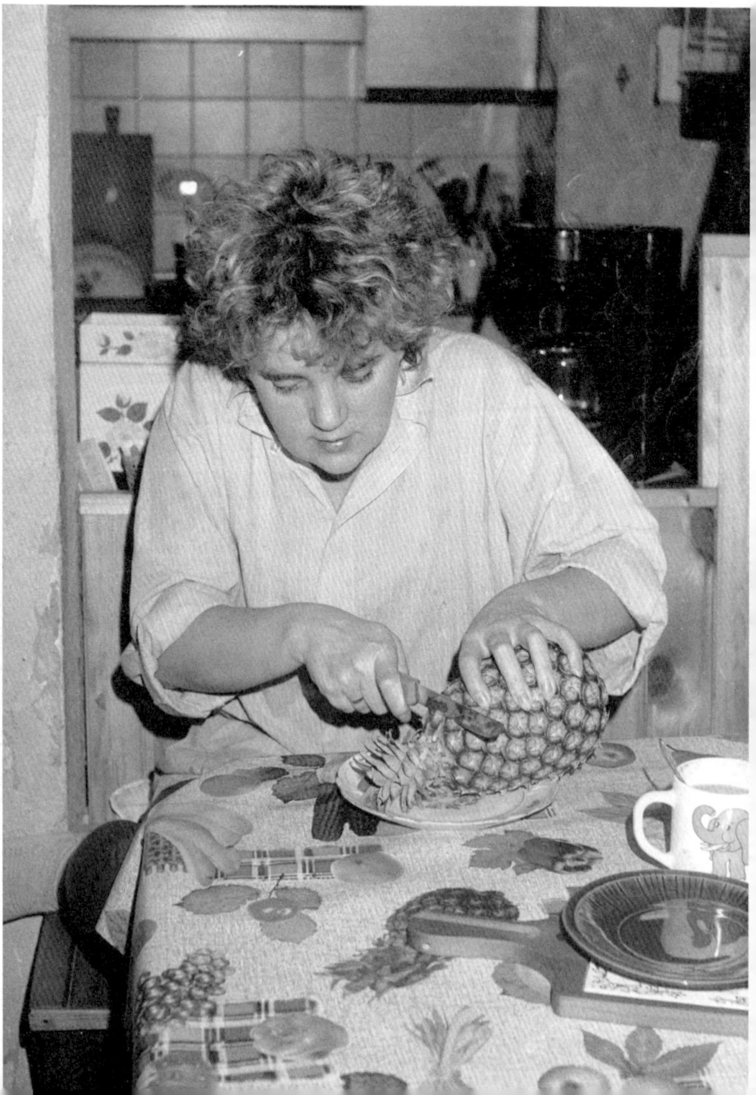

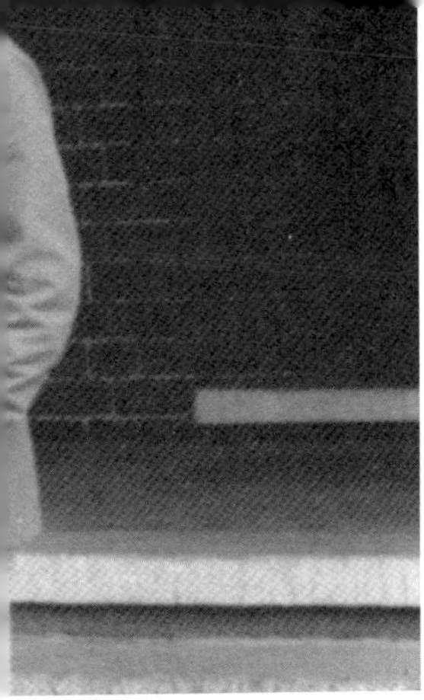
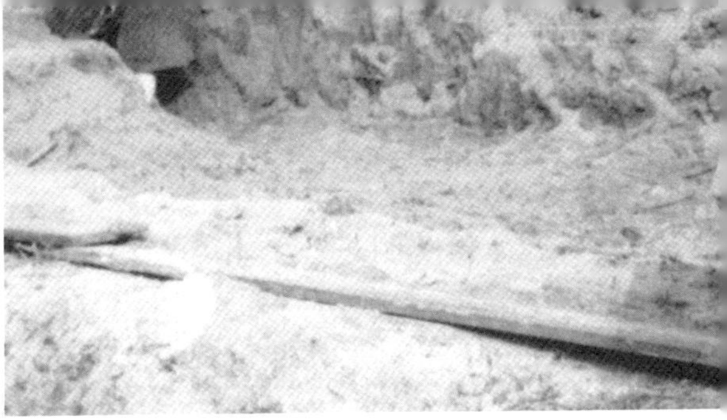
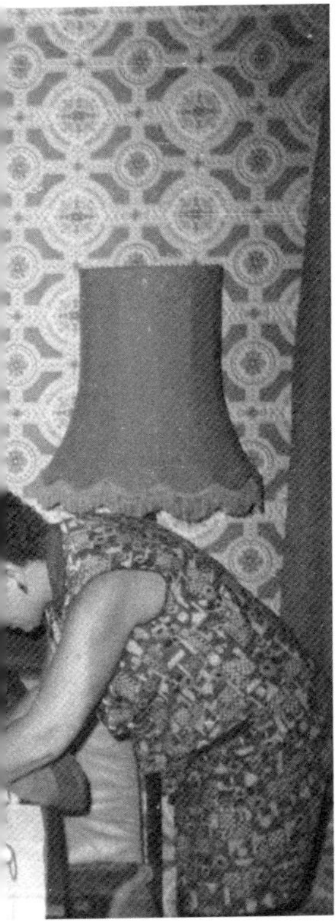
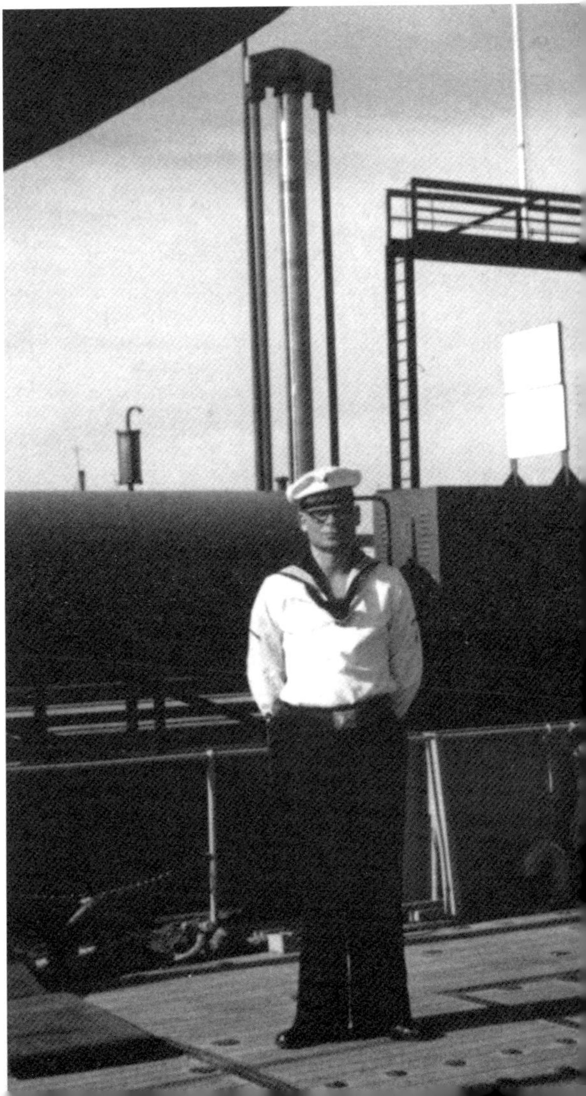

now went away when the photos were developed and enlarged externally. The standardized production is also evident in the uniformity of the prints in the album.

Margrit Specht sums it up and by saying that this also reveals the value the darkroom had in their own photographic practices: "Those are not photos we made ourselves … That is, didn't develop them ourselves."(23)

23 Album conversation with Margrit and Burghard Specht, Magdeburg, July 27, 2021, 1:41:00.

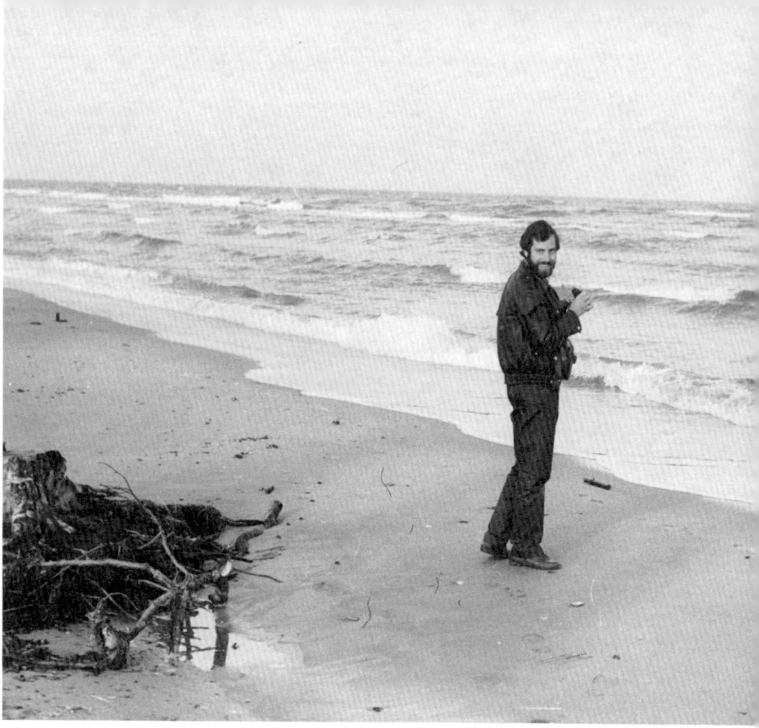

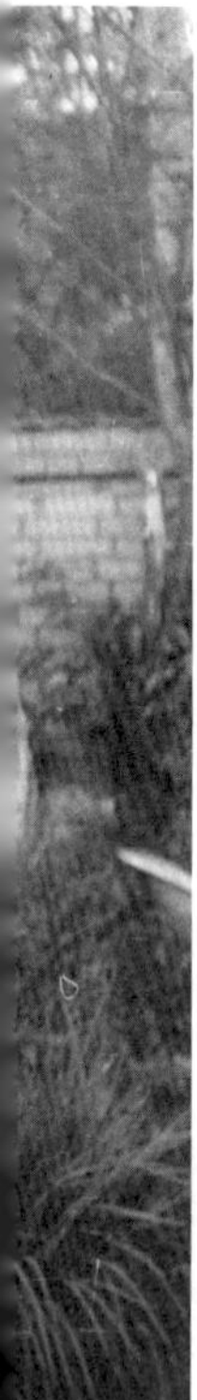

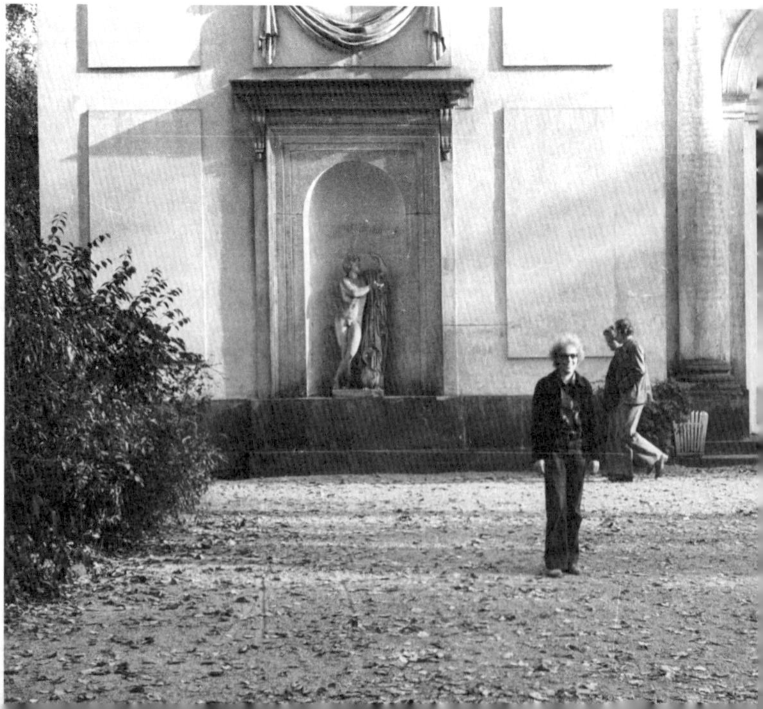

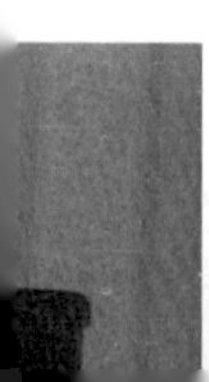

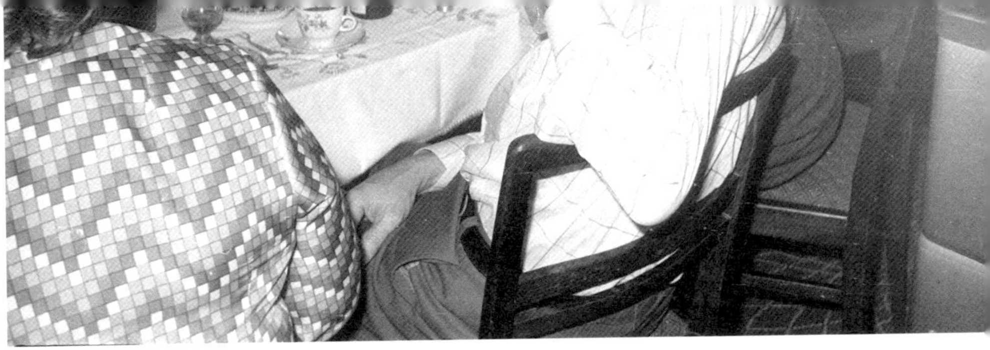

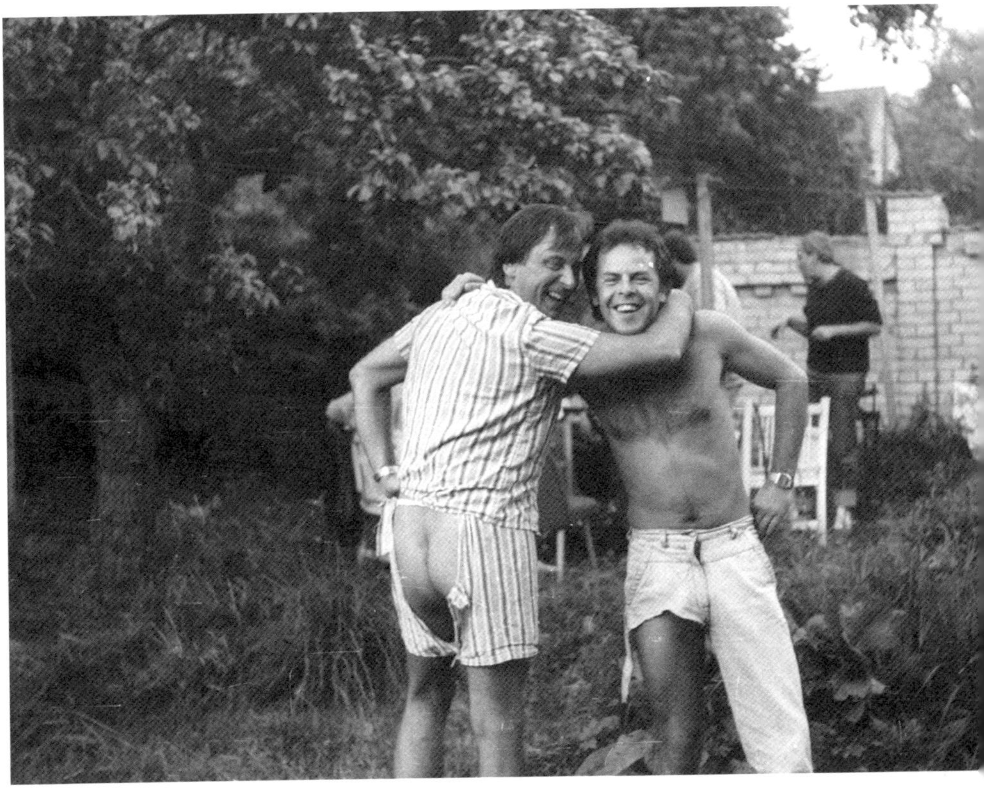

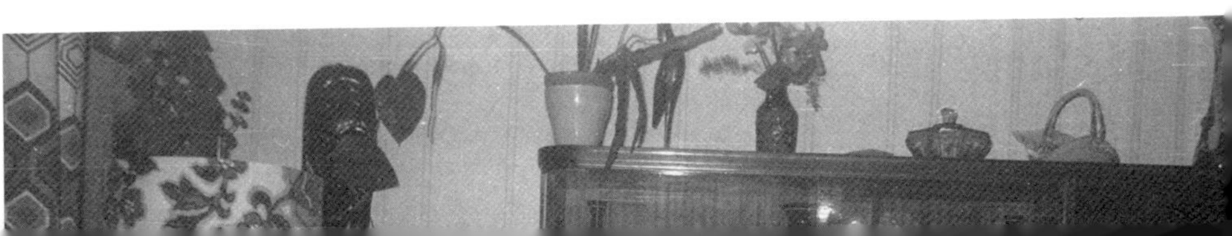

Oktober 1990 beim Theater Cottbus

Gitti und Harald

der neue West-
film ist da

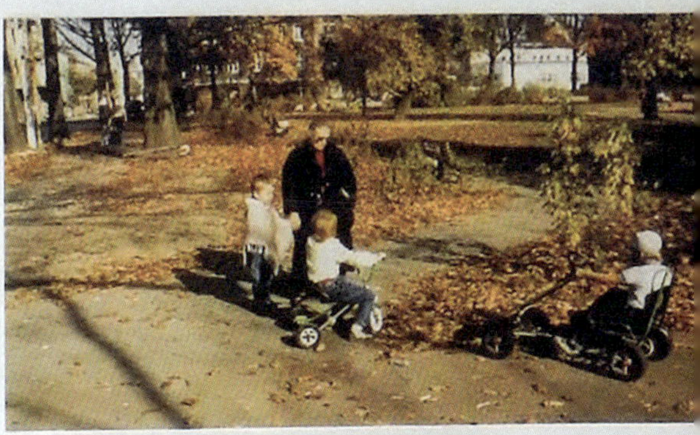

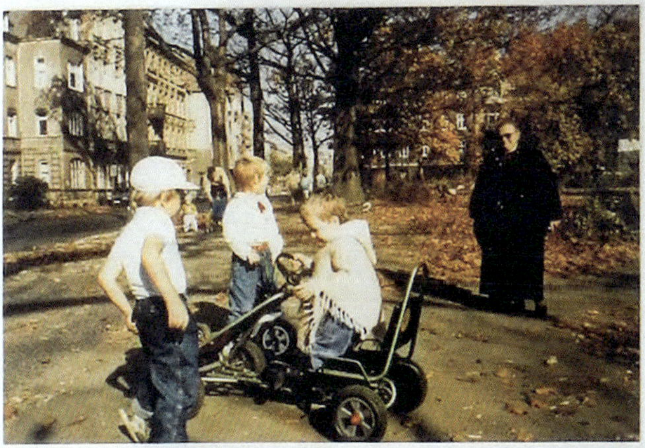

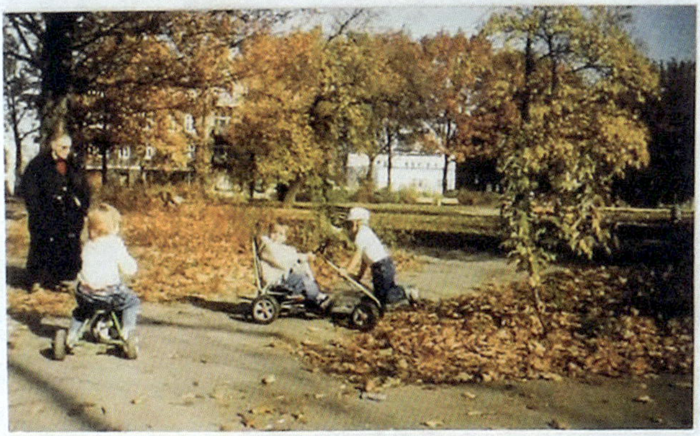

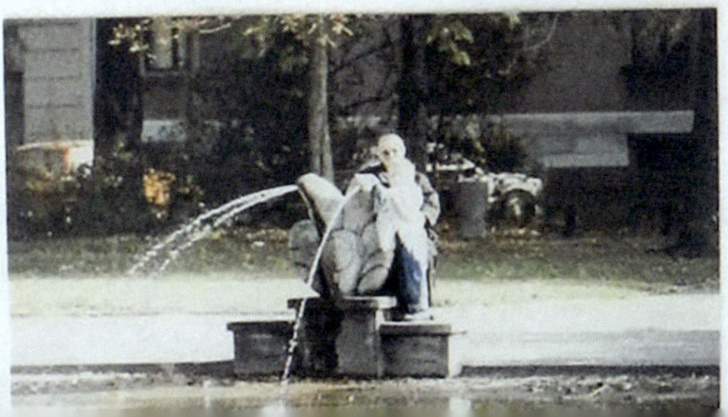

Birgit and Werner-Wolf Turski

Birgit and Werner-Wolf Turski

7-TAGESREISE IN DEN SPANISCHEN FRÜHLING

COSTA BRAVA

WIR REISEN mit Niveau

WIR-REISEN GmbH
Jakob-Sigle-Str. 2
8939 Türkheim
Telefon 0 82 45/10 14-1
Telefax 0 82 45/10 43

WIR-REISEN GmbH · Jakob-Sigle-Str. 2 · 8939 Türkheim

Ihre persönlichen Reiseunterlagen

für die Reise
23.5.91 am — 2 Personen — Hotel Unterbringung

Busunternehmen

7-Tagesreise "Costa Brava"

Reisetage: 7.5./15.5./23.5.91

Reisepreis: DM 199,--

Einzelzimmerzuschlag: DM 80,--

Reisepaß nicht vergessen!

Abfahrtsstellen: Bahnhof Cottbus

Abfahrtszeit: 16.45 Uhr

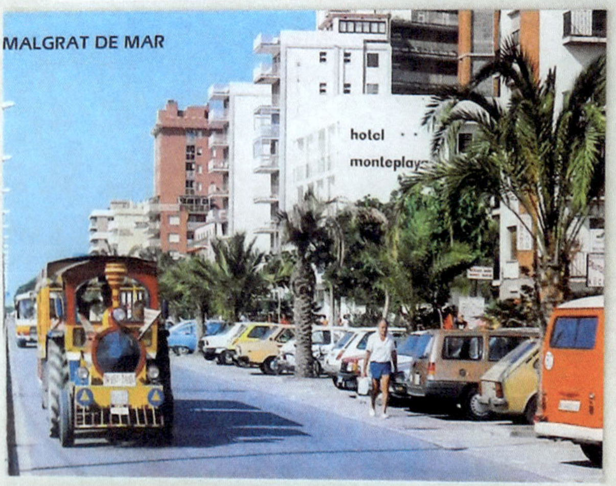

AQUAMARINA
PARK HOTE
Tel. 93/767 82 11 • SANTA SUSANNA (Barcelona) E

Sr. D. / M. / Mr. / Herr: RBA

Fecha entrada: 24-5 Fecha salida: 28

Agencia:

Habitación / Chambre / Room / Zimmer: 3313 N.º Pax

Régimen / Régime / Acommodation / Hotelleistung: H.P. Precio / Prix / Price / Preis

Desayuno / Déjeuner / Breakfast / Frühstück: 8- 10

Almuerzo / Diner / Lunch / Mittagessen:

Cena / Souper / Dinner / Abendessen: 18⁰⁰-21⁰

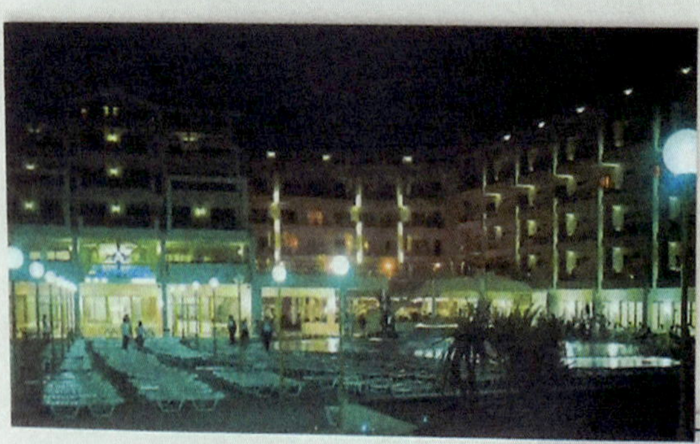

unser „Haus" in Malgrat de M

Aquamarina Park Hotel

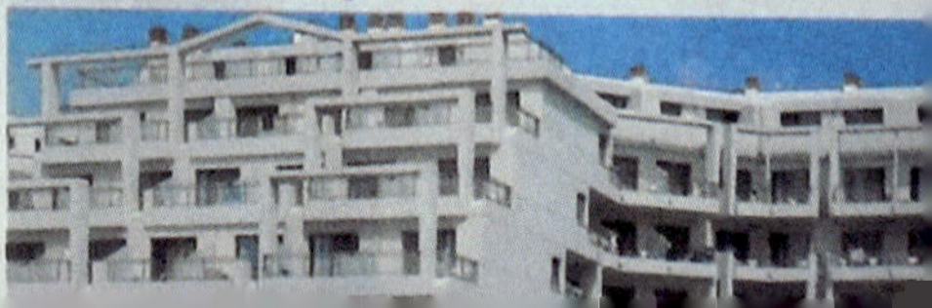

Hotel Riviera
El Carro
Piano Bar

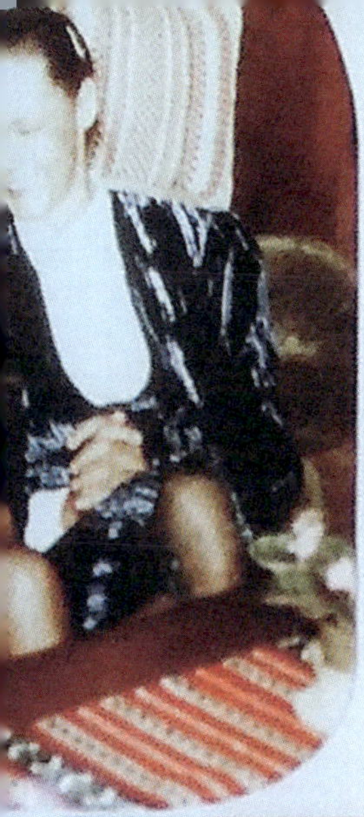

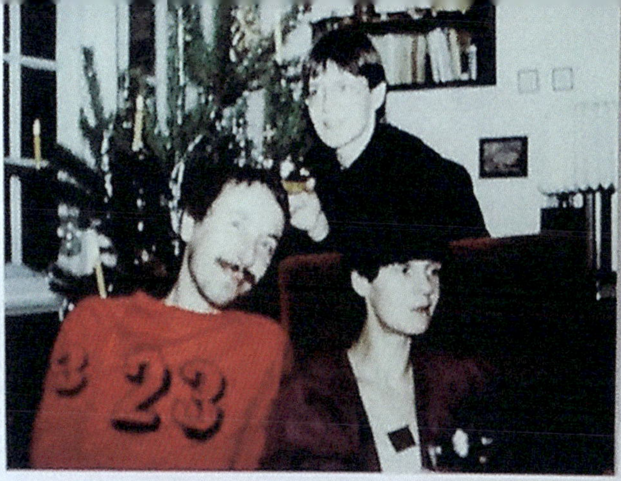

Nach 4 Tagen Weihnachten in Mulda und 1 Rückfahrt-Stop in Leipzig: mit LYNN zu Bielicks in die Klinikallee 56 nach Brandenburg – "Bye-bye '89" und "Hallo '90"

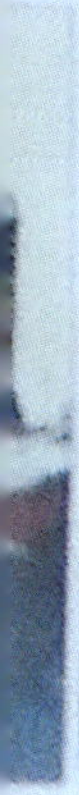

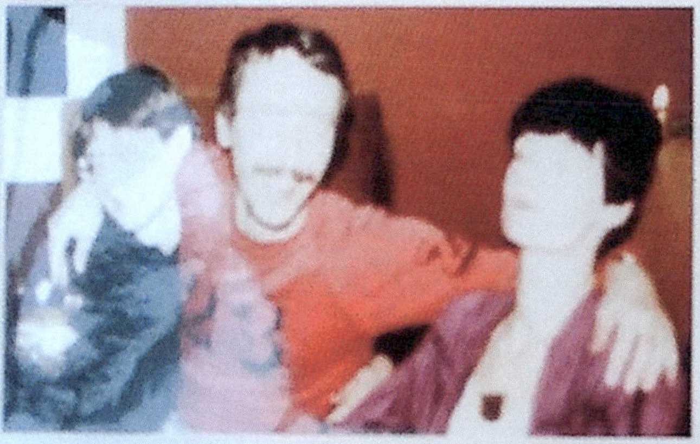

SYLVESTER 1989 ([illegible])

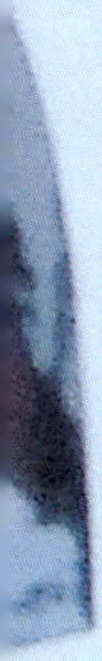

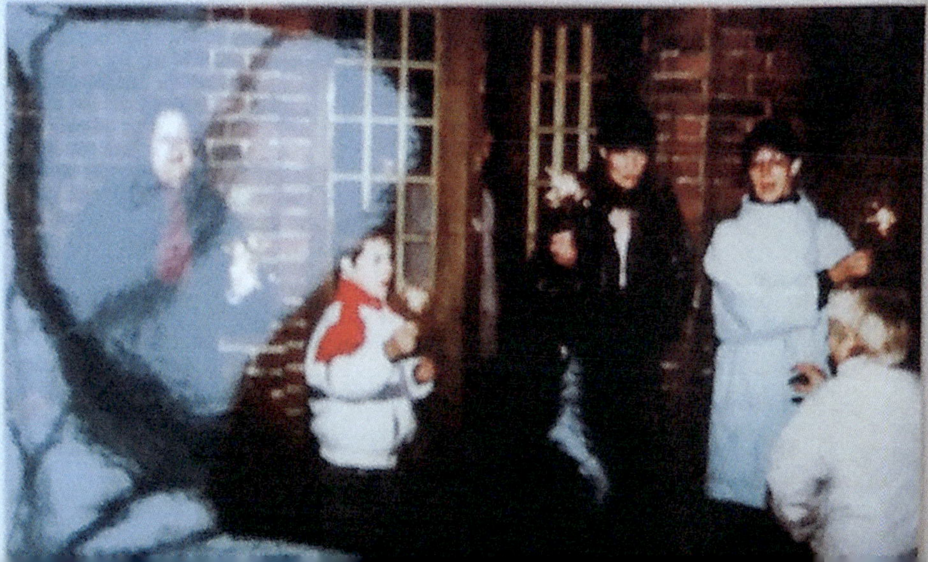

Beate and Jürgen Göldner

Beate and Jürgen Göldner

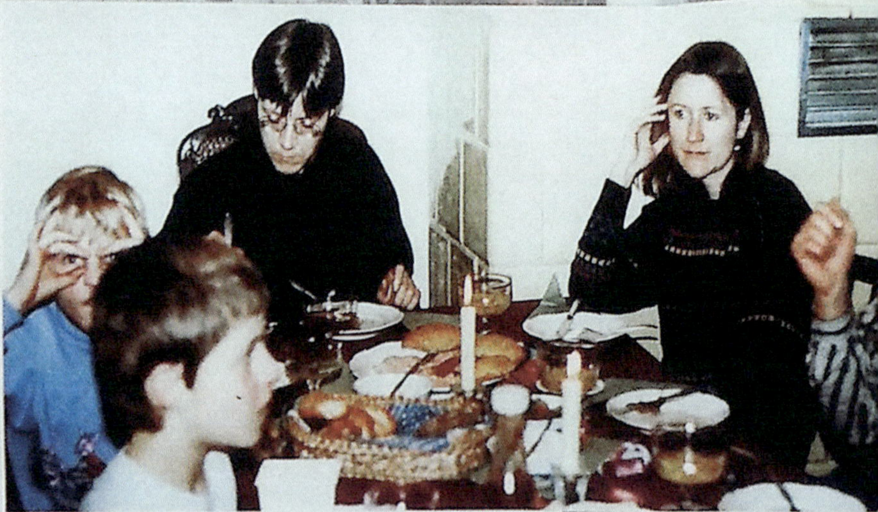

Neujahrsmorgen 1. Januar 1990:
Üppiges (Silvester –) Katerfrühstück
mit Miss LYNN G. bei IRIS, BERNHARD &
JAKOB

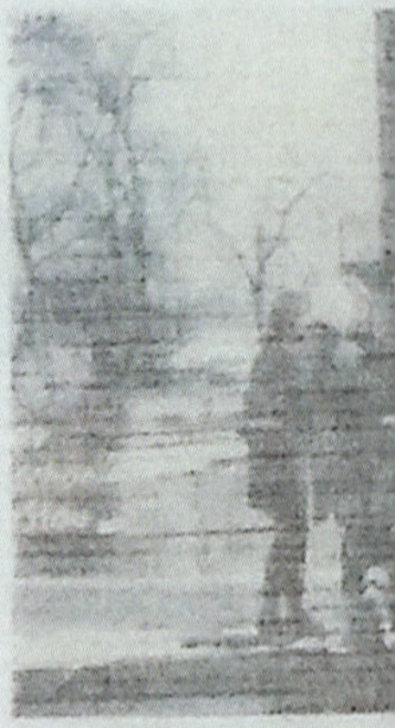

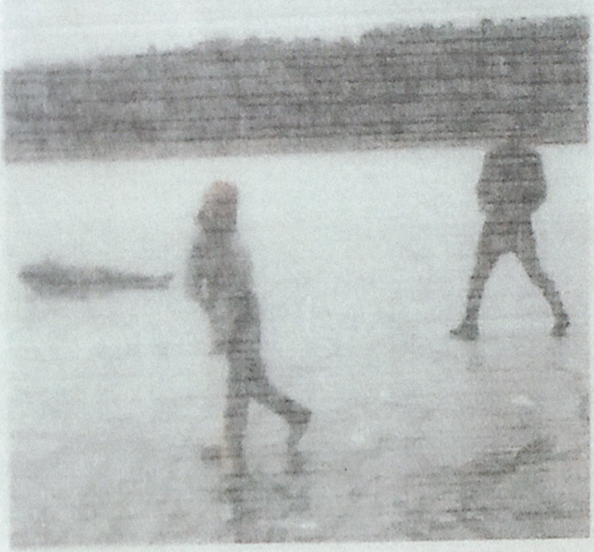

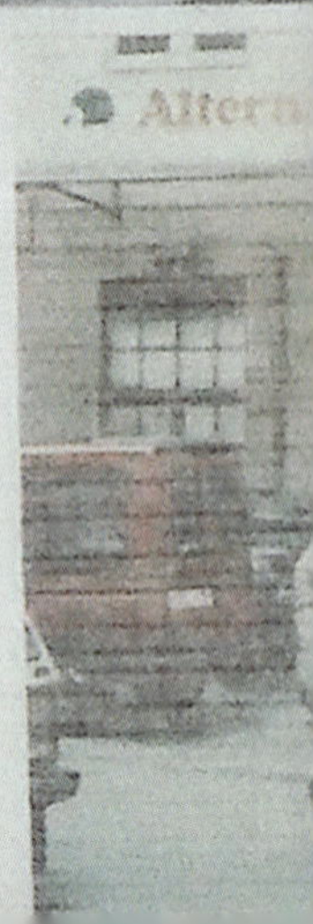

tember 1989

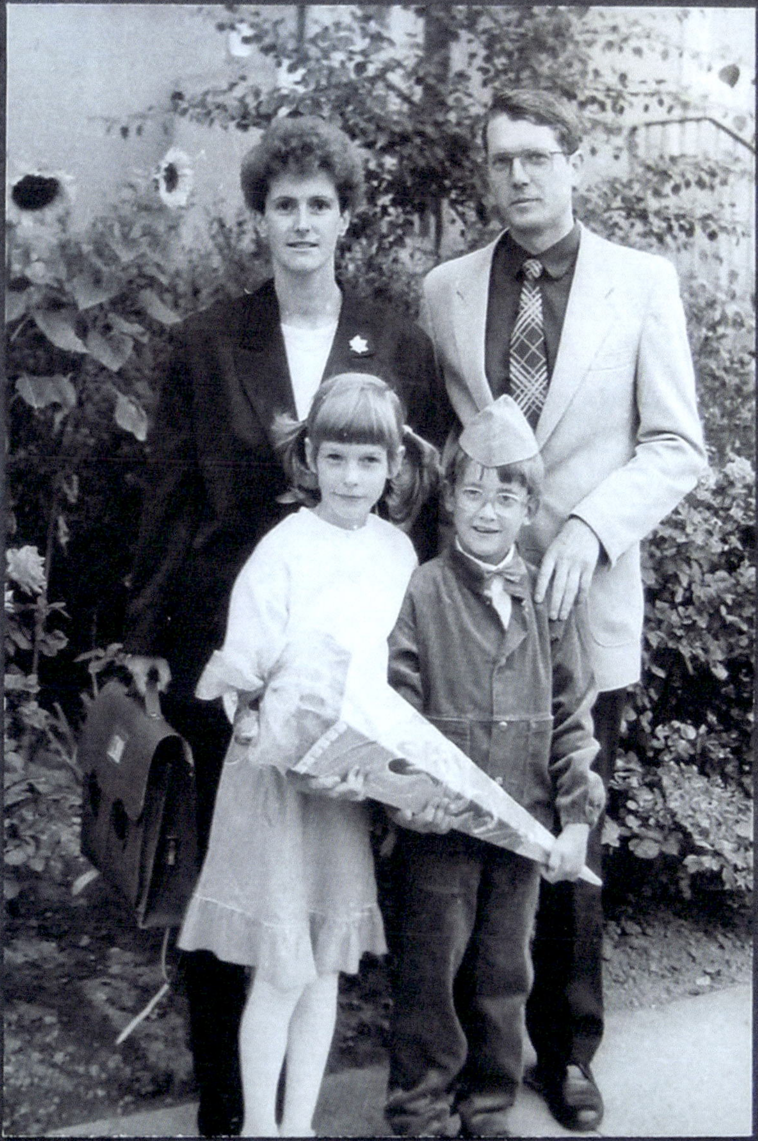

ule beginnt

Bettina and Manfred Simon

Bettina and Manfred Simon

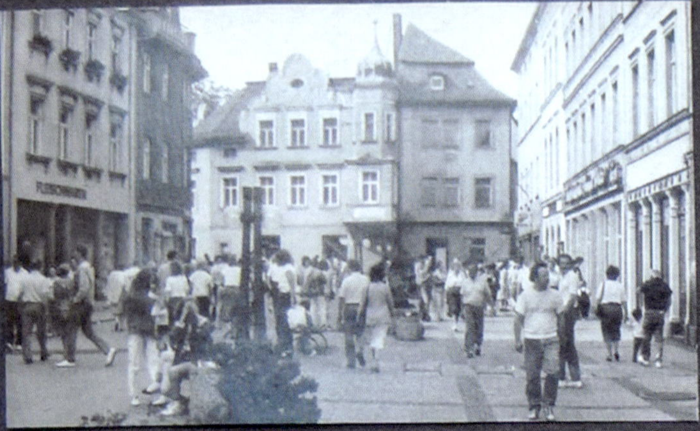

Währur

Es ist
Sonntag -
alle Geschäft
sind geschlo
ser

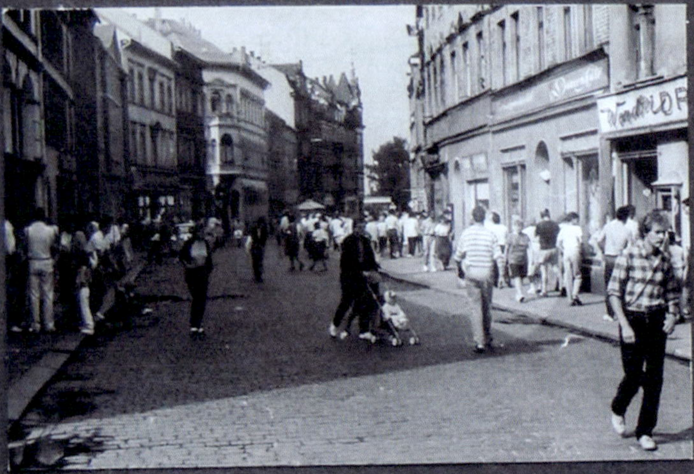

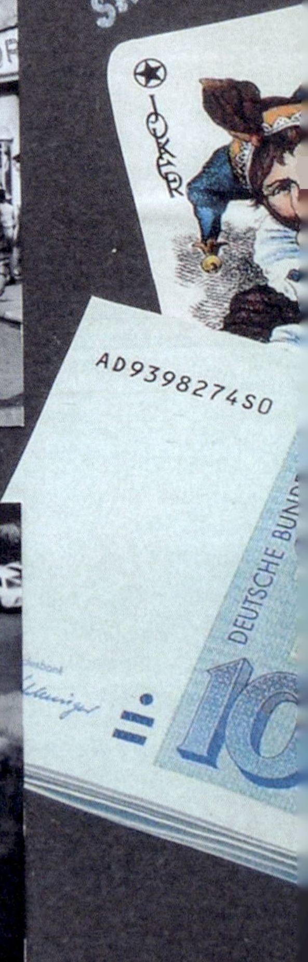

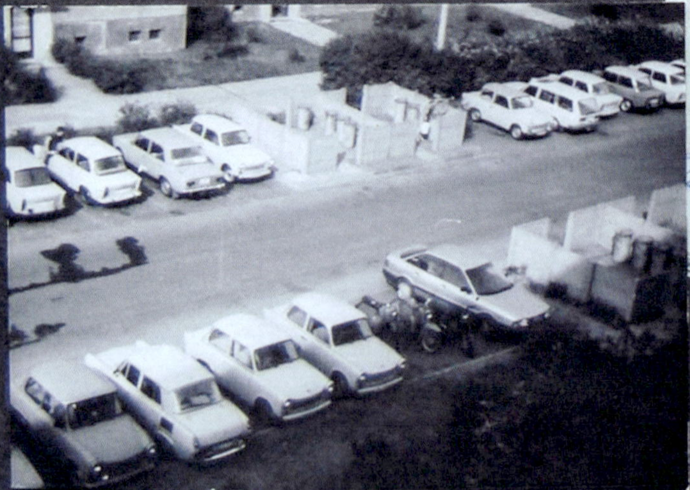

Das erste Westauto ist da!

The West in the East: On Four Motifs in Private Photographs from East Germany

Friedrich Tietjen

I.

"You were proud to have something like that,"(1) Martin Siebert from Ilmenau in Thuringia said of the images he had photographed from West German television programs—from the *Sportschau* (a sports broadcast), the quiz *Kennen Sie Kino?* (Do You Know Cinema?), the film *Flug in Gefahr* (Flight into Danger), and the German adaptation of the U.S. series *Dragnet*, among other programs. (fig. 1) Although there are no black bars across the screen, a frequent result of insufficient exposure times, picture noise and blurry movements could scarcely be avoided. Thus, the pictures are of rather middling quality. Admittedly, in private photography that is often a secondary criterion: when a photograph captures an important moment or an important person, flaws in the image make no difference. And yet… these photographs certainly do show something of private life, like most private photographs. But why does one photograph individual moments of ephemeral Western television broadcasts? And why would someone be proud of having "something like that"?

Photographing television screens is not a practice unique to East Germany; viewers in other countries also photographed broadcasts of particularly memorable events, such as the moon landing or the trial of Adolf Eichmann, sometimes just out of pride in the new tv-set they had just switched on. (2) What is striking, however, is that this practice appears to have been fairly widespread

1 Phone conversation with Martin Siebert, July 30, 2022.

2 See Friedrich Tietjen, "Documenting Witnessing: Two Cases of TV-Screen Photography," in: Winfried Gerling/Sebastian Möring/Marco De Mutiis (eds.), *Screen Images. In-Game Photography, Screenshots, Screencast*, Berlin: Kulturverlag Kadmos 2022, pp. 301–306.

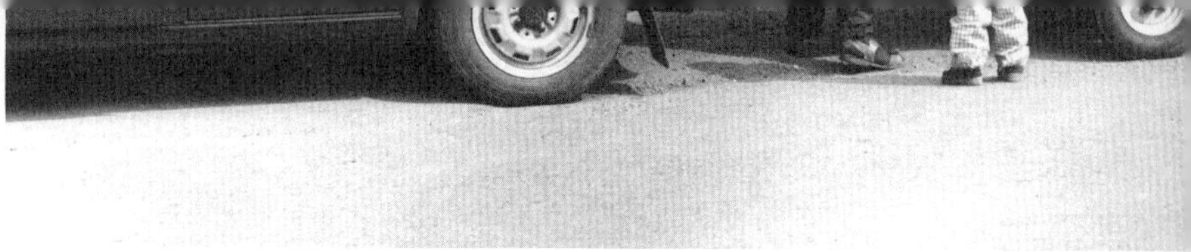

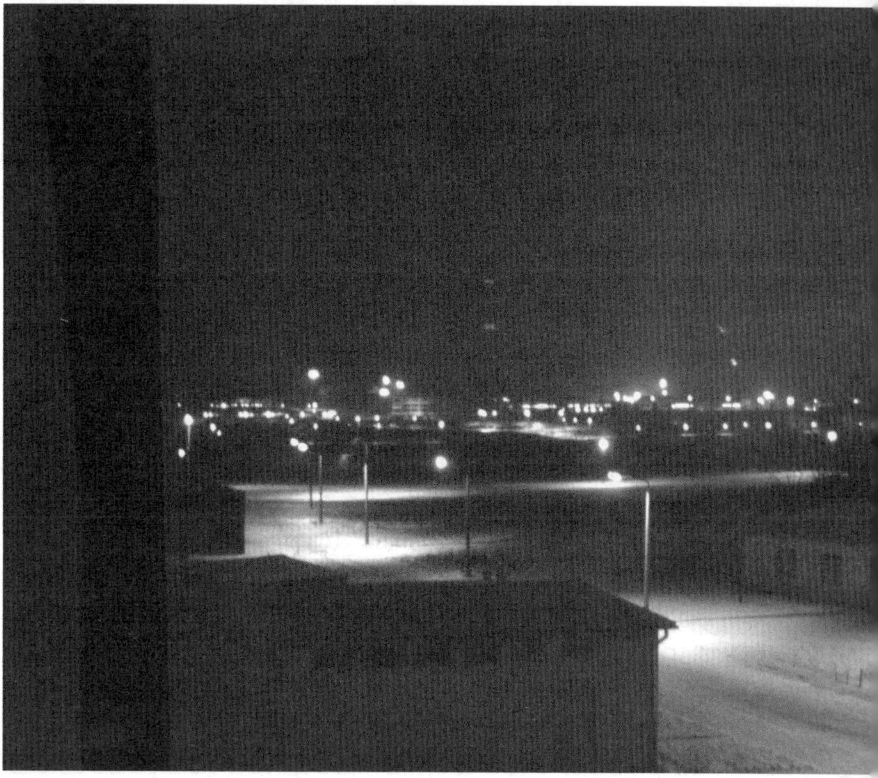

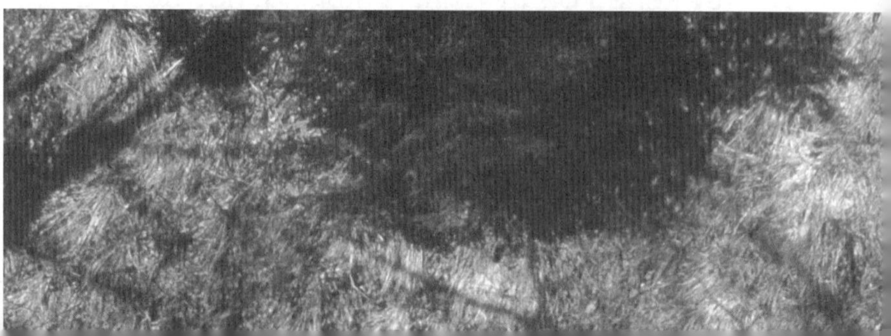

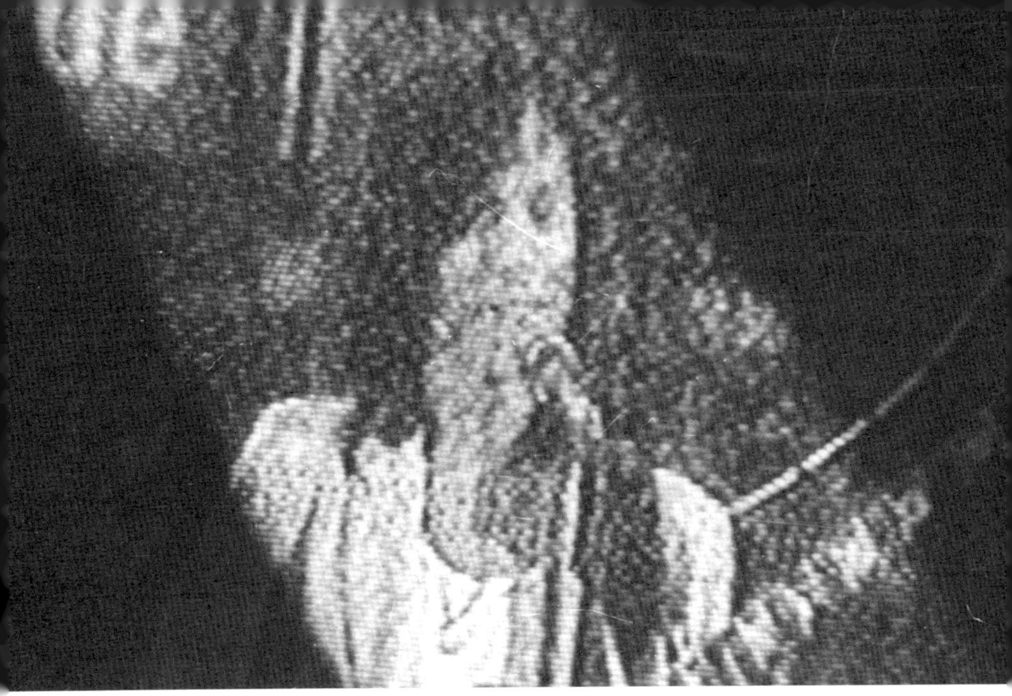

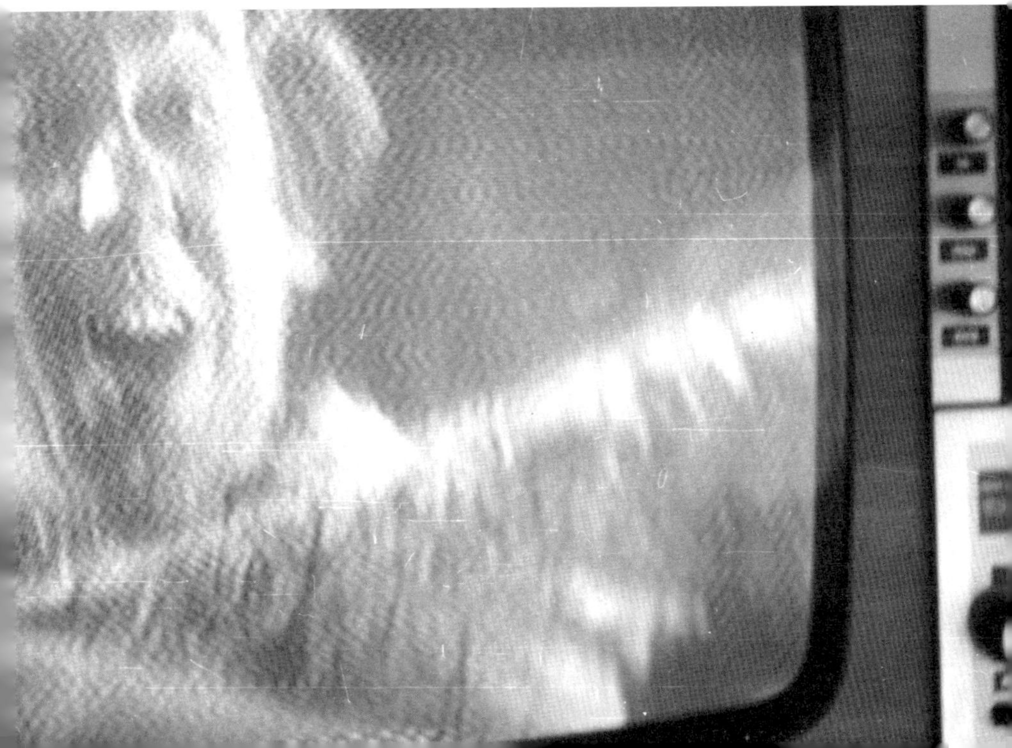

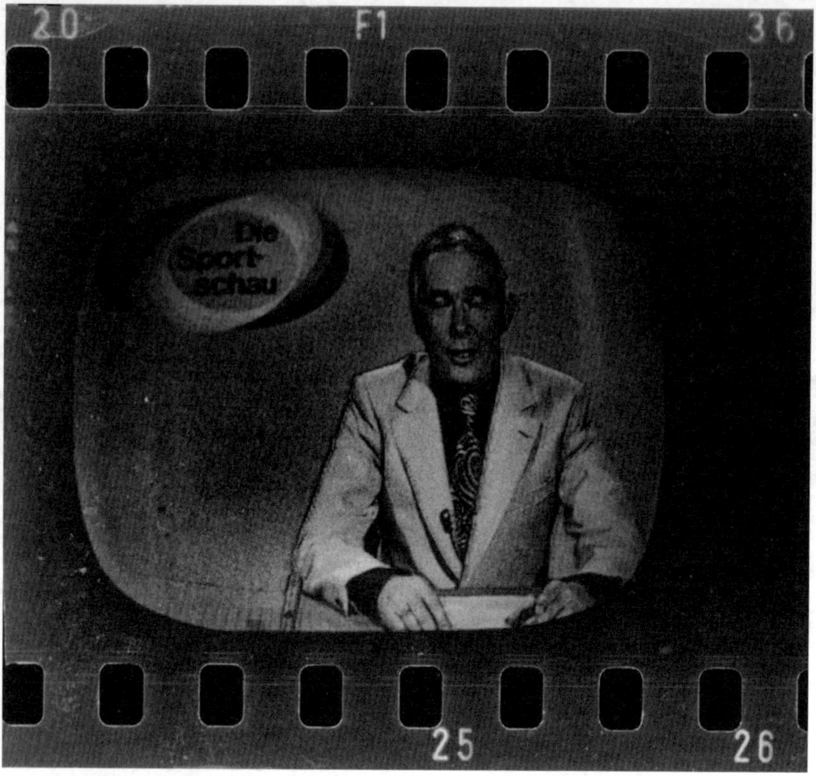

Fig. 1: *Sportschau.* Undated. Photo: Martin Siebert. Reproduced from the negative in the project's archive.

in East Germany. During the project we saw such pictures in two collections, and some of our interviewees told us about acquaintances and relatives who had also sat in front of the TV with the camera. Moreover, it seems that only television programs from the West, not from the East, were photographed. Despite this popular practice, hardly any prints have turned up so far—such photographs apparently had no place in family albums.

The fact that West German transmitters installed close to the borders were particularly powerful and thus covered a large part of the GDR's territory could not please the country's leadership. In 1961, therefore, the Central Committee of the Sozialistische Einheitspartei Deutschland (Socialist Unity Party, or SED) issued a directive that "organized Western television and the distribution of Western news" was to be "prosecuted criminally." No such law was ever passed and other more sporadic countermeasures, such as jamming broadcasts and taking down private reception antennas, proved to be of little help. A large part of the East German population watched or listened to Western stations on a more or less regular basis and could not be prevented from doing so by these means. Then, in May 1973, the GDR government let it be known that this practice would generally be tolerated. An eyewitness recalls: "In a speech at a Central Committee meeting [...], Honecker said in passing: 'The Western mass media, especially radio and television from the Federal Republic of Germany, which everyone here can switch on or off at will ...' That was the signal; reception was still forbidden, but it was no longer punished."(3)

How much political influence Western television had in East Germany before 1989 is a matter of

3 Deutscher Bundestag (ed.), Materialien der Enquete-Kommission "Aufarbeitung von Geschichte und Folgen der SED-Diktatur in Deutschland", Baden-Baden: Nomos Verlagsgesellschaft 1995, vol. VIII/1, p. 50.

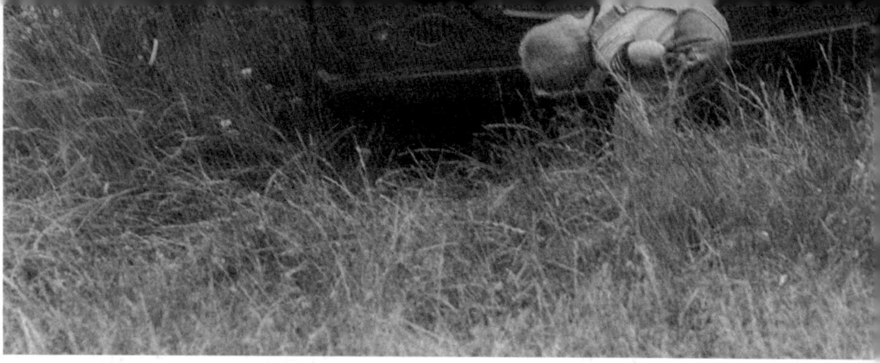

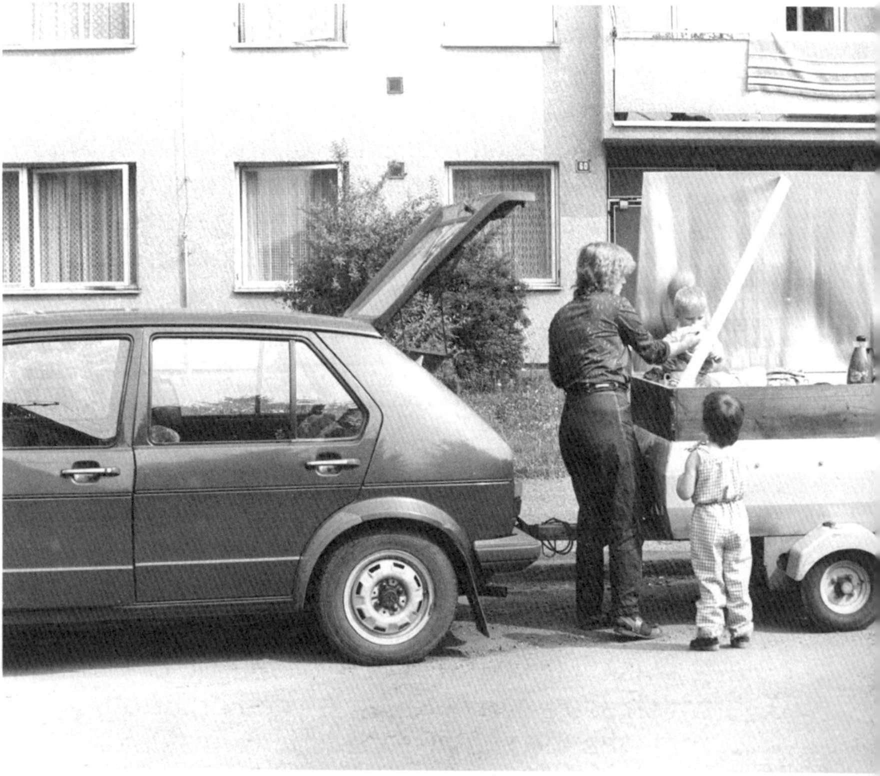

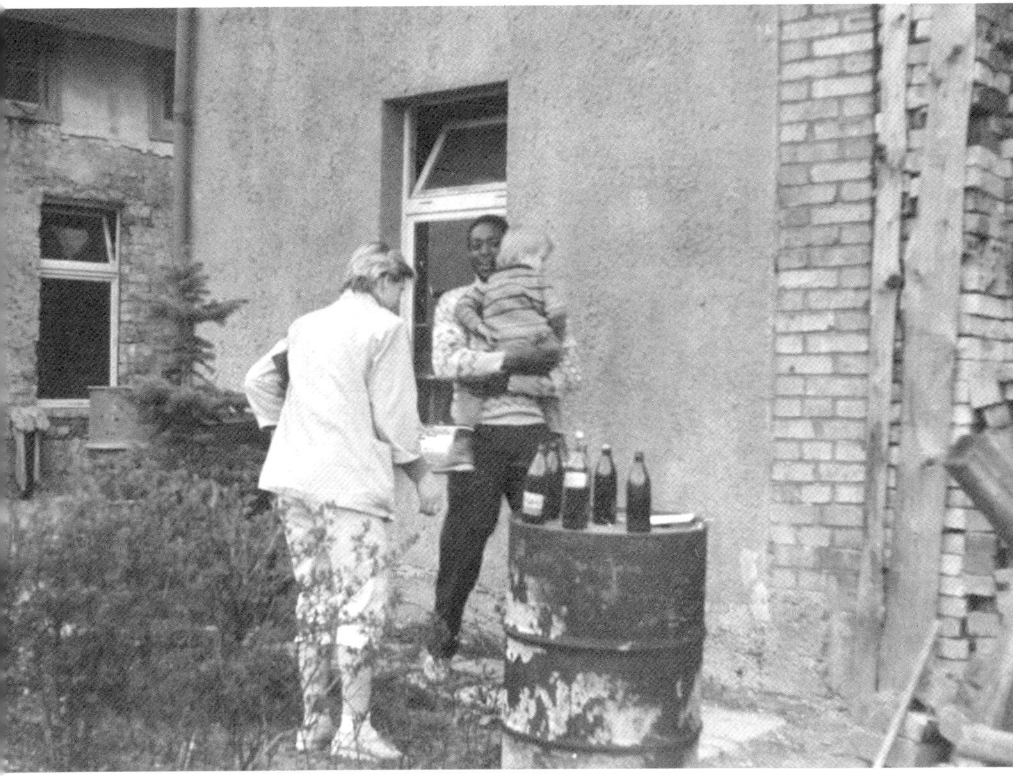

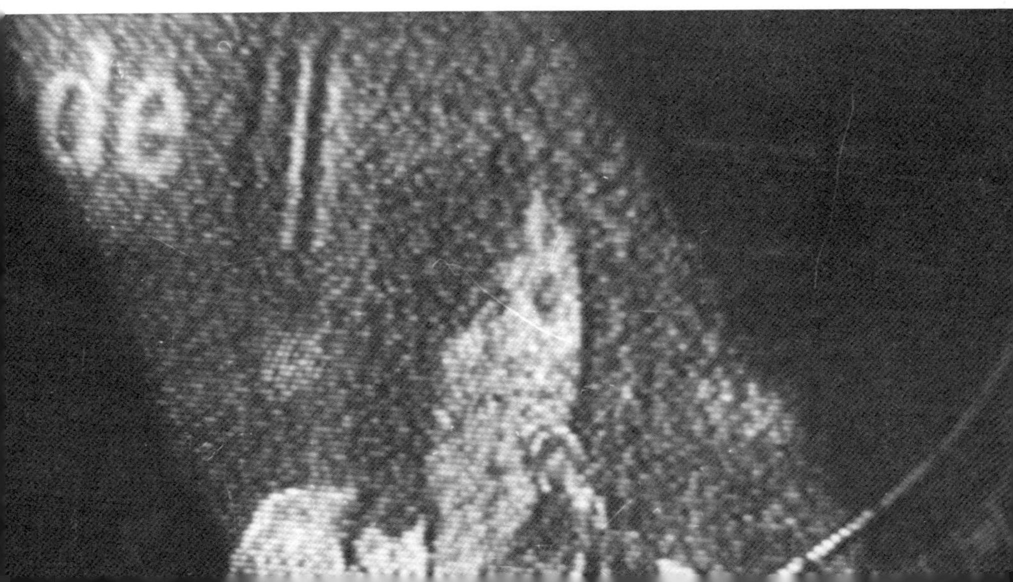

dispute.(4) Less controversial is that television was generally consumed primarily as a form of entertainment, and in this area the East German programs were certainly competitive. The advantage West German broadcasts had over these programs, however, was access to stories and music that were rarely available in the East: no series comparable to *Dallas* and *Dynasty* was filmed in East Germany, and the music presented in *disco*, *Rockpalast*, and *Hitparade* was played on GDR radio only in exceptional cases, and often enough was not available on records either. But regardless of whether the consumption of Western broadcasts was politically motivated or out of a need to relax in front of the TV after work, it was—even on a small scale—a decision against one's own country, or more precisely against the prevailing conditions there. It expressed a more or less vague desire that something could be different after all: different music, different stories, different conversations, different things, another world, another life.

Television from the West brought all of this into East German living rooms, in sound and image. Elsewhere in the interview, Martin Siebert described his photographs of these broadcasts as a form of "participation in West culture,"(5) and that is what they are: capturing the fleeting appearances of these images and their promise of a different life-world and in addition, a culture of commodities, variety, enjoyment, and excitement that was hardly available in this form in East Germany. Yet it is striking that such photo-

4 For his study published in 1988, Kurt R. Hesse asked migrants from the GDR about their television viewing habits and found that political broadcasts such as *Kennzeichen D*, *Report*, and similar news programs were watched frequently, far more so than in West Germany (see Kurt R. Hesse, *Westmedien in der DDR: Nutzung, Image und Auswirkungen bundesrepublikanischen Hörfunks und Fernsehens*, Cologne: Verlag Wissenschaft und Politik 1988, p. 52). Michael Meyen points out, by contrast, that in East Germany, too, televisions tended to be tuned on more for entertainment and not necessarily for political enlightenment (see Michael Meyen, "Kollektive Ausreise? Zur Reichweite ost- und westdeutscher Fernsehprogramme in der DDR," in: *Publizistik. Vierteljahreshefte für Kommunikationsforschung*, 47, pp. 200–220, June 2002).

5 Telephone conversation with Martin Siebert, July 30, 2022.

graphs were apparently hardly ever printed and pasted into albums—in short, not looked at at all (6), so why were they taken in the first place?

It is possible that their purpose was not necessarily to create a memory of a specific moment in life with an indeterminate future. The motifs of the photographs seem to confirm this, as they are of rather unspecific moments. In the case of *Flug in Gefahr*, for example, it is a scene with several passengers sitting in an airplane and in *Sportschau*, it is Ernst Huberty sitting like a newscaster next to the program's logo. More important than the pictures themselves might have been the act of taking them. Without being in the picture oneself, one photographs oneself doing something: watching (through the viewfinder) Western television.

The West German television program was one of the few spheres practically equally accessible to East and West Germans. Even if the social orders and milieus differed considerably, the sofa and armchair in front of the TV were one of the few places where Germans from both countries have similar experiences: enjoying the same music, loathing or loving *Dynasty*, knowing more than the contestants on quiz shows, or hoping and trembling with them, and watching with fascination as the first automobile drives through extraterrestrial dust on the Apollo 15 moon mission. Photographing the screen during these broadcasts certainly has something to do with cultural participation, as Martin Siebert put it, with appropriating something that was otherwise inaccessible. But beyond that, these photos do something similar to what many other private photographs do: they document a shared experience—only in this case, people are not sitting together on the sofa, but in two different countries.

6 Thus far I have only seen a single album (presumably West German, mid-1960s) into which photographs of a switched-on television had been pasted; the object of these images was, however, rather the—apparently new—television set and not so much the program being shown. Loose prints of such photographs of television screens are also quite rare.

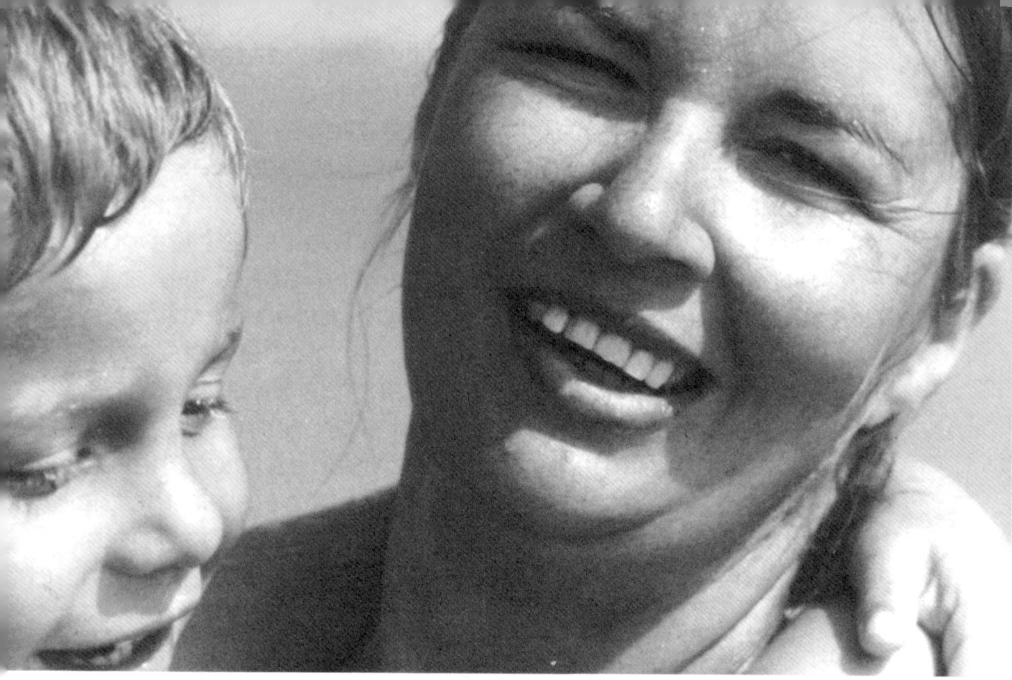

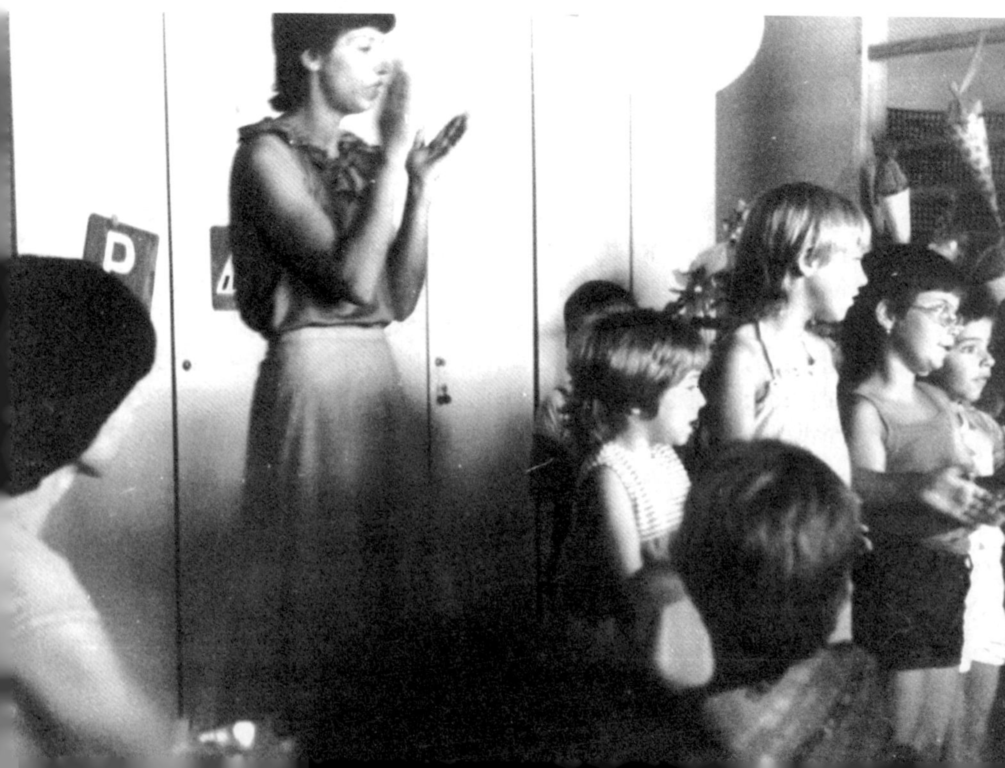

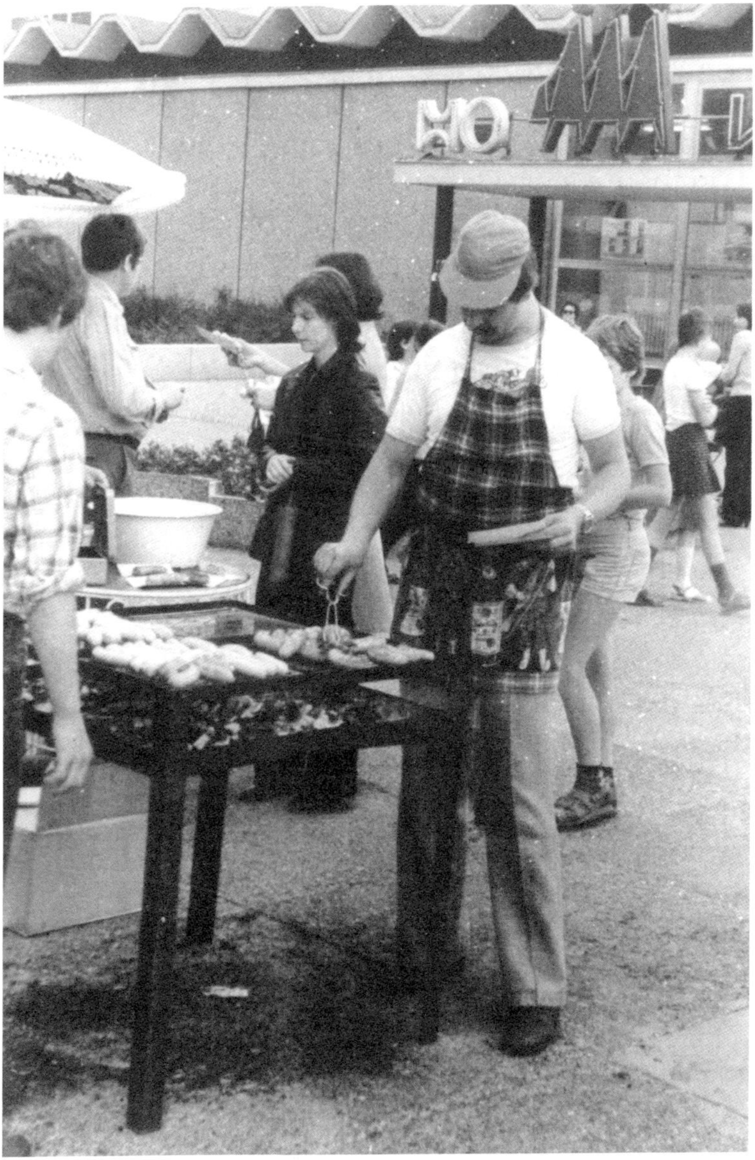

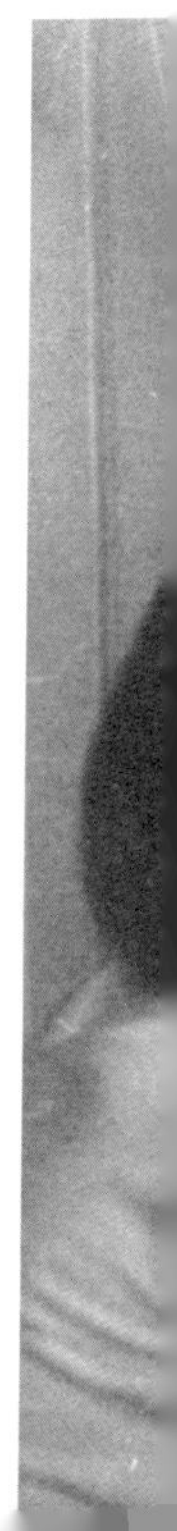

II.

Probably at the beginning of 1980, a young woman living in the Leipzig area got hold of some issues of the West German music magazines *Rocky* and *Bravo*. These magazines were not distributed in the GDR, and having them sent or brought from West Germany was forbidden.(7) (fig. 2) Unlike their East German counterpart *Melodie & Rhythmus*, *Rocky* and *Bravo* also reported on the music—British rock, German New Wave, and disco—that was broadcast by West German television and radio stations into the GDR, and was heard by many young people as well as taped on cassette recorders. These magazines also included regular inserts of autograph cards, posters, and were a coveted and at the same time scarce commodity for fans.

It is unclear whether these magazines belonged to the young woman or whether she had borrowed them from friends; small dog-ears and creases indicate that they had already passed through several hands before they came into hers. In any case, it is obvious that it was important to her to photograph the pages carefully—laid flat on the floor, the sometimes monochrome, sometimes patterned carpets as backgrounds look a bit unfortunate for a reproduction, but most of the shots are well-lit, while she placed the camera—perhaps with a tripod?—centered over the magazine, and she used several black-and-white films for her project.(8) It is neverthe-

7 West German instruction leaflets for gift packages being sent to East Germany listed goods whose sending was prohibited by GDR authorities. They explicitly include newspapers and magazines. For a detailed account, see Christian Härtel, "Ostdeutsche Bestimmungen für den Paketverkehr im Spiegel westdeutscher Merkblätter," in: Christian Härtel/Petra Kabus (eds.), *Das Westpaket: Geschenksendung, keine Handelsware*, Berlin: Ch. Links 2000, pp. 45–53.

8 I purchased these negatives at a flea market in Leipzig in the summer of 2020 as part of a set of twenty rolls. The sparse information cited here is from the images themselves and the details on several slips of paper enclosed with them. Like Martin Siebert, by the way, the unknown young woman also photographed Western broadcasts from the television screen. Martin Siebert, in turn, also photographed posters, album covers, and the like from the West.

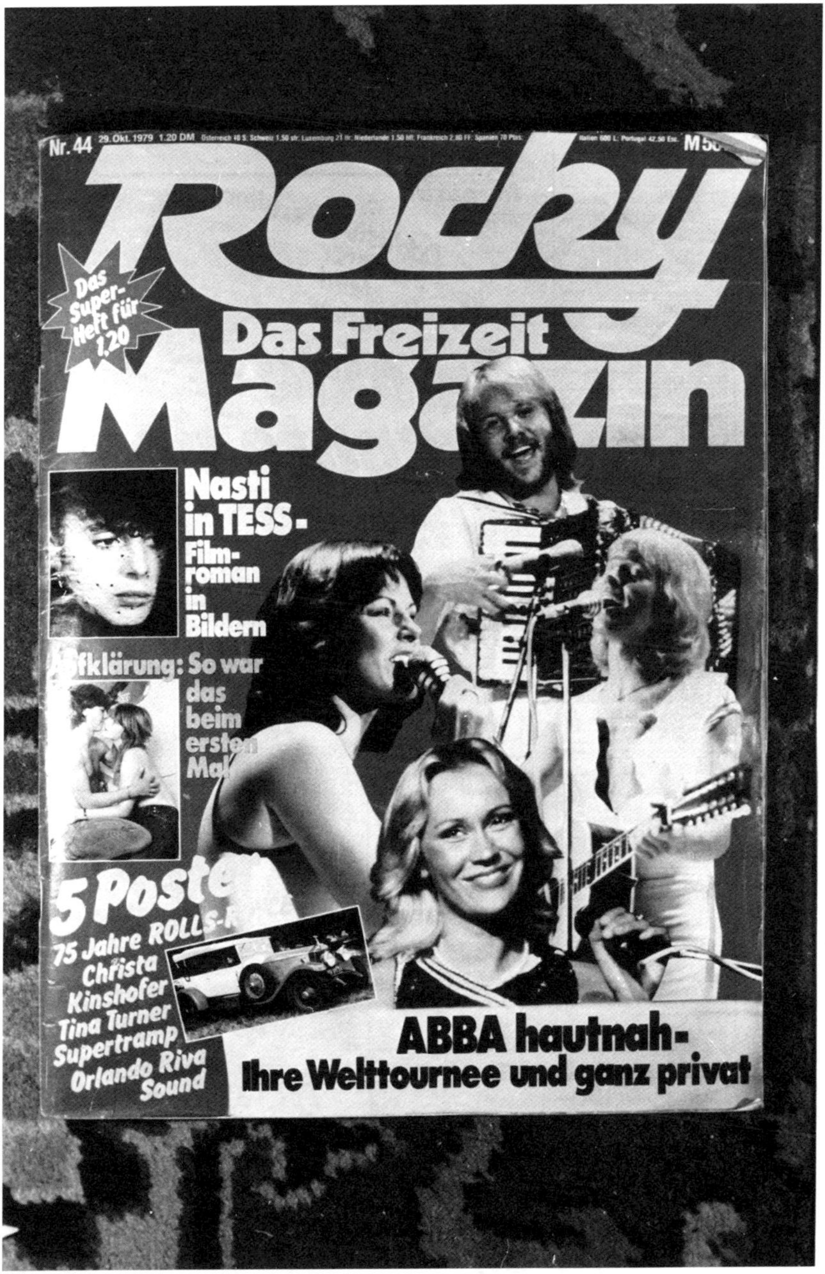

Fig. 2: Cover of *Rocky—Das Freizeit Magazin* (October 1979). Reproduced from the negative in the author's archive.

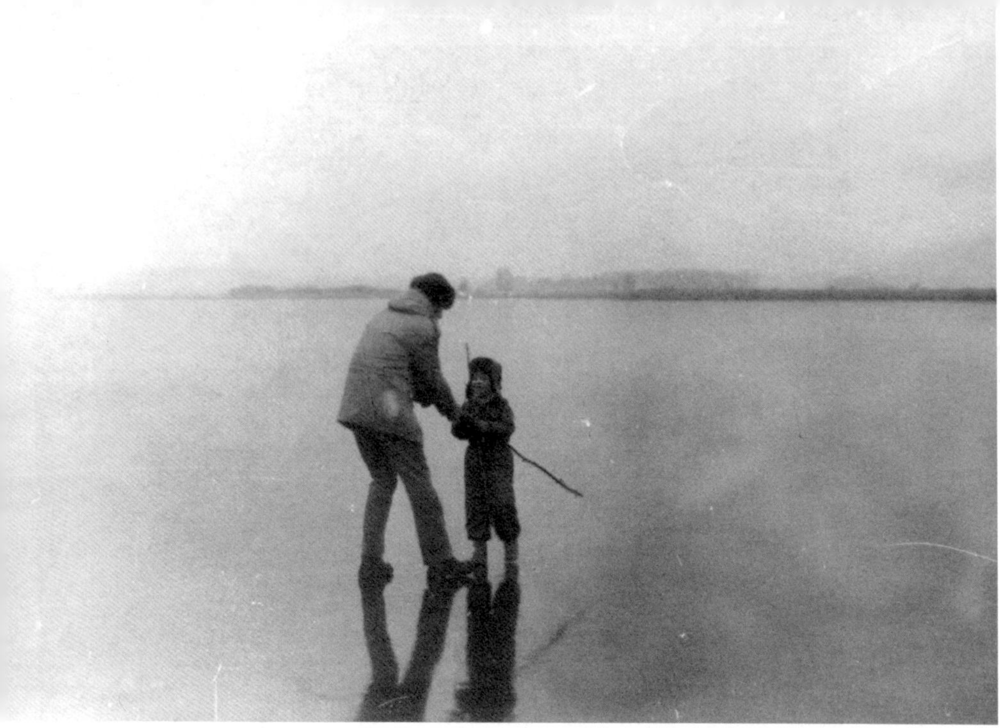

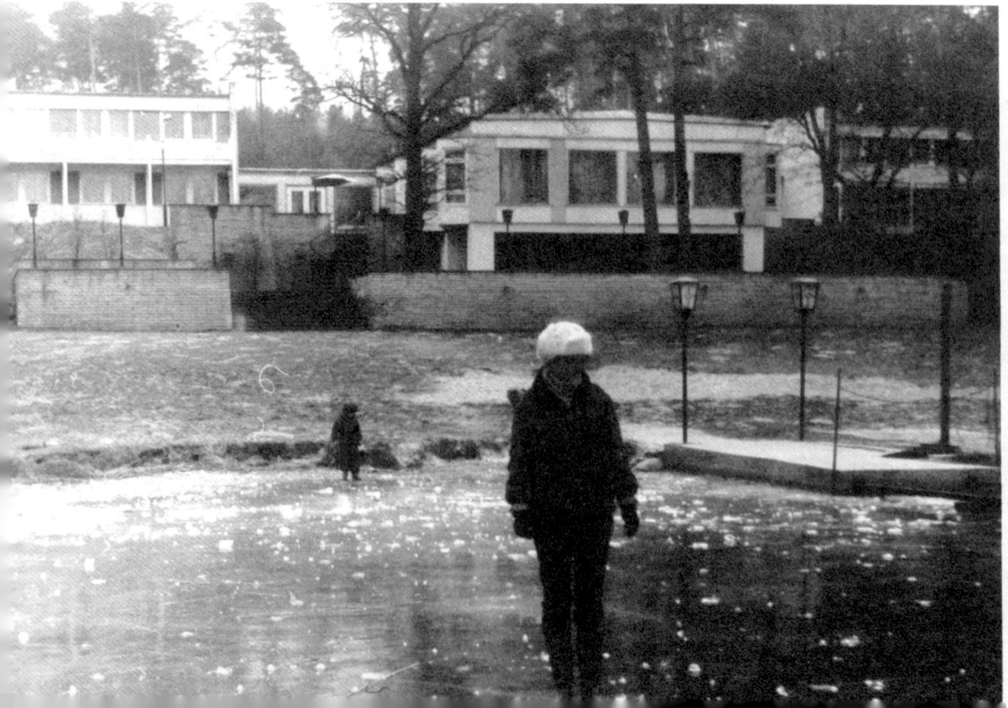

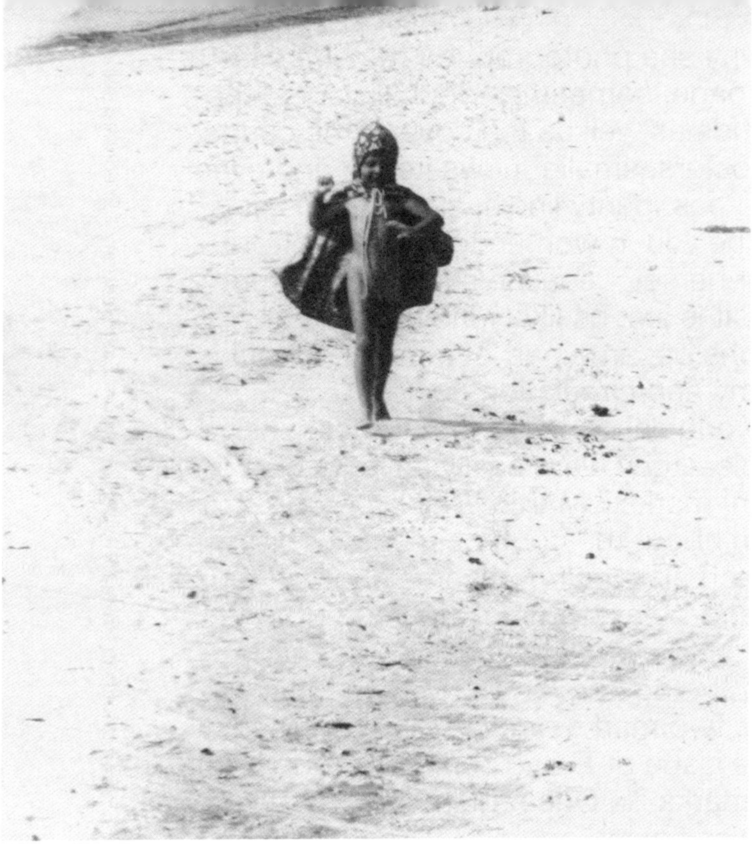

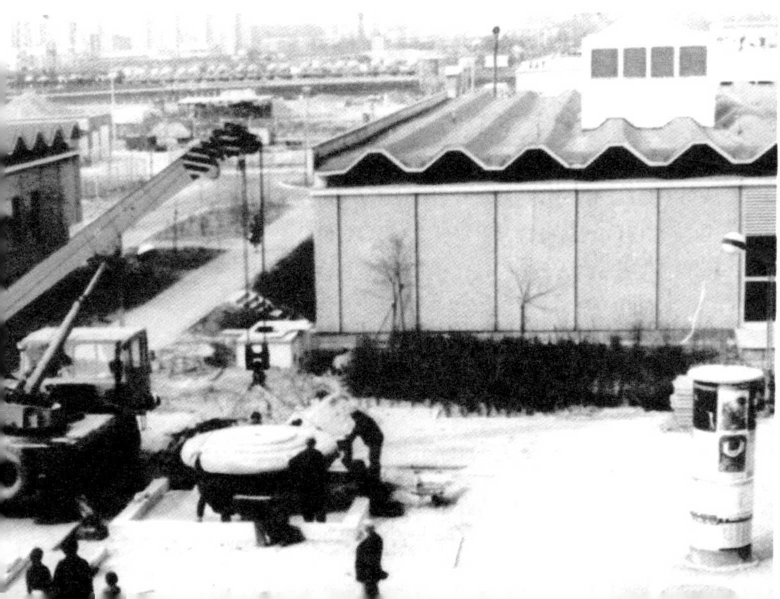

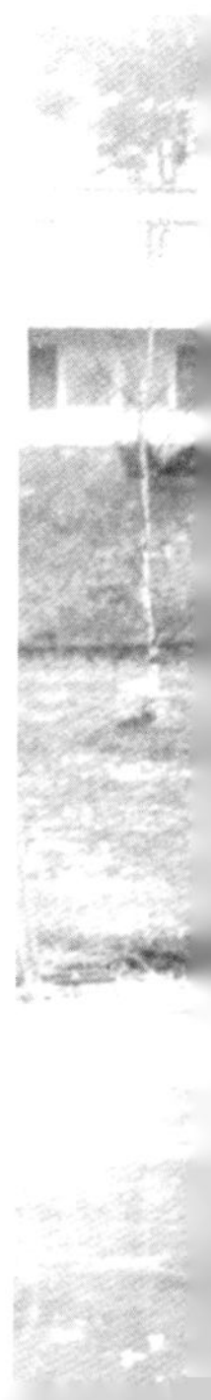

less unclear why she photographed the entire issue—mostly single page, sometimes double pages, the reports on bands as well as the covers, the charts, joke pages, posters, smaller news items, and even the ads for stereos, panty liners, and mopeds. It is possible that the young woman took these photographs just for herself because she had to return the magazine. It is just as likely, however, that her photographs became part of a rather specific image economy and circulation.

"The original posters were too expensive for most people—they were easily seventy or eighty [eastern] marks," Martin Weinhold says in a conversation about the contact sheets of his negatives, which also included some shots of music magazines, "and before you sold it, you photographed it, even the whole magazine. We made small prints of the posters and sold them at school for a fair price, two marks or so. Including these prints, a single issue of *Bravo* could be worth a total of about 600 marks."(9) One requirement for these transactions was having one's own dark room to be independent of professional photo labs. Martin Weinhold again: "I started working in my own lab relatively early; we had set it up in the attic [in his best friend's grandfather's house]. In winter it was difficult, the developer partly froze; in summer we put ice cubes in the baths to cool them down…"(10)

Thus, the private cameras and darkrooms served as a substitute for another Western commodity that was rare and difficult for ordinary citizens to access: the photocopier.(11) In fact, not only music magazines from the West were reproduced in this way, but also record covers, soccer magazines,

9 Album conversation with Martin Weinhold, Berlin, June 13, 2021. 0:06:24.

10 Album conversation with Martin Weinhold, Berlin, June 13, 2021. 0:05:37.

11 For texts in particular, there were also other reproduction processes, above all typewritten carbon copies and transfers.

pornographic images, and sometimes entire books.(12) The prints were sold at school, passed on to friends, and sometimes photographed again.(13) Unlike family pictures, they were not pasted into albums because they were hardly addressed to an audience other than the owner alone; moreover, they did not record a communal event, a subjective affect, a memory, but, like other reproductions, primarily ensured that otherwise inaccessible information was available. With the opening of the borders, the demise of the GDR, and the influx of goods from the West, which was no longer subject to controls, not only the preconditions for this practice of image production and circulation disappeared, but also the images themselves. Having become worthless, there was no reason to keep the loose prints. The photographs were only preserved if they were practically invisible—as negatives.(14)

III.

If *Dallas*, *Kennzeichen D*, and *Rockpalast* made it possible to spend a few evening hours in the West, at least with one's eyes and ears, consumer goods from there enabled their owners to have other sensual borderline experiences: "Yes, that was a beer!" is written on the back of a photograph of a can of *Beck's* beer, which was arranged with some care on an oil barrel so that the entire logo was visible. (fig. 3) The caption reflects both the long-ago pleasure as well as the lament that one could not drink such a beer every evening, but had to make do with the goods that were available at HO (Handelsorganisa-

12 This sort of reproduction was sometimes used outside of private contexts as well: for example, the library of the Hochschule für Grafik und Buchkunst (HGB) in Leipzig has an edition of the book of photographs *Family of Man* consisting of bound prints on baryta paper.

13 This appears to have been done with pornographic photos.

14 Although the practice itself was widespread, and we asked about it in many conversations about albums, we have not yet found a single print of such photographs.

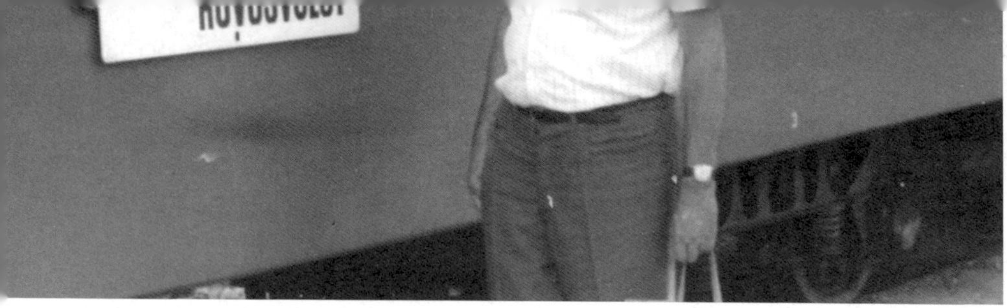

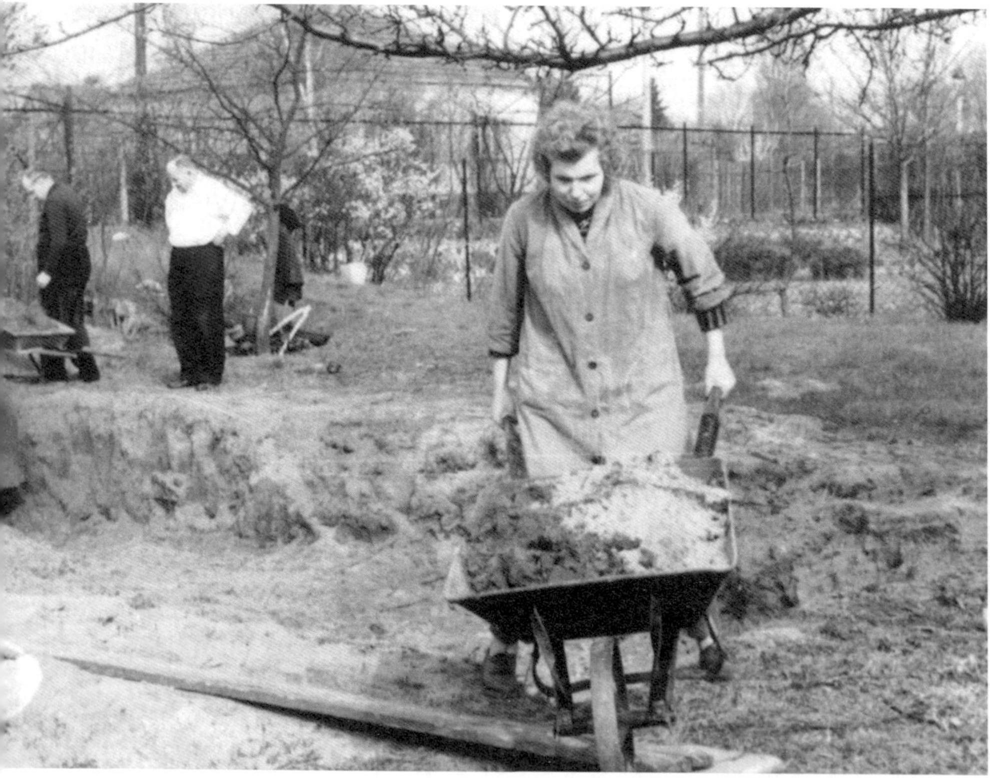

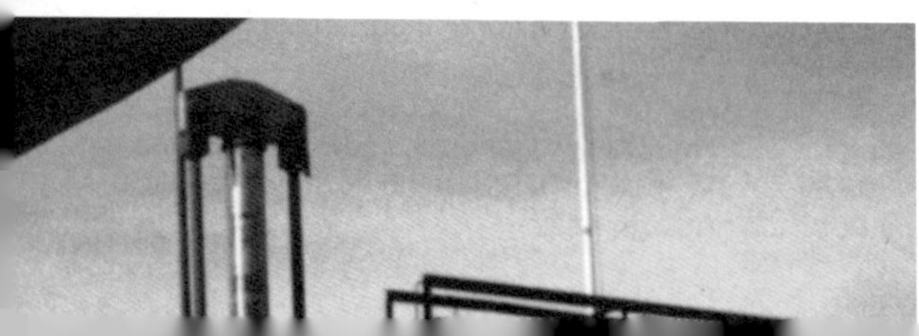

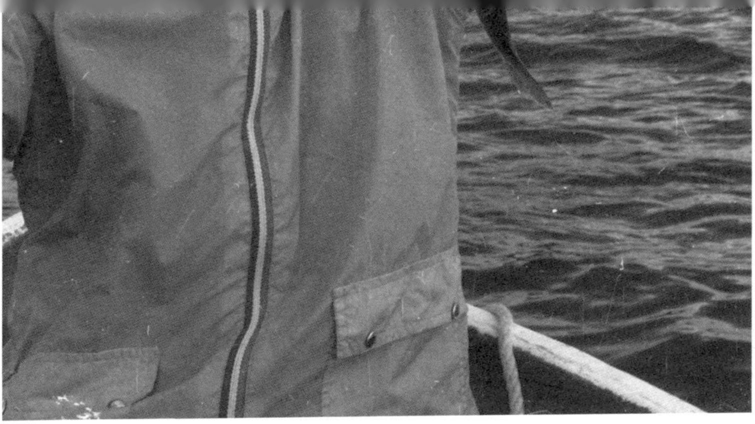

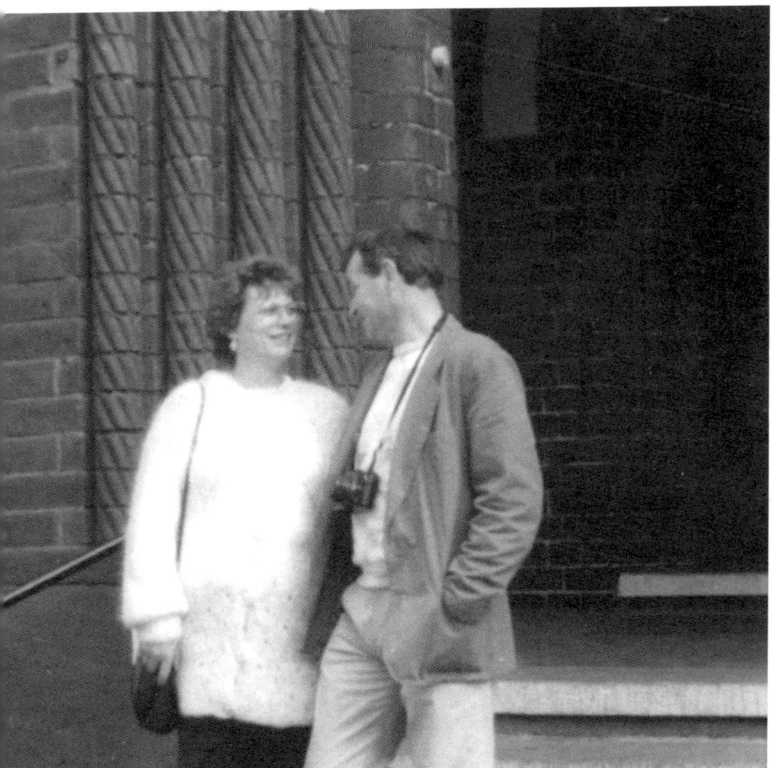

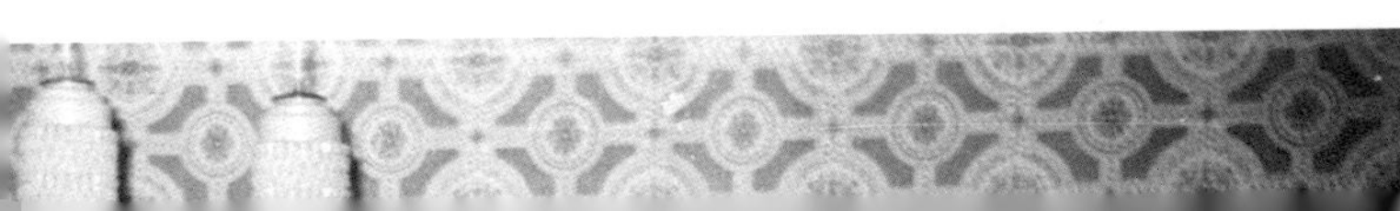

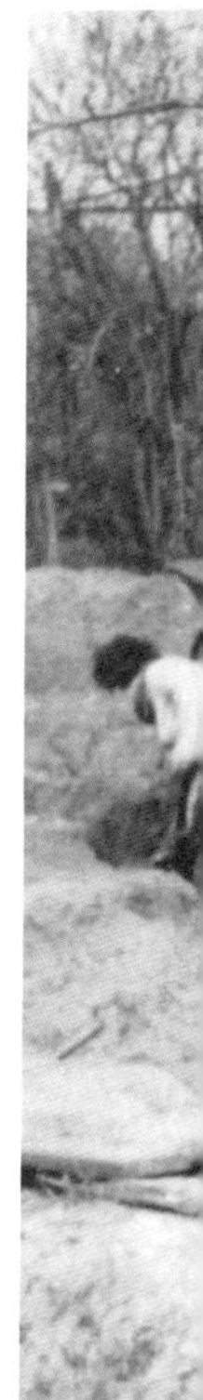

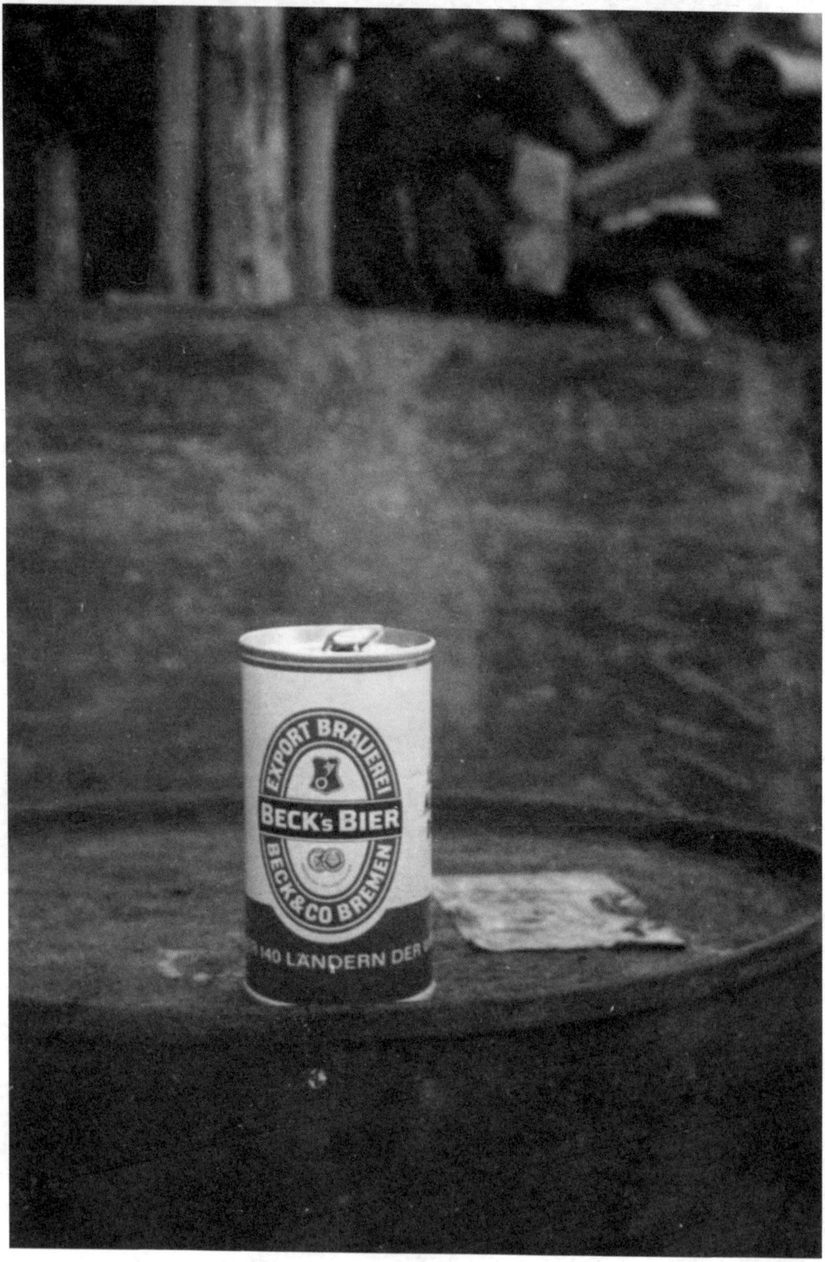

Fig. 3: *Beck's* beer can on an oil barrel. Undated print on baryta paper. Anonymous photographer. Author's archive.

tion, the state-owned retailer), which did not enjoy much of a reputation. (15) The attitude toward Western goods that can be read from this photograph and its caption applied quite generally. They were considered superior to Eastern products, a benchmark, and their rarity added to the pleasure. Just having access to them was prestigious. One had to have West German money to be able to shop in the Intershop, know sailors or so-called travel cadres, or have relatives or friends in West Germany who could also have West German goods delivered via the Genex gift service set up by GDR. This kind of supply was not always free of conflicts, for example, when the parcels contained used clothing or when the senders did not give a lot of thought to what the recipients might actually need. (16) Nevertheless, the supply of the GDR's population by relatives from the West was so essential that they were taken into account by the state leadership as an economic factor when planning the supply of the population with coffee and cocoa, for example (17) Goods received from the West were therefore used and

15 "The palates and stomachs of beer lovers in the GDR cannot have been all too refined until now. Radeberger, probably the best beer from the GDR, is brewed in the modest quantity of 400,000 hectoliters, and sold primarily abroad and in hard-currency hotels. The beer citizens of the GDR could obtain in HO stores was of a different quality. West German brewers tell real horror stories about their tours of the GDR. They hear talk of ox gall being substituting for the unavailable hops that are necessary to give beer its bitter flavor. Cuban sugar, they report with horror, is also in it." Anonymous, "Galle statt Hopfen," in: *Der Spiegel*, March 18, 1990.

16 See the reports by eyewitnesses in Härtel / Kabus, *Das Westpaket* (see note 6).

17 See Susanne Müller, *Von der Mangel- zur Marktwirtschaft. Analyse der Konsumbedingungen und des Konsumverhaltens in der DDR (Teilprojekt 1)*, Leipzig: Institut für Marktforschung 2000, enclosure 28/3, table 6. It indicates that the import of coffee via packages in 1978 was just under 9,000 metric tons, corresponding to 19% of the quantity calculated in the state's provision plan. That same year, 1,900 metric tons of cocoa powder arrived in the GDR in packets from the West, which amounted to 136% of the quantity in the provision plan. On this, see also Annette Kaminsky, "'Nieder mit den Alu-Chips': Die private Einfuhr von Westwaren in die DDR," in: Härtel / Kabus (eds.), *Das Westpaket* (see note 6), pp. 161–77, esp. p. 172.

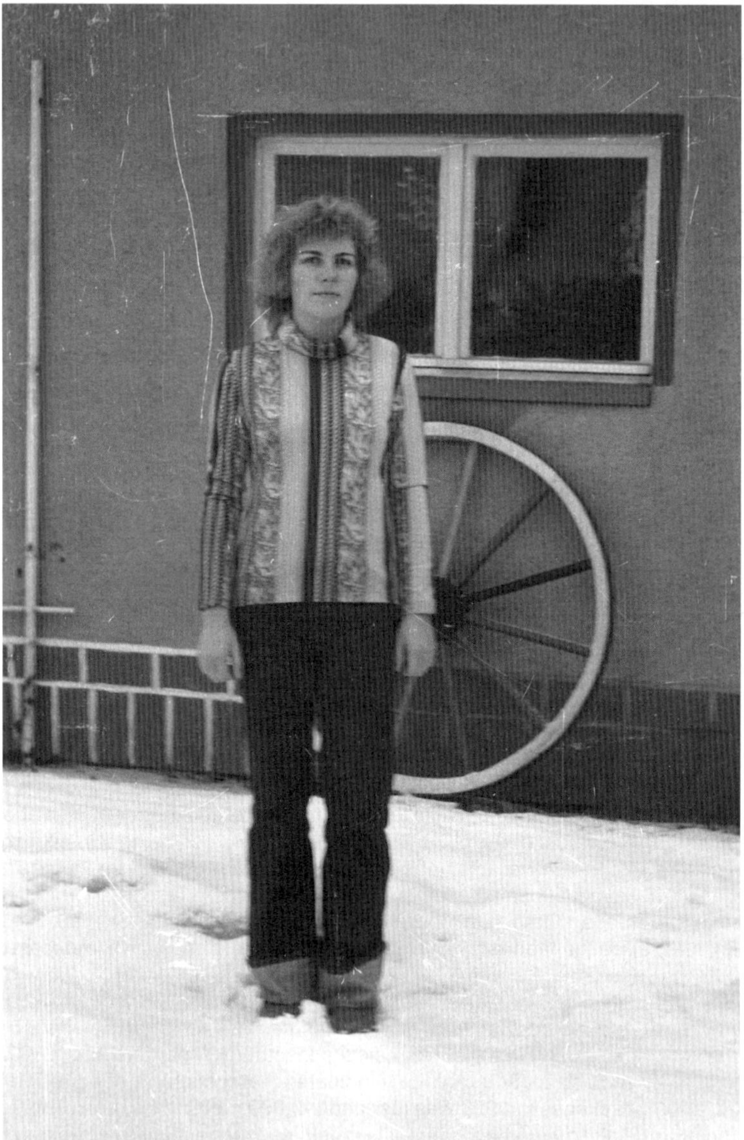

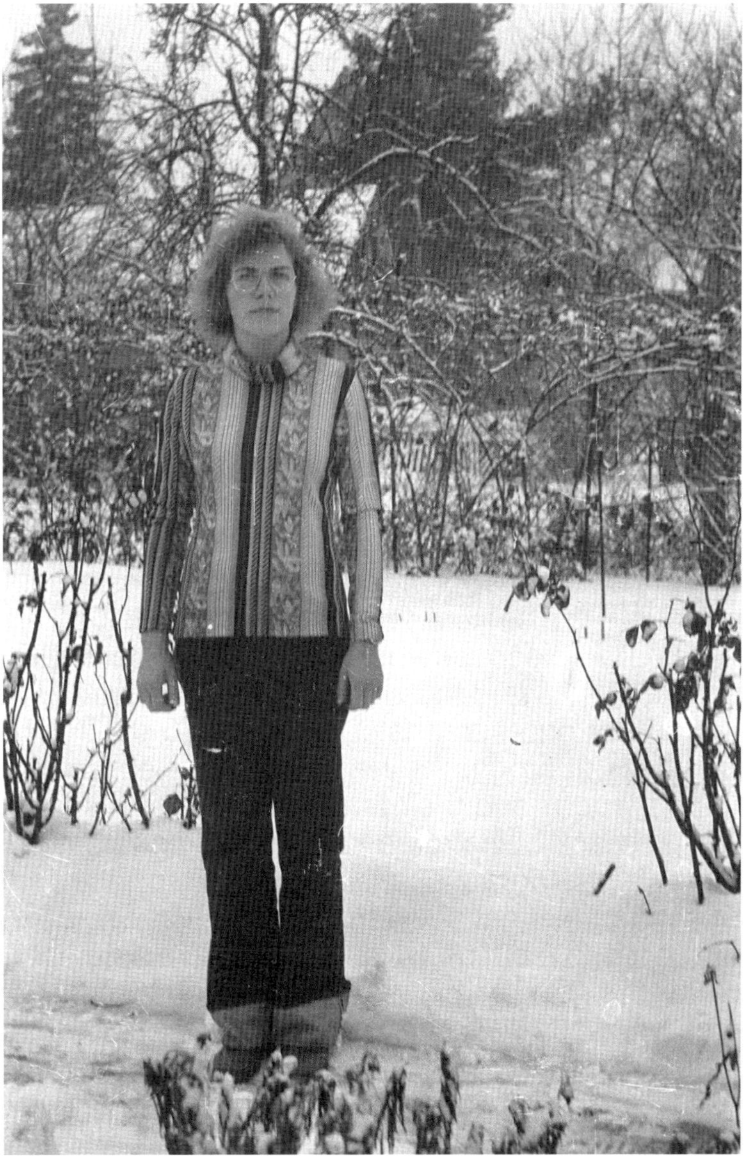

consumed sparingly, and enjoyment was sometimes postponed, staged or even even fetishistically prolonged. The soap was not unpacked at all but displayed in its box on the bathroom shelf as a status symbol while empty cans of coffee from the West were filled with coffee from the East to ennoble it. When the West beer was drunk, one cut off the lid of the empty can and made a pen holder for the desk out of it. They were washed and put in a showcase with all the other empty Western packages, or, as in this photograph, they were portrayed standing on a tin barrel, perhaps with the silent wish that it might be full of good beer and not stinky oil.

Photographing them is just one of the many ways in which Western goods were elevated to the status of luxury goods in the GDR—when the Western packages arrived, their unpacking was sometimes accompanied by the camera.(18) Then people posed with the new pair of jeans or cans of coffee; and anyone who received the gift of a Golf via Genex would sit in the car beaming with pride. But no less proudly smiled into the camera those who, after a long wait, were finally able to take delivery of a Wartburg. Goods from the West were thus not absolutely required in the GDR for photographs of this kind. To put it another way, these photographs were not just celebrating Western goods and their possession. They also documented a lack being remedied. Typologically, they resemble photographs taken in West Germany and other countries that show the joy of a first car, a new doll, or a bottle of fine whisky. They were different, however, insofar as this relative lack can also become indirectly visible in these photographs—what triggered such a melancholy, wistful sigh in the unknown beer lover was a rather ordinary part of everyday consumption for a West German beer drinker.

18 We have not encountered any such pictures of unpacking as part of our project. Härtel/Kabus, *Das Westpaket*, does, however, have several examples (see note 6).

IV.

"On November 9, they opened the border," Georg Mohr recounts, the corresponding album on the table, "and a week later, we went to Mölln. Actually, we wanted to go to Lübeck. But when we passed through Satow and came to the road that led to Lübeck, it was packed with cars, nothing but red taillights, and nothing but headlights behind us, and traffic went at a walking pace, a car length took two, three minutes. After we had moved forward a hundred meters in this way, we got fed up and said to ourselves: we are going to Mölln. […] Before that, we had been given fifteen marks in West German money at the State Bank of the GDR [in Rostock]." He taps on the photo of two banknotes in the album, "and then we went to the bank in Mölln and got our welcome money.(19) The crowds stood at the bank, there were at least another hundred more people in front of it. […] And then we marched through Mölln with our welcome money. My daughter grabbed a shopping basket and went into Aldi and loaded it up. And I stood there like an idiot, not knowing what to put in my basket. I was totally overwhelmed by what I saw there—not just impressed, I was overwhelmed. And then in the third store, the daughter said: 'Give it to me, father, give me your basket,' and then she loaded it up for me. And this is what she packed," says Georg Mohr pointing to a second photograph in the album: on a table in the apartment are marzipan, chocolate, licorice, canned fruit, toothpaste, two oranges, and three bunches of bananas. (fig. 4)

Surely Georg Mohr is not telling this story for the first time, but the astonishment has still not been exhausted: now what had been unattainable for years was within reach. One had money, one could go to the stores, one could choose something for oneself, and there was so much of everything, ultimately too much.

19 The welcome money or *Begrüßungsgeld* was paid by the government of the FRG to visitors and refugees from the GDR from 1970 to 1989.

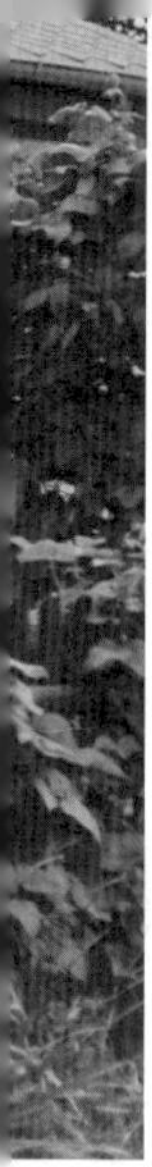
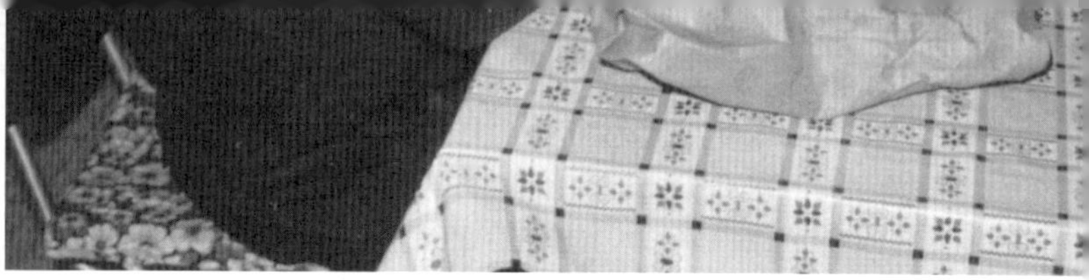
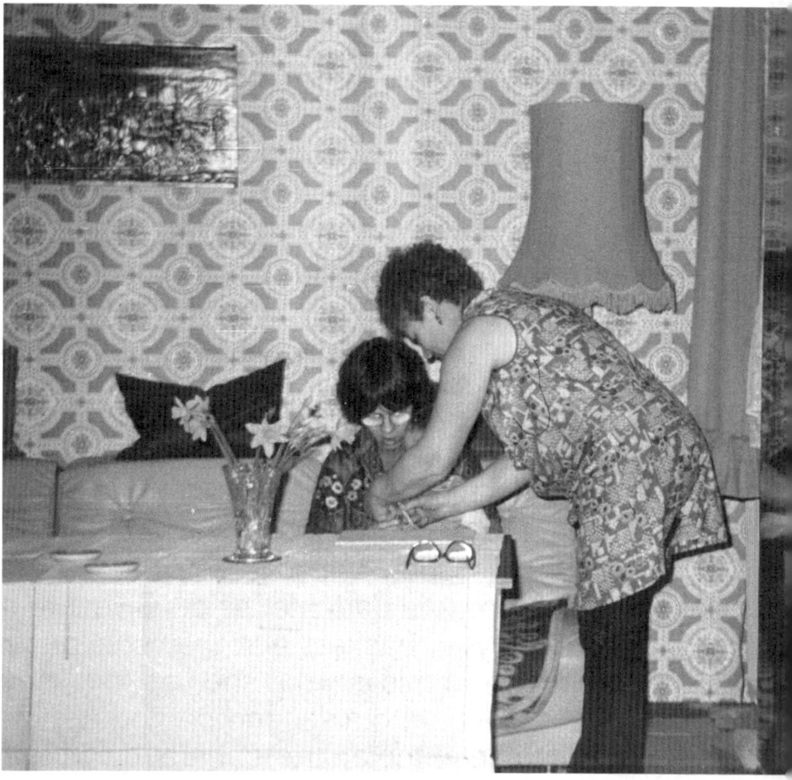
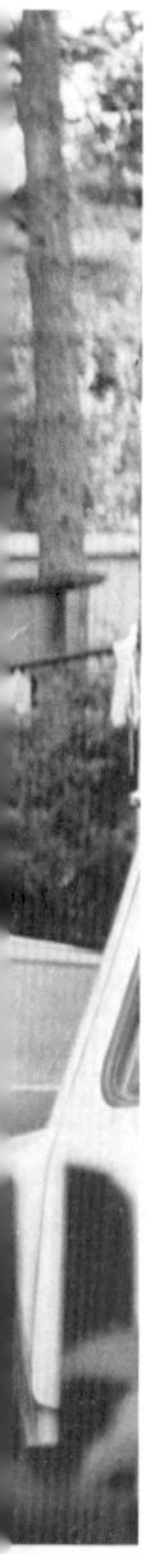
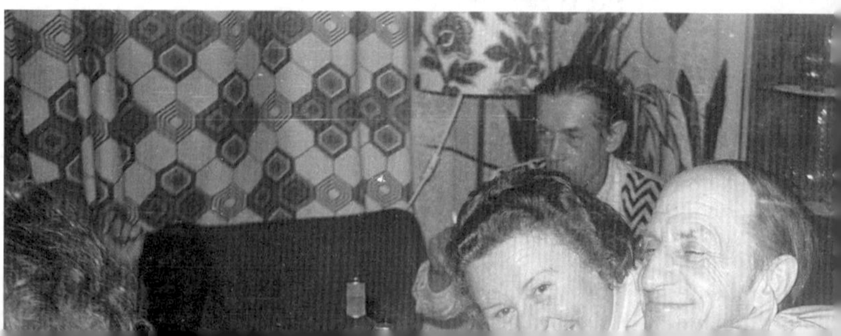

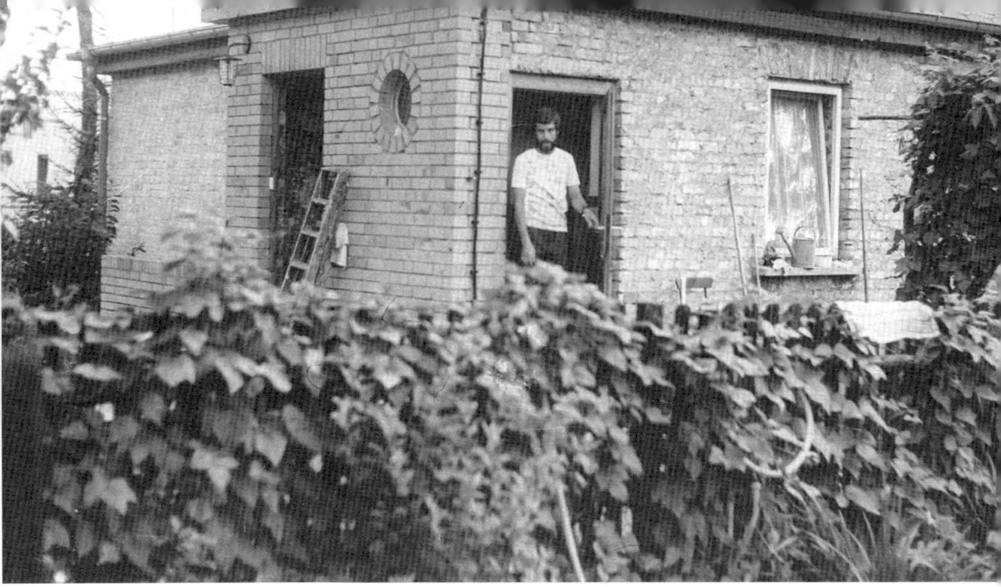

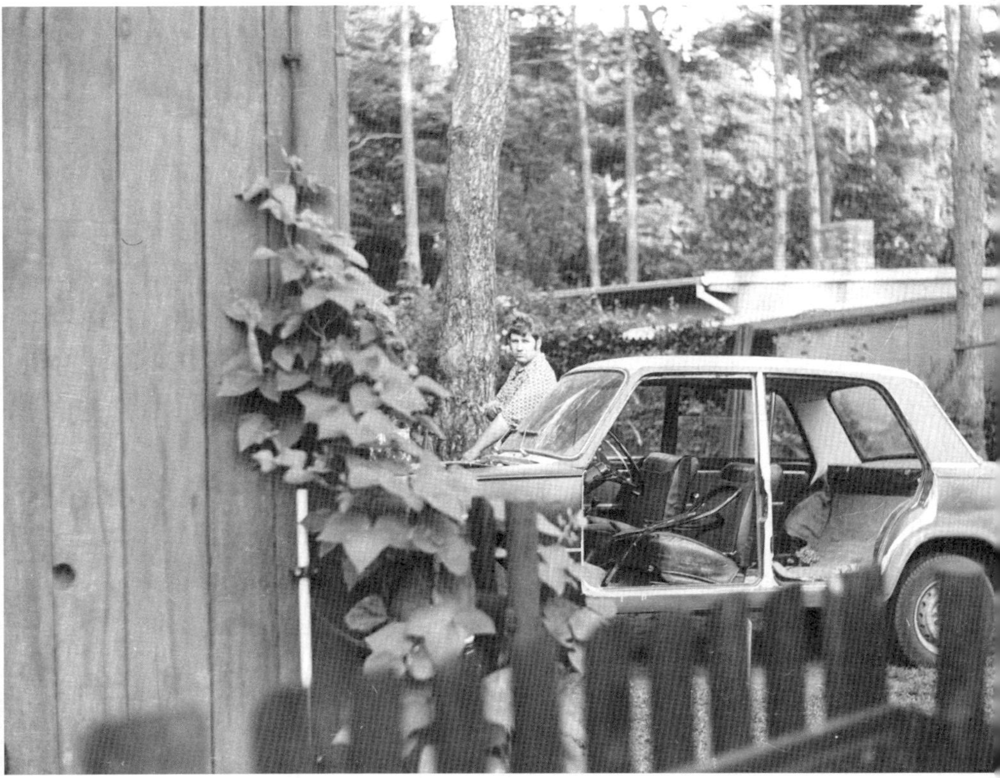

His daughter solved the problem pragmatically by loading up what probably had once been on wish lists and came into the house via packages from the West. Her father reacted by doing what he had always done when something was new, interesting, strange, beautiful, pleasing: he took photographs. Although not of the walk through the supermarket itself or the sense of being overwhelmed in front of the shelves, but between the two photographs mentioned in the conversation there is a shot (taken by the daughter) of her father looking away from a display window and into the camera, in addition to some views of the city. What Georg Mohr finally photographs and pasts in the album is his first purchase with West German money.

And it is presumably also the last, because with the opening of the border Western goods may not have lost their aura, but they did loose their unavailability. The first purchase in Mölln could be followed by any number of others, provided the appropriate funds were available. And what's more with the Monetary Union on July 1, 1990, goods from West Germany found their way onto East German supermarket shelves. What had been the exception and luxury became the normality of everyday life. And in everyday life private photography finds no subjects. Therefore, at the latest with the unification of the two German states on October 3, 1990, the photographic practices described above came to an end. Photographs of television shows, music magazines, or of Western goods were no longer needed. The West had arrived in the East and ultimately began to reshape it in its image.

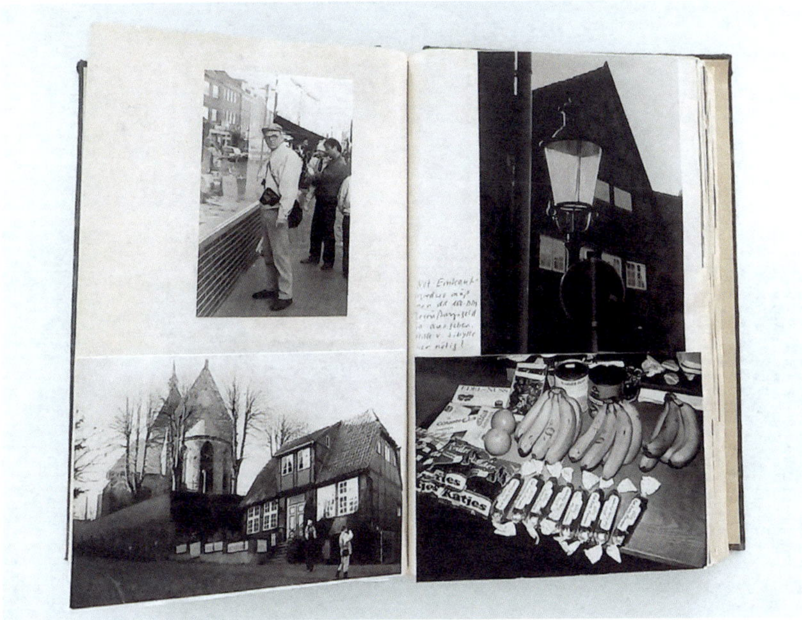

Fig. 4: Album conversation with Georg Mohr, Rostock, June 27, 2021. Videostill, 0:12:25.

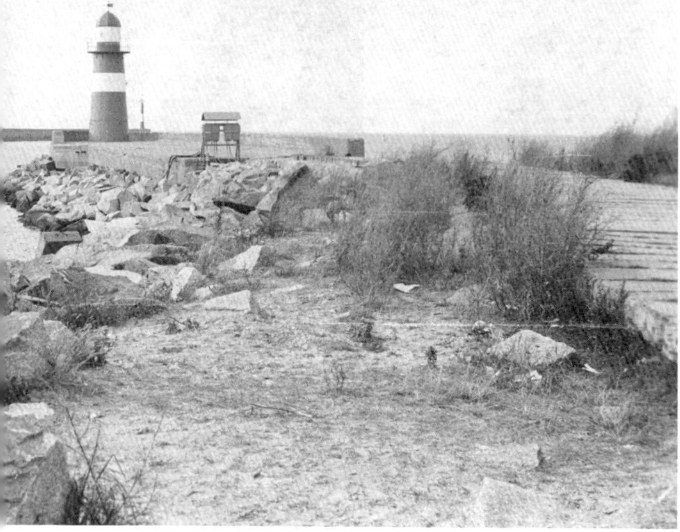

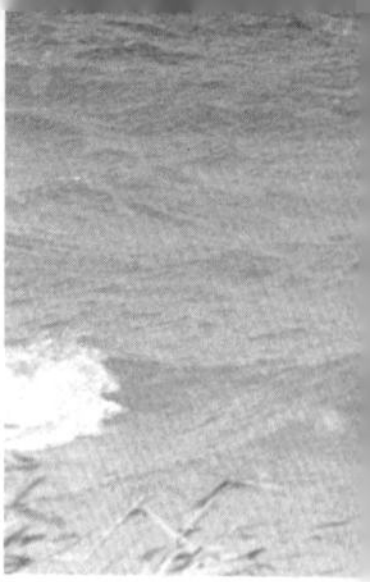

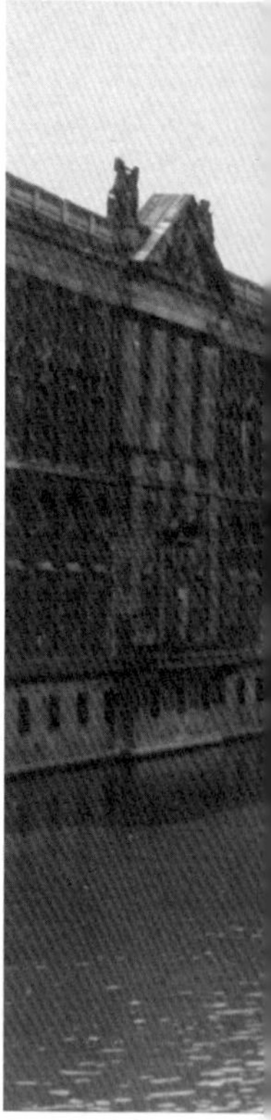

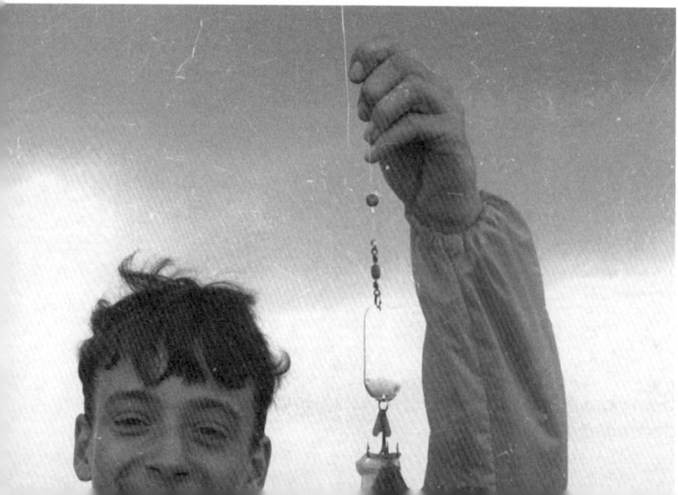

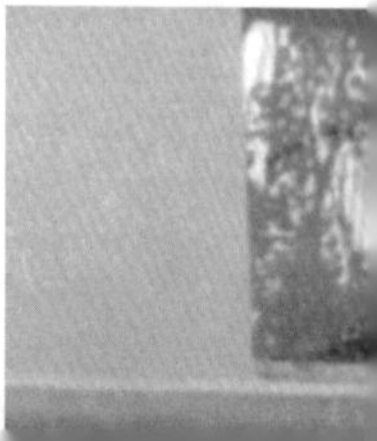

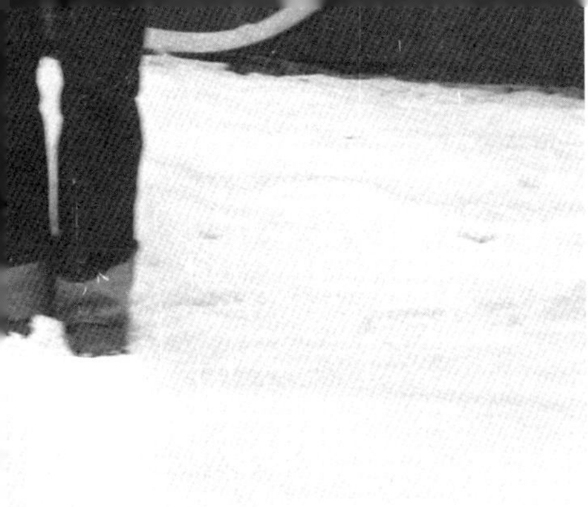

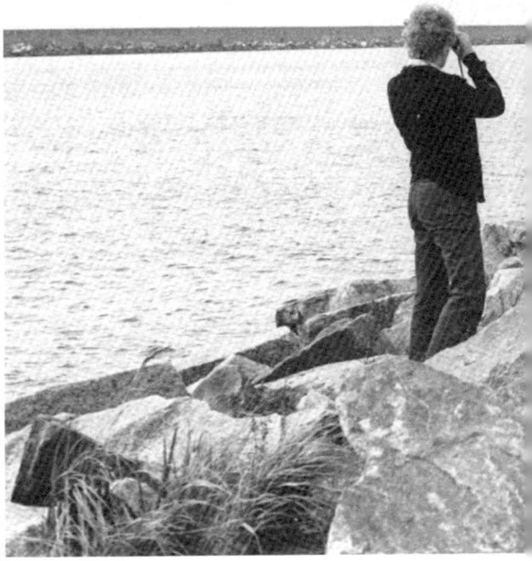

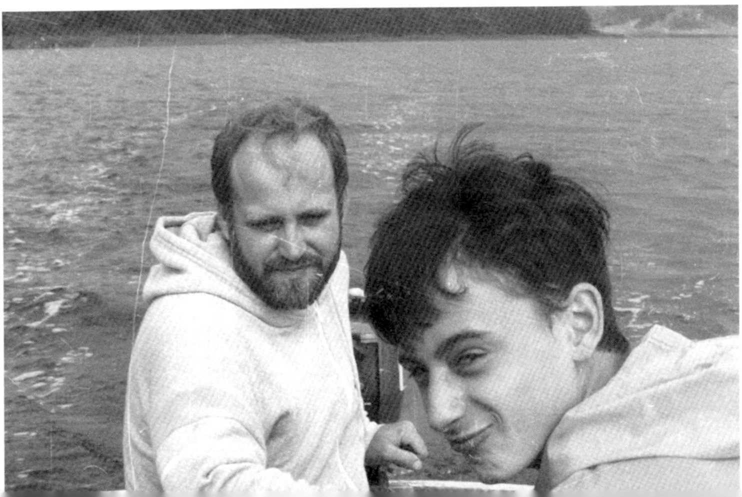

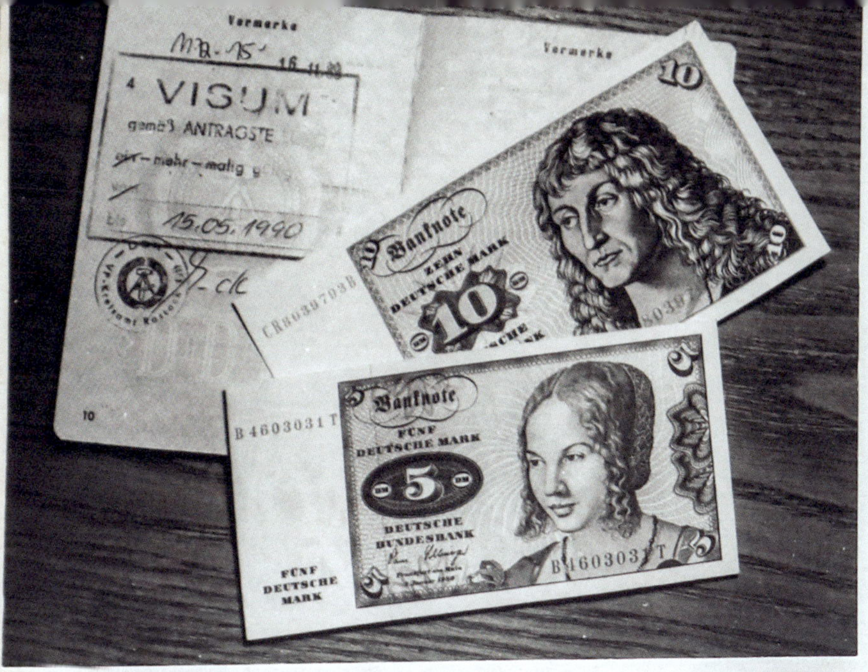
Vermerke
Vermerke
VISUM
gemäß ANTRAGSTE
15.05.1990
Banknote
ZEHN DEUTSCHE MARK
10
B4603031T
Banknote
FÜNF DEUTSCHE MARK
5
DEUTSCHE BUNDESBANK
B4603031T
FÜNF DEUTSCHE MARK

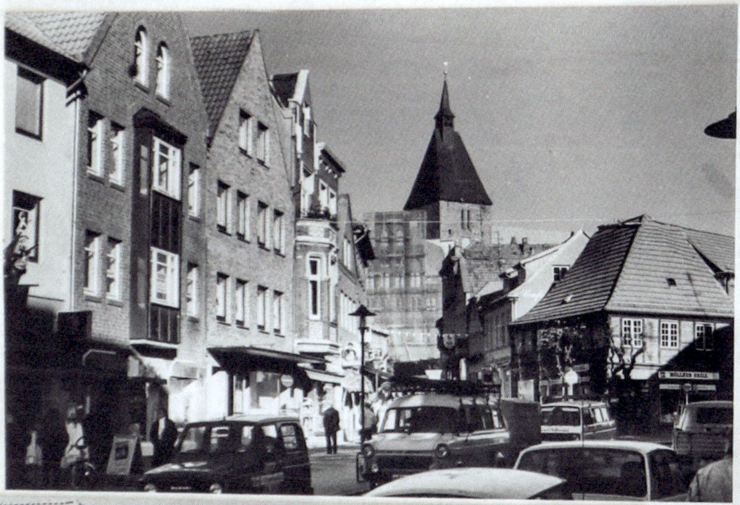

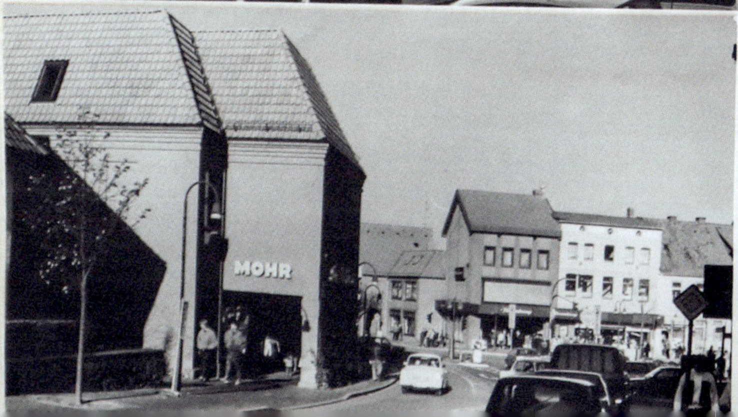
MOHR

Georg Mohr

Georg Mohr

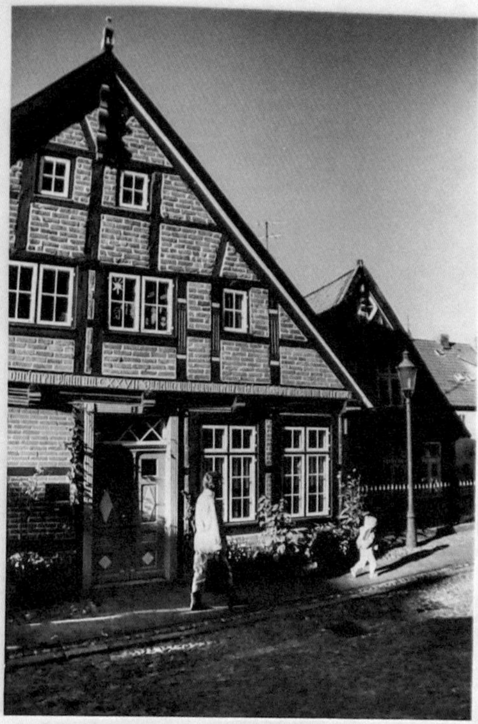

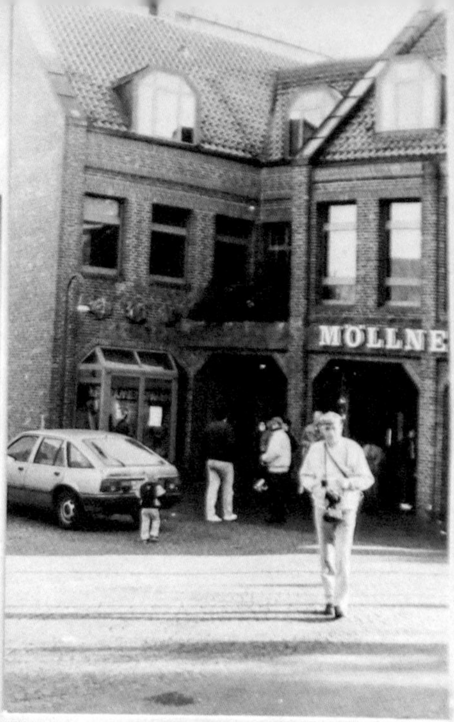

17.11.89 in Mölln/BRD
1 Woche nach Öffnung
der Grenze
1067

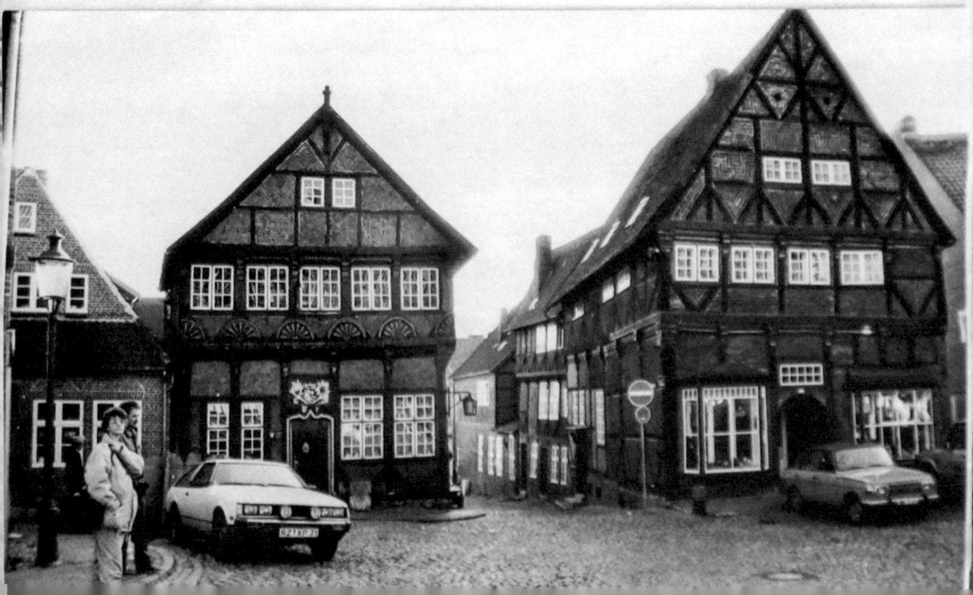

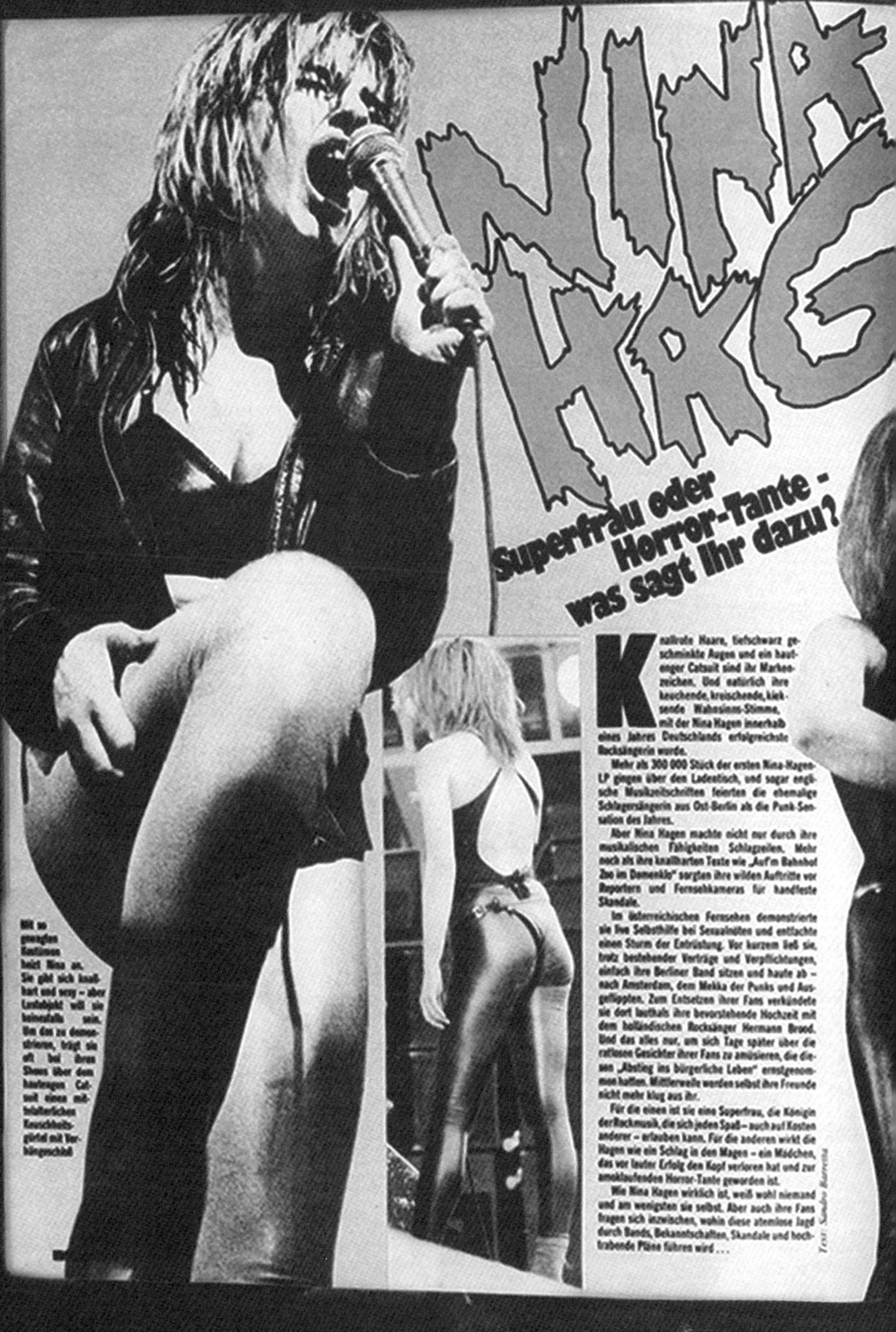

NINA HAGEN

Superfrau oder Horror-Tante – was sagt ihr dazu?

Knallrote Haare, tiefschwarz geschminkte Augen und ein hautenger Catsuit sind ihr Markenzeichen. Und natürlich ihre keuchende, kreischende, kieksende Wahnsinns-Stimme, mit der Nina Hagen innerhalb eines Jahres Deutschlands erfolgreichste Rocksängerin wurde.

Mehr als 300 000 Stück der ersten Nina-Hagen-LP gingen über den Ladentisch, und sogar englische Musikzeitschriften feierten die ehemalige Schlagersängerin aus Ost-Berlin als die Punk-Sensation des Jahres.

Aber Nina Hagen machte nicht nur durch ihre musikalischen Fähigkeiten Schlagzeilen. Mehr noch als ihre knallharten Texte wie „Auf'm Bahnhof Zoo im Damenklo" sorgten ihre wilden Auftritte vor Reportern und Fernsehkameras für handfeste Skandale.

Im österreichischen Fernsehen demonstrierte sie live Selbsthilfe bei Sexualnöten und entfachte einen Sturm der Entrüstung. Vor kurzem ließ sie, trotz bestehender Verträge und Verpflichtungen, einfach ihre Berliner Band sitzen und haute ab – nach Amsterdam, dem Mekka der Punks und Ausgeflippten. Zum Entsetzen ihrer Fans verkündete sie dort lauthals ihre bevorstehende Hochzeit mit dem holländischen Rocksänger Hermann Brood. Und das alles nur, um sich Tage später über die ratlosen Gesichter ihrer Fans zu amüsieren, die diesen „Abstieg ins bürgerliche Leben" ernstgenommen hatten. Mittlerweile werden selbst ihre Freunde nicht mehr klug aus ihr.

Für die einen ist sie eine Superfrau, die Königin der Rockmusik, die sich jeden Spaß – auch auf Kosten anderer – erlauben kann. Für die anderen wirkt die Hagen wie ein Schlag in den Magen – ein Mädchen, das vor lauter Erfolg den Kopf verloren hat und zur amoklaufenden Horror-Tante geworden ist.

Wie Nina Hagen wirklich ist, weiß wohl niemand und am wenigsten sie selbst. Aber auch ihre Fans fragen sich inzwischen, wohin diese atemlose Jagd durch Bands, Bekanntschaften, Skandale und hochtrabende Pläne führen wird …

Text: Sandra Barrera

Mit so gewagten Kostümen heizt Nina an. Sie gibt sich knallhart und sexy – aber Lustobjekt will sie keinesfalls sein. Um das zu demonstrieren, trägt sie oft bei ihren Shows über dem hautengen Catsuit einen mittelalterlichen Keuschheitsgürtel mit Vorhängeschloß

Archive Tietjen

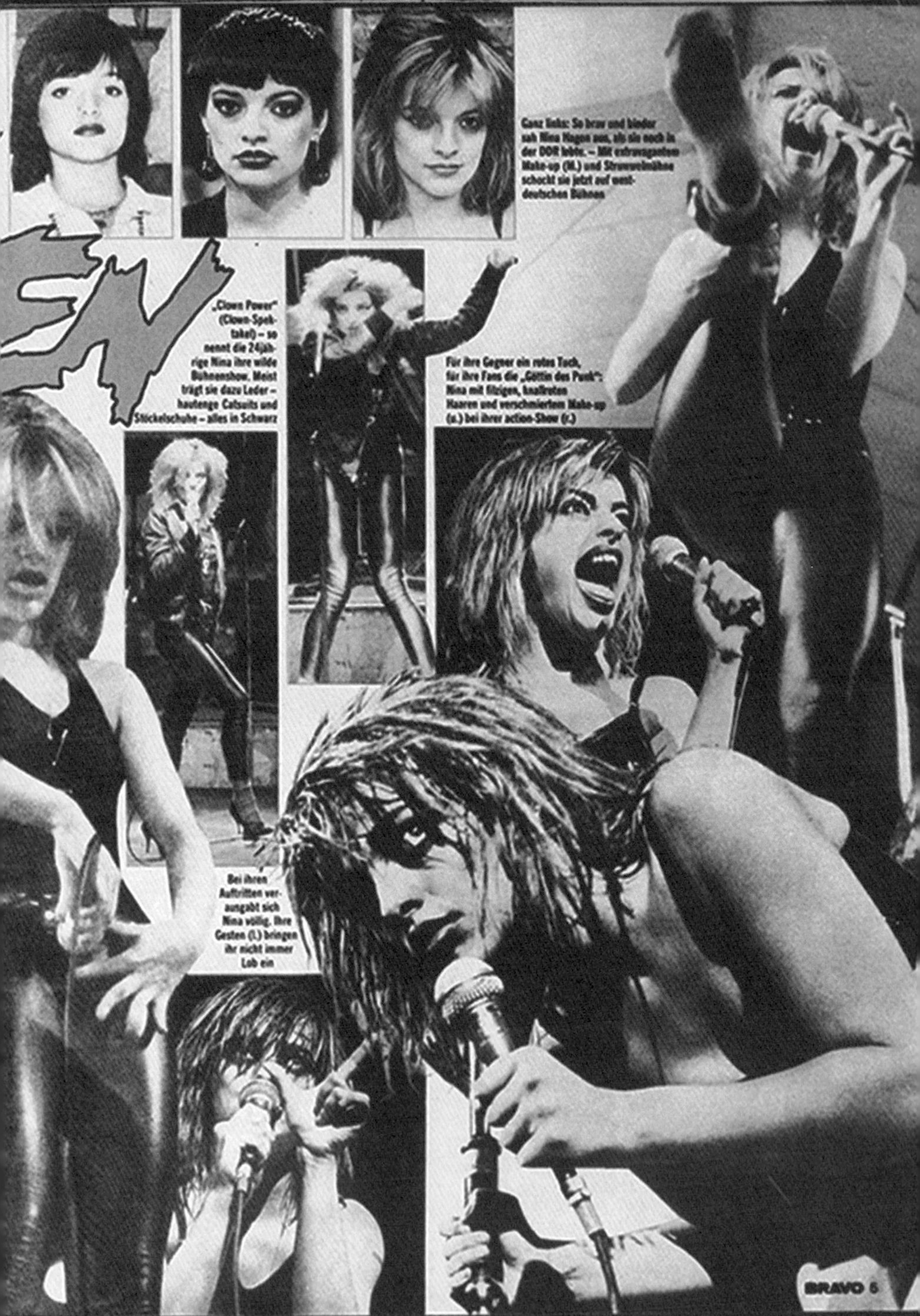

Ganz links: So brav und bieder sah Nina Hagen aus, als sie noch in der DDR lebte. – Mit extravagantem Make-up (M.) und Struwwelmähne schockt sie jetzt auf westdeutschen Bühnen

„Clown Power" (Clown-Spektakel) – so nennt die 24jährige Nina ihre wilde Bühnenshow. Meist trägt sie dazu Leder – hautenge Catsuits und Stöckelschuhe – alles in Schwarz

Für ihre Gegner ein rotes Tuch, für ihre Fans die „Göttin des Punk": Nina mit filzigen, knallroten Haaren und verschmiertem Make-up (u.) bei ihrer action-Show (r.)

Bei ihren Auftritten verausgabt sich Nina völlig. Ihre Gesten (l.) bringen ihr nicht immer Lob ein

Martin Weinhold

Martin Weinhold

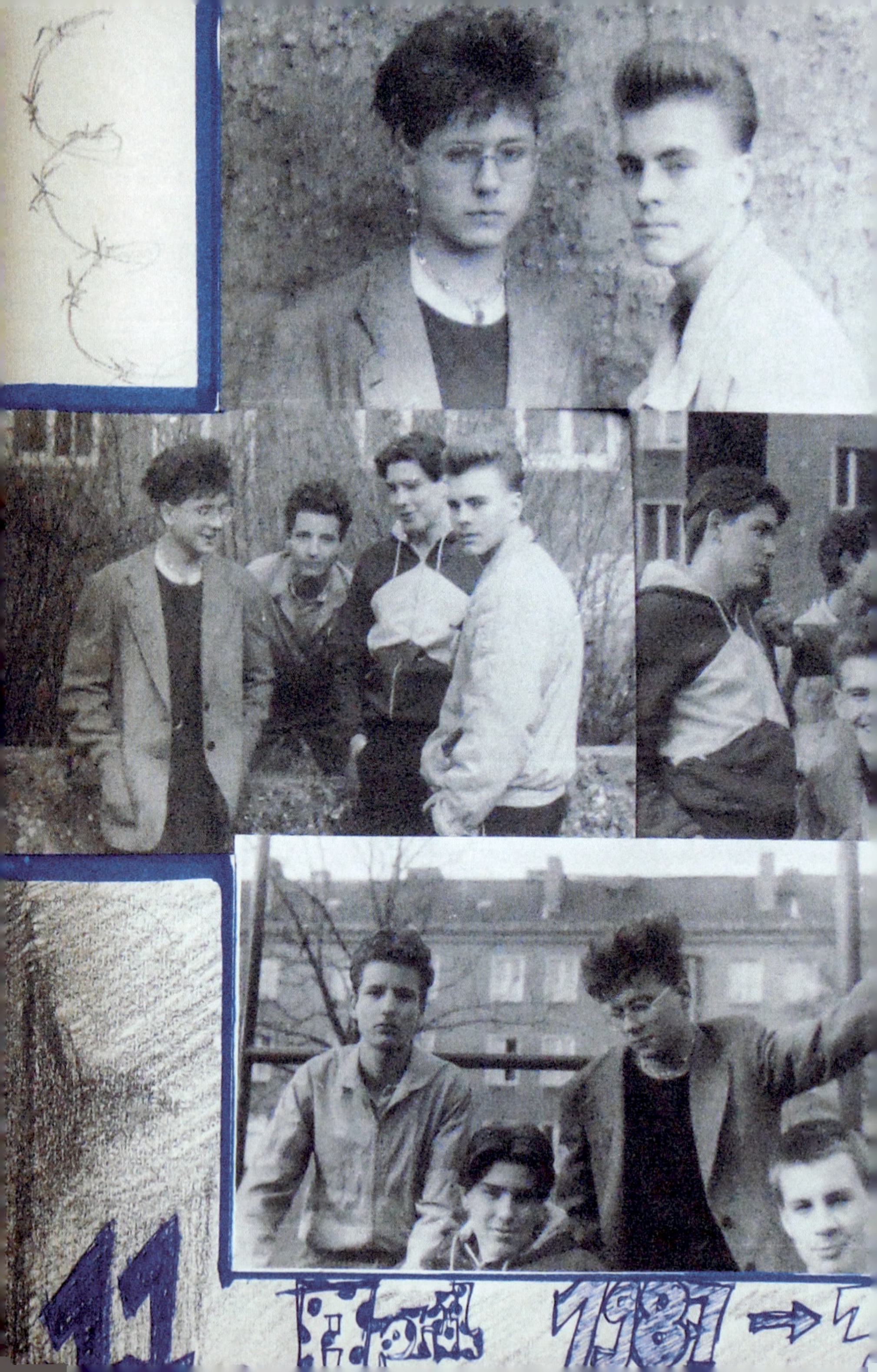
11
1981 →

On the following pages, ten collections of albums and photographs are presented. They were selected based on several criteria: the collections selected are relatively extensive; that is, they include many albums and/or photographs. They are diverse in terms of media: nearly all of them have not just black-and-white photographs but also other media such as postcards, purchased photographs, or ephemera such as tickets of all kinds, dried plants, and so on. The collections also differ in their structure: there are family albums and books of photographs as well as individual photographs, slides, and files with negatives. The collections are also thematically diverse; as a rule, they cover not only the familial and social milieu but also to varying degrees look at other aspects such as specific leisure activities or neighborhood developments. Finally, the collections are from different regions of Eastern Germany and from both larger and smaller towns; some go as far back in time as the nineteenth century, and some are still being continued today. This selection is, however, not representative, nor could it be, since several hundred albums and other visual media were examined as part of this project. In Eastern Germany, too, private photography is above all a mass medium of complex, contradictory, diverse practices, which therefore stubbornly evades most generalizations but also invites future studies that adopt not just qualitative but also quantitative perspectives.

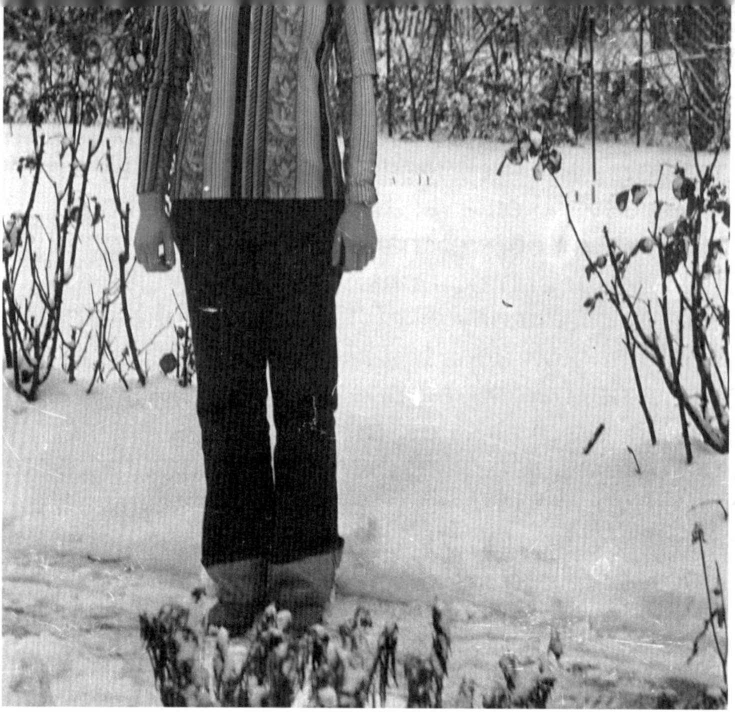

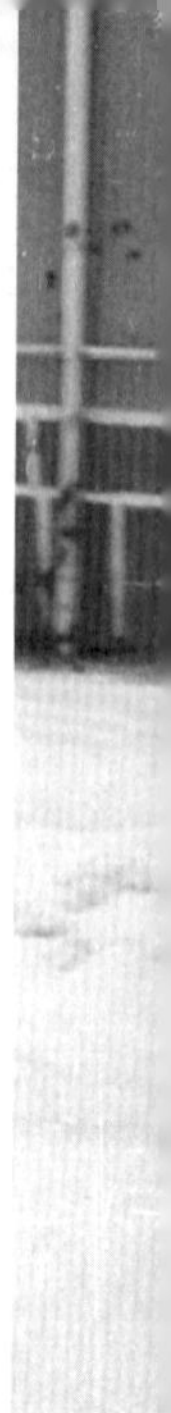

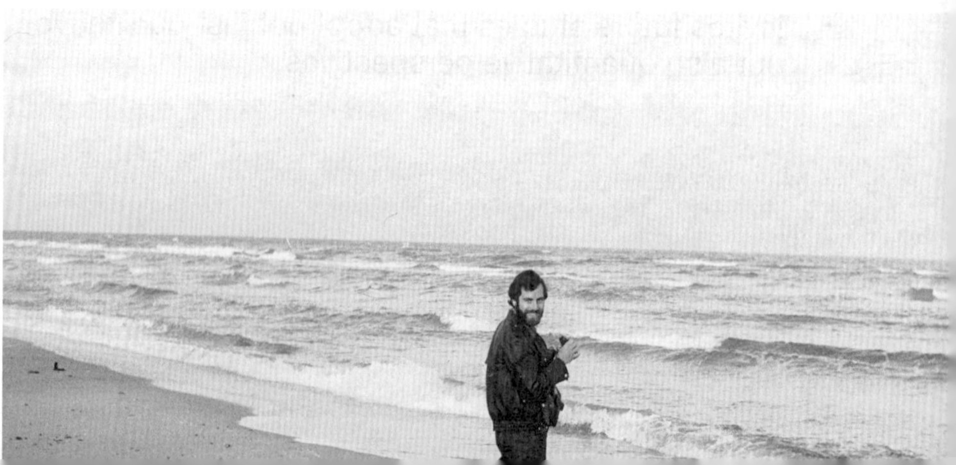

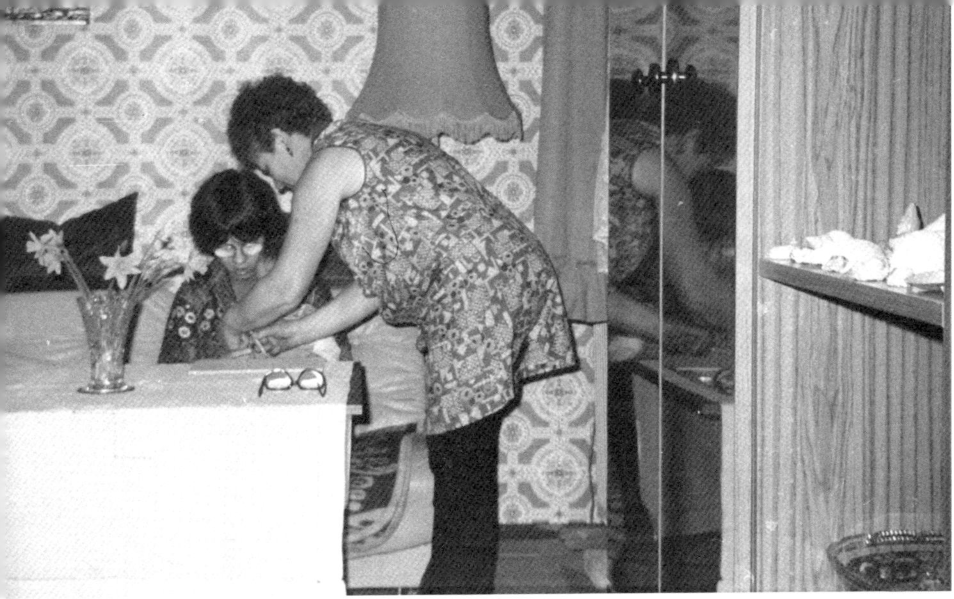

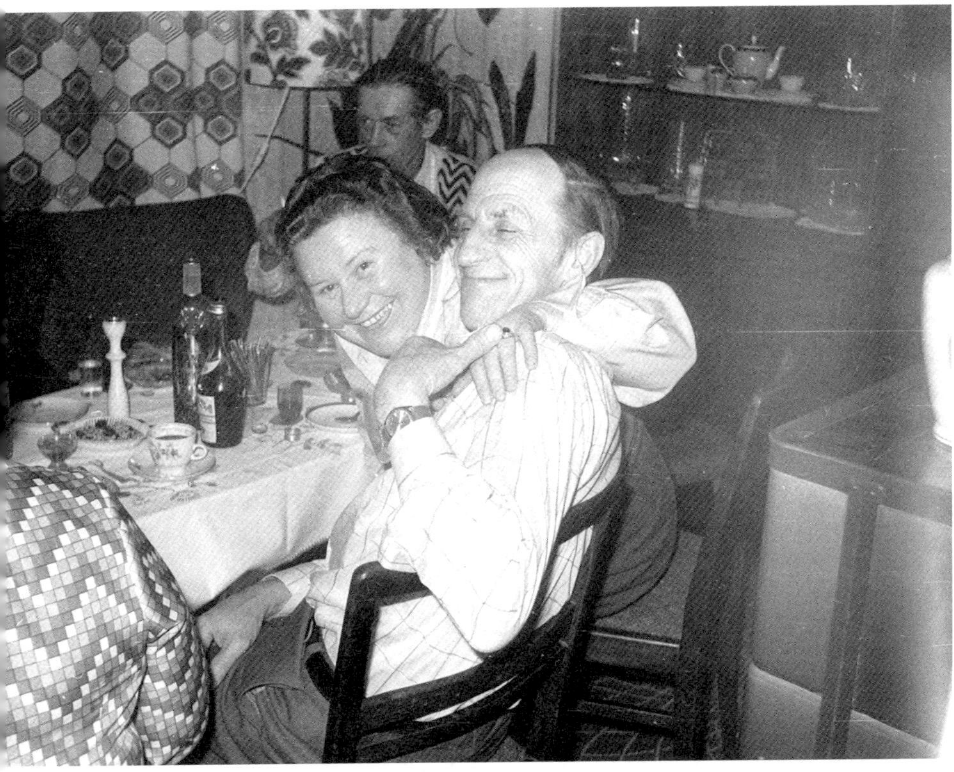

Borghild Carus, Berlin

Profession:	Archivist
Holdings:	About 50 albums, card index boxes, and envelopes with a total of around 4,000 photographs; arranged by places or themes and only then by year
Themes:	Above all Berlin's urban space and changes to it: architecture, street, demolition of buildings, as well as landscapes, nature, animals, clouds; occasional family events such as Jugendweihen (coming-of-age ceremonies) and other celebrations
Dates:	End of the 1960s to the present
Photo materials:	Black-and-white and color photographs, as well as postcards and ephemera such as brochures
Labeling:	Handwritten, usually identifying place, time, and sometimes the occasion
Storage:	Primarily in card index boxes; the general albums were split up

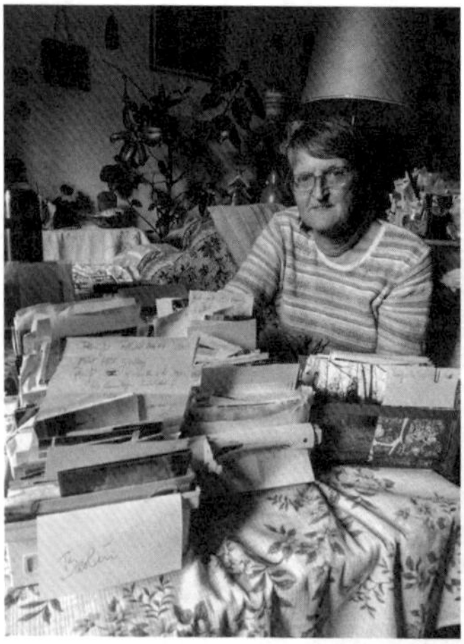

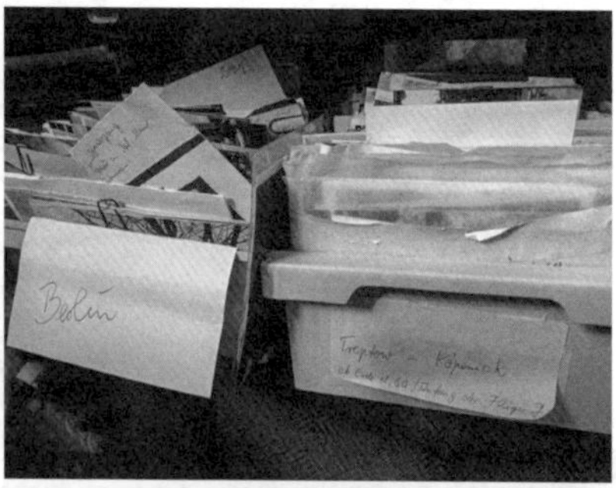

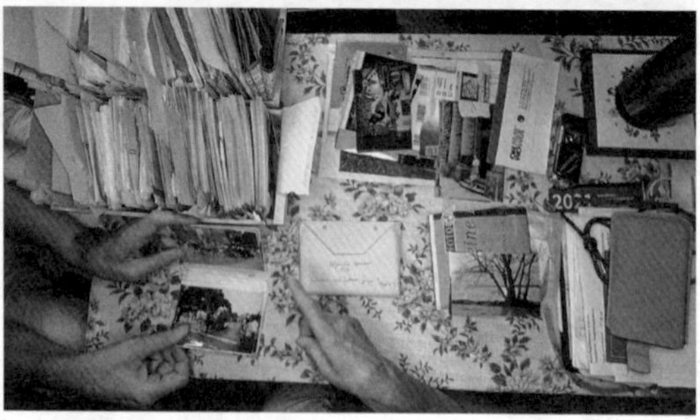

Fig. 1 Borghild Carus, Berlin, August 27, 2021. Photo: Project Archive.
Fig. 2 Archive boxes with photographs. Photo: Borghild Carus.
Fig. 3 Album conversation with Borghild Carus, Berlin, August 27, 2021. Video still.

13 Beate and Jürgen Göldner, Potsdam

Profession:	Research associate and engineer in urban development
Holdings:	Sixteen albums of 40 to 100 pages
Themes:	Primarily daily life and vacations (arranged chronologically)
Dates:	From 1950 to ca. 1994
Photo materials:	Black-and-white photographs, early color photographs, color prints from slides as well as plane and train tickets, admission tickets, hostel IDs, brochures, postcards, slips of paper, poems, and other ephemera
Type of reproduction:	A few photographs were developed in a friend's private darkroom
Labeling:	Handwritten in ink or ballpoint pen
Additional holdings of private photographs:	About 10,000 slides from 1973 to 2014
Storage:	Overwhelmingly in albums, but also in files, boxes, and slide boxes; in addition, there is a "House and Garden Book" that has been kept since 2009 with photographs and weather reports from the media; annually designed calendars with their own photographs; individual images on the walls of the room and on shelves (living and deceased family members from 1910 onward, individual vacation impressions and the like)

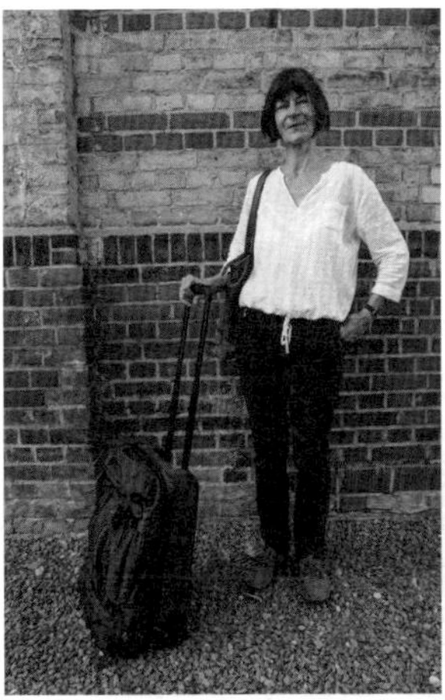

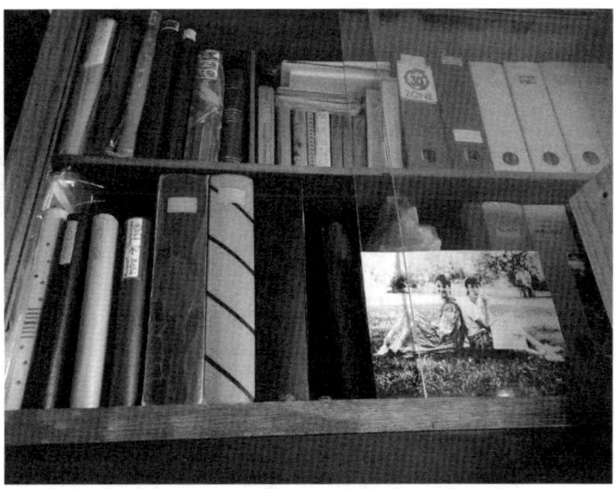

Fig. 1 Beate Göldner, Potsdam, July 24, 2020. Photo: Project Archive.
Fig. 2 Beate and Jürgen Göldner: Cabinets with photo albums. Photo: Project Archive.

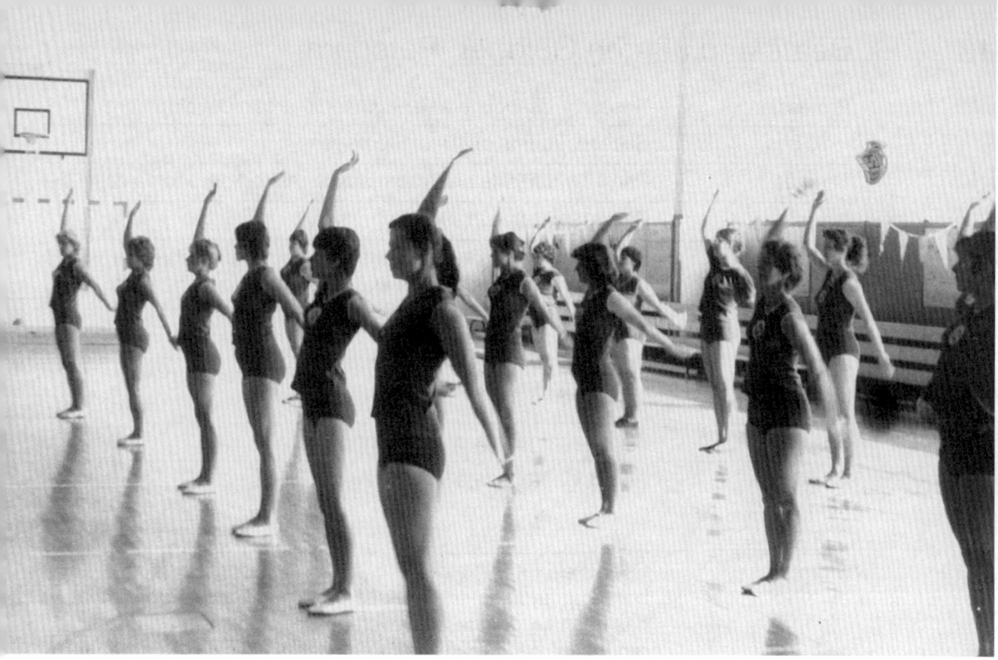

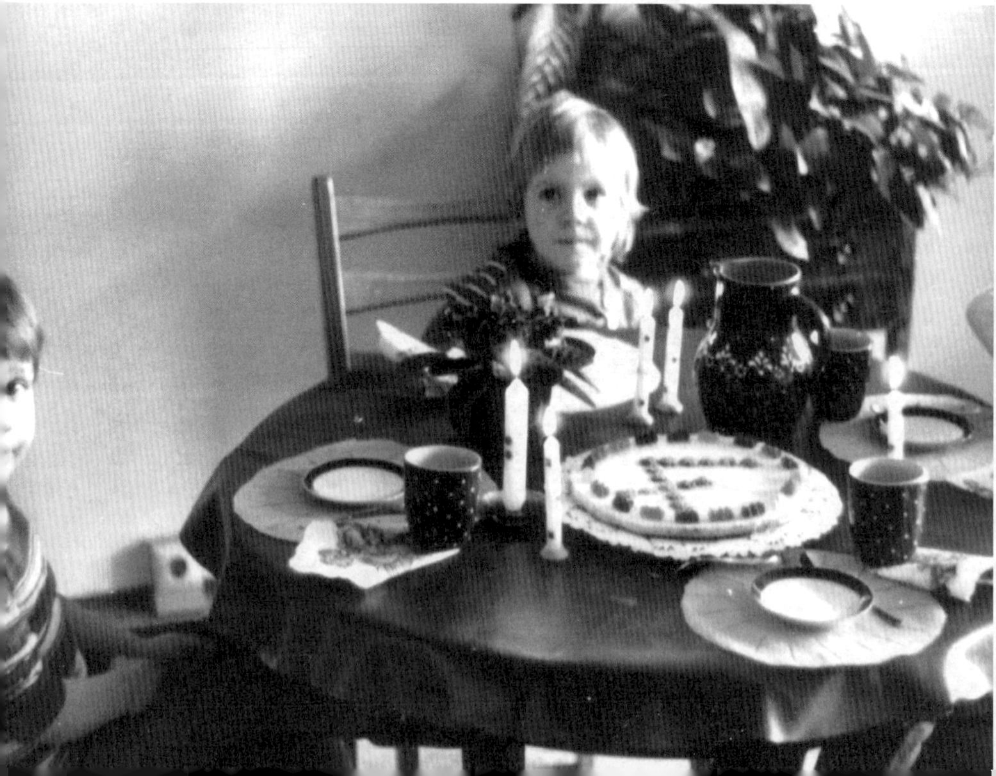

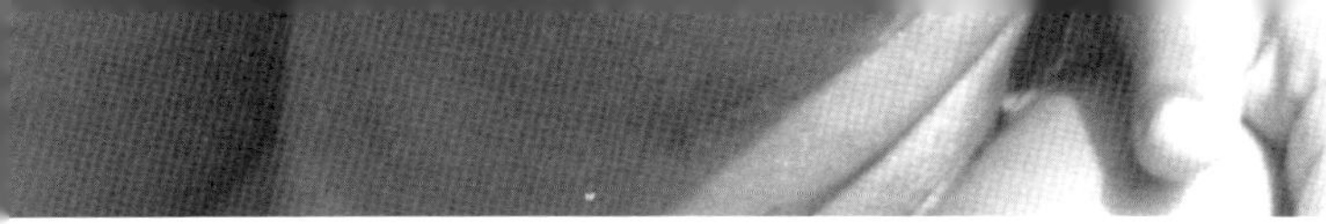

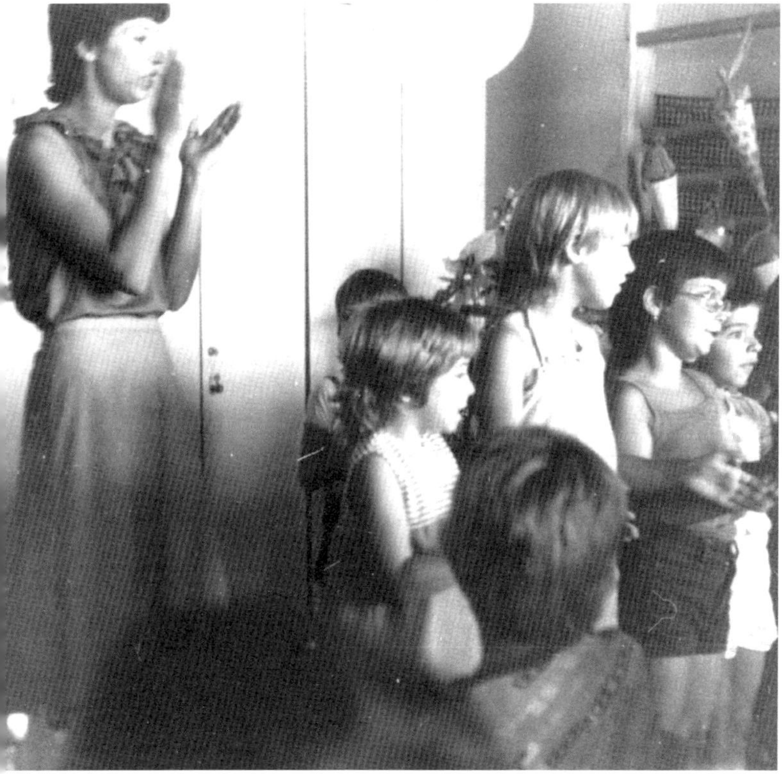

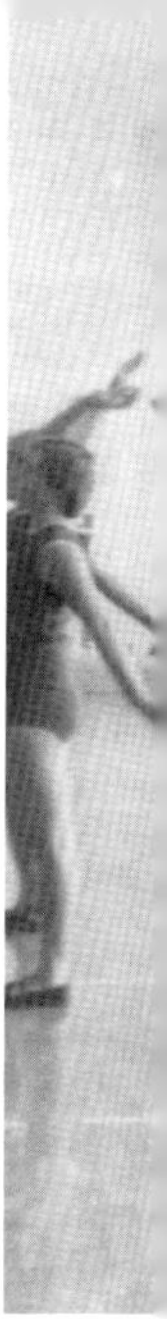

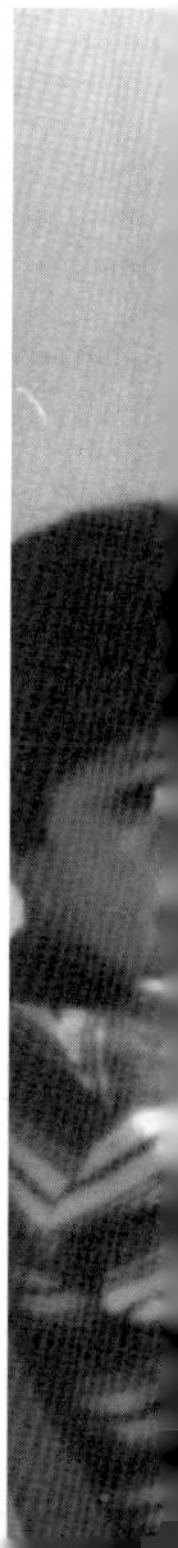

Jürgen Jabs, Berlin

Profession:	Geologist
Holdings:	25 files with about 70 black-and-white strips of negatives each and associated contact sheets; digital photographs from 2017 onward
Themes:	Amateur soccer in the metropolis and in the country; paintings with chalk or paint until ca. 1990; old façade signage on the walls of buildings; portraits; children playing; street photography in East Berlin, Amsterdam, Paris, London, Brussels, Vienna, and Cuba; bicycles; landscapes in the Uckermark; buildings in Brandenburg; people on the beach at the Baltic Sea; people watching trotting races in Berlin-Karlshorst
Dates:	From 1978 onward, more frequently from 1990 to the present
Photo materials:	Analogue black-and-white photographs and printed digital color photographs
Type of reproduction:	Black-and-white photographs were developed and enlarged in their own dark room; they printed the digital color photographs themselves
Labeling:	On the back of each print is a registration number and sometimes details of use; the contract sheets also have writing and markings
Additional holdings of private photographs:	Several strips of slides and color negatives; many photographs were turned into postcards, booklets of photographs, calendars, posters, and the like
Storage:	Most of the prints are stored in a wide variety of boxes

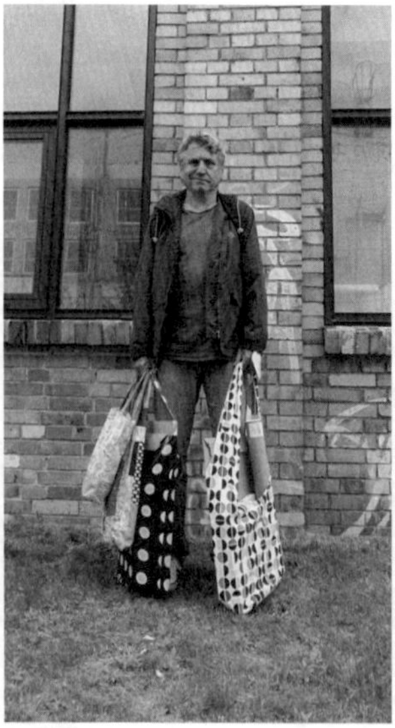

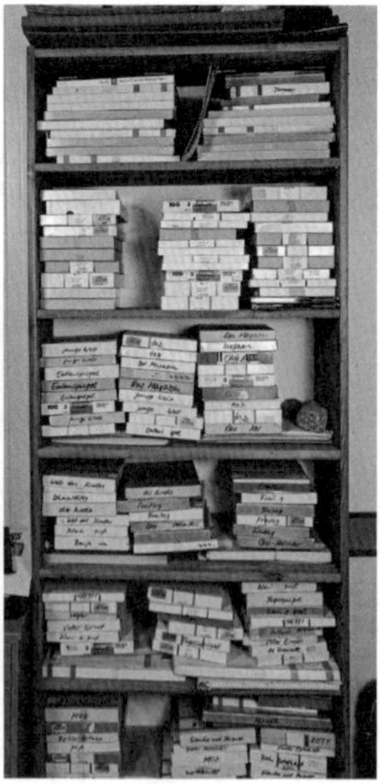

Fig. 1 Jürgen Jabs, June 13, 2021. Photo: Project Archive.
Fig. 2 Cabinet with boxes of photos. Photo: Jürgen Jabs.

115 Karin and Andreas Koven, Berlin

Profession:	Architect and mathematician
Holdings:	66 albums in all; from childhood and youth, one album for Andreas and eight albums for Karin Koven, some put together by their parents, others by themselves; 57 numbered joint albums with around 28,500 photographs from about 85,000 photographs taken; the latest album, from the fourth quarter of 2012, is volume 57, albums from later years are still being put together
Themes:	Parties and celebrations; children, grandchildren, family, and friends; many travel pictures; work, leisure (exhibitions, visits to opera, operetta, variety show, ballet, theater, concerts, cinema), hobbies (music, dancing) and sports; photographs of flowers and details; protests and the like (few from the period around the fall of the Wall); area around their home
Dates:	Self-compiled albums beginning in 1951 or 1952; also occasional albums and photographs of parents and grandparents from earlier years
Photo materials:	Black-and-white photographs, color photographs, postcards, tickets, brochures, invitations, a few cards/letters, business cards, labels from bottles and other products, etc.
Type of reproduction:	Black-and-white photographs were developed in their own darkroom from the 1970s to the early 1990s
Labeling:	Handwritten, usually in black with color for emphasis
Additional holdings of private photographs:	Slides, later also color photographs, also video sequences taken with a digital camera of grandchildren, animals, dancers, moving art objects and the like
Storage:	Slides in boxes, black-and-white photographs in boxes, digital images on hard drives with backup copies; albums on a shelf in the study

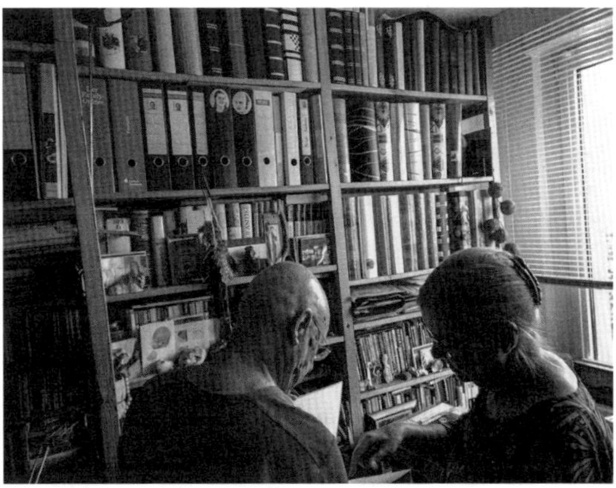

Fig. 1 Karin and Andreas Koven in front of their shelves with albums. Photo: Project Archive.

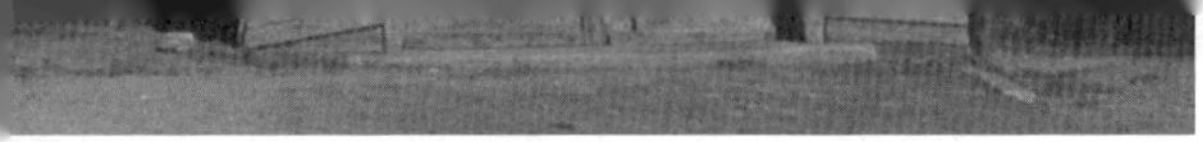
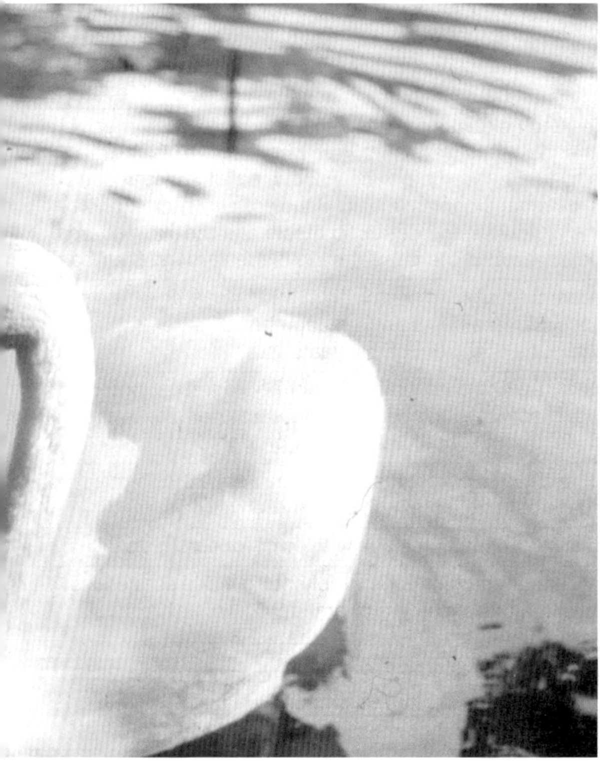
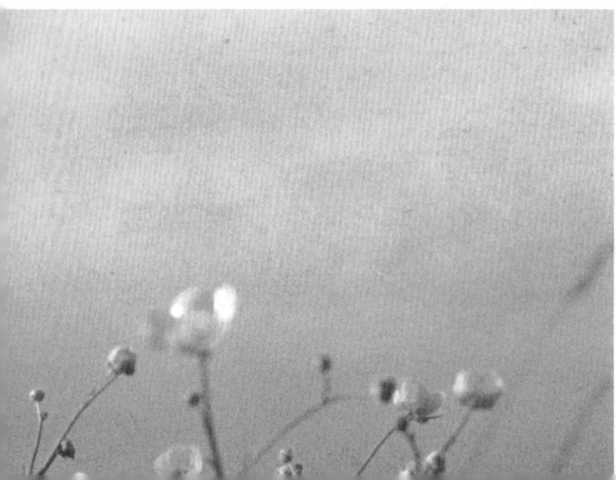
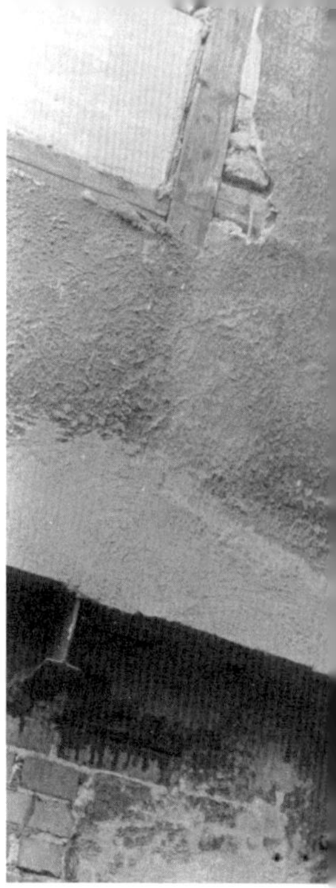
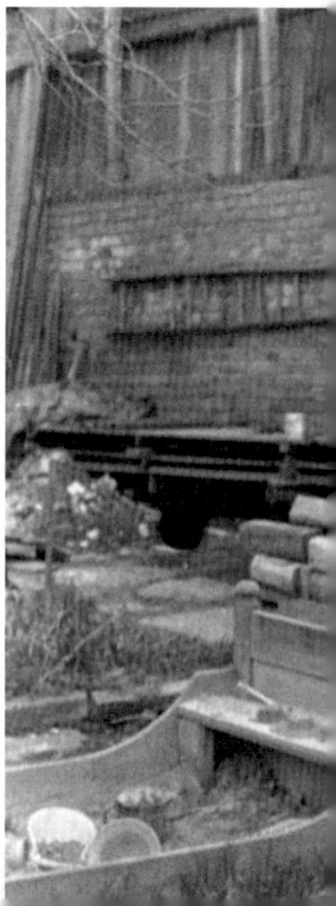

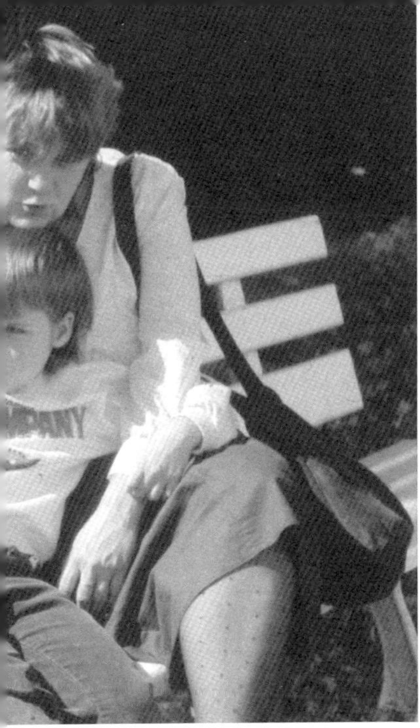

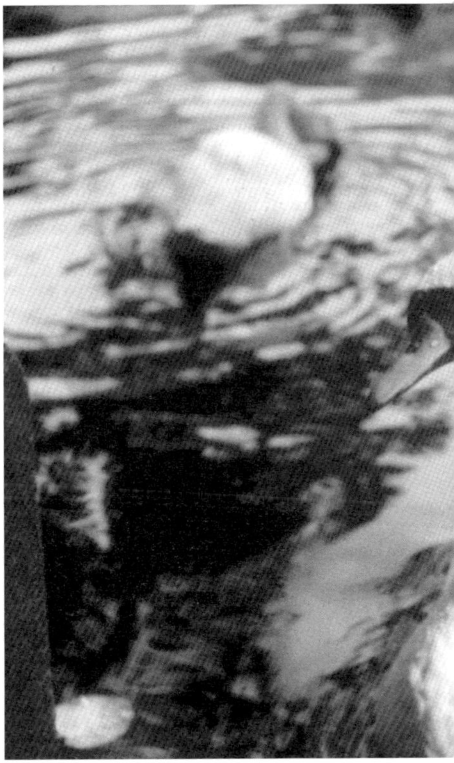

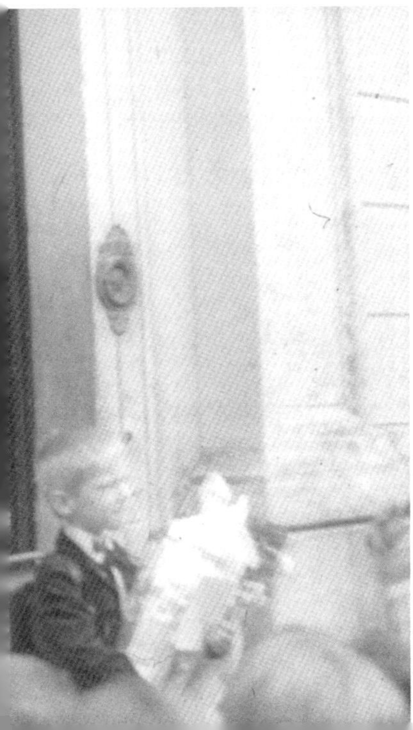

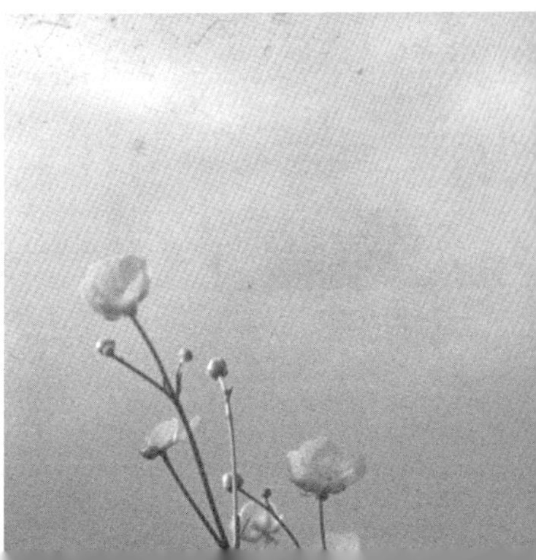

Georg Mohr, Rostock

Profession:	Marine engineer
Holdings:	230 albums
Themes:	Landscape, family, construction projects in Rostock, documentation of the decline of the Neptun shipyard in Rostock
Dates:	From 1954 to the present; older family albums date as far back as ca. 1870
Photo materials:	Until 1989, almost exclusively black-and-white photographs, then increasingly color photographs
Type of reproduction:	The black-and-white photographs were printed in his own darkroom installed in the bathroom
Labeling:	Concise with date and brief comments on the subject of the picture
Additional holdings of private photographs:	Color slides

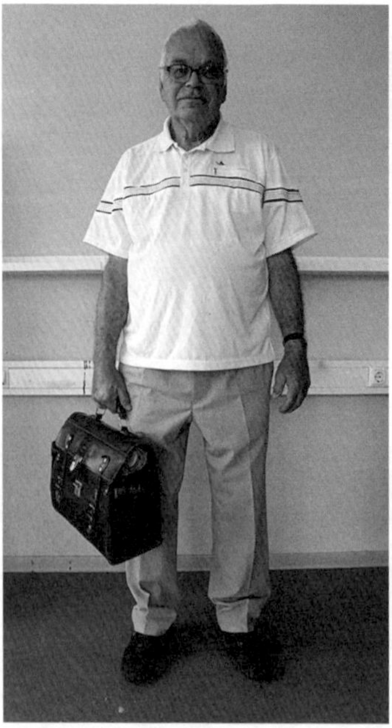

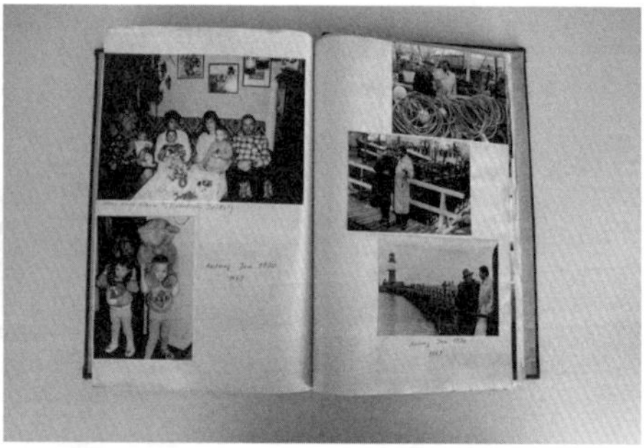

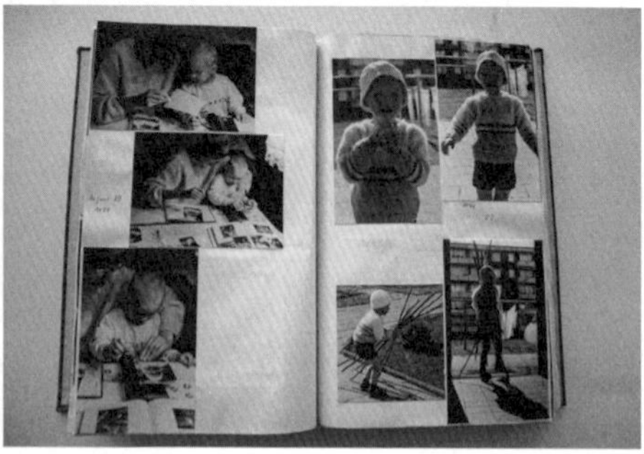

Fig. 1 Georg Mohr, June 27, 2020. Photo: Project Archive.
Fig. 2 Open photo album from January 1990. Photo: Project Archive.
Fig. 3 Open photo album from August 1989. Photo: Project Archive.

117 Gabi and Martin Siebert, Ilmenau

Profession:	Optician and electrical engineer
Holdings:	Nearly forty albums with about 10,000 photographs, including a digital archive with keywords of scans of about 80,000 photographs; about 100 sheets of black-and-white negatives transferred to the Deutsches Historisches Museum
Themes:	Overwhelmingly family photographs but also trips and other events
Dates:	From the early 1970s onward, from 2000 onward, gradually switching to digital photography
Photo materials:	Analog black-and-white photographs, along with several color prints; in addition, postcards, admission tickets, maps, etc.
Type of reproduction:	Until 2000, overwhelmingly black-and-white photographs printed in their own darkroom; in addition, postcards, admission tickets, maps, etc.
Labeling:	Very meticulous, especially in the case of the travel photographs
Additional holdings of private photographs:	Several color slides
Storage:	In addition to the albums, there are several boxes of photographs

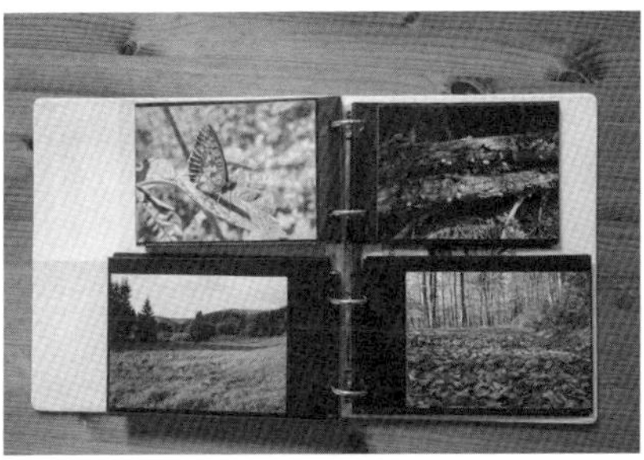

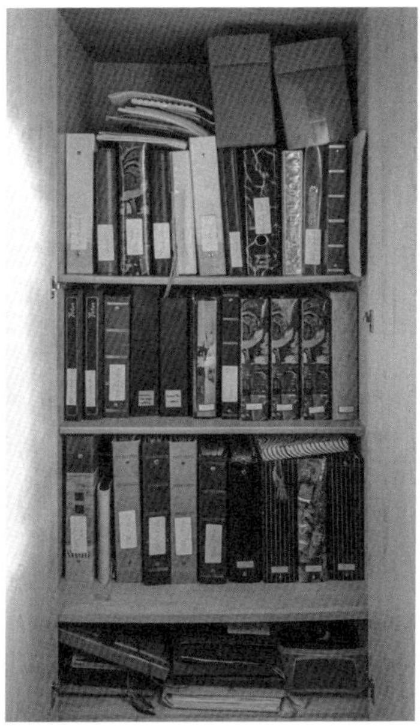

Fig. 1 Gabi and Martin Siebert: Open album. Photo: Project Archive.
Fig. 2 Cabinet with photo albums, Ilmenau, September 11, 2021. Photo: Project Archive.

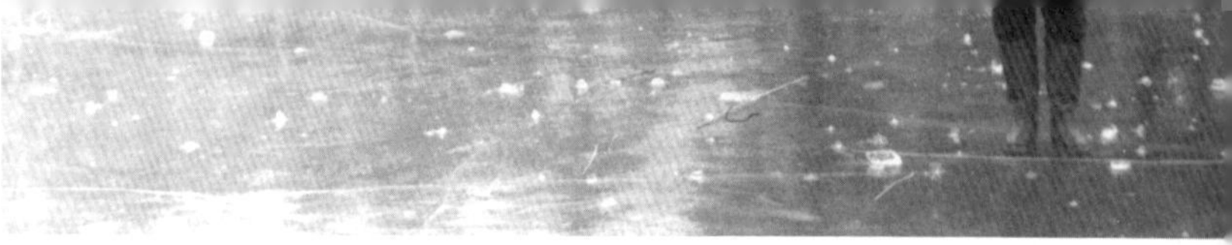

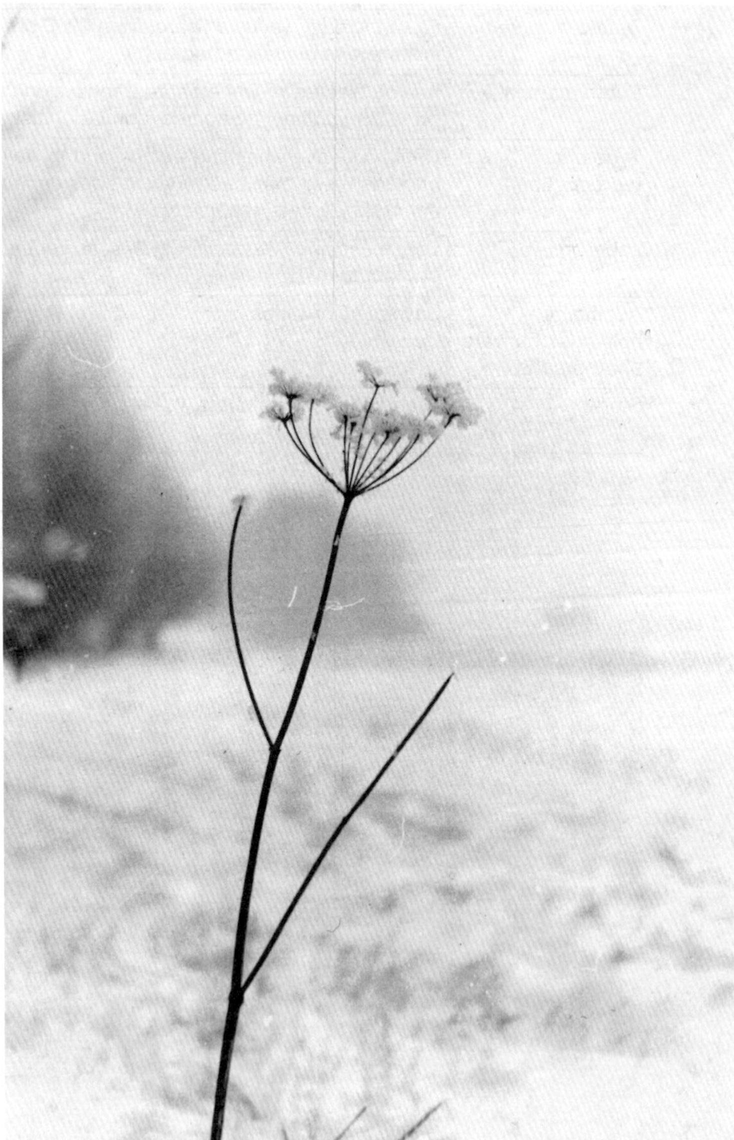

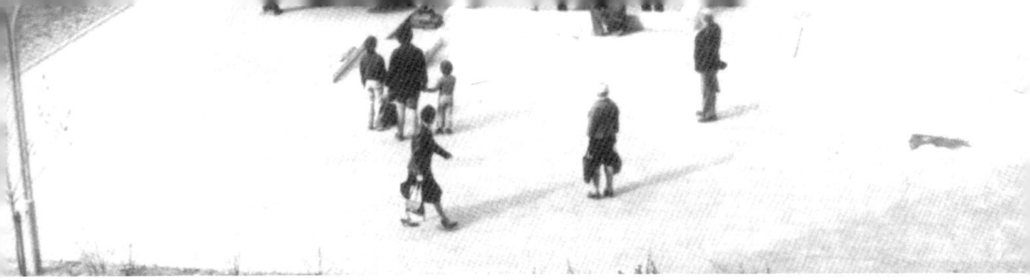

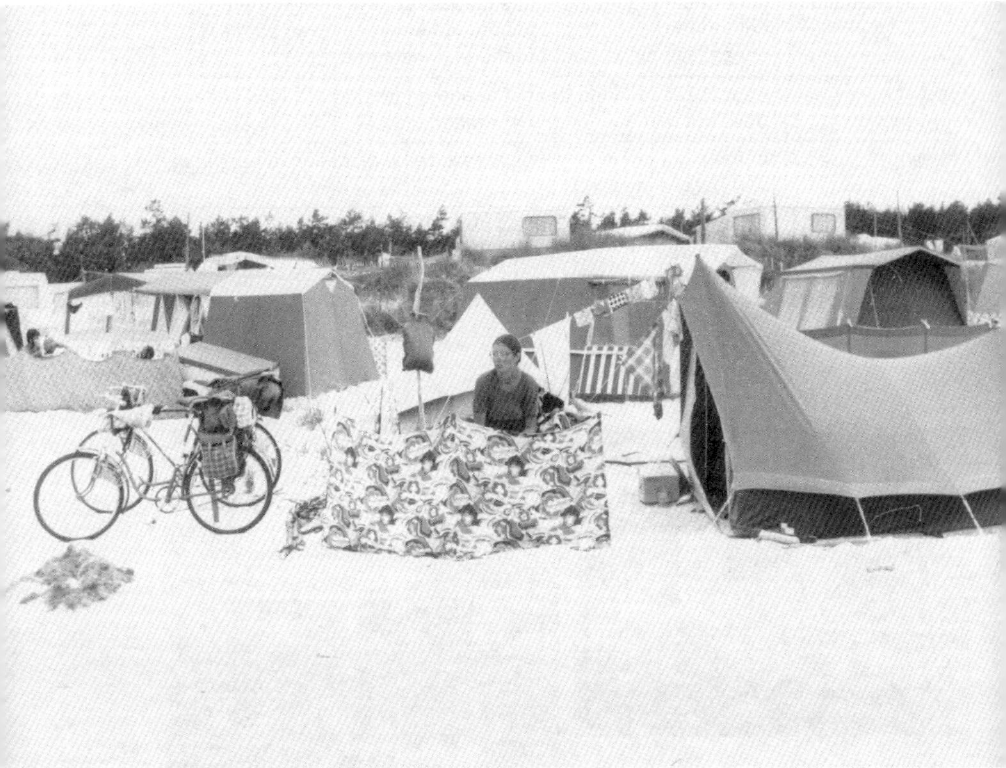

Profession:	Council member in Stadt Löbau (Saxony) and commissioned officer
Holdings:	A total of 25 albums; nine albums of the history of the Simon family. Five albums of Manfred Simon's childhood and youth, four of Bettina Simon, and several albums of her parents; eight file folders with additional photographs
Themes:	Primarily family events such as births, birthdays, celebrations, vacations; in addition, of their professions and especially from 1989–90 of political events
Dates:	From the 1930s onward
Photo materials:	Until 1992, black-and-white photographs and from then on color photographs; in addition, ephemera such as admission tickets, clippings from brochures, postcards, etc.
Type of reproduction:	From 1973 to 1992, the black-and-white photographs were developed in their own darkroom
Labeling:	In the albums, usually indications of the occasion, time, place, and people involved
Additional holdings of private photographs:	Color slides from the period up to 1989; several videos from later years
Storage:	Arranged in albums and files

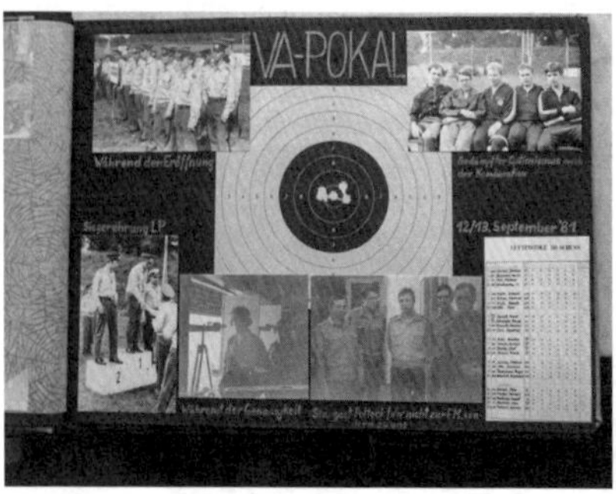

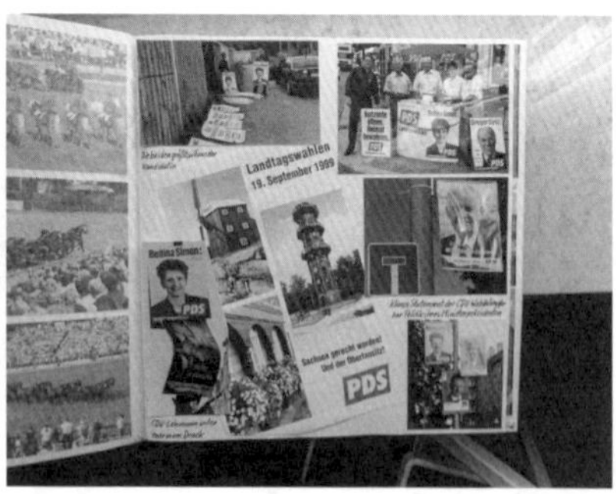

Fig. 1 Open photo album from September 1981. Photo: Manfred and Bettina Simon.

Fig. 2 Open photo album from September 1999. Photo: Manfred and Bettina Simon.

119 Margrit and Burghard Specht, Burg

Profession:	Painter/secretary and operations manager
Holdings:	75 albums and 13 books of photographs
Themes:	Stages of life such as school, teaching, and the army; in addition, portraits, landscapes, sports, animals, and works produced in connection with photography clubs; beginning with the founding of the family in 1977, chronological albums with a separate album for each of their two daughters kept in parallel
Dates:	From 1968 to present
Photo materials:	Primarily black-and-white photographs but later also color photographs; a small number of postcards, tickets, and brochures
Type of reproduction:	All color and black-and-white photographs up to 1990 were developed themselves in their private darkroom; large-format photographs (up to 30×40 cm) were mounted on cardboard
Labeling:	Handwritten
Additional holdings of private photographs:	A few slides
Storage:	In portfolios and cases

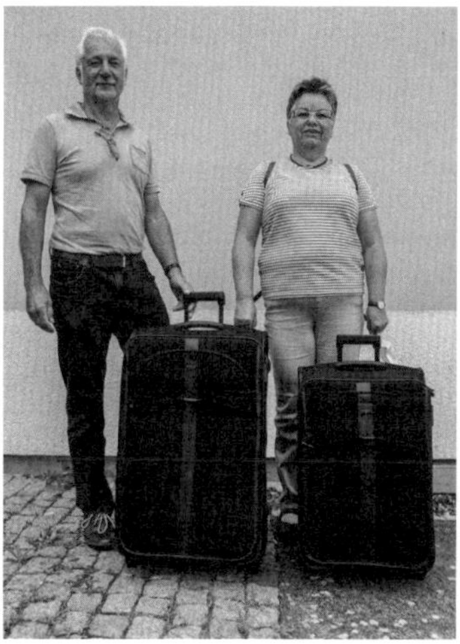

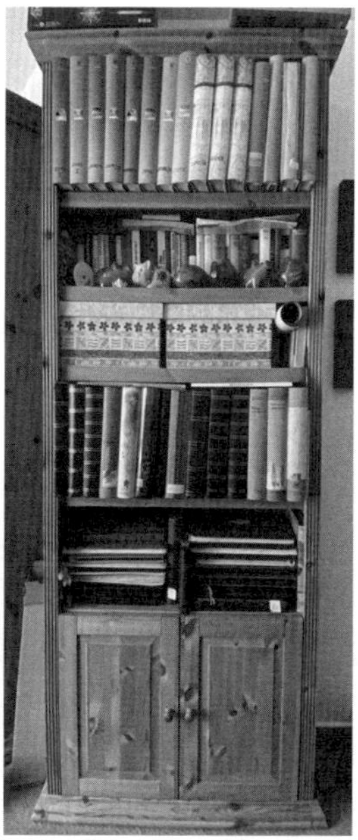

Fig. 1 Margrit and Burghard Specht. Magdeburg, July 20, 2020. Photo: Project Archive.

Fig. 2 Cabinet with photo albums. Photo: Margrit and Burghard Specht.

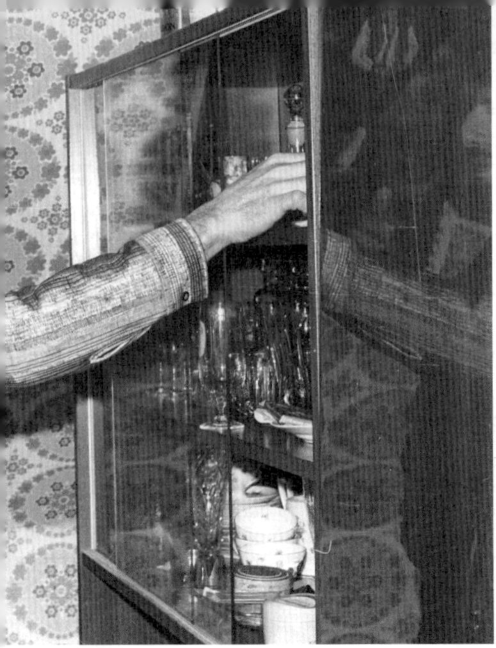

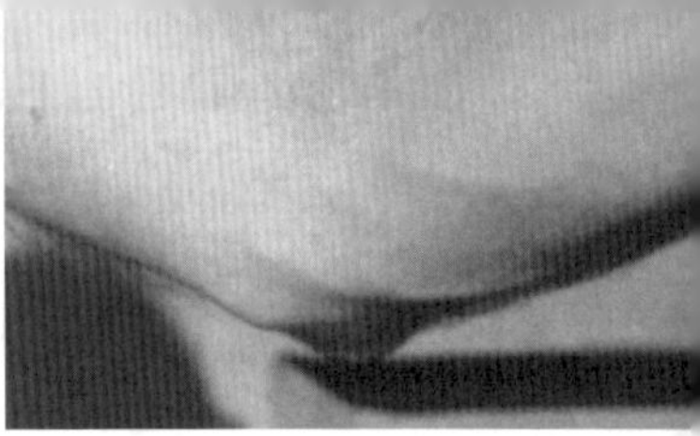

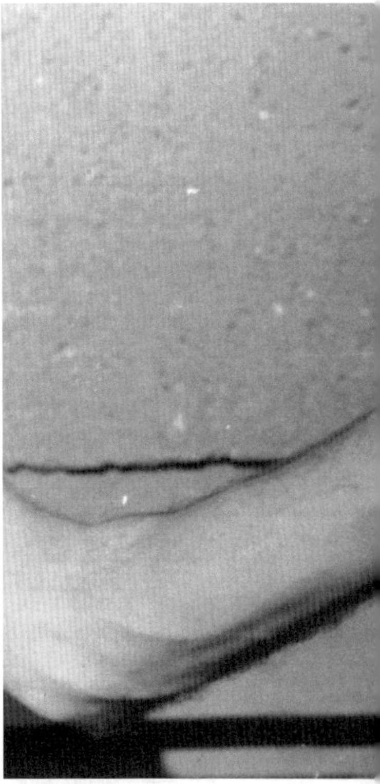

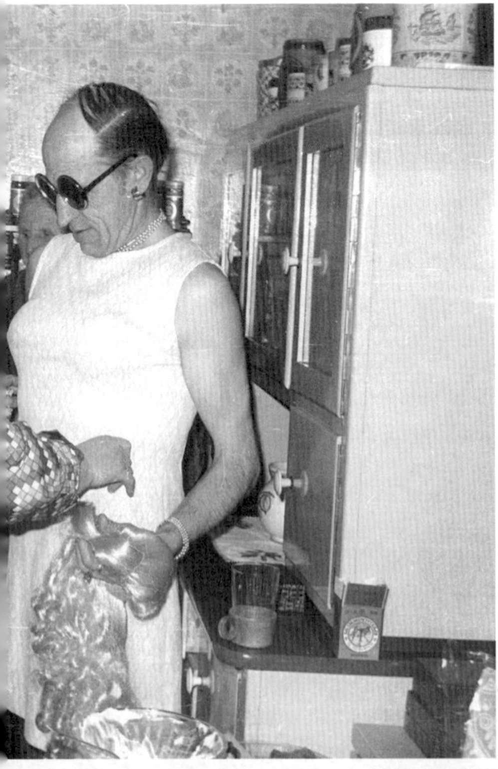

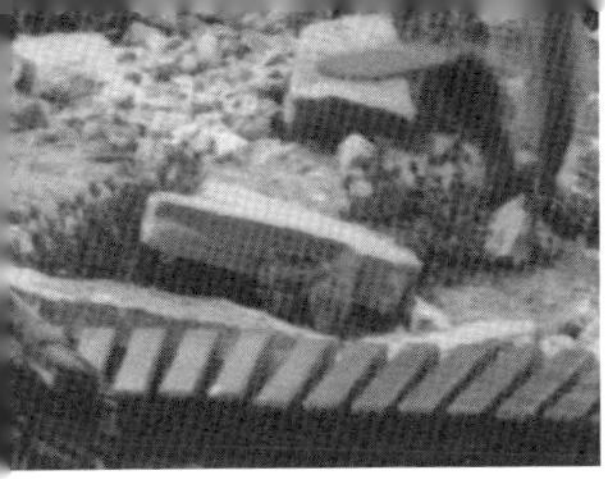

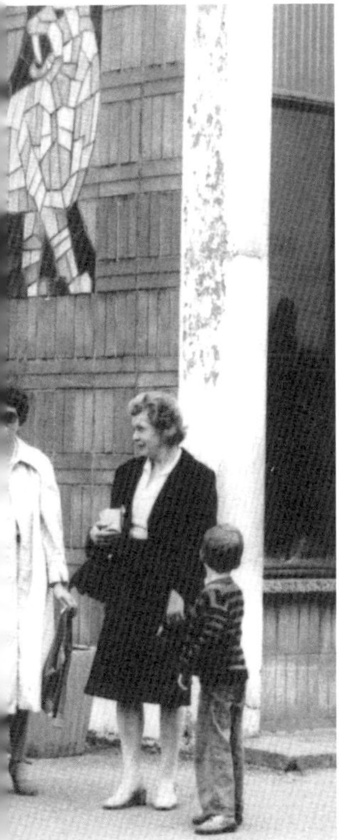

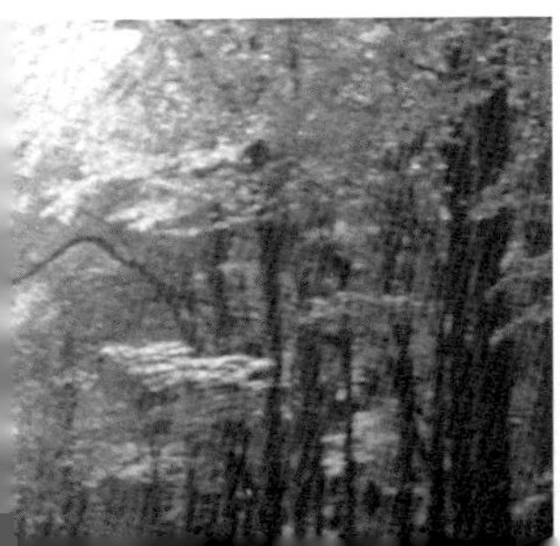

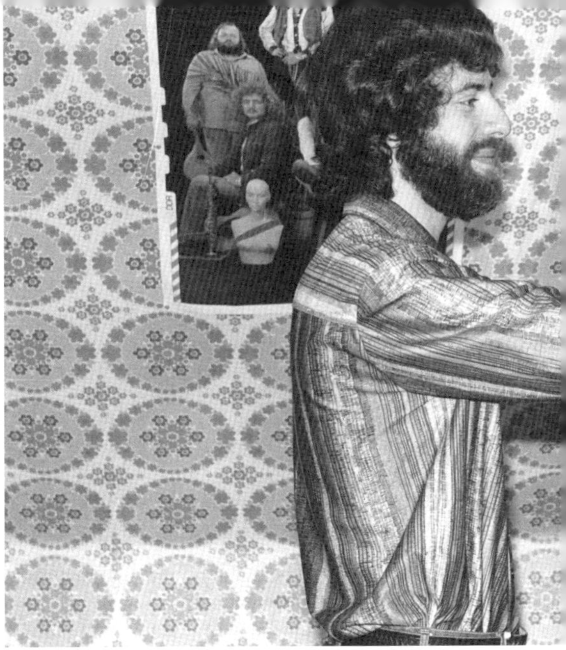

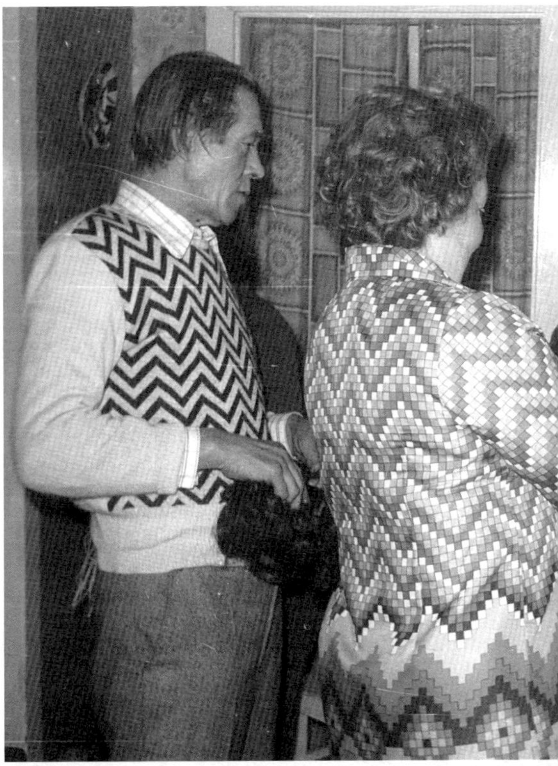

Birgit and Werner-Wolf Turski, Heidenau 120

Profession:	Cultural scientist and mining engineer
Holdings:	30 photo albums in A3 format, bound with about 20,000 photographs; nine smaller albums
Themes:	History of the Zemann family (Birgit Turski's family) from 1906 to 1999 (three albums); life of Werner-Wolf Turski from 1944 to 1969 (five albums); history of the Turski Jr. family from 1969 to 2020 (22 albums): the children growing up and the associated events and experiences, family and brigade parties and excursions, museum visits, cultural events at the Stadthalle Cottbus with national ensembles from all over the world; travel photos, primarily from places in the Soviet Union (e.g., Murmansk, Vorkuta, Alma Ata, Tashkent, Fergana, Ashgabat, Baku, Leningrad, Veliky Novgorod, Mos-cow, Kyiv, Marhanets / Nikopol); photographs from the Pedro Bissonette youth club for Indianism and of the Indianist scene in the GDR and later; photographs from work life, especially brown-coal mining from 1963 onward (Werner-Wolf Turski was a mining engineer working in strip mining)
Dates:	From 1906 to 2020; a few earlier photographs dating as far back as the nineteenth century
Photo materials:	Until 1990, almost exclusively black-and-white photographs; after 1990, color photographs; in addition to their own photographs, they used photographs taken by their sons, friends, relatives, and others; color copies of some of the photographs from earlier albums were pasted in the albums; in addition, postcards, images clipped from catalogues; a few tickets and other ephemera such as dried plant parts
Type of reproduction:	Until 1990, the black-and-white photographs were developed by Brigit Turski in her own darkroom; from 1990, the color photographs were developed by outside labs
Labeling:	Handwritten, later printed out from the computer and pasted in
Storage:	Albums are stored on a shelf; a few photographs are stored in bags

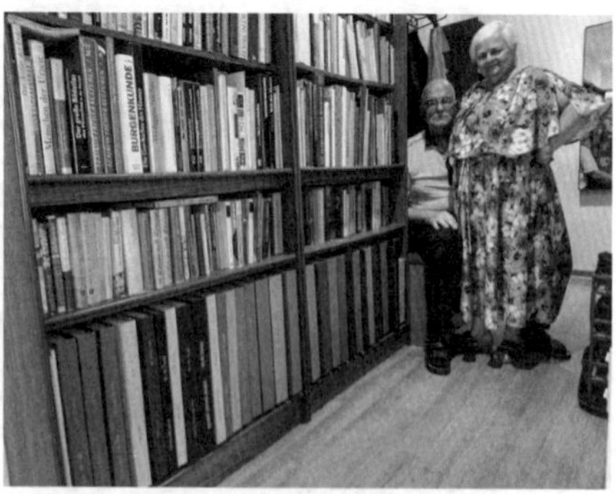

Fig. 1 Werner-Wolf and Birgit Turski in front of a cabinet with their photo albums, Heidenau, June 25, 2020. Photo: Project Archive.

Martin Weinhold, Berlin

Profession:	Photographer
Holdings:	Two albums with around 40 photographs each; one album with about 50 negatives and contact sheets; in addition, numerous individual prints
Themes:	An East Berlin new wave/punk clique; family photographs; some urban photography
Dates:	From 1986 to 1992
Photo materials:	Black-and-white photographs
Type of reproduction:	From 1987 onward, printed himself in his private darkroom
Labeling:	Sometimes the lyrics of songs by current bands; drawings in felt-tip pen; no labeling in the archival or chronological sense; the album of negatives was compiled later and is organized as an archive
Storage:	A small part of the collection is in files/albums; the individual prints are kept in archival boxes for photographs

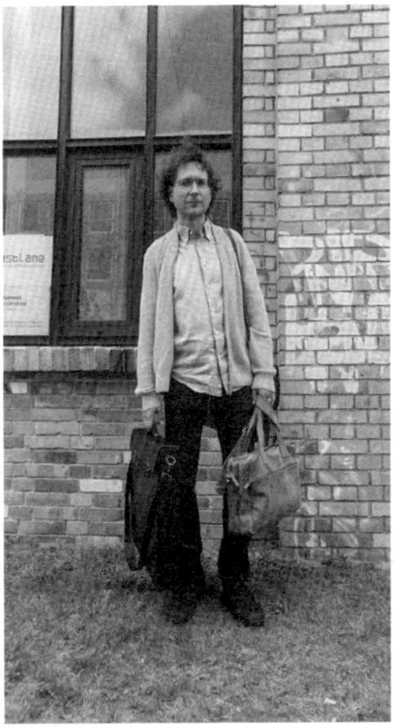

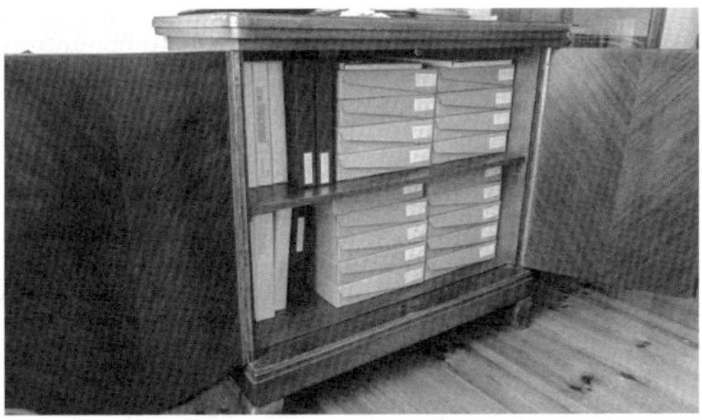

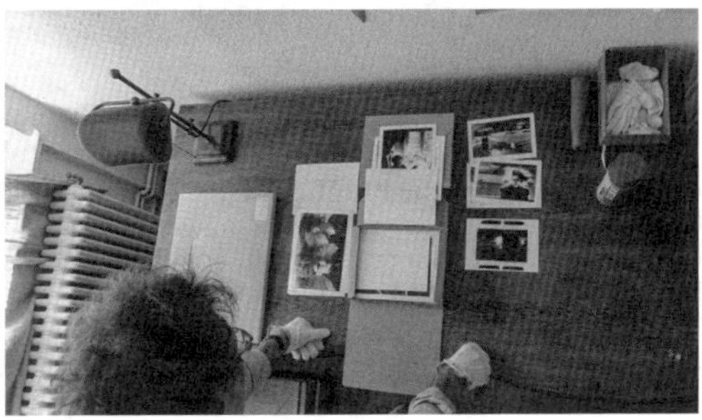

Fig. 1 Martin Weinhold, Berlin, June 13, 2020. Photo: Project Archive.
Fig. 2 Archive cabinet. Photo: Project Archive.
Fig. 3 Martin Weinhold with photographs. Photo: Project Archive.

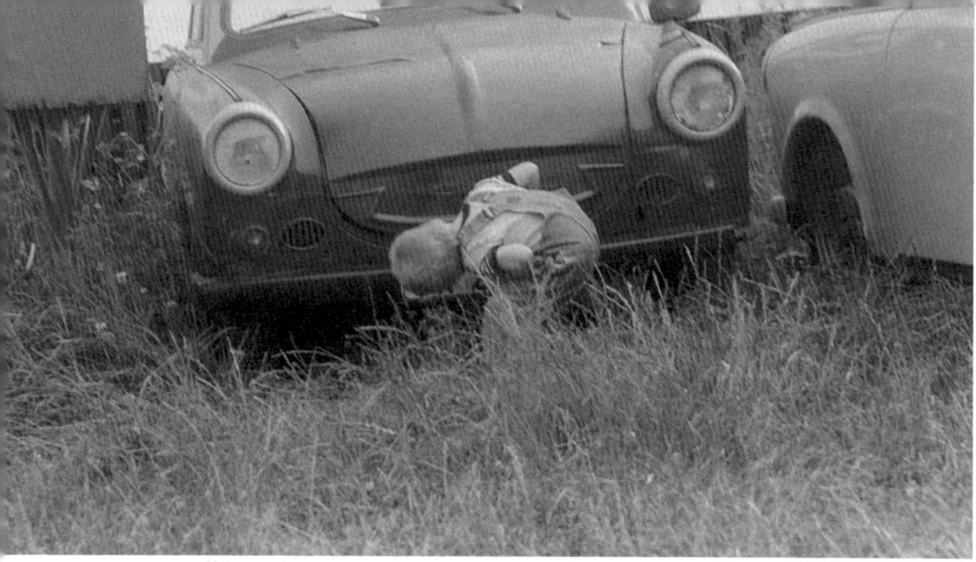

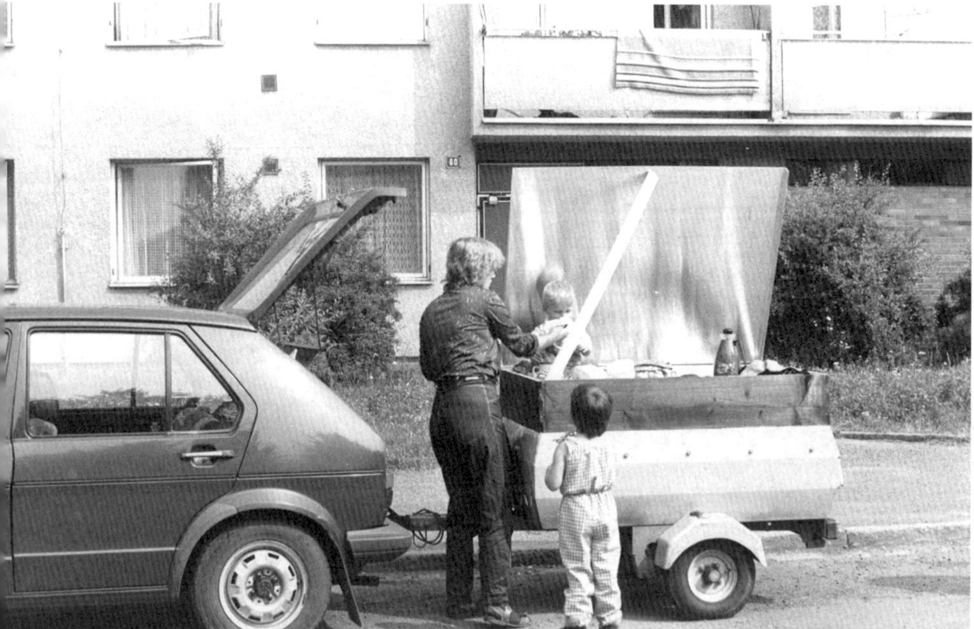

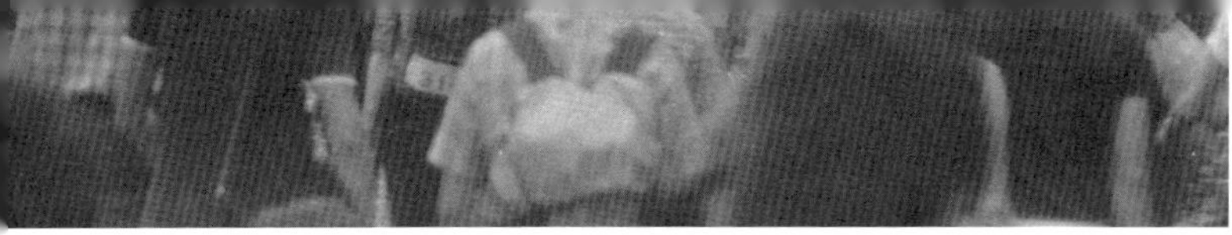

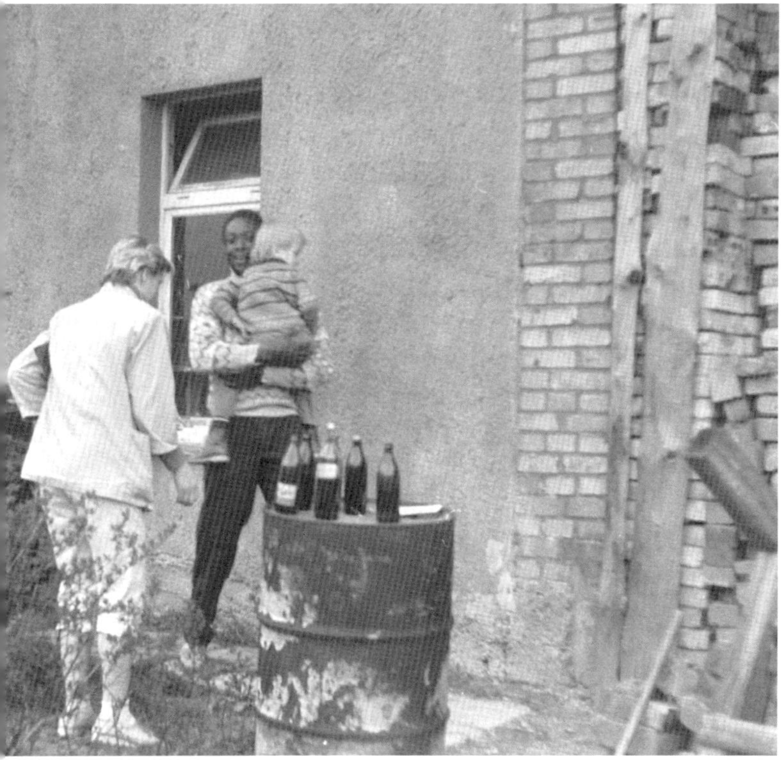

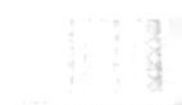

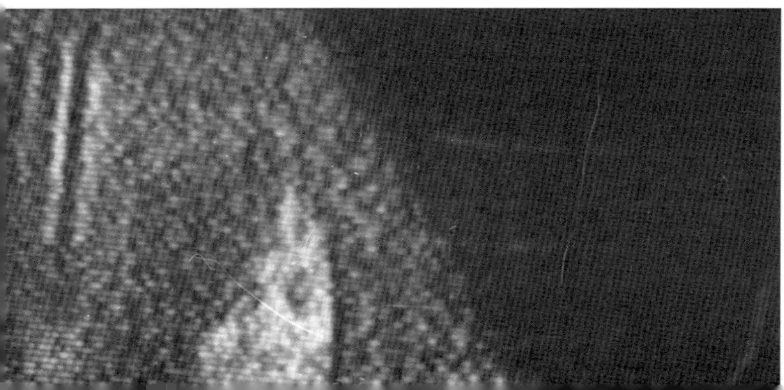

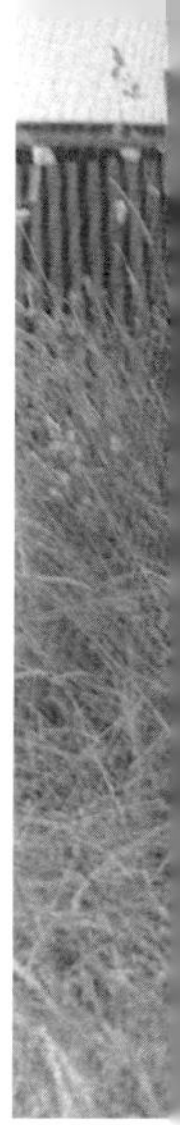

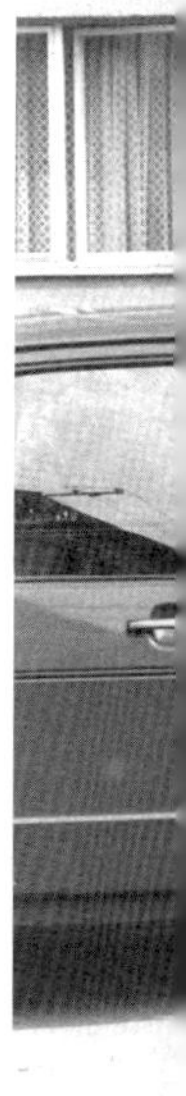

We would like to thank our many interviewees, who opened their albums and boxes for us and who told us their private photography stories: Gabriele Adam, Gudrun Baer, Sibylle Besmehn, Heinrich Bechmann, Martina Behn, Borghild Carus, Annabel Dukes, Evelyn Gebhardt, Victor Gehring, Ingrid Gietz, Beate and Jürgen Göldner, Detlef Groth and Elke Schulz-Groth, Michael Günther, Wolfgang Haensel, Udo Hill, Egon Höcker, Jürgen Jabs, Pertina Karczewsky, Arno Kiehl, Barbara Klage and Thomas Klage, Christine Koschmieder, Karin Koven and Andreas Koven, Anita Liethmann, Stefanie Lürtzing, Gudrun Matschenz, Georg and Katrin Mohr, Gabriele Parakeninks, Klaus Parnow, Günther Römer, Siegfried Rommel, Gudrun and Gundula Sachse, Petra Scheibe, Bettina Schinko, Hilmar Schmundt, Jan Schneppe, Andreas Schütz, Olaf Schwarz, Martin and Gabi Siebert, Bettina and Manfred Simon, Christa and Gerd Simon, Margrit and Burghard Specht, Patricia Strohmaier, Kathrin Stöver, Birgit and Werner-Wolf Turski, Jörn Vorwald, Manfred Wagner, Martin Weinhold, Hans Westphal, Rudolf Winterfeldt, Ralph Wittmann, Lothar Wölfel, Petra Worf and Wolfgang Worf, Margot Ziemann.

This project would not have been possible without the kind support of Giulia Artusa, Loubna Baba Ahmed, Simon Bichler, Agnete Bay Blichfeldt, Ann-Kristin Block, Magdalena Boesch, Annekathrin Böttcher, Gereon Budéus, Anja Buenning, Natalia Buerkle, Nadine Butigan, Daniel Chinellato, Marian Cramm, Johanna Dietz, Ha Van Dinh, Marie Egger, Gianna Ehrke, Veronika Epple, Friedrich Severin Fetzer, Nikolas Geier, Julia Globig, Aletta Haniel, Marit Herrmann, Sven Herrmann, Felix Hoffmann, Alina Elena Hosu, Andrea Hubin, Leonie Hugendubel, Carola Jüllig, Herbert Justnik, Seoyoung Kim, Matthias Klos, Karsten Knobbe, Laura Koepp, Matteo Anthony Kramer, Franziska Kuschel, Viviane Linda Linek, Solange Lingnau, Sten Linnert, Paul Lissner, Candice M. Hamelin, Yi Ma, Mariette Minnemann, Aloisia Moser, Katja Müller-Helle, Maria Neff, Valentina Plotnikova, Doreen Reichenbach, Julia Dumstrei Reidy, Judith Riemer, Yifan Ruan, Claire-Elisa Rueffer, Georg Schelbert, Natascha Scholl, Sandra Schubert, Sophie Schulz, Véronique Seibert, Marlene Sichelschmidt, Romy Isabella Simon, Pia Spengler, Jana Leonora Storch, Charlotte Tietjen, Brigitte Trimper, Linh Truong, Sophia Uckmann, Siri van den Berg, Frederique van Staalen, Leander Verse, Mona von Homeyer, Juliane Wenzl, Frank Wingens, Jamaludin Yousef and Carolina Zamfirescu. Many, many thanks for this.

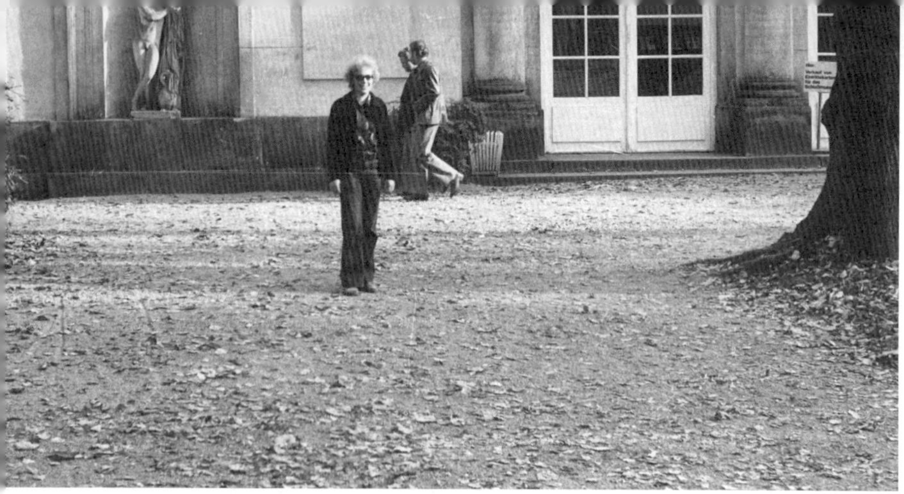

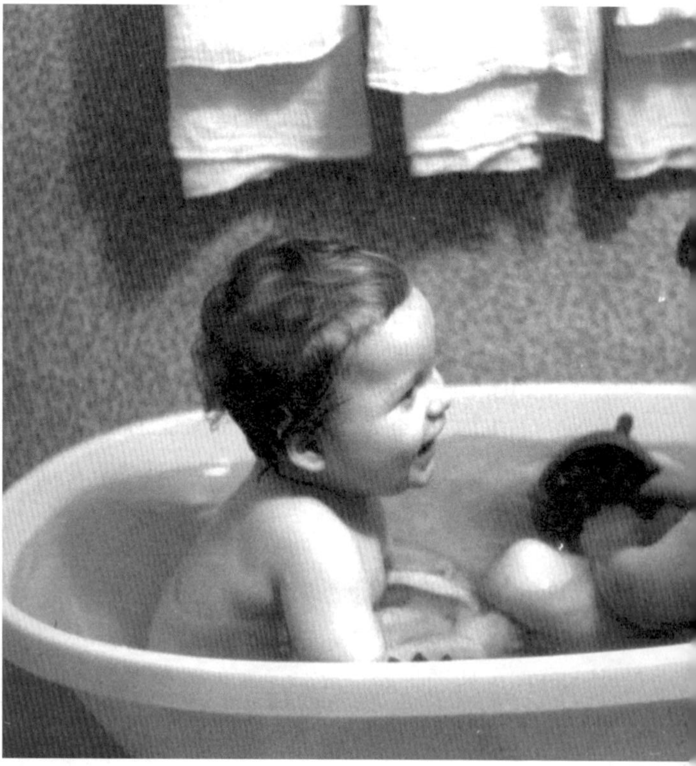

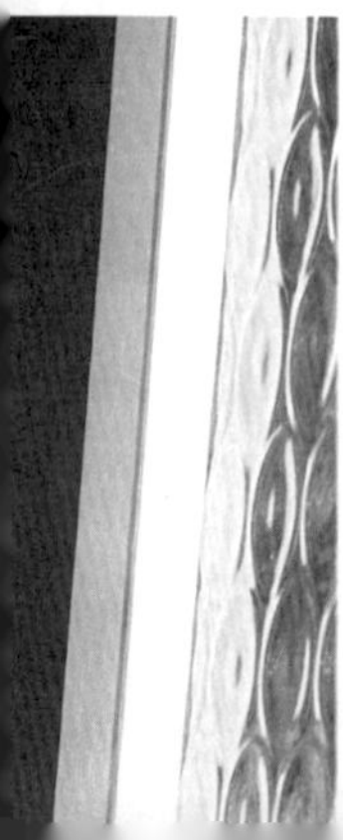

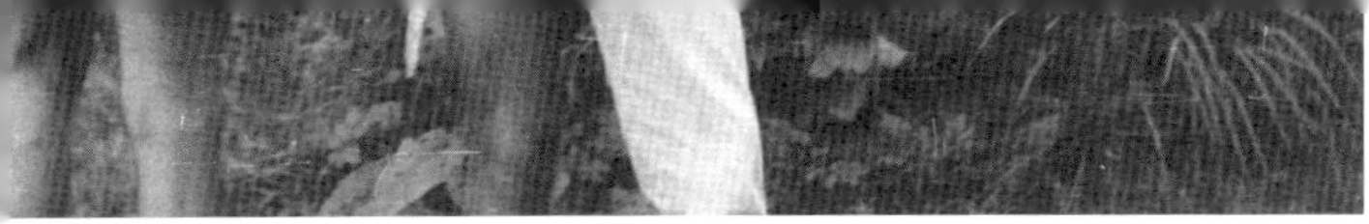

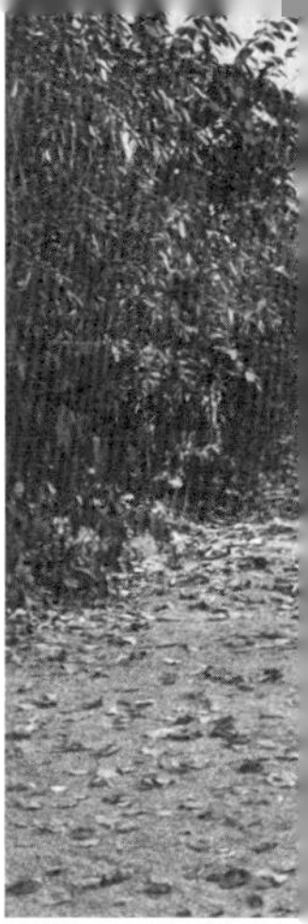

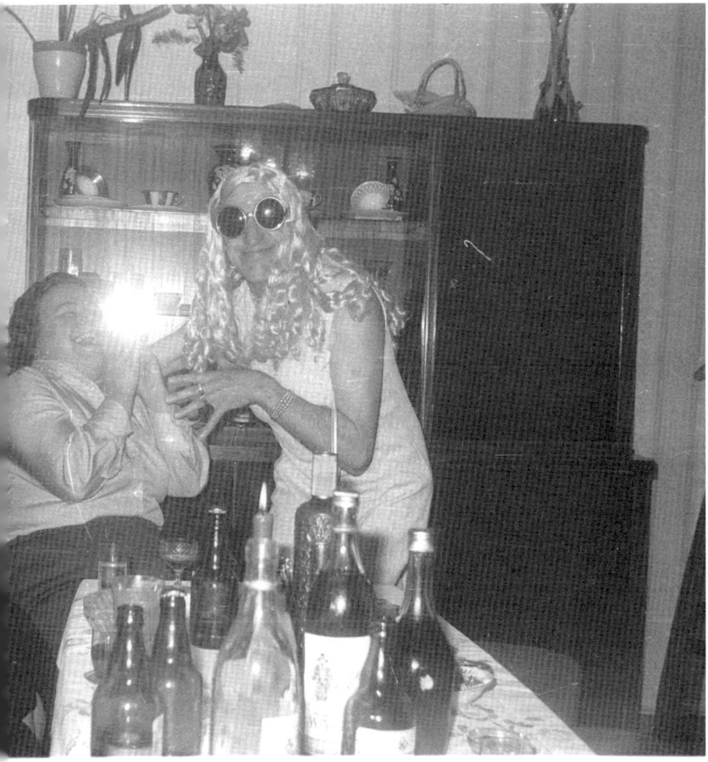

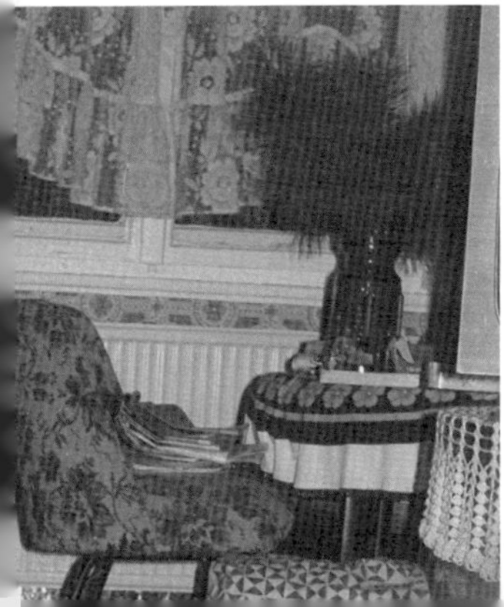

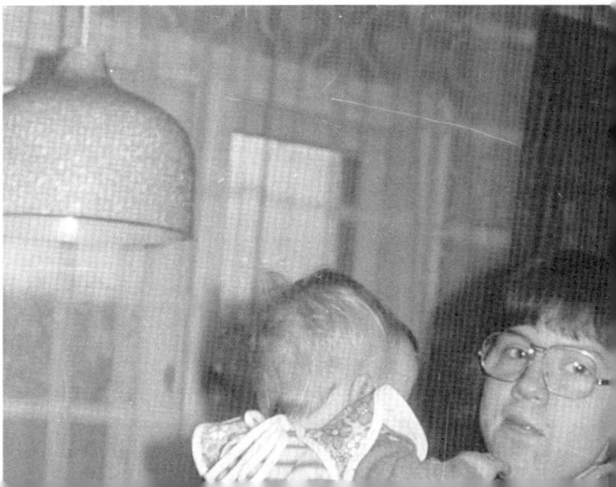